REPUTATION MANAGEMENT

University of Liverpool

Withdrawn from stock

Reputation Management is a how-to guide for students and professionals, as well as CEOs and other business leaders. It rests on the premise that reputation can be measured, monitored, and managed. Organized by corporate communication units including media relations, employee communication, government relations, and investor relations, the book provides a field-tested guide to corporate reputation problems such as leaked memos, unfair treatment by the press, and negative rumors, and focuses on practical solutions. Each chapter is fleshed out with the real-world experience of the authors and contributors, who come from a wide range of professional corporate communication backgrounds.

Updates to the third edition include:

- Global content has been incorporated and expanded throughout the book, rather than being restricted to only one chapter.
- Opening vignettes, examples, and case studies in each chapter have been updated.
- Additional case studies and examples with an international focus have been added.

John Doorley, head of corporate communications for Merck & Co. Inc. until 2000, most recently built and directed for ten years the Master of Science Degree Program in Public Relations and Corporate Communication at the New York University School of Professional Studies. He is now with the London-based company Mindful Reputation.

Helio Fred Garcia is president of Logos Consulting Group. He is an adjunct professor in the Executive MBA program of New York University's Stern School of Business, and teaches courses in NYU's MS in Public Relations and Corporate Communication program at the university's School of Professional Studies. He is the author of *The Power of Communication: Skills to Build Trust, Inspire Loyalty, and Lead Effectively* (FT Press, 2012) and of *Crisis Communications* (AAAA Publications, 1999).

REPUTATION MANAGEMENT

3RD EDITION

The Key to Successful Public Relations and Corporate Communication

**John Doorley
and
Helio Fred Garcia**

 Routledge
Taylor & Francis Group

NEW YORK AND LONDON

Third edition published 2015
by Routledge
711 Third Avenue, New York, NY 10017

and by Routledge
2 Park Square, Milton Park, Abingdon, Oxon, OX14 4RN

Routledge is an imprint of the Taylor & Francis Group, an informa business

First edition published by Routledge 2006
Second edition published by Routledge 2010

Library of Congress Cataloging in Publication Data
Doorley, John.
  Reputation management: the key to successful public relations and
  corporate communication / John Doorley, Helio Fred Garcia. —
  Third edition.
    pages cm
  1. Public relations. 2. Communication in organizations.
  I. Garcia, Helio Fred. II. Title.
  HD59.D66 2015
  659.2—dc23   2014029488

ISBN: 978-0-415-71627-7 (hbk)
ISBN: 978-0-415-71628-4 (pbk)
ISBN: 978-1-315-87998-7 (ebk)

Typeset in Aldine and Zurich
by Keystroke, Station Road, Codsall, Wolverhampton

Printed and bound in the United States of America by Sheridan Books, Inc. (a Sheridan Group Company).

TABLE OF CONTENTS

3 Media Relations — 92

4 Social Media — 126

10   Issues Management   268

11   Crisis Communication   295

PREFACE

"GOOD BOOK, DUMB TITLE"

We heard that more than a few times when the first edition of *Reputation Management* was published in 2006. This despite the fact that the text was peer-reviewed and published by one of the world's leading academic publishers.

On the surface, the logic of the detractors was irrefutable: reputation is an intangible asset; therefore, it cannot be managed. That logic, more pervasive than not at the time, presupposed that intangible things, say interpersonal relationships, cannot be managed. We would argue that if intangible things are not managed their value will go south, just as will always be the case with unmanaged tangible assets. Do we need a case study to prove that if an individual does not care for and cultivate his or her personal relationships, the sum of how that individual is perceived and regarded— something called reputation—will deteriorate?

In fact, the authors believed then and more so now that one reason so many organizations—from corporations, to governments, religions, universities, and non-profits—continue to set records for destroying their own reputations is that they think of reputation as unmanageable. Nonsense!

One reason we like the Abraham Lincoln quote on page 1 is that the tree's shadow can be shaped, by fertilizing and pruning the tree for instance. The shadow (reputation) can be shaped and even controlled, at least to some degree, despite the wind, the sun, pestilence and so on. It is hard to argue with the proposition that the continued existence of the shadow is more likely with cultivation of the tree than without.

The other reason we and communicators of substance love the Lincoln quote is its emphasis on substance: "Character is like a tree . . . the tree is the real thing."

The lesson we take from Lincoln is that if an organization takes care of the important things—performance, behavior, communication and identity—then reputation will flourish, at least over the long term. Reputation may get blown around and even distorted from time to time, but the alternative to care and nurturing of the things that matter most is scandal, failure, unemployment, poverty, a loss of faith in government and religions, and on and on. A kind of reputational anarchy.

Here's an update on the emerging field of reputation management and why we predict it will, eventually, become its eponymous self:

- The term reputation management, seldom used in 2006 without derision, now produces millions of search engine hits.
- There are thousands of firms that bill themselves as reputation managers yet most by far stop at measurement or analysis.
- Many of the "reputation management" firms monitor on-line mentions of a company or brand, and many do that very well. But they monitor—not manage.
- Over the last nine years the number of public relations firms that list reputation management among their capabilities has increased exponentially.
- Some of the large management consulting firms have entered the field.
- The field has been moving from measurement to analysis to management. Most companies in the field are stuck at measurement or analysis.
- Since the first edition of *Reputation Management*, researchers have done great work to validate the benefits of a good reputation (see Chapter 1). That argument is settled.
- If the parts of reputation can be managed so too can the whole. We think this book, with special thanks to our many contributors, will help solidify that argument.

There are still leading executives and academics who say reputation cannot be managed. Some of them are successful and highly regarded in the reputation field, marketing academic offerings or their services to students and companies. And so, before we set the foundation for this edition, we would ask them this question:

If one cannot do anything about reputation, what the heck are you selling?

DEFINITIONS AND BASIC PREMISE

Public Relations:

> The management of communication and relationships between an organization and its publics. It is also the selling of ideas, policies, products and services through often uncontrolled media and two-way communication that complement or replace the controlled media and often one-way communication of advertising.
>
> – Doorley / Garcia

The above definition is built on the seminal, ten-word definition by Grunig and Hunt—"the management of communication between an organization and its publics."

Corporate and Organizational Communication:

> The centralized management of communication on behalf of the organization; the function is a critical contributor to an organization's reputation—and thereby its competitiveness, productivity, and financial success. It is a subset of public relations.
>
> – Doorley / Garcia

Corporate Reputation:

> How the corporation is perceived.
>
> – Doorley / Garcia

Product Brand:

> How the (marketing) organization wants the product to be perceived.
>
> – Doorley / Garcia

Corporate Brand:

> How the corporation wants to be perceived. Success, at least from the perspective of those who lead the company, would have corporate reputation equal to corporate brand.
>
> – Doorley / Garcia

This book on public relations and corporate and organizational communication is grounded on the simple premise that everything communicators do should be respectful of, if not geared toward, the long-term interests of the organization. Organizations that manage their reputations well benefit not just in so-called soft, feel-good ways, but in quantifiable, bottom-line ways as well. Organizations that ignore the reputational effects of their actions pay the consequences over the long term, as the rash of business scandals has shown. And the consequences range from soft, embarrassing ones to dissolution of the organization.

This book is unique because:

- It covers each of the major disciplines in the field of corporate and organizational communication, bridging real-world practice with communication theory and history.
- It covers the field from the perspective of reputation management, and provides a new framework for managing reputation into the future.
- Every chapter and sidebar article is written by someone who has practiced the craft successfully at a high level.
- The authors cite personal experiences, including both successes and failures.
- Each of the chapters include some history and theory, real-world how-to information, and the perspective of a practitioner other than the chapter's author.
- Each chapter concludes with best practices, resources for further study, and questions for further discussion.

It is our hope that this book will help advance the practice of public relations and corporate and organizational communication by helping practitioners and students become more knowledgeable about the history, theory, and practice of their craft. Ours is not a primer—for example, we do not show readers how to write a press release. Our book presumes a basic knowledge

What we have tried to produce is a how-to book, based on solid academic principles and written by leaders from the communication professions.

of communication theory and practice appropriate to professional communicators, executives, and students at the advanced undergraduate or graduate levels. There are good basic public relations and communication texts on the market. What we have tried to produce is a how-to book, based on solid academic principles and written by leaders from the communication professions—a book that addresses communication problems and opportunities in a thoughtful, thoroughgoing, practical way.

This book is a team project. John and Fred have collaborated on the entire book, and have shared responsibility for drafting individual chapters. John has taken the lead in drafting the chapters on "Reputation Management," "Media Relations," and "Community Relations," and has done much of the liaison and editing work with outside authors. Fred has taken the lead in drafting the chapters on "Communication Ethics," "Investor Relations," "Issue Management," "Crisis Management," and "Challenges and Opportunities." John wrote the proposal for the book and secured the agreement with the publisher.

We have also sought the help of many prominent practitioners whose perspectives and experiences complement ours. These contributions come in two forms: authorship or coauthorship of individual chapters, and contributions of sidebars or case studies within chapters.

To keep clear who wrote what, the chapters written by John and Fred have no author attribution at the beginning of the chapter; each chapter written by a contributor begins with the contributor's byline.

ILLUSTRATIONS

Back in 2006 when we were beginning to wrap up the first edition, we approached an illustrator who had done many of the wonderful *New Yorker* cartoons. Fred and John asked for his fee and were about to budget for it when we thought it would be nice to retain one of our students. Long story short, we found Julie Osborn, a graduate student in the Center for Advanced Digital Applications Program in New York University's School of Continuing and Professional Studies. Lucky us! Julie's work, though Jules Pfeiffer-like, is original, sometimes humorous, always engaging. Since our first edition was published, Julie has earned her graduate degree and landed a job with George Lucas (the *Star Wars* Lucas). Lucky George! It was Julie who conceived Mr. ProCom and Ms. ProCom shown in the book's chapter openers. But then the question for John and Fred became: Which person to use with which chapter? Being quite the serious professional communicators ourselves, we pondered the media relations challenges, the looming issues to manage. Should we prepare a crisis communication contingency plan? In the end, we decided to have Ms. ProCom adorn the cover of each of the chapters of editions 1, 2, and 3. Why? Perhaps because we have a few more male contributors in our book than female; perhaps because women communicators now have a population edge in the PR profession; or perhaps because Fred and John found Ms. ProCom to be better company. And if any of this is upsetting to anyone anywhere—well, even after three editions, we still have, excuse the expression, no comment!

STRUCTURE OF THE BOOK

Chapter 1 includes "The Ten Precepts of Reputation Management," with the tenth stipulating that reputation should be managed like any other asset—that is, in a strategic way. The rest of the chapter includes a copyrighted framework for implementing Comprehensive Reputation Management. It is remarkable, but very few organizations approach reputation management in a comprehensive way, as they would any other asset; in fact, most organizations do not know what their reputations are worth. Corporate communication professionals should make it their business to understand the value of reputation, and ways to support, enhance, and measure it. Chapter 1 also includes a discussion of the Pushmi-Pullyu syndrome, whose schizophrenic tug has been felt by every communication professional.

Chapter 2 focuses on ethics. The subject is up front in the book, right where it belongs. The ethical practice of communication is neither an oxymoron nor an afterthought, but should be an integral part of practicing the craft. And it has a tangible effect on reputation. Failure to keep ethical issues always in mind can cause predictable, negative consequences. At New York University's Center for Marketing, whose students are working professionals, Fred used to teach communication ethics in the fall semester and crisis communication in the spring semester. Students invariably wanted to discuss the same case studies in both semesters; they noticed a meaningful overlap in companies with ethical challenges and crises. That led some students to note: "Better pay attention during fall or you'll be quite busy in the spring." This chapter includes general principles of communication ethics, the normative standards of behavior embodied in the codes of ethics of major professional organizations, accounts of recent scandals in communication ethics, and two historical sidebars showing that such ethical issues have been part of professional communication for many, many years.

Chapters 3–13 are organized according to the corporate and organizational communication disciplines (for example, media relations, organizational communication, and government relations), or around issues or functions that protect reputation (such as corporate responsibility, issue management, and crisis communication).

Each of the chapters begins with a true anecdote that reflects the essence of the chapter.

Chapter 14 looks ahead, and frames criteria for the successful practice of public relations and corporate and organizational communication in the future. It also describes ways to enhance the credibility of the communication function among senior leaders. It provides a framework for thinking strategically about the impact of communication, and on assuring that all the organizational communication functions are aligned not only with each other but also with the bigger enterprise.

For those who wish to compare this third edition with editions 1 and 2, you will notice that the chapter entitled Global Corporate Communication is gone. That isn't because global is no longer relevant. Rather, the practice of public relations is so global that we've incorporated international case studies and techniques throughout the book, in each chapter.

We hope that students and professional communicators will find the personal, anecdotal approach an interesting and informative complement to other books in the field, most of which take a third-person, definitional approach. This book should also be helpful to people—from managers to CEOs—who supervise or work with professional communicators. Communication is not rocket science, but it is not easy either, and it can make or break an organization, perhaps faster than any other function.

Today, those who communicate on behalf of institutions have greater power than ever before, because communication media are both more powerful and more widespread than ever. And professional communicators are under greater pressure to use their power in the right and responsible way to meet the pressing requirements of laws and regulations, corporate and organizational governance, and a more vigilant society. Paradoxically, pressures to compromise the forthrightness standard are also becoming greater in this increasingly competitive and fast-paced world.

In order for organizations to build solid, sustainable reputations and avoid the kinds of scandals that have recently affected so many of them, organizational communication, like organizational performance, must be proficient and ethical, because communication and performance are major components of reputation. An organization must speak with all its constituencies with one voice that is highly trained and true; and although more people within the organization are joining many "conversations," thanks to social media, the need for the organization to speak with one voice remains critical, if only to meet regulatory and legal obligations, not to mention the ethical ones. It is our hope that those with a stake in corporate and organizational communication, as well as students and aspiring communicators, will find in this book sound, ethical communication principles and practices that they can believe in and adhere to over the long term.

YOU SAY COMMUNICATIONS . . . WE STILL SAY COMMUNICATION

This is a stylistic point, of course, but some logic can be brought to the discussion. Most academics label their disciplines and their courses as singular. They are professors of communication, and they teach organizational communication, intercultural communication, and so on. On the other hand, practitioners most often use the plural, and they work in departments of corporate communications, employee communications, and so on. We're afraid the academics have it. Communication covers the entire spectrum. It is a discipline, like art or language, and is therefore singular. And to label it and think of it as singular is to help elevate what is too often perceived as tactical—for example, issuing press releases and publishing newsletters. Most unabridged dictionaries make only a few exceptions to the use of communication. They refer to the various means of sending messages as plural, so that radio, television, telephones, and the Internet are communications media. And they refer to multiple messages as communications. In the 1980s, when Fred headed "communications" for a large investment bank, he was often approached by bankers who wanted to add a phone extension or install a computer. "Communications" sounds like the phone company.

This book will go with logic, and the unabridged dictionaries, and use communication. We will use the plural only in referring to the media, and to the titles of practitioners and the names of their departments, because that is how practitioners usually refer to themselves. Everywhere else, it will be communication.

John Doorley and Helio Fred Garcia

ACKNOWLEDGMENTS

This book would not have been possible without the active support and encouragement of many people in addition to the two primary authors and all of the contributors. We wish to thank all those who have supported us, our work, and the book. We wish in particular to thank our development editor at the venerable publisher Routledge, Taylor & Francis Group, Darcy Bullock, for her steady hand in helping us shape this book, offering many suggestions for improvement along the way.

We wish also to take a moment, individually, to acknowledge and thank those who have helped each of us in our task.

JOHN DOORLEY'S ACKNOWLEDGMENTS

To Carole Doorley, with love and gratitude.

To these executives, former executives, and friends who have done the profession of public relations proud by communicating strategically, ethically, and very successfully over the years. I appreciate your reading the various iterations of the manuscript, the fervent discussions, and the insights Fred and I could not have brought by ourselves.

Albert D. Angel
Mike Atieh
John Baruch (deceased)
Kenneth P. Berkowitz
Rich Coyle
Ernie Grigg
Robert Pellet
Randy Poe
Richard D. Trabert
Paul Verbinnen

To these communication scholars for their encouragement, editing, and scholarly insights:

Boston College:
Edmund M. Burke (deceased)

Boston University
James Katz

New York University:
William E. Burrows
Lou Capozzi
Helen Ostrowski
Fraser Seitel

Purdue University:
Stacey Connaughton

Rutgers University:
Todd Hunt
Brent D. Ruben

University of California Santa Barbara:
Ronald Rice

University of Missouri:
Donald Ranly

Western Michigan University:
Maureen Taylor

To Lisa Ryan and Jim Masuga of Heyman Associates for helping to recruit contributors and co-authors. To Michael Cushny of NYU for sending us Julie Osborn, our illustrator.

To the following family, friends, and colleagues for their logistical, proofreading, editing and moral support: Carole Doorley, Jonathan Doorley, Nanci Doorley, Clark Landale, Madeline Najdzin, Nick Kornick, Dr. Charles P. Yezbak, and Sam and Jean Davis.

HELIO FRED GARCIA'S ACKNOWLEDGMENTS

Much of the content of the chapters I drafted was honed over thirty-five years of advising clients and twenty-seven years of teaching students, mostly at NYU. I thank those clients and students, whose insights and challenges allowed me to grapple with the issues distilled here.

I thank my colleagues at Logos Consulting Group and the Logos Institute for Crisis Management and Executive Leadership, especially Barbara Greene, Anthony Ewing,

Laurel Hart, Oxana Trush, Raleigh Mayer, Kristin Johnson, Adam Tiouririne, Katie Garcia, and Evan Chethik. I wish to particularly thank those who helped me with the specific content of the book. These include Katie Garcia, Adam Tiouririne, and Evan Chethik, who helped develop case studies, fact checked, and confirmed citations for the footnotes. I extend special thanks to two of my graduate students who helped me with case studies on events that took place in Asia: Yvonne Xiaoqian Du and Iris Wenting Xue (Iris also prepared the index). Elizabeth Jacques did much of the fact checking and research for the first edition, some part of which remains reflected in this edition. And the late Lisa Wagner designed the graphics for the ethics, issues, crisis, and challenges section.

I also thank colleagues who contributed to this volume in their own rights as chapter author, chapter coauthor, or sidebar author. These include my Logos colleagues and friends Anthony Ewing (Chapter 12, Corporate Responsibility), Laurel Hart (Chapter 4, Social Media), and Raleigh Mayer (Sidebar, Chapter 3, The Art of the Pitch); my friends Jeff Grimshaw and Tanya Mann (Chapter 5, Organizational Communication); my friend and colleague Gene Donati (coauthor with me of Chapter 8, Investor Relations), and Judy Voss (Sidebar, Chapter 14, Challenges Facing the Public Relations Practitioner Today).

And finally I wish to thank my family: my wife, Laurel Garcia Colvin, and our daughters, Katie and Juliana. They are the loves of my life and I count my blessings every day. And my mom, Anezia MC Garcia, and my brothers, Tom Garcia and Chuck Garcia.

ABOUT THE AUTHORS

JOHN DOORLEY

 John Doorley joined the new London-based company Mindful Reputation in 2013 after almost ten years at New York University as founding academic director and clinical assistant professor of the master of science degree program in Public Relations and Corporate Communication. Under his leadership the NYU program became the world's largest graduate program in its field and the one named America's Best Public Relations Education Program in 2009 and 2010. Before joining NYU he was a full-time faculty member in the School of Communication at Rutgers University.

Previously, until 2000, John was head of corporate communication at Merck & Co., Inc., which was named America's Most Admired Company seven of his 12 years there (annual *Fortune Magazine* survey). Before joining Merck, he was a director of public relations and a speechwriter at Hoffmann-LaRoche Inc.

At NYU in 2012, he developed and taught the world's first graduate course in reputation management. He coauthored with Helio Fred Garcia the first text on reputation management (*Reputation Management*, from Routledge, Taylor & Francis), the third edition of which will be released in 2015, and copyrighted a process, Comprehensive Reputation Management, to help organizations measure, analyze, monitor, and manage their reputations. John's most recent book, *Rethinking Reputation*, from St. Martin's Press, written with Fraser Seitel, premiered at number 12 on the Amazon list of best-selling business management books.

While at Merck, John designed and directed reputation management initiatives that cultivated solid relationships with internal and external stakeholders, especially the press. He helped lead many policy initiatives for Merck and the healthcare industry, most notably in AIDS, healthcare reform and managed care, and directed the company's communication programs for each of its business development initiatives, including acquisitions and joint ventures. John wrote the proposal for the Merck

Manual Home Edition, the first edition of which sold two million copies. He won the Merck Chairman's Award, the company's coveted top honor.

In 2009 he worked with the communication leadership at Johnson & Johnson to found the Academy for Communication Excellence & Leadership (ACCEL), now one of industry's most successful career development initiatives for communicators.

John earned a bachelor's degree in Biology from St. Vincent College in Latrobe, PA., a master's degree in Journalism from New York University, and he completed the Harvard-Merck Executive Business Program. He has won numerous writing awards, and been recognized by the New Jersey Governor's Office for his pro bono work with pediatric cancer patients.

He and his wife, Carole, have two grown children, Nanci and Jonathan.

John can be reached at johnd@mindfulreputation.com

HELIO FRED GARCIA

For 35 years Helio Fred Garcia has helped leaders build trust, inspire loyalty, and lead effectively. He is a coach, counselor, teacher, writer, and speaker whose clients include some of the largest and best-known companies and organizations in the world. Fred is the president of Logos Consulting Group and the executive director of The Logos Institute for Crisis Management & Executive Leadership.

Fred has been on the New York University faculty since 1988 and has received his school's awards for teaching excellence, for outstanding service, and for twenty-five years service in teaching. He is an adjunct professor of management in NYU's Stern School of Business Executive MBA program, where he teaches crisis management. He is an adjunct associate professor of management and communication in NYU's master's in Corporate Communication program in the School of Professional Studies. In that program he teaches courses in communication strategy; in communication ethics, law, and regulation; and in crisis communication.

Fred is also on the adjunct faculty of the Starr King School for the Ministry—Graduate Theological Union in Berkeley, CA, where he teaches a seminar on religious leadership for social change. And he is on the leadership faculty of the Center for Security Studies of the Swiss Federal Institute of Technology, Zurich, Switzerland. In that program he teaches an intensive seminar in the master's in Advanced Studies in Crisis Management and Security Policy.

In 2011 Fred was designated an International Distinguished Scholar at Tsinghua University in Beijing, where he gave a series of lectures and workshops on effective crisis response for graduate students and senior government, corporate, and NGO leaders. He is a frequent guest lecturer at the Wharton School of Business of the University of Pennsylvania, the U.S. Defense Information School, U.S. Marine

Corps Command and Staff College, U.S. Marine Corps Officer Candidate School, Universidad de San Martin de Porres (Lima), and other universities.

In addition to working with John on *Reputation Management*, Fred is the author, most recently, of *The Power of Communication: Skills to Build Trust, Inspire Loyalty, and Lead Effectively*, FT Press, 2012. That book was named to the United States Marine Corps Commandant's Professional Reading List for 2013 and 2014. A Chinese language edition of *The Power of Communication* was published jointly in 2014 by Pearson Education Asia Ltd. in Hong Kong and by Publishing House of Electronics Industry in Beijing. His two-volume book *Crisis Communications* was published by AAAA Publications in 1999.

Fred is accredited by the Public Relations Society of America, and received the Society's New York Chapter's Philip Dorf Award for mentoring.

Fred has master of arts in Philosophy from Columbia University and two graduate certificates in classical Greek language and literature from the Latin/Greek Institute of the City University of New York Graduate Center. He has a BA with honors in politics and philosophy from New York University, where he was elected to Phi Beta Kappa. He received an honorary doctorate in Humane Letters from Mount Saint Mary College.

Fred can be reached at HFGarcia@logosconsulting.net

ABOUT THE CONTRIBUTORS

Chapter Contributor Biographies

Chapter 3, Media Relations, by the authors with significant input and writing from Jennifer Hauser of Edelman, the world's largest public relations agency.

Jennifer Hauser is an executive vice president at Edelman. Through her twenty-three-year career in the public relations industry, she's worked with leading global brands and organizations across multiple sectors including health, food/nutrition and consumer goods, and technology. She actively represents clients including Merck Consumer Healthcare, Glaxo SmithKline, Pfizer, Johnson & Johnson, The Dannon Company, Microsoft, and the American Heart Association. Jennifer is also on the faculty at New York University in the School of Continuing & Professional Studies. Prior to joining Edelman, Ms. Hauser owned a public relations agency she started in 1993. She sold her agency in 2002 to Havas/Euro RSCG Magnet.

Chapter 4, Social Media, by Laurel Hart, Logos Consulting Group

Laurel Hart is a senior advisor at Logos Consulting Group, where she counsels clients on social media, crisis communication and strategic communication. She has over 15 years of communication experience, at Logos and for companies and non-profits in Seattle and New York City. Laurel was also an adjunct instructor at NYU until 2013, where she helped develop and taught a course on social media in the MS in Public Relations and Corporate Communication program. In addition, she has been a regular guest lecturer at the Wharton School of Business of the University of Pennsylvania. She has a BA in English from Colby College and an MS in Public Relations and Corporate Communication from NYU.

Chapter 5, Organizational Communication, by Jeff Grimshaw, Tanya Mann and Lynne Viscio of MG Strategy

Jeff Grimshaw, a partner at MGStrategy, is an expert on accountability, alignment, and leadership effectiveness. Over two decades, he's helped hundreds of executives deliver the results on which they've staked their reputations. His clients include senior leaders in dozens of Fortune 500 companies. In March 2010, McGraw-Hill published

Jeff's book, *Leadership Without Excuses: How to Create Accountability and High Performance (Instead of Just Talking about It)*, now in second printing.

Tanya Mann, a partner at MGStrategy, helps leaders elevate their effectiveness, especially when it comes to aligning and engaging employees in pursuit of important outcomes. Across engagements, she has built a consistent track record of helping clients address their immediate needs—while leaving behind stronger teams, greatly improved communication processes, and increased leadership capability. She has a bachelor's degree in Communication Studies and a master's degree in Interpersonal Communication, both with honors from the University of Texas at Austin.

Lynne Viscio, a principal at MGStrategy, consults with clients on organizational effectiveness, organizational design, internal communication strategy, and leadership development. Lynne brings focused problem-solving skills, facilitation expertise, and deep organizational experience to a broad range of situations and challenges. She works to drive business results by removing barriers, strengthening processes, and developing leaders and team members. She has a bachelor's degree in Education from the University of Connecticut and graduate degrees from the University of New Hampshire (MS), New York Medical College (MPH), and Temple University (M.Ed.).

Chapter 6, Government Relations, by Ed Ingle, managing director of government affairs, Microsoft Corporation

Ed Ingle joined Microsoft Corporation in 2003 as managing director of government affairs, and has over twenty-five years of public policy and political experience. He previously served in the White House as a senior aide to President George W. Bush. Ed was a consultant for twelve years with the Wexler & Walker government relations firm (owned by WPP Group plc), where he lobbied Congress and the Executive Branch on behalf of corporate clients. He served in the Reagan White House Office of Management and Budget from 1985–1989. Ed has a bachelor's degree in Journalism and Public Relations from the University of Tennessee, and a master's in Public Administration and Policy from Indiana University.

Chapter 8, Investor Relations, by the authors and Eugene Donati of Lycoming College

Eugene L. Donati is an assistant professor and director of the corporate communication program at Lycoming College, Williamsport, PA. His research interests include the communication of financial information and the role of public relations in public policy formulation and political campaign management. He is also an adjunct professor at New York University, where he teaches investor relations. Gene is a graduate of the Universities of Toronto and Pittsburgh and the American University, Washington. He began his thirty-year public relations career as a press secretary on Capitol Hill and, later, was managing director at the consulting firm Clark & Weinstock, New York.

Chapter 9, Integrated Communication, by Tim McMahon of Creighton University

Tim P. McMahon is a member of the full-time faculty in the Business School of Creighton University as well as a management consultant at McMahon Marketing LLC. He has been on the full-time faculty at New York University, St Joseph University and Elon University. Previously, he headed corporate marketing and communication at ConAgra Foods, Inc., then a Fortune 100 company. Before that, he founded and managed an award-winning advertising and public relations firm for twelve years. Also, he has headed national advertising for Pizza Hut, Inc. and was the founding marketing director for Godfather's Pizza, Inc., then one of the country's fastest-growing restaurant chains. He holds a Ph.D. from Gonzaga University, a master of arts from Seton Hall University and a bachelor of arts from the University of Nebraska. He is an expert in a number of communication areas including organizational communication, integrated communication and social media.

Chapter 12, Corporate Responsibility, by Anthony P. Ewing of Columbia University and Logos Consulting

Anthony P. Ewing is a lawyer, consultant, and teacher. As a senior advisor at Logos Consulting Group, Anthony counsels senior executives on corporate responsibility, crisis management, and communication strategy. Anthony has helped companies to engage stakeholders, conduct due diligence, and implement policies to understand and manage the risk of adverse human rights impacts. Anthony teaches a graduate seminar on corporate responsibility at Columbia Law School. He has served as an independent expert for the International Labour Organization and is a member of the United Nations Global Compact Human Rights and Labour Working Group. Anthony holds a BA in political science from Yale University and a law degree from Columbia University.

Chapter 13, Public Relations Consulting, By Louis Capozzi, President PRSA Foundation

Louis Capozzi has a broad background in issues and crisis management and communications, working at major public relations firms, with large multinational companies and as an educator.

As Chairman of the MSL Group, Lou managed all of the $4 billion Group's PR and corporate communications businesses. His responsibilities encompassed firms in forty cities around the world, with a total of 2000 employees and more than $200 million in revenues. Before joining MSL, Lou was vice president of corporate communications for Aetna Life & Casualty where he managed a 150-person corporate communications department with a budget of more than $80 million. Today, he is a widely respected educator and the president of the PRSA Foundation, working to drive ethnic and racial diversity in the public relations profession.

Expert Perspectives and Case Study Contributor Biographies

Karan Bhatia serves as Vice President of Global Government Affairs and Policy for General Electric overseeing GE's engagement on commercial and public policy issues with governments around the world.

Before joining GE, he was Deputy U.S. Trade Representative, Assistant Secretary of Transportation for Aviation and International Affairs, and Deputy Under Secretary of Commerce for the Bureau of Industry and Security. Prior to his government service, he was a partner at Wilmer Cutler & Pickering.

Bhatia holds a bachelor's degree from Princeton University, a master's from the London School of Economics, and a law degree from Columbia University.

Sandra Combs Boyette is senior advisor to the president at Wake Forest University. Prior to that appointment, she was Wake Forest's vice president for public affairs and then vice president for university advancement. A graduate of the University of North Carolina at Charlotte, she holds a master's degree in Education from Converse College and earned her MBA at Wake Forest. She has more than thirty-one years of experience in higher education public relations and fundraising.

Simon Cole's career in brand, advertising and communications consultancy has spanned nearly thirty years. Originally a mathematician he has held senior positions in Saatchi & Saatchi, the brand consultancy Interbrand and corporate communications consultancy Financial Dynamics (now FTI). In 2009 he founded Reputation Dividend, the corporate reputation and branding firm specializing in applying quantitative analytics to reputation management (see www.reputationdividend.com). His working life has taken in some of the disciplines of the communications industry and he has advised many of the world's largest and best known brand owners. He has both published and spoken widely on the management and economics of brands and branding.

Bob DeFillippo is chief communications officer for Prudential Financial, a global financial institution with operations in the United States, Asia, Europe, and Latin America, where he directs the company's public relations, crisis communications, event planning, internet and social media editorial content, video production, and company-wide employee engagement communications. DeFillippo is also an adjunct professor at NYU's School of Professional Studies, and has previously served as director of public affairs for the American Association of Retired Persons (AARP), press secretary to U.S. Rep. Hamilton Fish Jr., and as a newspaper reporter and editor. He graduated from Long Island University's Brooklyn Center with a bachelor's degree in Journalism.

Paul Gennaro is the senior vice president and chief communications officer for AECOM Technology Corp., an $8 billion global provider of professional services, with 45,000 employees operating 140 countries. He leads all aspects of the company's global corporate communication efforts, including: corporate brand and reputation management, public and media relations, internal communications, crisis and issue management, investor relations, philanthropy and community relations, and government relations. Mr. Gennaro was named one of the "100 Most Influential in Business Ethics" by the Ethisphere Institute and one of the "50 Most Powerful People in PR" by *PRWeek*.

Phil Gomes' career in the communications field is characterized by his passionate interest in technology, media, and emerging forms of communication. As a senior vice president with Edelman Digital, Phil challenges teams and companies to engage with online communities in ways that are compelling, persuasive, and parallel with "digital citizenship" expectations. These instincts for online community mores have also made Phil a consistent go-to resource at the firm for online crisis communications. Phil co-founded Corporate Representatives for Ethical Wikipedia Engagement (CREWE), a group of PR professionals and Wikipedians who seek to cooperate in the public interest of accurate articles about corporations and organizations. He earned a bachelor of arts in Communications from Saint Mary's College of California and an MBA from Purdue University.

Sandra Macleod, CEO of Mindful Reputation, has provided evidence-based counsel and worked to build the professionalism of communications and reputation management for over 25 years. She is one of the founders of the International Association of Measurement and Evaluation Companies (AMEC), a Companion of the Chartered Institute of Management, a member of the McKinsey Women as Leaders' Forum and has been is cited as "among the 100 most influential people in PR" by *PRWeek*. From an early career at Edelman Public Relations in London and Information et Enterprise in Paris, Sandra went on to become head of communications at PA Management Consulting before setting up the first international franchise for media analysis company, CARMA International, in 1989. Ten years later, she founded Echo Research as a full-service research firm with offices in the London, Paris, New York, and Singapore. Winning a record-breaking eighty-nine industry awards for innovation and excellence in research, the Echo group was acquired by Ebiquity PLC in 2011 and rebranded under the same name in 2013. She founded Mindful Reputation in 2013.

Raleigh Mayer, the "Gravitas Guru" and principal of Raleigh Mayer Consulting, helps senior executives elevate presence, speak persuasively, and become more sophisticated at managing their relationships and reputations. A senior fellow at the Logos Institute for Crisis Management and Executive Leadership, Raleigh is an instructor at Barnard College's Athena Center for Women's Leadership, lecturer at Harvard Business School, presenter at Columbia University's MBA programs, coach for New York University's Stern School of Business, and adjunct professor of marketing and management at NYU for over twenty years. Raleigh is executive presence correspondent for The Glass Hammer, an online community for women executives in financial services, law, and business.

Michael Neuwirth is senior director of PR for Dannon, the U.S. subsidiary of global food maker Danone. Michael joined Dannon in 2005 and directs corporate communications, including crisis communications. Michael began his career at Porter

Novelli (1990–1994) and then established the corporate communications role within Danone's North American bottled water and specialty food businesses (1994–2001). Michael returned to Danone and Dannon in 2005 after working for two years (2003–2005) as senior vice president of Ruder Finn, and prior to this for an organic food company (2001–2003). Michael is an honors graduate of Vassar College and lives in New York City with his wife and children.

Julie M. Osborn is currently working at Mattel on Playground Productions' animated Barbie feature films in Los Angeles, where she moved after spending four years in northern California at Lucasfilm. She had the great pleasure there to work on the two-time Emmy-winning children's animated television series *Star Wars: The Clone Wars* under the tutelage of George Lucas himself. She earlier received her bachelor of arts in Studio Art with a minor in Japanese Language from the University of California, San Diego, after which she moved to New York for a change of pace at New York University where she received an MS in Digital Imaging and Design. While earning her degree, she met one of the authors of this book, John Doorley, and happily accepted the challenge of becoming the illustrator.

Katja Schroeder is the president of Expedition PR and an adjunct professor for Marketing at St. Francis College. She has led award-winning communication programs for global brands across regions and created local programs onsite in Germany, China, France, and North America. Before founding Expedition PR, Katja serviced global brands at Burson-Marsteller and Ruder Finn in New York and China. She holds a master of arts in Communications and Business Administration from the FU Berlin, Germany, and a master of arts in Communications and Information Sciences from CELSA, Sorbonne, Paris, France. She sits on the board of the Center for Entrepreneurship of St. Francis College.

Gary Sheffer oversees external and internal communications and provides strategic communications advice to GE executives on issues related to culture, reputation, and strategy. He also works with external groups and individuals to foster understanding of GE policies and businesses. Sheffer joined GE in 1999 after seventeen years in journalism and government communications, including serving as a press aide to two New York governors. Before working in government, Sheffer was a reporter and editor at several newspapers winning many awards for his reporting. Sheffer is chairman of the board of the Arthur W. Page Society, a membership organization for senior public relations and corporate communications executives. He also serves on the board of the Institute for Public Relations and is a member of the boards of the GE Foundation and the GE-Reagan Scholarship Program. He earned a bachelor of arts degree in English from Siena College in Loudonville, New York.

Claude Singer is a brand strategist known for his creative flair in brand positioning, naming and narratives. He has worked for the big agencies Siegel+Gale and Lippincott, and has served clients as an independent consultant known as Brandsinger. Claude began his career writing speeches for the chairman of Chase. He did stints as vice president of corporate communications at Chemical Bank and Aetna. Today, he is EVP at Siegelvision. Claude is an active teacher. Out of graduate school he taught history at Boise State. Later he taught a graduate course in brand strategy at University of Hartford. Today he is Adjunct Faculty at NYU teaching advanced writing. Claude has a bachelor of arts from Reed College and a PhD in History from University of Washington.

Judy Voss is director of professional development for the Public Relations Society of America, the world's largest organization for public relations professionals. She provides direction and support for PRSA's seminars and more than fifty training webinars annually. She is heavily involved in developing, managing, and evaluating the annual PRSA International Conference sessions. Previously she held communications positions with both for-profit and non-profit organizations including the American Hospital Association, Perkin-Elmer and Woodhead Industries, Inc. Her titles have ranged from marketing communications specialist, to advertising manager, to manager of corporate communications. Previous responsibilities have also included branding and corporate identity work with subsidiaries through her position at a corporate headquarters. She earned her bachelor's degree from Northwestern University in Chicago, majoring in communications, and earned her Accreditation in Public Relations designation in spring 2003.

Thanks to Katherine for her input and support:

Katherine Pitney holds a master's of science in public relations and corporate communication from New York University. Prior to obtaining her master's degree, she graduated magna cum laude from Binghamton University with an advanced honor's degree in English. At only 23-years-old, she is working as a communications specialist for a manhattan staffing firm, where she manages both internal and external communication.

A very special thank you to Jeanne for preparing the accompanying electronic materials and Instructor's Manual.

Jeanne Templeton is an Account Executive in the Technology Practice at Weber Shandwick. She supports strategic public relations programs and media relations outreach across consumer technology accounts. She holds a M.S. in Public Relations and Corporate Communication from New York University's School of Continuing and Professional Studies.

1 REPUTATION MANAGEMENT

*Character is like a tree and
reputation like its shadow.
The shadow is what we think
of it; the tree is the real thing.*
                    – Abraham Lincoln

■ ■ ■

SQUANDERING THE REPUTATION ASSET: DAYS OF RECKONING DRAW NEAR

Warren Buffett famously said to new employees: "If you lose dollars for the firm by bad decisions I will be very understanding. If you lose reputation for the firm, I will be ruthless."[1] It seems the oracle of Omaha was paraphrasing the bard of the ages, whose Othello said: "He who steals my purse steals trash . . . but he that filches from me my good name . . . makes me poor indeed."

For many years CEOs and other leaders have echoed a similar mantra: "Reputation is our most important asset." So why is it that so many have let the asset be "trashed"? It will surely take years of cascading scandal and investigation to determine which and how many General Motors (GM) employees reacted negligently or worse to the ignition switch defect. While that is a stark illustration, others occur with shocking frequency and in the extreme—almost as if negligent management of the reputation asset does not really matter to those in charge. *That is about to change.*

An unmanaged asset will decline in value over time, inevitably moving to the liability column, and this is one reason for the decline in corporate reputation. Whereas most large companies today have a risk and crisis management framework in place, few have a process to manage the overall reputation asset, both the upside as well as the potential downside.

And of the companies that have risk management frameworks in place, few, as the GM recall demonstrates, coordinate and communicate the various risks residing in various parts of the organization. In her Congressional testimony of April 3, 2014 GM CEO Mary Barra acknowledged that, over the years of the ignition switch problem, internal communication was poor, with engineering and legal, for instance, not sharing information that might have saved lives.[2] (Whether that was an illustration of the George Bernard Shaw principle—"The greatest challenge of communication is the illusion that it has taken place"—or of something more sinister is a matter for the investigators.)

Is poor stewardship of reputation the result of senior executives not really believing in the importance of reputation? Or is it because they think there is no way to measure or manage reputation?

Reputation is a corporate asset of substantial and measurable value. The view that it is an intangible asset is not a constructive perspective, and it helps explain why so many senior executives who achieved success through smart management of company assets have no idea what their company's reputation is worth or how to manage it.

Over recent years the intuitive has been proven true: Companies with better reputations attract more and better employees, pay less for goods and services, accrue measurable competitive advantages, and can charge more for their own products. The argument over whether or not reputation has tangible worth is settled.

How much? Since the early 1980s the "Most Admired Companies" surveys have been providing what is generally seen as reliable benchmark data for comparing how one company is viewed versus others. Measurement analytics continue to improve. The 2014 Reputation Dividend Report indicated that the reputations of the Standard and Poor's (S&P) 500 companies accounted for 21 percent of the combined market cap of those companies.

Over the last several years, the growing desire to measure, analyze, and manage reputation has spawned numerous firms that claim to do those three things—an internet search of "reputation management" now yields over two million results—but most do little more than monitor for what is being reported and opined. The major public relations agencies and some of the large consultancies also list "reputation management" in their portfolios of offerings but they usually stop short at measurement or analysis.

The good news is that the growing market is also producing thoughtful ways of helping to build and protect reputation. Reputation can be managed, not perfectly but well. Research indicates that in companies with a process in place for managing reputation, reputation rankings are higher.

The fact is that some companies are undervalued on certain drivers of reputation—for instance, long-term investment value or corporate social responsibility—and such a problem can often be addressed through a targeted communication strategy. In other cases companies are overvalued on such drivers, which then presents a performance or a behavior challenge. To manage the components of reputation—performance, behavior, communication and intrinsic identity (what the organization stands for)—is to manage the whole. To manage relationships with groups and individuals that have a stake in the company is to manage the sum of those relationships, something called reputation.

If there had been in place at GM a rigorous, audited, reputation management, and reporting process—including objectives and strategies for accentuating the company's tremendous accomplishments in engineering and safety, as well as dealing with its problems and vulnerabilities—the chances of admitting and addressing the ignition switch problem early would have been enhanced.

This year, and more so the coming years, senior executives will succeed or fail on their ability to build and guard reputation. In the latest annual survey by the Conference Board, chief executives included reputation among their top five strategies for "driving enterprise growth and achieving better performance."

Now that there are validated ways to measure and manage the reputation asset, accountability will follow. Company leaders who are negligent in their management of reputation will meet "ruthless" consequences. Companies headed by good reputation stewards will reap the benefits of a good reputation, the greatest of which is trust, the future equity that conveys a competitive advantage of enormous value.

■ ■ ■

The business scandals of the first years of the twenty-first century demonstrated how important it is to build and guard reputation. The scandals spread to nonprofits, government, universities, and sports, and the public seemed to tire of the news reports. But fatigue did not convey immunity, so people demanded change: tougher laws, more governance, and greater accountability. At the same time, academic researchers and public relations professionals intensified efforts to quantify and manage reputation, often thought of in the past as an intangible asset.

Reputation scholar Charles Fombrun, professor emeritus, Stern School of Business, New York University, an editor-in-chief of the journal *Corporate Reputation Review*, defines reputation as the sum of the images the various constituencies have of an organization.[3]

John Doorley and Fred Garcia (this book's coauthors) accept that definition but also like their own—which leads us to:

**Reputation = Sum of Images =
Performance + Behavior + Communication**

This definition helps make it clear that performance and behavior, as well as communication, are critical components of reputation.

REPUTATIONAL CAPITAL

Just as people develop social capital that helps them build relationships and careers, corporations and other organizations develop reputational capital that helps them build relationships and grow their organizations.

A good reputation has both intangible and tangible benefits. It is important for stakeholders, from customers to employees to consumer advocates, to feel good about an organization, and it is important to build a good reputation to sustain an organization through the tough times. But a reputation is worth much more than that. Companies with the better reputations attract more and better candidates for employment, pay less for supplies, gain essentially free press and social media coverage that can be worth much more than advertising, and accrue other benefits that actually contribute to profits. Reputation adds value to the actual worth of a company—that is, market capitalization (the number of shares outstanding times the price per share) is often greater than just the book value or liquidation value of assets. The reputation component of market capitalization, reputational capital, is a concept closely related to "goodwill," and it is worth many billions of dollars in many large corporations. It has a value in not-for-profits, government, and universities as well. For instance, a good reputation helps a university attract students and donors.

Although CEOs agree that reputation has a value—is an asset—few firms actually treat it as such. Few companies or nonprofits take a rigorous, quantifiable approach to reputation management—measuring, monitoring and managing reputation assets and liabilities—yet such an approach is intrinsic to the concept of asset management. Most organizations have no idea what their reputations are worth, yet reasonable measurement can be agreed upon and taken. Most companies do not have a system in place for regular, periodic accountability on variations in reputation, yet without such a system opportunities will be missed and problems will become magnified. Measurement, acknowledgment, and planning make possible proactive behaviors and communications to take advantage of reputational opportunities and minimize problems—thereby building reputational capital.

At the same time, in other countries, developed and emerging, leaders of business, government, non-profits, universities and religions continued to demonstrate that inappropriate, even vile behavior seems to have no limits.

The formula—$R = P + B + C$—applies to the reputations of individuals as well as organizations. Within a period of weeks in the late summer of 2009, for example, four Americans behaved badly in an extraordinary way in public: tennis great Serena Williams threatened and verbally assailed a judge at the U.S. Open; Kanye West jumped on stage at the MTV Video Music Awards to wrest the microphone from one artist because he thought another deserved the VMA; Michael Jordan retraced decades-old interpersonal squabbles at his induction into the Basketball Hall of Fame; and Congressman Joe Wilson of North Carolina yelled, "You lie" when U.S. President Obama was addressing a joint session of Congress in what is usually a reverential forum. At the same time, in other countries, developed and emerging, leaders of business, government, non-profits, universities and religions continued to demonstrate that inappropriate, even vile behavior seems to have no limits.

The formula demonstrates that reputation is cumulative. So when a famous individual behaves badly, he or she cannot generally make up for it with a press conference, tweet or blog, no matter how sincere or eloquent the apology. Similarly with organizations, communication is not enough to right a wrong. A reputation is built on performance, behavior and communication and it can generally be repaired only by working on all three aspects.

EXPERT PERSPECTIVES: CORPORATE CHARACTER: THE HEART OF A DYNAMIC APPROACH TO COMMUNICATION AND REPUTATION MANAGEMENT

Leading a Transparent, Engaged General Electric

By Gary Sheffer

The world has changed quickly and significantly for corporate communicators in the past decade: The global population is on the rise; natural disasters are wreaking havoc at unprecedented rates; and the global economy is still recovering from the Great Recession. At the same time, digital technologies have democratized thought leadership and reputation, giving millions of people a voice in your reputation and brand. As a result, the communications landscape has been forced to respond to align with these new realities.

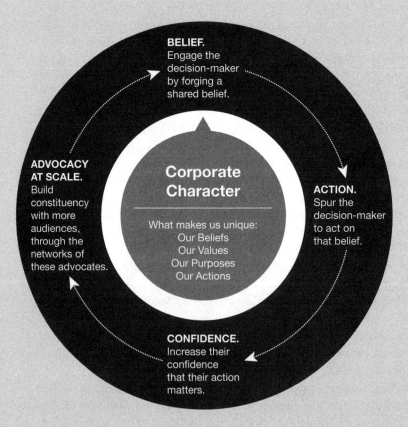

Figure 1.1 Page Society New Model for Enterprise Communications

Reprinted with permission from the Arthur W. Page Society

Communicators now play a more critical role in ensuring the reputation of their organization is protected and enhanced amidst a global landscape that is defined by high risk, low trust and little patience for nuance.

To succeed in developing a sustainable corporate reputation in this environment, a company must define and know itself. No matter how volatile the environment becomes, a strong sense of self—or "corporate character"—will help build value inside an enterprise as well as trust and good will externally. This thesis is the heart of a dynamic approach to communications and reputation management, the Corporate Communications Model, released in 2012 by the Arthur W. Page Society.

Defining Corporate Character

Corporate character is defined as the unique purpose, beliefs, mission and values that are at the center of your company culture. Critical to the strength of any corporate communications function is the ability to understand the values of the company, to clearly define it and to engage employees as authentic advocates for the brand.

The Page Society introduced the New Model for Enterprise Communications as a new framework for how communicators can define and activate their companies' unique corporate character and build "advocacy at scale."

At GE a few years ago we realized the world we once knew had shifted. A decade of significant growth and change across GE's portfolio, lingering fallout from a deep recession and loss of trust in Corporate America, a challenging and skeptical media with a keen eye on taxes and business outside the U.S., and a natural disaster in Japan created a volatile and challenging communications environment for us.

We were being defined by narrow issues that ignored the GE we knew—a company that is committed to taking on tough challenges, to invent and build what the world needs and to do so with an enduring commitment to integrity. While our highly successful tagline, "imagination at work," spoke to the hard work and wonder of our company, we knew it was time to change the emphasis to reflect the seriousness of the times.

We hung on to "imagination at work" but focused more emphasis on "work." We reframed and restated our identity, purpose, and value by first listening to our employees around the world. They told us that they came to work every day to try to make things better in energy, transportation, healthcare, aviation, and finance. That they were committed to delivering results for their customers, society and our shareowners—that they wanted to do nothing less than move, power, build and cure the world.

These passionate contributions from our colleagues defined the strong foundation for a new communications platform—GE Works. We liked it because it authentically reflected the company culture, its people and the impact of their work. In developing GE Works, we were often guided by the Page model, which puts corporate character at its center.

Putting Corporate Character into Practice

Once corporate character is defined and there is internal buy-in, it is important to communicate externally with transparency. In other words, we decided to take our culture beyond the GE "fire wall." By defining a set of strategic imperatives that align with our corporate character, we could determine what kinds of engagement would authentically and persuasively deliver the company message.

To reach all target audiences with GE Works, we knew we needed to activate around these strategic imperatives:

- Put employees at the heart of storytelling to demystify the work that GE does and underscore its impact
- Micro-target those we want to reach—employees, investors, science geeks, entrepreneurs—and resist the big company urge to target everyone
- Illustrate GE's role as a leading technology company and leverage our heritage in manufacturing to drive perception of innovation and increase favorability
- Align GE's message with public debate by focusing on America's economic future and to drive meaningful and honest dialogue about American competitiveness
- Engage at a hyper-local level through thought leadership events, factory tours, and employee town halls, for example bringing Chairman Jeffrey Immelt and senior executives to dozens of communities to highlight the powerful combination of employees, technology and community that make GE work
- Develop new advertising to humanize the company and show GE at work through the lens of its employees, demonstrating the value and impact of their work
- Drive online engagement through GE-owned channels and external platforms, often in a humorous and unexpected way

We introduced GE Works externally through a robust campaign tying together advertising, digital/social, public affairs, communications, executive positioning, and employee engagement in order to align with our strategic imperatives and reach our target audiences.

Results

Two years later, our reputation and brand are stronger, our employees are proud and, frankly, the communications team is having a lot more fun. Sitting down with our colleagues to define a clear corporate character was quite satisfying. Creating our own content—storytelling every day—energized a team weary of talking points and superficial debate. Today, you will find GE weighing in on tough public issues but also inviting the world's innovators to share ideas through campaigns like "Six Second Science."

At GE, we used the external environment to discuss who we are and to connect our people to a broader mission—we are advocating at scale and leading a transparent, engaged enterprise. Ironically, the volatile environment has strengthened our culture, as GE people have coalesced around our challenges, re-examined our values and clarified our purpose.

Keys to success:

1. Define your company's corporate character.
2. Engage internal stakeholders as authentic advocates.
3. Determine how you communicate your corporate character externally and micro target your audiences.
4. Activate the appropriate elements of engagement that reach your core audiences in an authentic way.
5. Remain open, transparent and true to your corporate character through all your communications.

IDENTITY

To academics in communication, "identity" is the raison d'etre of an organization. It is, simply, what the organization stands for above all else. To distinguish this concept from other uses of the term (such as corporate identity programs that try to position the company in a particular way through all its communications and graphic vehicles), Paul Verbinnen of Sard Verbinnen coined the term "intrinsic identity." (We use that term in this book.)

> "Identity" is the raison d'etre of an organization. It is, simply, what the organization stands for above all else.

Of course organizations, like individuals, have multiple identities. Research by George Cheney of the University of Colorado, in *Rhetoric in an Organizational Society: Managing Multiple Identities*, is consistent with the proposition that multiple identities need not pose any conflicts, as long as there is a clear, dominant identity.[4] Companies such as the venerable General Electric and the relative upstart Starbucks, have each stayed true to a dominant identity: respectively developing and marketing consumer and technology products of the highest quality, and employing the best people to obtain, market, and sell quality coffee and collateral products in a warm and welcoming venue. Starbucks is not at all embarrassed to proclaim the ideals of mutually beneficial and profitable relationships with employees and communities.

Other organizations and industries, sadly and notably, have recently failed to stay true to the dominant identities that made them successful. Some learned from their failings; the verdict is not yet in on others.

Dairy Scandals in India and China. The problems were similar in both countries and occurred at about the same time, circa 2008–2013. In India, where cows have been thought of with reverence, the problem was impurities in almost three-fourths of the milk tested by the Indian Food Safety and Standards Authority, impurities that included urea and formaldehyde. In China, dairy products from major providers were found to contain chemicals that can cause kidney stones and liver cancer. Observers in both countries attributed the abysmal failures to ensure quality to overzealous dedication to market growth and profiteering. Quickly, though, at least one major producer in each country took a leadership role, with excellent results.

The Indian company, Pride of Cows, stepped up its quality control, and then marked its milk as a premium product that costs more but is of better quality. This company's cows are now treated humanely, almost with reverence, and other Indian manufacturers are following. Already, it seems clear that Indians are willing to pay more for pure milk.

> But when subprime mortgages presented the opportunity to earn large amounts of money quickly, the Lehman executives ignored those values and lost in the end.

Mengniu Dairy Group was China's largest dairy company in 2011 when its milk was found to be contaminated with melamine, a toxin that can cause liver cancer. Quickly, Mengniu invested huge resources in addressing the quality control failures in a comprehensive way that touched all parts of the company. The accompanying communication campaign that stressed employee engagement and buy-in helped bring the company back to its core values—remedying the quality problems within months.

Lehman Brothers was one of the oldest and most respected investment banks in the United States. After posting record high earnings in 2007, the bank firmly entrenched itself in the following year's subprime mortgage crisis caused by bad mortgage loans and borrowers defaulting on payments. Lehman folded resulting in the largest bankruptcy filing in U.S. history. An exchange of emails disclosed by the House Oversight Committee reveals one major cause of the collapse. A memo from managers suggested that top executives forgo their 2008 multimillion dollar bonuses. The email said, "It would send a strong message to both employees and investors that management is not shirking accountability for recent performance."[5] The Lehman executive committee dismissed the memo as a joke, and CEO Dick Fuld even told his top people not to "worry." Throughout its history, Lehman had a reputation for making values-driven decisions. But when subprime mortgages presented the opportunity to earn large amounts of money quickly, the Lehman executives ignored those values and lost in the end.

The Catholic Church. The scandals over the sexual abuse of young children by some priests, which came to light starting in the Boston Archdiocese in 2002, were shocking and horrible enough. Catholics and non-Catholics recognized that evil could exist anywhere. But what drove many Catholics away from the church was the cover-up by the church hierarchy, from bishops to cardinals. In numerous instances, they knowingly sent offending priests to other parishes without telling the legal authorities or the people in the new parish, leaving the priests free to commit the same crimes over and over. The average priest believes he exists to give spiritual and emotional guidance to the people in his parish, but many of the bishops and cardinals chose to ignore that intrinsic identity, trying to protect the church's image at all cost.

In 2003, in his first public statement as Boston's new archbishop, Sean P. O'Malley made explicit reference to the need to return to the Church's intrinsic identity:

> We can only hope that the bitter medicine we have had to take to remedy
> our mismanagement of the problem of sexual abuse will prove beneficial,
> making all of us more aware of the dreadful consequences of this crime

and more vigilant and effective in eradicating this evil from our midst. How we ultimately deal with the present crisis in our Church will do much to define us as Catholics of the future. If we do not flee from the cross of pain and humiliation, if we stand firm in who we are and what we stand for, if we work together, hierarchy, priests, religious and laity, to live our faith and fulfill our mission, then we will be a stronger and a holier Church.[6]

Many believe that the pope at that time, John Paul II, did not do enough to recognize the victims of these crimes; from a public relations standpoint, he did not. He attempted to minimize the issue with general statements and expected his American bishops to manage the problem.

His successor, Pope Benedict XVI, understood that this strategy was not working. In almost every public appearance during his first papal trip to the U.S. in 2008, he acknowledged the horror and encouraged victims and others alienated by the scandals to find comfort in their faith. He publicly apologized. In Washington, DC, Pope Benedict met privately with victims from the Archdiocese of Boston where the public exposure of the scandal began. He assured the victims that he understood the problem on an emotional level and promised to stop the abuse.

By 2013 when Francis became pope, stories of abuse by priests had come from every corner of the world. The Church had instilled numerous safeguards and provided financial compensation to thousands of victims. And while Pope Francis reached out to people from many countries and all walks of society, abandoning the trappings of the office, he was slow to address the pedophilia scandal. On July 7, 2014, he met in private with six victims, two each from Ireland, Germany and Britain. He acknowledged that the scandal had harmed the Church to its core—producing a "toxic effect on faith and hope in God." He begged forgiveness and pledged to ensure that Church hierarchy no longer would protect abusers.[7]

The New York Times. To its credit, *The New York Times* broke the story itself in a front-page exposé on May 11, 2003. Reporter Jayson Blair had plagiarized content from other newspapers, had fabricated whole stories, and had invented scenes for stories that appeared in the paper, including major front-page ones over a period of years. There were warning signs bold and numerous enough to have stopped him early on, but the top editors ignored them. Why did the people charged with seeing that the country's "newspaper of record," the one that exists to report "all the news that's fit to print," publish the unfit? An explanation that makes sense is that one of the paper's other identities—including its commitment to affirmative action (Blair is African American) and a desire not to rock the boat about a reporter thought to be a favorite of the executive editor—superseded, in this case, its commitment to quality. So while the paper can be proud of its various identities, it cannot be anything but humbled by its failure to live up to its commitment to quality journalism, above all else.

In the wake of the Blair scandal, *The Times* has reaffirmed its commitment to its intrinsic identity, and has established numerous structures, including a public editor and a standards editor, to try to assure that it is not distracted from its mission again.

It is important for employees to understand and be committed to the organization's dominant intrinsic identity. For example, if the CEO truly believes the organization is committed above all else to quality products, but the average sales person believes the dominant identity is the sales quota, there exists a prescription for disaster. For in difficult times, what the employees believe the organization stands for will determine what they will do.

Another benefit of a clear identity is that it can drive behavior, performance, and communication, as it should. Then, internal and external constituencies will all understand what the organization is about.

"INTANGIBLE ASSETT"—THE WRONG PERSPECTIVE

The historical view of reputation as an intangible asset is the wrong approach.

The reason most organizations do not have formal programs to manage reputation is that they view it as something "soft"—intangible. Yet as nebulous as reputation can seem, it has real, tangible value (dollars, for example) that can be measured. So the historical view of reputation as an intangible asset is the wrong approach. Moreover, such a view is analogous to that of some parents who say they need not be that concerned about their young children's character, because "they will be influenced by their peers anyway when they become teenagers." Such laissez-faireism—whether in parenting children or organizations—is a prescription for disaster, as history continues to demonstrate.

Like all other assets—a building or a product, for example—reputation has its liability side. So any reputation management plan has to measure, monitor, and establish a plan for managing both the reputation assets and vulnerabilities/liabilities. The important thing is to have a plan. If the following is not an ancient proverb, it should be: "If you don't know where you're going, any road will take you there." And you might end up in the wrong place.

CAN REPUTATION BE MEASURED?

In the 1990s some reputation scholars defined reputational capital as the difference, averaged over time, between market capitalization and the liquidation value of assets. Many chief financial officers disagreed with that formula, believing that the difference overstates the value of reputational capital. But even those CFOs agree that much of that difference is reputational capital. Since then, much progress has been made in quantifying the value of reputation. (See the text box on the opposite page: "The Economic Case for Corporate Reputation Management.")

A common approach to measuring reputation is to take comparative measures against similar organizations. The annual *Fortune* magazine survey of The World's Most Admired Companies is among the most widely known and respected by both industry leaders and academics. But it surveys only three constituencies: senior executives, (outside) board members, and securities analysts. A more comprehensive approach would include surveying all the major constituencies, including employees, customers, and the press.

Another is the Harris-Fombrun Reputation Quotient (by Harris Interactive in association with Charles Fombrun). It evaluates reputation among "multiple audiences," according to twenty attributes that are grouped into what are referred to as "dimensions of reputation": products and services; financial performance; workplace environment; social responsibility; vision and leadership; and emotional appeal. The results of that survey are widely covered by the press and discussed in social media.

EXPERT PERSPECTIVES: THE ECONOMIC CASE FOR CORPORATE REPUTATION MANAGEMENT

By Simon Cole and Sandra Macleod

> *If this business were split up, I would give you the land and bricks and mortar, and I would take the brands and trademarks, and I would fare better than you.*
> *– John Stuart, CEO, Quaker Oats Co. 1922–1953*

Investors tend to think of themselves as objective souls making decisions based on hard facts and rigorous analysis. They will readily agree that a company's reputation can have a considerable bearing on its value, but struggle to put a figure on just how much. The question is often avoided, dismissed under the banner of sentiment or bundled up into an equally vague box labeled goodwill. As a result, value-based assessments of companies' reputations have been ignored on the grounds that if you can't measure it, you can't account for it.

Something had to change. The sheer volume of shareholder value tied up under the all-too-amorphous banner of "intangibles" has soared in recent years to the point where by the start of 2014, the very tangible book or net asset value of companies in the S&P 500 accounted for just 41 per cent of the market capitalization. Black and Carnes reasoned as long ago as 2000 that corporate reputation makes up much of the difference because it must have worth "to the investor since it results in financial benefits to the corporation."[8] They argued that reputation contributes to the firm's value by reducing the mobility of rivals, supporting premium prices and enhancing access to capital but stopped short of identifying "a method for evaluating and measuring, in dollar terms, an individual firm's reputation."

Unlike consumer brands, the primary source of value creation from corporate brands, or, more accurately, their reputations, derives from investors. Traditional brands are valuable to their owners because of the influence they exert in guiding and securing customer transactions. Corporate reputations, however, impact primarily on investors who buy or hold a company's stock on the basis of the economic returns they expect from either capital growth or dividends. This is the key to effective reputation measurement. Understanding the mechanism by which a company's reputation returns value to its shareholders not only provides an objective means to structure communications and messaging, but also, an instrument to gauge the performance of reputation management and the return on investment.

Measuring Reputation Value

Reputation value analysis is based upon the notion that a company's market capitalization and so stock price can be explained by factors including financial indicators combined with corporate reputation. It is designed to fulfill a number of criteria; to be logically sound, transparent and based on empirical evidence; to be sensitive to the constantly changing interests of investors; and to be capable of withstanding the inevitable scrutiny of the boardroom.

The process, employing statistical regression, comprises four stages.

1. Data definition and capture

Analysis to date has been focused on leading publicly quoted corporations from two jurisdictions, the US and the UK. The modeling was designed to explain companies' market capitalizations (the "response" variable) by testing a wide selection of potential "predictor" variables over a number of years (sourced from Factset and Bloomberg) including reported and consensus forecasts of:

- EBITDA (Earnings before Interest, Tax, Depreciation and Amortization)
- EBIT (Earnings before Interest and Tax)
- EPS (Earnings per share)
- Return on assets
- Dividend yield
- Beta
- Assets
- Liabilities
- Earnings per share
- Stock liquidity

Reputation data are derived from the Most Admired Companies studies published by *Fortune* magazine in the U.S. and *Management Today* in the U.K. Although independent, the studies are highly comparable insofar as they are conducted among C-suite professionals (senior and board level executives including chief executive officers, chief communications officers, and chief financial officers) from many of the largest public companies in each market along with selected investment analysts. The main difference is in the companies covered which are by definition oriented to their respective jurisdictions.

Although by no means perfect, the Most Admired studies boast decades-long track records of consistency and are widely judged to be authoritative. Most importantly, they are, unlike other syndicated studies of corporate reputation, polling the impressions of "professional observers"—i.e., people who have a view of the business as a whole not just from the perspective of its products or services. Those views represent a close proxy for the investment community and as such can reasonably be judged to reflect investor sentiment. Other studies tend to focus on the views of consumers and, while possibly relevant to more traditional brand valuation metrics, have little useful bearing on corporate reputation in its principle role.

The Most Admired studies capture perceptions of nine different factors judged to be among the main components of corporate reputation. In the U.S. they include:

- Quality of management
- Innovation
- Quality of goods/products and services
- Social responsibility
- Financial soundness
- Long-term investment value
- Use of corporate assets
- People management
- Global competitiveness

Note: "People management" and "global competitiveness" are replaced by "ability to attract talent" and quality of "marketing" in the UK.

2. Econometric analysis

Technical analysis is structured around cross-sectional step-wise regression. Raw data are tested for independence using simple correlation analysis. Variables exhibiting signs of any relationship with market capitalization are designated possible predictor variables and prioritized. Variables showing high levels of correlation with each other are either consolidated or removed. Analysis explores the relationships between possible predictors and the response variable and identifies requirements for further variable transformation and or compounding.

Once the role of reputation has been established at the overall level it is introduced though each of its nine component drivers. Modeling uses the general form as the framework re-running the regression with the individual measures substituted for the headline rating. This determines which of the nine factors are most influential and, more importantly, their relative impact.

3. Individual company outputs

"Interrogation" of the model facilitates the creation of a combination of reputation metrics for each of the companies in the analysis. Predicted values of each company's market capitalization can then be calculated and from that a series of leading indicators. These include the following.

- *Reputation Contribution.* The proportion of a company's market cap attributable to its reputation. The primary measure of its reputation value.
- *Reputation Risk Profile.* Spelling out how any reputation value is distributed between the individual component drivers.
- *Reputation Leverage.* The extent of the economic return that can be expected from specific increases in overall reputation strength (expressed in terms of projected increases in market cap).

4. Market behavior

Finally, armed with a detailed explanation of the individual reputation assets of a cross-section of leading U.S. and U.K. companies, pictures of the overall state of corporate reputation can be compiled. These include the scale of the reputation assets as a whole, how they are trending, the individual company winners and losers and the overall potential to deploy reputation to grow shareholder value.

Note: A more detailed explanation can be found in *World Economics Journal*, vol. 13, no. 3.[9]

Learnings—The Evidence for Reputation Value

Corporate reputation is a major contributor to shareholder return.

The implications of the analysis built up over the seven years since the tracking began in 2008 are clear; company reputations are, as many already believe, real, present, and

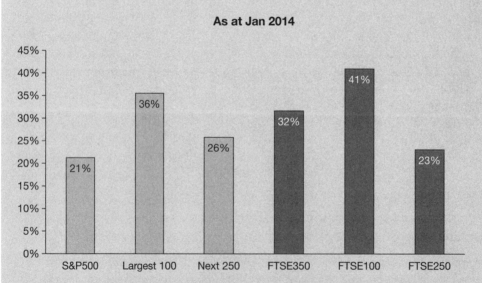

Figure 1.2 Reputation Contribution—U.S. vs U.K. Averages

Source: Reputation Dividend

often very substantial economic assets. Indeed, they rank among the most important repositories of corporate value in both the U.S. and the U.K. where they accounted for nearly $3.7 trillion of shareholder value in the S&P 500 and $1.5 trillion in the U.K.'s FTSE 100 at the start of 2014.[10]

Reputation Contribution, the proportion of a company's market capitalization attributable to its reputation, varies in broad terms by company size. It would appear that even the hardest-nosed investors infer a degree of "success" from company size and in that are consigning greater judgment to the thoughts and impressions that by definition constitute bigger companies' reputations. Size matters, but it is by no means everything.[11]

Reputation returns vary from company to company.

Individual Reputation Contributions among the 300+ U.S. companies tracked at the start of 2014 ranged from as much as nearly 50 percent of the market capitalization to a little as 1 percent. Within that, five companies commanded reputation assets contributing more than 45 percent of their market capitalization—Walt Disney (50 percent), Apple (50 percent), Google (49 percent), Exxon Mobil (47 percent) and Occidental Petroleum (47 percent)—with a combined reputation value of $973bn.

At the other end of the spectrum six companies commanded reputation assets delivering less than 10 percent of market capitalization; Becton Dickinson (8 percent), WellCare Health Plans (8 percent), Owens and Minor (7 percent), Ford Motor Co. (7 percent), Safeway (2 percent) and Southwest Airlines (1 percent). The combined value of their reputation assets stood at just $7bn.

In most cases, reputation is a force for good and creating shareholder value, but in others it can destroy it. Investors need to look beyond the simple headline

Table 1.1 Leading U.S. Corporate Reputations by Contribution

The Top Ten	Reputation Contribution	Reputation Value ($m as at Jan 2014)
Walt Disney	49.8%	$65,081
Apple	49.7%	$240,011
Google	48.8%	$184,873
Exxon Mobil	47.1%	$202,172
Occidental Petroleum	46.6%	$34,300
Chevron	43.9%	$101,382
Caterpillar	42.9%	$24,621
International Paper	42.9%	$9,125
Qualcomm	42.7%	$53,260
Comcast	42.4%	$58,260

Source: Reputation Dividend

measures if they want to understand the impact of corporate reputation and optimize value.

The value of reputation, like any investment, can fall as well as rise.

The importance of corporate reputation was further evidenced by the part it played in supporting stock price value through the recent economic downturn. Reputation Contributions were subdued in the immediate aftermath of the Lehman's collapse when nervousness spread and investors looked to more tangible evidence. It wasn't long, however, before they went up in response among other things, the wider flight to safety and the anticipated fortunes of individual companies ability to deal with the recession. Investor interest in component drivers can change relatively quickly as events unfold and reputation managers need to keep an eye to that in order to ensure their charges are optimized.

Reputation management is a means to grow shareholder returns.

Over and above being a repository of shareholder value, corporate reputation can be an important source of growth. The 2014 analysis of US corporations indicated that a 5 percent improvement in the strength of a company's reputations would yield an average market capitalization increase of 1.6 percent, a return on investment of around $552m for the average sized S&P 500 company at the start of 2014.

The extent of any potential to leverage individual reputation assets depends upon the structure of the company's reputation and the general nature of investor interest

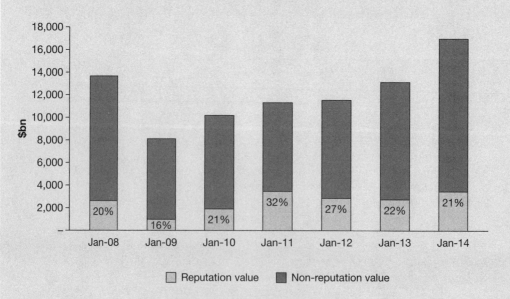

Figure 1.3 Reputation Value Development—S&P 500

Source: Reputation Dividend

at the time. Together, they define a company's unique reputation driver profile and determine the value gain that can be expected from improvements to perceptions of any of its component drivers.

In Sum

Reputation value analysis reveals the scale and location of shareholder value residing in a company's reputation asset and provides an objective basis for both securing and growing it.

It presents reputation owners with a uniquely objective basis to organize communications and wider operational activities. It reveals whether or not the company is being unfairly underrated or could benefit from a stronger reputation, it explains where the communications, performance or behavior opportunities lie, and answers the question as to whether or not the return on the investment required is justifiable. This is the foundation for Reputation Value Management.

Reputation value analysis may not be a panacea for a company's reputational shortcomings, however, it can reveal the most pressing value-generating or value-destroying components. And, in providing hard numbers that reflect the magnitude of the reputation drivers in a language that is both straightforward and immediately relevant to corporate leaders, reputation management can take on the truly strategic role it undoubtedly deserves.

(**Disclosure:** John Doorley is a director of the London-based company Mindful Reputation, which collaborates with Reputation Dividend on a variety of projects.)

CAN REPUTATION BE MANAGED?

> *Anything built to last must be well engineered.*
> *– Gay Talese, in his book* The Bridge, *about*
> *construction of New York's Verrazano Bridge*

One thing is certain, as recent business scandals have demonstrated in the sharpest relief: reputations can surely be mismanaged, and in many cases, not managed at all. There is a clear need for a new approach that will help companies and other organizations measure, monitor, and manage their reputations, and the factors that contribute to reputation, organization-wide, over the long term.

So a major question for leaders of organizations is: Can reputation be managed? It follows that those who believe it can be managed—perhaps not totally, but which asset can be?—must establish a plan to do so, as they would for any other asset.

COMPREHENSIVE REPUTATION MANAGEMENT

Comprehensive Reputation
Management is one way for
an organization to get its
arms around this asset, and
a way to manage reputation
problems, vulnerabilities, and
opportunities.

"Comprehensive Reputation Management" provides a formal framework for managing reputation (copyright 2003, John Doorley). It is one way for an organization to get its arms around this asset, and a way to manage reputation problems, vulnerabilities, and opportunities. It has been vetted before the leadership of the Conference Board, many industry leaders and CEOs, numerous academic researchers, and heads of corporate communications at 30 major companies. Paul Verbinnen and Rich Coyle of Sard Verbinnen made significant contributions.

Comprehensive Reputation Management =

A long-term strategy for measuring, auditing, and managing an organization's reputation as an asset.

This strategy results in the management of an organization's intrinsic identity (what it stands for) and external images, giving an organization a methodology for working to bring the two together. The Comprehensive Reputation Management methodology is applied to the major areas of an organization—for example, finance, human resources, investor relations, manufacturing, marketing, and public affairs. Each area gets involved in a process that is a way of approaching total reputation management—(performance and behavior) + communication—and is distinct from brand management (the marketing value of a name) or corporate identity programs (which usually boil down to institutional advertising).

These are the seven major components of Comprehensive Reputation Management:

1. *Customized Reputation Template.* The measurement tool begins with a basic template that is then customized for each organization. In some cases, the organization may simply want to improve its ranking in an established poll, such as Fortune magazine's. Certain of the financial measures may be more important to some companies than to others, as might be environmental performance and community relations (under "social responsibility") and so on.

    Reputation Criteria: Basic Template for Comprehensive Reputation Management program includes:

    *   Innovation
    *   Quality of management
    *   Employee talent
    *   Financial performance
    *   Social responsibility

- Product quality
- Global competitiveness
- Communicativeness (transparency)
- Governance
- Integrity (responsibility, reliability, credibility, trustworthiness)

The first seven are the time-tested *Fortune* criteria, with the three financial measures collapsed to one. Communicativeness is part of the template because there has now been more work done to demonstrate the link between an organization's transparency and its reputation. (See reference to *Corporate Reputation Review* paper on page 34. Governance is listed because it is now, especially post Sarbanes-Oxley, an important part of the reputation mix. Integrity is this model's way of encompassing the four character traits that research by Fombrun and others has shown to have a direct effect on reputation: responsibility, reliability, credibility, and trustworthiness.

The basic template can then be customized for the particular organization, and the resultant customized template becomes senior management's acknowledgment of which reputation factors are most important. The customized template becomes the tool for measuring changes in reputational capital. The template can also be customized by constituency, because different constituencies care more about different attributes.

2. *Reputation Audits of Internal and External Constituencies.* One audit assesses what employees believe to be the intrinsic identity (what the organization stands for) and compares that with what senior leadership believes the intrinsic identity to be. The gap between the two views is analyzed and a plan (part of the Reputation Management Plan) to converge them is created. A second audit measures how external constituencies view the organization, and the sum of those constituency images constitutes reputation. The gap between identity and reputation is analyzed, and a plan (part of the Reputation Management Plan) to converge the two is created.

3. *Reputational Capital Goals.* Goals are established for performance within an industry group, for example, or versus competitors. A company might establish a goal of moving up into the top quartile of its industry sector. Progress toward that goal can then be measured, monitored, and managed.

4. *Accountability Formula.* This is based on changes in reputation measured against the customized template. If the organization is slipping according to one reputation attribute (for example, communicativeness) particular departments, such as public relations, can be given the responsibility of correcting that impression through proactive communication initiatives.

5. *A Reputation Management Plan.* This is the deliverable that the Comprehensive Reputation Management process produces. It is a strategic performance, behavior and communication plan for convergence of identity and reputation—a plan to move the images the various constituencies hold about the organization closer to the intrinsic identity.

The very act of having to list their reputational assets and liabilities helps the various units focus on reputation management. The Reputation Management

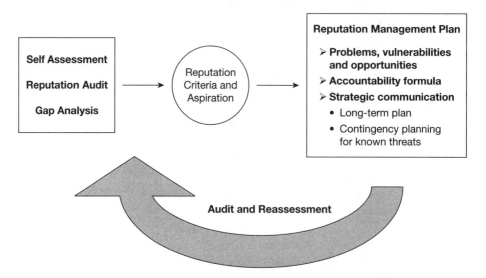

Figure 1.4 Comprehensive Reputation Management

Plan includes: a summary of the internal and external audits; measures of reputational capital; a statement of reputation challenges and potential problem areas by company or organizational unit; the respective goals and opportunities; and corporate or organizational message strategies. With objectives, strategies, timelines, and so forth, the Reputation Management Plan becomes a strategic guide for units of the organization to follow, short-and-long term.

6. *Annual Follow-Up Audit and Assessment According to the Standards in the Reputation Management Plan.*

7. "Stakeholder Overview"—This document (two pages per stakeholder group) is a key component of the copyrighted Comprehensive Reputation Management process. It lists for the organization's main stakeholders (seven to ten for a large organization) the opportunities, vulnerabilities, goals, and strategies. Importantly, it lists (*"reveals"* is usually the case even in organizations where reputation is a priority) the various internal staffs and functions that interact with each stakeholder group.

CONFUSING COMMUNICATION WITH PERFORMANCE AND BEHAVIOR

Pushmi-pullyu

In Kurt Eichenwald's *Conspiracy of Fools*, Enron CEO Kenneth Lay proclaims to his public relations officer Mark Palmer, not long before the collapse of the company: "The reason we can't right the ship is we're not doing a good job in dealing with the press."[12] In other words, Lay saw a communication problem, not a performance or behavior problem.

In the contest between the steak and the sizzle the steak will, inevitably, prove more important.

Or, as in Enron's case, the sizzle will always evaporate. Wendy's television commercial from the 1980s, "Where's the beef?" said it best.

In *The Story of Doctor Doolittle*, by renowned children's author Hugh Lofting, the good doctor comes across a mythical, rare animal in Africa. It is a llama-like creature with one head at the front, where it would normally be, and one at the base of its spine, and it is called Pushmi-pullyu. "Lord save us," cries the duck. "How does it make up its mind?"[13]

The Pushmi-pullyu metaphor (devised by John Baruch, LittD, former CEO of Reed & Carnrick) is a fitting one to represent the problem that public relations and corporate communication practitioners face: the confusion of behavior or performance with communication—of the substantive issue with the communication about it. While the communication objectives and strategies should always be in synch with the business objectives and strategies, they are distinct. Communication cannot make a bad product good, at least over the long run. Of course it can make a good or fair product seem worse, as it did with the Exxon Valdez crisis in 1989. Many observers agreed that Exxon did a pretty good job operationally in cleaning up the oil spill, but the communications were a disaster. A similar assessment applied to the BP oil spill in the Gulf of Mexico in 2009. In 2006, the mishandling of communication regarding the hunting accident involving U.S. Vice President Dick Cheney clearly made the matter worse, and played right into the hands of the press and its insatiable appetite for sensationalism.

Pushmi-pullyu is a syndrome that explains the generations-old lament of corporate and organizational communicators about their lack of a "seat at the table." The reason this has been a problem, of course, is that, too often, an organization develops an ill-advised product or position, or takes such an action, and then asks the communications group to justify it. The performance/behavior head is turning in one direction and saying one thing, and then it expects the communication head to turn and speak in a different direction.

> **The Pushmi-pullyu syndrome:** "A pattern of behavior whereby an organization performs or behaves in one way but expects the communications professionals to explain that performance away. Assembled in that fashion, two heads are not better than one—and they should be merged so that performance/behavior and communication can turn and talk in a confluent direction."

Reframing the Problem

In 2002 this book's coauthor Fred Garcia was called into a company to consult on what the communication people called a "*Fortune* magazine problem." They said *Fortune* was working on a story about the company's chairman, a flamboyant, politically connected executive who had borrowed millions of dollars from the company to support a lavish lifestyle. The chairman's business and political enemies were pointing to the lifestyle, and to other personal foibles and business failures, and the company's stock was suffering. Investors and analysts were asking questions but getting no satisfactory answers. It seemed like the worst mix of Enron, Tyco, and WorldCom. Company leadership was also concerned that the weakening stock price could lead to a hostile takeover.

Fred asked the company leadership what would happen if *Fortune* magazine should be persuaded not to run a story: would the problem be solved? They acknowledged that they would still be as vulnerable to takeover and to critics' capitalizing on the company's weakness in other ways. "You don't have a *Fortune* magazine problem," Fred told them, "you have a governance problem." He met with the general counsel and several board members. They discussed various scenarios under which they could remedy the company's weaknesses. Regardless of the scenario, one thing was consistent: success required the chairman to resign and to repay his loans to the company. The only meaningful question was timing: Could he leave before the company suffered more harm, or would he resist, leading to calls by shareholders and others for his resignation, declines in the stock price, and eventually his ouster? Given the alternatives, the Board persuaded the chairman to leave quickly. He resigned within two weeks, and repaid his loan. The company's stock price rebounded. There was no takeover. And no *Fortune* article.

The solution to the struggle represented by the Pushmi-pullyu metaphor—the solution to the push and pull of substance and communication—is to have the entire organization behave and communicate as one.

REPUTATION MISMANAGEMENT: LESSONS FROM THE FINANCIAL CRISIS

The causes and effects of the Great Recession of the last years of the first decade of the new millennium were many and, admittedly, complex—including, arcane financial instruments, and massive greed on the part of not just bankers and business leaders but also average consumers. Data have been compiled, analyzed, peer reviewed, and published. The tomes already published will be followed by PhD theses, Pulitzer Prize winning series, and best sellers.

The complicit parties, from consumers to banks to governments to regulatory agencies, failed to live up to the intrinsic identities that had served them well over the ages.

Out of this morass of facts and theories has emerged a consensus that the seminal causes were with the real estate industry and the banks, who often collaborated to sell property to people who could be expected to pay for it only if the value of property continued to rise. With American consumers leading the way— spurred on by government policies that fostered home ownership with or without the ability to pay—the cycle of profligate lending and spending spread worldwide. When property values leveled off and then plunged, so too did the worldwide economy.

While it is true that the financial instruments that accompanied this cycle were novel and complex, and while it is true that the greed that arose was novel in its creativity and pervasiveness, there is a simplicity to be found in the story that explains how it happened and how a similar catastrophe might be prevented from happening again. And for professional communicators, the lesson to be learned is only partly one of communication. For in the final analysis, the complicit parties, from consumers to banks to governments to regulatory agencies, failed to live up to the intrinsic identities that had served them well over the ages. And they failed to protect their reputations, by failing to protect the component parts.

Reputation = Performance (P) + Behavior (B) + Communication (C)

The Performance Failure

When property values and other economic indicators fell, the reputations of the real estate and banking industries fell, and then, as was inevitable, business overall. The 2008 Reputation Quotient Report by Harris Interactive concluded that Americans had an extremely low opinion of banks. According to the survey, the financial services sector had such little public support that even the tobacco industry enjoyed a better reputation.[14] The road is still rocky. On April 28, 2014 America's largest bank, Bank of America, revealed that it had made a $4 billion accounting error that went unreported for months.

The Behavior Failure

Leading up to the Great Recession, when the economy was on the ascent, executive compensation continued to rise. It became a caricature of unfairness, viewed much like outsized pay to top athletes, except that consumers often felt they had no recourse, could not even withhold the price of a ticket to the game. Even though executive compensation outpaced by far the rate of growth in wages for average workers, the protests were not strong enough to force more moderate executive pay practices based on performance.

As people started to lose their jobs and savings, leading business figures seemed unaware of public sentiment. Witness the infamous jet rides of the Detroit auto executives to the Congressional hearings in November 2009.

The Occupy Wall Street movement of 2012 was sparked by similar concerns over income inequality. But it never achieved focus or critical mass, and suffered from its own behavior problems.

The Communication Failure

Were the Detroit corporate communicators consulted in March 2008 before the CEOs took their private jets to Washington as the financial system was collapsing? Were they consulted over the decades of collapse of an industry that had once led the United States economy and the world? Were they just seen as communicators, whereas they should have been involved in the performance and behavior considerations as well?

Of course many industries lost reputation during the financial crisis. In general, the closer the consumer connection, the greater the loss—to wit, energy, apparel, food, and retail in general.

In his September 2009 speech on the anniversary of the Lehman collapse, President Obama praised community banks for "being responsible lenders [and] doing the right thing."[15] During the early months of the financial crisis, banks with assets of less than $5 billion outperformed their larger competitors in nearly every measure important to stakeholders. While it is still too early to make definitive conclusions about the economic mess, analysts are closely monitoring the practices of small banks. Even after accepting money from the Troubled Asset Relief Program (TARP) because the government deemed them too big to fail, a number of the larger institutions remain at a collective low point. On the other hand, many of the small banks, which simply rely on maintaining accountability and making sensible business decisions, are weathering the crisis with relative ease.

The investment bank Goldman Sachs accepted $10 billion in TARP funds in October 2008, but paid it back with interest in June 2009 as soon as the U.S. government would allow repayment. During the worst months of the Great Recession, Goldman reported positive earnings results that were much better than the other major investment banks. It seemed that the better Goldman performed the more criticism it received from journalists, bloggers, and the traditional media. In 2009, major exposés appeared in *Vanity Fair, New York* magazine and *Rolling Stone*, among others, criticizing the firm for relentless profiteering and perpetuating all of the major market bubbles in the last century and a half. It was called, "a great vampire squid wrapped around the face of humanity."[16]

But Goldman leadership views reputation through a different lens. The *New York Times*'s DealBook blog reported that, during an August 2009 meeting with a CreditSights analyst, Goldman executives claimed that the "negative image of the firm portrayed in the popular press had not damaged its franchise with its institutional clients nor adversely impacted its funding levels, liquidity access or stock valuation." The analyst said that, "Goldman Sachs's view is that it must keep striving to deliver value for its shareholders and doing what it thinks is in the best interests of the firm in spite of some recent negative press in the media." Goldman's own perspective considers the views of securities analysts, Goldman customers, and others to whom financial performance is the major criterion.

But if one views reputation as singular, the way some reputation scholars do—that is, an organization, or an individual, has just one reputation, which is the sum of the views of all its stakeholders—then the company leadership should not be so sanguine. For example, its executive bonuses seem way out of bounds to most people. Goldman, despite its remarkable strengths, has been tarred by the same brush that painted the entire investment banking industry.

The Identity Failure

For millennia, banks made loans only to people who had enough resources and income to repay them. What banks stood for, simply, was soundness in lending and investing. In the late 1980s, one bank after another started making loans on the prospect that the properties offered as collateral would appreciate. Often, the banks sold the dangerous loans to other banks, absolving the original lender of vulnerability—for a while. The practice became so lucrative that too many banks felt they could not pass it up. Smart consumers—who had always stood for hard work and living thriftily—bought into the illusion that they could live in a house they could not afford.

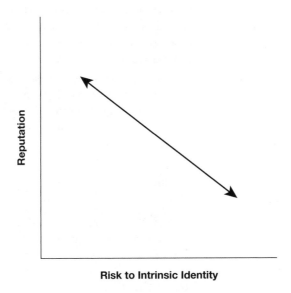

Figure 1.5 Tom Matteini was president of Jeffrey and Foster, a small printing company that held its own for sixty years against the behemoths—in the New York City market no less. He conceived this chart: "Actions that put at risk what you stand for—with us it's printing quality, reliability, and competitive pricing—inevitably lower reputation. But you have to be willing to lose some of the bids and some revenue. Sometimes, you just cannot compete on price."

CASE STUDY: REPUTATION BE DAMNED

In 1998 Abercrombie and Fitch published a back-to-school catalog with a section advocating that college students drink creatively, rather than just participate in the standard beer binge. The section headed "Drinking 101" contained recipes for the Woo-Woo, the Beach Hemorrhage, and other potent mixtures. The organization Mothers Against Drunk Driving was irate. Within days, NBC's *Today Show* was set to interview MADD's president, but the clothing company refused to send a spokesperson (issuing just a brief statement). The question is: Should the company have sent a spokesperson?[17]

When that question is asked of communication or PR majors (this book's coauthor John Doorley has done this with many classes) most students say yes; often the teacher is the only dissenter. The reason for dissent: The company had not formulated any policy expressing embarrassment, let alone shame, and there was no commitment to mitigate the damage—for example, recall the catalog and help wage responsibility-in-drinking campaigns. Most college students are not of drinking age, and the company appeared to care little about the health of the people who wear their clothing. What could the spokesperson have said, in lieu of repudiation and correction, that would not have made the matter worse? For as Will Rogers was fond of saying: "When you find yourself in a hole, the first thing to do is stop digging."

Eventually, of course, the company had to issue statements and provide stickers for existing catalogs that advocated responsibility in drinking. MADD and most PR observers agreed it was too little too late.

It turns out that A & F has published catalogs for its young audiences with nude models and been criticized for not featuring people of color. The company discontinued its 2003 "Christmas Field Guide" catalog after it caused more controversy over the sexually explicit nature of several articles. Since then, A & F has launched a slightly more responsible version of the catalog in Europe, but slogans on its products have offended many different groups in the United States. A sample list of boycotters includes Asian American groups, women's organizations, Christian schools, the State of West Virginia, and USA Gymnastics.

However, it seems that A & F is not concerned about its reputation with older audiences, believing perhaps that the younger audiences will not care about the social issues and may even want their clothing all the more. One has to hand it to the company: it is a bold marketing strategy, and a very risky reputation strategy, especially over the long term. Creating demand is one thing, but alienating the people who pay the bills, as well as groups that devote their lives to a cause, is another. (Illustration: the organization of mothers against drunk driving, MADD, almost single-handedly forced the U.S. government into the nationwide drinking-age limit of 21.)

THE TEN PRECEPTS OF REPUTATION MANAGEMENT

These precepts are meant to help professionals who spend their workdays communicating on behalf of organizations. Because the precepts are intended to help with reputation management, they have as much to do with performance and behavior as with communication. These precepts are the same ones the authors listed in the first edition, with some new examples for currency. We ask the reader to review them to see how well they have stood the tests of the financial crisis and other reputational challenges that have occurred since the first edition of this book in 2006.

> We ask the reader to review the precepts to see how well they have stood the tests of the financial crisis and other reputational challenges that have occurred since the first edition

1. *Know and honor your organization's intrinsic identity.*

Organizations have multiple identities (for example, quality products and competitive profitability), but as George Cheney and other researchers have demonstrated, the identities must be compatible, and one must be dominant. That dominant, or intrinsic, identity must be clear to the members of the organization. It is what the organization stands for, and it will often determine what the employees will do as a first resort, in good times and bad. The Johnson and Johnson Credo expresses the company's intrinsic identity in terms of its responsibilities, first to those who use its products. Its basic principles guided the company during the Tylenol tampering cases of 1982 and 1986.[18]

> That dominant, or intrinsic, identity must be clear to the members of the organization. It is what the organization stands for, and it will often determine what the employees will do as a first resort, in good times and bad.

2. *Know and honor your constituents.*

The American Red Cross, among the most successful and highly regarded charities in U.S. history, had good intentions when it decided to withhold from the families of the victims of 9/11 some of the monies donated for them. The fund had generated an overwhelmingly generous response, and the leadership of the Red Cross reasoned that not all the monies were needed by the families, and that it would be prudent to save some to help when future disasters, man- and God-made, strike. Donors were outraged, and a major crisis ensued.

The moral: Do not presume to know the will of your constituents, and do not presume that good intentions alone are sufficient to protect against criticism that the organization is acting against the interests of its key constituents.

3. *Build the safeguards strong and durable, for they are the infrastructure of a strong reputation.*

Former U.S. Federal Reserve Chairman Alan Greenspan maintains that greed was the root cause of most of the recent business scandals, but he acknowledges that weakened safeguards let the greed flourish. Former Wall Street financier Bernard Madoff pleaded guilty to eleven federal crimes tied to charges that he defrauded his clients of $65 billion in a Ponzi scheme. In spite of several SEC investigations and red flags raised by analysts and competitors, Madoff's operation remained intact for twenty years. According to reports, authorities only made cursory investigations into his business practices and usually in search of specific offences. The moral: Strong, efficient safeguards, internal and external, are in an organization's best interests.

4. Beware the conflict of interest, for it can mortally wound your organization.

Few firms in history had better reputations than Arthur Andersen, and a statue of the company namesake and founder stood tall at the company's training facility as a reminder of what he stood for: the meticulous and rigorous auditing and reporting of a client's finances. Andersen's primary duty was to the shareholders of companies whose books it audited. But by 2001 Andersen's imperative to boost revenues and profits had eroded structures intended to assure the independence of auditors. Andersen allowed itself to act in its own short-term interest and against the interests of its clients' shareholders. The compromising of audit standards and auditor independence was discussed publicly within and outside the firm for years before the damage became apparent and severe.

After the Enron/Andersen scandal broke in late 2001 and early 2002, a committee of some of society's most respected leaders, including former U.S. Federal Reserve Chairman Paul Volker and former Merck CEO P. Roy Vagelos, was convened to save it. But by then the firm's intrinsic identity—meticulous, honest auditing—had already been so compromised that the core had been ruined; Andersen was convicted of a crime and soon closed its doors. The conviction was later reversed, but by then the firm had gone out of business and thousands of employees had lost their jobs.

Paul Volker once said that it is only the people or organizations that have not accomplished very much who could be free of all potential conflicts. Nevertheless, the test for labeling something as a major conflict of interest might be as simple as the one used by U.S. Supreme Court Justice Potter Stewart to label pornography: it may be hard to define, but you know it when you see it.

5. Beware of the "CEO Disease," because there is no treatment for it.

It is the same malady the Greek gods said destroyed so many tragic figures, and it is called hubris. Chief executives command tremendous incomes, power, and prestige. Thousands of employees almost genuflect when they walk by, and powerful people from all sectors of society treat them with deference. It must be difficult not to fall into certain traps, such as wanting to be surrounded by employees who always agree with them. Ask anyone who has worked in corporate communication for a long time: There is a "CEO Disease" (and heads of governments, nonprofits, and universities are not immune).

One of the manifestations of hubris is an inability to see that a looming problem requires immediate attention. Many CEOs mishandle initial phases of a crisis out of either arrogance or willful blindness, caused by a misplaced sense of invincibility. The outcome is otherwise manageable crises that result, ultimately and after much hardship, in the CEO's ouster. The year 2004 saw more forced CEO turnover than any year since such statistics have been compiled. According to the consulting firm Booz & Company's annual CEO succession survey, the "giant sucking sound heard in the business world during 2004 was the extraction of chief executives from seats of power . . . The first quarter of 2005 brought headline-generating forced successions at Disney, Hewlett-Packard, Boeing, and AIG, linked to shareholder dissatisfaction, scandal, or both."[19] The trend continued until the beginnings of the most recent recession, when further Booz surveys discovered that "the nature of the recession is leading boards of directors of Western companies to stick with the leaders they know." However, government intervention and market volatility, as well as performance, can determine CEO turnover in the new economic climate.

6. *Beware of organizational myopia, for it will obscure the long-term view.*

Especially during times of crisis, organizations tend to focus on the short term. It is part of the corporate and organization condition, and not falling into that trap is one of the lessons of crisis management (Chapter 12). Sometimes organizations are given plenty of advance notice of issues looming large, but few heed the warning signs.

7. *Be slow to forgive an action or inaction that hurts reputation.*

Enough said.

8. *Do not lie.*

People tell lies, most of which are small and harmless, and some of which may even be good things ("Honey, do I look heavy in this suit?"). Similarly, organizations are not always completely forthcoming with information and, indeed, that is sometimes a very good thing (see Media Relations, Chapter 3). But lying is of course a slippery slope, eventually dragging the organization into a deep hole from which there is no extrication. Organizations can often get away with lying for a while, but that's all. Sometimes, efforts to mislead have significant adverse consequences, a lesson learned by President Nixon with Watergate, President Clinton in the Monica Lewinsky scandal, and by Martha Stewart, who was prosecuted, convicted, and imprisoned for lying to law enforcement officers.

9. *Dance with the one that "brung" you.*

This aphorism, popular within sports teams, applies to organizations as well as individuals. By the fall of 2000, it was becoming clear that Firestone tires were leading to traffic accidents, and many of them were on the Ford Explorer. Bridgestone-Firestone blamed Ford and vice versa. A business and public relations crisis ensued, and in May 2001 the two companies severed their business relationship that had endured for almost 100 years. Most analysts agreed that the crisis was compounded by the lack of cooperation, and although the relationship was later revived, the damage had been done. Likewise, it is not uncommon today for a firm that is downsizing to give

A family-owned company based near Stuttgart, Germany, that employs 8000 people manufacturing laser tools for the automobile industry, was able to avoid layoffs.

pink slips to employees, and then have a security guard publicly usher them to the gate—even those employees with excellent, long-term records.

Many other companies take monumental initiatives to be loyal to their employees, customers, and other constituencies. Aaron Feurstein, owner of Malden Mills in Lawrence, Massachusetts, was able to retain all his employees after a fire destroyed his factory in 1995. He said he would simply not abandon his employees, and quoted from the Torah, or Jewish Law: "He is poor and needy, whether he be thy brethren or a stranger."

Similarly, a family-owned company based near Stuttgart, Germany, that employs 8000 people manufacturing laser tools for the automobile industry, was able to avoid layoffs during The Great Recession. "The responsibility I have for our employees is what is dearest to my heart," Nicola Leibinger-Kammuller, the family member who heads the company, told *The New York Times*. "It's not the family wealth. It's not our standing with the public."[20]

10. *Reputation is an asset and must be managed like other assets.*

Reputation is intangible, but it has great, tangible value (worth many billions of dollars in large corporations, for instance). It is therefore an asset. Failure to acknowledge reputation as an asset can be self-fulfilling. By ignoring reputation and factors that harm or help it, companies often behave and communicate in ways that cause harm to the reputation. Successful stewardship of reputation not only protects against the downside, but can affirmatively enhance the enterprise value of an organization. Because the component parts of reputation (performance/behavior and communication) can be managed, one should devise a strategy and plan to measure, audit, and manage reputation on an ongoing basis.

> **Reputation = Sum of Images =**
> **Performance and Behavior + Communication**

REPUTATION MANAGEMENT: THE BEST CORPORATE COMMUNICATION STRATEGY

The remaining chapters of this book flow from a discussion of ethics (Chapter 2), to a discussion of approaches to working with the various corporate communication constituencies (Chapters 3–11), to ways of handling certain major responsibilities (Chapters 12 and 13), to the challenges facing those who seek to build a career in corporate and organizational communication (Chapter 14).

The premise of Chapter 1—that reputation can be measured, monitored, and managed—begs for the adoption by corporate communications departments of a long-term strategy of reputation management, customized for the particular constituencies, and in synch with an intrinsic identity that the entire organization understands and believes in.

A growing body of scholarship shows links between reputation and business performance, and the ability of public relations, particularly corporate communications, to impact reputation. Such studies include the following.

> A growing body of scholarship shows links between reputation and business performance, and the ability of public relations, particularly corporate communications, to impact reputation.

- *The Institute for Public Relations*, "Corporate Reputation Management in the U.S. Pharmaceutical Industry," Goldstein and Doorley et al., 2011. The reputations of firms may be linked to the degree to which they have formal reputation management programs. To examine that hypothesis the authors surveyed firms in the U.S. pharmaceutical industry where reputation is a highly visible challenge. We compared the reputation measurement and management efforts of the most admired firms with those of less admired firms. The data indicate a positive correlation in five areas—that is, between reputation and having an ongoing reputation measurement program; having an active reputation management program; having a formal reputation management plan; having an individual or unit charged with responsibility for coordinating / overseeing reputation management; and having the chief communication officer as a member of the company's executive committee.[21]
- *Harvard Business Review*, "Reputation and its risks," Eccles, et al., 2007. "This article provides a framework for proactively managing reputational risks. It explains the factors that affect the levels of such risks and then explores how a company can sufficiently quantify and control them." The authors of this article maintain, unlike the positions taken by the authors of most articles on reputation management, that corporate communication is not the best department to oversee the reputation management process, since corporate communication has too large an interest in communication. But as the formula for reputation given in this chapter illustrates, communication is just one of the three components of reputation (along with performance and behavior). Another weakness with this *HBR* article is that it focuses exclusively on the risks to reputation, with never a mention of the fact that reputation management calls for capitalizing on the positive aspects of reputation as well as minimizing the risks.
- *Journal of Public Relations Research*, "Measuring the economic value of public relations," Yungwook Kim, 2001. "This study established a two-step model to measure the economic value of public relations by testing two relationships: the impact on reputation as a goal of public relations, and the economic impact of reputation on companies' bottom lines." The study showed a positive causal relationship between public relations and reputation, and a positive causal relationship between reputation and revenue.
- *Southern Economic Journal*, "A latent structure approach to measuring reputation," Quagrainie et al., 2003. "The study provides estimates of reputation as a dynamic latent variable that is determined by price premiums and market data." It showed a positive effect between reputation and the prices a company can charge.

- *Corporate Communications*, "Measuring corporate reputation," Bradford, Stewart Lewis, 2001. "This paper considers how corporate reputation is most influenced by the actions of an organization rather than a successful (or otherwise) PR campaign, and how a communication strategy can best influence reputation." The paper established that it is important to measure and manage reputation by constituency.
- *Corporate Reputation Review*, "The concept and measurement of corporate reputation . . .," de la Fuente Sabate et al., Winter 2003. "This paper . . . leads us to a new definition of corporate reputation, one that not only introduces the perceptions of how the firm behaves towards its stakeholders, but also takes into account the degree of transparency with which the firm develops relations with them." The paper established that information transparency (communicativeness) affects reputation and the ability to do business. Positive reputations have a positive effect on a company's ability to do business.

Since reputation is the sum of performance/behavior and communication, an effective corporate communication strategy must be that inclusive. As with individuals, the relationships an organization has will succeed or fail based on performance/behavior and communication. In other words, relationships must be sound and aggressively fostered. Such a strategy can ensure that the organization moves forward, avoiding the Pushmi-pullyu syndrome (see earlier section) and the reputation pitfalls.

BRAND (NOT REPUTATION) MANAGEMENT

> Reputation: The sum of perceptions that individuals or groups have of a specific individual or organization.
>
> Brand: How an individual or organization wants to be perceived.[22]

In the fall of 2011 John Doorley, one of this book's coauthors, was asked by the Conference Board to address a group of senior brand management executives from major companies. At a November 11 meeting hosted by Mayo Clinic in Phoenix, Arizona, he began with the thesis that the principles governing corporate reputation management apply to brand management—challenging the brand executives to agree or disagree. Among the seventeen senior executives in attendance, there was no disagreement with the basic principles—that performance, behavior and communication, linked to intrinsic identity—are key. In the best of worlds, they agreed—a kind of quixotic goal but one worth striving for—the organization's reputation equals its brand.

THE EXPANDED REPUTATION FORMULA

In 2009 Ray Jordan, then vice president of public affairs and corporate communication at Johnson & Johnson and now senior vice president of corporate affairs at Amgen, told authors Doorley and Garcia that he believes professional communicators should

EXPERT PERSPECTIVES: EVERYBODY'S GOT BRAND

By Claude Singer, PhD

The term "brand" used to be associated primarily with objects wrapped in foil paper—candy, cigarettes, and such. Today almost every human activity is being viewed through the lens of branding. Political parties nurture brands that rise and fall in voter esteem. Exceptional athletes—along with rock stars and politicians—are brands that wax like Shaq or wane like Tiger.

Even a new pope for the Catholic Church is hailed for his ability to reinvigorate the Roman Catholic brand, which was tarnished by man-made evil and scandal, and criticized for its unyielding stance on social issues.

The 2014 crisis in Syria and Iraq shed light on extremist groups differentiating themselves as unique brands. One militant brand featured the authoritative name Islamist State of Iraq and Syria (ISIS), with high-profile leadership, and a narrative that framed its victories as triumphs for religious purity. In the summer of 2014 ISIS "re-branded itself," as the media put it, to become a caliphate named the Islamic State.

Today, university officials—devoted to creating and disseminating knowledge—do not mind being associated with such tawdry entities as commercial brands. Universities openly speak of their "brands" and market themselves as such. Harvard is considered a blue-chip brand with the drawing power of a Google, Apple, or Walmart. The Tisch School, Stern, Wagner, and other components of New York University comprise prestigious product brands within NYU's complex brand architecture.

In this contemporary landscape of branding, three generalizations apply:

First, the rush to create a unique brand has opened the field to amateurish attempts to show differentiation. In the fall of 2010 Drake University launched a branding campaign centered on a jaunty plus symbol: Drake + You. Your passion + Our experience. Your potential + Our opportunities.

What sparked titters across the Internet was the central visual motif: A large, proudly drawn "D+"—academia's symbol for dismal work. D+ became—briefly—a joke in marketing circles. Some waggishly observed that Drake should have at least shot high and gone for a C. This was a marketing gimmick gone awry.

Drake's mistake was a common one: Thinking of brand marketing as if it's a tactical campaign. Missed was a disciplined search for the authentic Drake University, the true heart and soul of a respected institution. Clever word games and visual devices only diminish an institution's stature and should be avoided. Brands have to be built on solid foundations, and silly campaigns trivialize an institution's unique strengths.

Second point: Just as non-profits are trying to build their brand reputations, so for-profit enterprises develop non-profit activities for the public good. Starbucks funds online higher education for all its employees. The College Board, under fire for sustaining the status of wealthy students who can afford tutors, offers free test prep to all students via the Khan Academy. Whole Foods is famous for supporting local farmers, protecting farmland, and promoting fair trade sourcing of food.

Perhaps the most amazing commitment of a commercial organization is the community outreach of Univision Communications Inc., the largest diversified media company targeting Hispanic peoples. Univision's services aimed at this audience range from career fairs to scholarships to smart card initiatives to healthcare services. It is well known throughout the company that immigrant Hispanics call its radio stations for doctor referrals, financial advice, and even response to house fires.

Initiatives likes those of Whole Foods and Univision are not undertaken for profit in the short term, but are central to building a brand that lives its concern for people which in turn enhances brand and business reputation. Marketers call the strategy "CSR"—corporate social responsibility. But it might just as well be considered essential brand extension and enrichment.

A **third point** to keep in mind is the inextricable link between brand communications and brand behavior. That link has never been stronger. What you say must be backed up by what you do. Walk must be aligned with talk as never before. The digital age lets no claim go unchallenged in the public eye. A restaurant cooks and serves food for money and for a reputation that is vetted daily by opinion-sharing consumers. Modern terrorists use sophisticated media channels to create a brand narrative to fire up recruits and instill terror, but their reputations are won or lost on the battlefield.

The horrendous and deadly disaster of BP's *Deepwater Horizon* oil well perfectly illustrated the disconnect between word (we are a new, environmentally sensitive energy company!—2009) and deed (a series of accidents on pipelines, bays and drilling platforms—2005 through 2011) that revealed BP's failure to establish a true culture of safety.

All in all, it is easy to see why the term brand is both gushingly overused and, by some experts, snobbishly disdained. The term is a convenient, ubiquitous framing device for defining and comparing institutions. Its employment in communication is only as successful as its alignment with actual behavior.

understand the reputation formula, first postulated in the first edition of this book: $R = P + B + C$. But he challenged us to include a consideration of intrinsic identity: "Isn't it always true that what an organization stands for, and how well it lives up to that standard, will significantly affect its reputation?"

So we took up that charge, starting with the word "authenticity," which the Arthur W. Page Society calls the "coin of the realm for successful corporations and for those (including the communication officers) who lead them." In its 2007 report, *The Authentic Enterprise*, the Page Society states that any corporation that wants to establish a distinctive brand (reputation) must, "more than ever before, be grounded in a sure sense of what defines it—why it exists, what it stands for and what differentiates it in a marketplace of customers, investors and workers."

To be authentic is to have "integrity" and it follows then that a failure to live up to what one stands for is a failure of integrity or authenticity. The word integrity is linked with being whole, or undivided, which explains why everything inevitably falls apart once integrity or authenticity fails. "Once you lose integrity," John Haldeman said of his role in the Watergate scandal, "the rest is easy." Put more positively, an organization's reputation will be in direct proportion to its authenticity.

The Authenticity Factor (Af)—the authors' response to Ray Jordan's challenge—is the indicator of how well an organization (or person) lives up to its intrinsic identity. When there is authenticity, the organization is whole, undiminished. On the other hand, when integrity or authenticity fails, the Authenticity factor is a fraction. The organization is divided, and its reputation will decline, because it will be a fraction of the sum of $P + B + C$.

It is not important to try to assign numbers to the factors in the following equation. What is important for communicators and other leaders to understand is that reputation depends on each of the factors. Therefore, reputation can only be managed by managing all the components in the equation. Communicators, in order to do their jobs, need that "seat at the table," need to be involved not just in the communication.

After much thought, research and peer review, we got back to Ray Jordan with the following formula:

> **Reputation = (Performance + Behavior + Communication) x Authenticity factor**
> **R = (P + B + C) x Af**

Ray thought it represents a "step forward—it has simplicity and applicability."

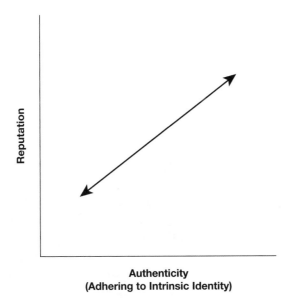

Authenticity
(Adhering to Intrinsic Identity)

Figure 1.6

SYSTEMS THEORY

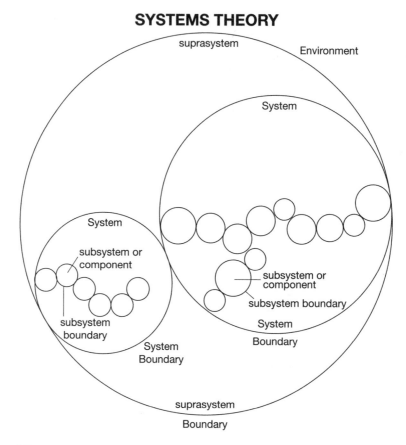

Figure 1.7

SYSTEMS THEORY

Communication is the means by which an organization functions, and it is axiomatic that the better the communication the more productive the organization. That proposition is supported by communication theories, most notably in the case of corporate communication by General Systems Theory. It provides a communication framework which conceives of organizations as living things composed of interrelated components or parts. It provides a way of thinking of an organization not as an amalgam of distinct, seemingly unrelated disciplines, such as finance, customer service, or research, but rather as a whole that comprises components bound together by certain commonalities. As a system, the organization is part of a community that is part of other communities and they all interact, wittingly or unwittingly, in a planned or unplanned way. Systems Theory can help communicators and leaders of organizations adopt a working philosophy that communication is the only way to unity and synergy within the organization, and to openness and harmony with systems (for instance, publics) in the environment outside the organization.

"One of the fundamental concepts of General Systems Theory can be traced to Aristotle," explains Rutgers University Communication Professor Brent Ruben, "who said in *Politics* that a state is composed of villages, which are in turn made up of households, which contain families.[23] Conceiving of entities in terms of wholes and interrelated parts is a basic concept in the general system framework of today."

The modern-day father of Systems Theory in organizational communication was Ludwig von Bertanffly, who conducted his research in the 1950s and 1960s. He was influenced by researchers who were working at the time to identify and express the generalities that tie the scientific disciplines together, so that biology and physics, for example, could be viewed in an interrelated way, rather than as separate, highly specialized fields. For example, cybernetics, which can produce a self-regulated machine that can perform functions greater than any part could, represents a specific application in the physical sciences; Gestalt psychology, which approaches psychotherapy from the perspective of the whole person, including the diverse systems of which he is a part, as opposed to an analytical approach, represents an application in psychotherapy.

Within the communication framework of Systems Theory, an organization can be pictured as a series of systems and subsystems within a supra system (see Figure 1.7). For example, a company could be pictured as a system, the departments as subsystems, and the particular industry as the supra system that functions within the environment of society. Of course, each supra system, system, and subsystem has a boundary and contains components (individuals). The boundaries are porous, opening subsystems to systems to supra systems to the environment. Subsystems and components are identified by the processes they perform. (Systems figure reproduced with the permission of Ruben, Gibson et al. of Rutgers University.)

> Systems Theory: A framework that supports many of the principles expressed in the following chapters.

Systems theory provides a framework for organizational communication based on the following properties and principles common to all systems. The properties and principles have implications for all communication enterprises, with employee communication, media relations, government relations, investor relations, and community relations being among the most obvious:

- Just as in a **biological system** where information flows from one cell to another, information in an organization flows across the borders in what theorists like Professor Ruben call the "metabolism of information." It follows that the more effective the communication, the more productive the organization.
- No part of a system, no person within an organization, can exist by himself or herself. This is the theoretical basis for tearing down the "silos," which became a theme throughout industry in the 1990s.
- Systems are dynamic. Feedback, from one component to another and with the environment, is essential. Implications for dialogue and engagement are clear in communication enterprises ranging from classroom learning to employee communication. The old communication model of sender–receiver may work for thinking in terms of transferring information; it is not helpful for understanding more complex processes involved with

attitudes and behavior. Participation in the system is mandatory. One cannot not communicate. (That is the phrase attributed to communication scholars Watzlawick, Beavin, Bavelas, and Jackson).[24] Engagement is essential.

- Human communication systems are "open systems." As opposed to closed, self-contained systems, which, for example, produce predictable chemical reactions in a test tube, the reactions of the things that go into an open system cannot be precisely calculated in advance; that is, the output cannot be calculated from the input. The open system has properties distinct from its parts; the total, therefore, is not equal to the sum of the parts.

- There are generalities that tie the parts together but one must be careful here. To say something meaningful about the whole—for example, the employee audience is to omit specifics about the parts. "The key is to find the optimum degree of generality," Professor Ruben states. The implications for audience segmentation (internal or external audiences) are clear.

- The environments within and surrounding the supra system, systems, and subsystems shape those parts, and the reverse is true as well. Likewise, the environment shapes the individual's view of reality, and the individual actually shapes the environment. That is, the environments of a company (everything from the physical and cultural environments within and around the company to the country in which the company is based) shape the employees and vice versa. This point illustrates the great potential of communication.

"The systems approach," Professor Ruben states, "has been a particularly useful foundation for what may be thought of as the quality approach to organizations. The dominant metaphor for the Quality School is team, which relies on communication for success." Sports metaphors about teamwork may be clichéd, but they have solid foundation in theory as well as practice. Professor Ruben: "Communication is the lifeblood of human systems. It is the means through which leadership functions, the mechanism by which parts relate to one another, the process by which systems relate and adapt to their environments. In organizations, quality and effective multidirectional communication go hand in hand."

▶ BEST PRACTICES: REPUTATION MANAGEMENT

1. Understand and value the components of reputation, including integrity, governance, and communicativeness (transparency).

2. Establish a formal mechanism to periodically moniter, measure, and manage reputation.

3. Establish a formal mechanism—for example, a regularly scheduled meeting of senior officers, and a "Reputation Management Plan"—to manage reputation on an ongoing basis. The very act of establishing and adhering to a formal mechanism clearly expresses leadership's commitment to protecting the reputation asset.

4. A formal mechanism (for example, a Reputation Management Plan) can help your organization corporate brand and corporate reputation with intrinsic identity (what the organization stands for).

5. The value of individual corporate reputations varies considerably.

6. Reputations create shareholder value, but can also destroy it.

7. Every company has a unique reputation profile which, when matched to prevailing investor interest, creates a level of confidence in the company's ability to deliver the economic returns expected.

8. The economic impact of reputation depends on what a company is known for rather than simply how well it's known.

9. Corporate reputation is a means to grow value: on average, a 5 percent improvement in the strength of an S&P500 company's reputation would yield a market capitalization growth of 1.6 percent, or some US$552m on average.

10. Identifying major stakeholder groups is key to managing reputation.

11. To manage stakeholder relationships is to manage reputation (to manage the parts is to manage the whole). Preparing a "Stakeholder Overview" with objectives, opportunities vulnerabilities, and strategies, gets everyone in the organization on the same page.

▶ RESOURCES FOR FURTHER STUDY

Alsop, Ronald J., *The 18 Immutable Laws of Corporate Reputation, A Wall Street Journal Book*, New York: Free Press, 2004.

Argenti, Paul, *Corporate Communication*, Dartmouth University, The Amos Tuck School of Business Administration: McGraw-Hill, 1998.

Arthur W. Page Society, www.awpagesociety.com

Conference Board CEO Challenge® 2014: People and Performance

The Corporate Communication Institute at Fairleigh Dickinson University.

The Corporate Reputation, an electronic newsletter by Peter Firestein, president of Global Strategic Communications Inc., at http://www.firesteinco.com/reputation.

Corporate Reputation Review: An International Journal, Henry Stewart Publications.

Edelman, Richard, "Public Engagement," *Richard Edelman 6 A.M.*, October 30, 2008, http://www.edelman.com/speak_up/blog/archives/2008/10/public_engageme.html

Fombrun, Charles J., *Reputation: Realizing Value from the Corporate Brand* (Boston: Harvard Business School Press, 1996).

Garcia, Helio Fred, *The Power of Communication: Skills to Build Trust, Inspire Loyalty, and Lead Effectively*, New York: FT Press/Pearson, 2012.

The Institute of Public Relations, http://www.ipr.org.uk/reputation.

Matthews, Chris, *Life's A Campaign: What Politics Has Taught Me About Friendship, Rivalry, Reputation and Success*, New York: Random House, 2007.

Measurement of "intangible assets." Refer to the work of Professor Baruch Lev of New York University, the Stern School, http://www.stern.nyu.edu/~blev/main.html - 9k.

Morley, Michael, *How to Manage Your Global Reputation: A Guide to the Dynamics of International Public Relations*, New York: New York University Press, 2002.

Morley, Michael, *The Global Corporate Brand Book*, London: Palgrave Macmillan, 2009.

Ross, Leslie Gaines, *CEO Capital: A Guide to Building CEO Reputation and Company Success*, New York: John Wiley & Sons, 2003.

Schultz, Majken, et al., *The Expressive Organization: Linking Identity, Reputation and the Corporate Brand*, London: Oxford University Press, 2000.

Seitel, Fraser and John Doorley, *Rethinking Reputation*, New York: St. Martin's Press, Palgrave Macmillan, 2012.

The Trust Barometer, annual survey by Edelman public relations.

▶ QUESTIONS FOR FURTHER DISCUSSION

1. Can you name several major stakeholder groups for Exxon Mobil? For the government of Mumbai? For the national Brazil soccer team?

2. Why do you think *The New York Times* was for so long blind to reporter Jayson Blair's plagiarism and fabrications?

3. Why is it that most by far of the organizations that claim to provide reputation management services are really selling reputation measurement? Do they really not know the difference?

4. Can you think of examples of the Pushmi-pullyu syndrome in your organization? Should that animal, exciting though it may be to watch, ever be permitted to exist in an organization?

5. Are companies whose products largely share the company name (Coca-Cola, Johnson & Johnson, etc.) at an advantage or disadvantage in terms of reputation management? Is it easier to manage the reputation of an organization in a free or totalitarian society?

6. During the Great Recession, many great enterprises collapsed—including: Fannie Mae, Freddie Mac, Lehman Brothers, Bear Stearns, AIG, General Motors, Chrysler and scores of banks. Is it an oversimplification to say it all happened because of a failure to manage reputation?

7. Arcane fields like physics, economics and chemistry build stature and credibility by offering formulas—for example, if you mix these chemicals together, the following result will occur. Why do you think there are so few formulas (for instance, $R = A \times (P + B + C)$ in public relations and corporate communication?

8. Public relations is an emerging social science. Draw some similarities and lessons from other social sciences?

9. Certain stakeholder groups—for example, employees and the media—are more influential than others. Would the views of employees or the media be a proxy for a company's overall reputation?

10. Why do you think there are not many published research papers on how companies have rebounded from reputational crises?

▶ NOTES

1 Charles J. Fombrun, *Reputation: Realizing Value From the Corporate Brand* (Boston: Harvard Business School Press, 1996), 376.

2 U.S. Congressional Record.

3 Charles J. Fombrun, *Reputation: Realizing Value From the Corporate Brand* (Boston: Harvard Business School Press, 1996), 9.

4 George Cheney, *Rhetoric in an Organizational Society* (Columbia, SC: University of South Carolina Press, 1991).

5 Lehman Brothers e-mail regarding suspending executive compensation, at Committee on Oversight and Government Reform,, http://oversight.house.gov/documents/20081006 141219.pdf.

6 Homily by Archbishop Sean P. O'Malley, July 30, 2003, at Archdiocese of Boston, http://www.rcab.org/News/homily030730.html.

7 *New York Times*, July 8, 2014.

8 E.L Black and T.A. Carnes, "The market value of corporate reputation," *Corporate Reputation Review*, 2000, 3 1, pp. 31–42.

9 S. Cole , "The impact of reputation of market value," *World Economics Journal*, 2012, vol .13, no. 3, pp. 47–68.

10 Reputation Dividend, Summary of 2014 UK Reputation Dividend Report, http://reputationdividend.com/files/3014/0048/4237/Summary_of_2014_US_Reputation_Dividend_Report.pdf.

11 Reputation Dividend, Summary of 2014 US Reputation Dividend Report, http://reputationdividend.com/files/2413/9029/4988/2013-2014 UK_Reputation_Dividend_Report.pdf.

12 Kurt Eichenwald, *Conspiracy of Fools: A True Story* (New York: Broadway Books, 2005), 590.

13 Hugh Lofting, *The Story of Doctor Doolittle* (A Yearling Book, May 1988), 76.

14 Harris Interactive, *The 10th Annual RQ: The 60 Most Visible Companies*, http://www.harrisinteractive.com/services/pubs/HI_BSC_REPORT_AnnualRQ2008_Summary Report.pdf.

15 Rob Cox, "Too Small to Bail Has a Nice Ring to It," *New York Times*, September 28, 2009, http://www.nytimes.com/2009/09/29/business/29views.html.

16 Matt Taibbi, "Inside the Great American Bubble Machine," *Rolling Stone*, July 2, 2009, http://www.rollingstone.com/politics/story/28816321/inside_the_great_american_bubble_machine.

17 David W. Guth and Charles Marsh, *Public Relations, A Values-Driven Approach* (Needham Heoghts, MA: Pearson Education, Allyn and Bacon, 2000), 292–4.

18 Johnson & Johnson Credo at http://www.jnj.com/our_credo/index.htm.

19 Booz & Company, "CEOs Hold Steady in the Storm," May 12, 2009, http://www.booz.com/global/home/what_we_think/reports_and_white_papers/article/45574145.

20 Carter Dougherty, "A Happy Family of 8,000, But For How Long?," *New York Times,* July 11, 2009, BU1.

21 "Corporate Reputation Management in the US Pharmaceutical Industry," April 25, 2011, http://www. instituteforpr.org/topics/corporate-reputation-management-in-the-us-pharmaceutical-industry/.

22 Fraser P. Seitel and John Doorley, *Rethinking Reputation* (New York: Palgrave Macmillan, 2012), 1.

23 Brent D. Ruben, Linda Lederman, and David W. Gibson, eds., *Communication Theory: A Casebook Approach* (Dubuque, IA: Kendall Hunt, 2000), 173–201.

24 Paul Watzlawick, Janet Beavin Bavelas, and Donald D. Jackson, *Pragmatics of Human Communication* (New York: Norton 1967).

2 ETHICS AND COMMUNICATION

Management is doing things right; leadership is doing the right things.
— Peter F. Drucker

■ ■ ■

TRUTH OR CONSQUENCES

Scott McClellan hadn't even begun his new job, but he knew it would be a challenge.

McClellan, deputy press secretary to President George W. Bush since the president took office in January 2001, had just been promoted to succeed press secretary Ari Fleisher, in July 2003. The U.S. had invaded Iraq in March, ostensibly to prevent Saddam Hussein from being able to use weapons of mass destruction. In the run-up to the war, senior administration officials had warned of grave consequences of leaving Hussein in power, including assertions that "the smoking gun may well be a mushroom cloud."

Just before McClellan took the top spokesperson job, *The New York Times* had published an op-ed by former ambassador Joseph C. Wilson IV, who had been dispatched by the U.S. government to investigate concerns that the African nation of Niger may have provided uranium to Iraq. The op-ed took exception to a statement President Bush had made in his 2003 State of the Union address, suggesting that there was credible evidence that Niger had provided materials to Iraq that could be used to make nuclear weapons. Wilson noted that his 2002 trip concluded that the concerns were unfounded; that Niger did not have such a capacity. It noted that Wilson was convinced that the White House had been so informed. He further concluded that the administration had twisted the intelligence to exaggerate the Iraqi threat.

According to McClellan, in his 2008 book *What Happened: Inside the Bush White House and Washington's Culture of Deception*, "To defend itself against the accusations of deliberate dishonesty leveled by Joe Wilson, Vice President (Richard) Cheney and his staff were leading a White House effort to discredit Joe Wilson himself." Wilson's article had appeared on July 6. On July 14, conservative pundit Robert Novak authored a column about how Wilson's trip had come about and what it concluded. It ended with "Wilson never worked for the CIA, but his wife, Valerie Plame, is an agent, an operative on weapons of mass destruction. Two senior administration officials told me that Wilson's wife suggested sending him to Niger to investigate [the report about uranium]."

As it happens, Wilson's wife was indeed a CIA agent, working under cover—in particular, under non-official cover, meaning that she posed as a business person, not a member of an embassy staff. Revealing the identity of a covert CIA agent is a crime. Novak's column provoked a firestorm of criticism, and ultimately led to an investigation by a special prosecutor.

As McClellan began his press secretary duties, the media was focused on questions about who leaked Plame's identity. By October,

> the emerging narrative in the Washington press was that the White House had deliberately blown [Plame's] cover. Administration officials had anonymously leaked her identity to reporters in order to punish (at worst) or discredit (at best) her husband, who was publicly alleging that the administration had misled the country into a war in Iraq. News stories suggested that White House aides had disclosed Plame's identity to at least five reporters. A concerted effort to disclose her identity would have meant that the officials involved, knowingly or not, had leaked classified national security information.

McClellan spoke directly to the two senior-most aides in the White House: Karl Rove, President Bush's closest advisor, and Lewis "'Scooter" Libby, Vice President Cheney's chief of staff. Both denied any role (for themselves or their bosses) in the outing of Plame's identity. Confident in their assurances, McClellan addressed the October 10 press briefing with this definitive statement: "I spoke with those individuals, as I pointed out, and those individuals assured me they were not involved in this, and that's where it stands.'"

McClellan would later write:

> The public assurances I provided that October 10 would be my final statements from the podium denying that Rove and Libby had been involved in the outing of a covert CIA official, and my final comments on any other matters which might be part of the criminal investigation that the leak of Plame's name had already spawned.
>
> There was just one problem. What I said was not true.
>
> I had unknowingly passed along false information. And five of the highest ranking officials in the administration were involved in my doing so: Rove, Libby, Vice President Cheney, the president's chief of staff Andrew Card, and the president himself.
>
> For my next two years as press secretary, the false words I uttered at Friday's briefing would stand as the official White House position on the Plame case. Little did I know at the time that what I said, and the pervasive deceit underlying it, would be my undoing as the president's chief spokesman.
>
> I had allowed myself to be deceived into unknowingly passing along a falsehood. It would ultimately prove fatal to my ability to serve the president effectively.
>
> I didn't learn that what I'd said was untrue until the media began to find it out almost two years later. Neither, I believe, did President Bush. He too had been deceived, and therefore became unwittingly involved in deceiving. But the top White House officials who knew the truth—including Rove, Libby, and possibly Vice President Cheney—allowed me, even encouraged me, to repeat a lie.

Public relations professionals in particular are subject to severe consequences of conveying falsehoods.

McClellan discovered the hard way a constant reality of public relations. Communication takes place in a climate of belief. Effective persuasion over time requires not merely truthfulness but intentionality about truthfulness.

Public relations professionals in particular are subject to severe consequences of conveying falsehoods, whether intentionally lying or, like McClellan, unintentionally passing along false information. But public relations professionals who are seen to lie or to be unconcerned with the truth, often find themselves marginalized by the media and other stakeholders. Trust can plummet when stakeholders discover they have been treated dishonestly.

The ethical challenge of professional public relations is dealing with truth, falsity, and ambiguity, and managing through the muddle with integrity.

Public relations professionals' occupational hazard is that clients, bosses, and even journalists will sometimes be dishonest with them in pursuit of their own goals. But it's the PR people whose credibility suffers when the lie is discovered. The ethical challenge of professional public relations is dealing with truth, falsity, and ambiguity, and managing through the muddle with integrity.

■ ■ ■

Communication ethics =

Normative standards of behavior that govern the practice of public relations with integrity

---

INTRODUCTION: WHY ETHICS MATTERS

The ethical practice of corporate communication and public relations is a given for many professional communicators.

But to much of the outside world there is something vaguely unethical about the entire enterprise. Such phrases as "just PR" or "spin" suggest that people see a meaningful difference between truthful and candid discussion and the kinds of activities that professional communicators are thought to engage in.

This has been a perennial concern for practitioners of the craft—from the roots of professional communication in the fourth century BC through the formative years of the modern practice of public relations in the twentieth century AD, to the present.

The irony is that most professional communicators not only practice ethically but deliberately want to do so. And many corporations, learning the lessons from celebrated corporate scandals of the 2000s, now recognize that inattention to ethical issues exposes them to far worse consequences than they may have previously understood.

Inattention to ethics risks significant harm to reputation and to other important intangible corporate assets—including employee morale and productivity, demand for a company's products, confidence in a company's executives, and stock price performance. Ethical lapses also lead directly to changes in senior leadership of a company. Inattention to ethics and the consequences of unethical behavior can even affect an organization's ability to survive.

> Inattention to ethics risks significant harm to reputation and to other important intangible corporate assets.

WHAT IS ETHICS?

Despite a general desire to practice corporate communication ethically, many professional communicators have only a passing knowledge of ethics and the way ethical standards have evolved in business generally and in the professional practice of communication in particular.

Individuals and companies often get into ethically murky situations because they confuse ethics with morality, legality, etiquette, or aesthetics—that is, they confuse actions with motives, crimes, politeness, or feelings.

Many people associate the word "ethics" with some sense of morality, and often use the words "ethics" and "morality" interchangeably. And although there is a high degree of overlap between the words, they mean different things and should not be confused. Ethics concerns behavior—what people do—and the behavior at issue is often public.

"Morality" concerns motivation—why people do things. And because morality involves intention and attitudes, it is generally within the realm of personal conscience, and is typically private. Sometimes morality drives ethics; that is, sometimes personal conscience leads to admirable public behavior. But sometimes the admirable public behavior takes place for other reasons.

> From an ethical perspective motives are less important than the actual behaviors.

Although some people might wish that all actions be done for the right reasons, from an ethical perspective motives are less important than the actual behaviors. Take a simple example: lying. As an ethical issue, it is a matter of indifference whether people refuse to lie because they are afraid of getting caught, because they have become habituated to not lie, or because of a strong moral commitment to honesty. From an ethical perspective, a person who doesn't lie—for whatever reason—is behaving ethically. Similarly, someone who lies for benevolent reasons—for example, from a desire not to hurt someone's feelings—commits an ethical offense. It doesn't matter that the motive was positive, even that the motive was moral. All that matters in such a case is that the lie—the public behavior—is unethical.

The same applies in the corporate world. It is more important that a company insist on ethical behavior by its employees than that it do so for some moral reason. Some companies' leaders are genuinely driven by a moral desire to practice business ethically—to do what's right. Others are driven by a desire to avoid the distraction and costs associated with ethical lapses. And some insist on ethical behavior because they know that having and policing a strong code of ethics protects them under U.S.

federal sentencing guidelines should they or their employees be convicted of a crime. But the motive for a company's behavior is less important than recognizing whether its behavior is acceptable or unacceptable. And because morality is a private matter, it is often difficult to discern a company's, or an individual's, true motive. Sometimes people and companies act from a mixture of both moral and practical motives.

Ethics is also often confused with legality; unethical behavior with illegal behavior.

In broad overview, morality, ethics, and the law are part of a continuum of sometimes overlapping considerations. Take again, for example, lying—telling a deliberate untruth with the intention of deceiving. Lying can be seen to be a moral failing. Lying to someone in a business context can be seen to be an ethical lapse, the violation of a codified or implied rule stating that people in business not lie to each other. And in some circumstances—such as lying under oath or to a criminal investigator—lying may trigger legal action. In the Valerie Plame example that began the chapter, Lewis "Scooter" Libby, the vice president's chief of staff, was convicted of lying under oath to investigators. Libby's lying could be considered a moral lapse, and it may also have been an ethical lapse. But he was prosecuted, convicted, and sentenced to prison not for moral or ethical lapses but for violation of the criminal law. (President Bush later commuted Libby's sentence.)

> It may be useful to think of morality, ethics, and legality as three circles of a Venn diagram, with some overlap among the three areas.

It may be useful to think of morality, ethics, and legality as three circles of a Venn diagram (see Figure 2.1), with some overlap among the three areas, but each comprising a distinct set of issues with its own distinct worldviews, considerations, and consequences.

Sometimes people compartmentalize the three, and miss the overlap; they fail to recognize that the violation of one of these may also be a violation of others. For example, in 2002 it became widely known that many Catholic priests in the U.S. had sexually abused children, and that the bishops who ran the Church in the U.S. had known about the problems for years and had done little to stop the abuse.

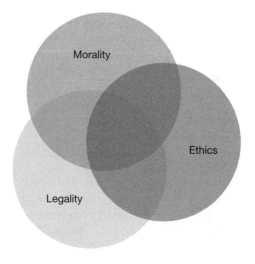

Figure 2.1

Abusing children was clearly immoral—in the vocabulary of the Church, a sin. And it was also a clear violation of priests' own codes of ethics, particularly their vows of celibacy and their duty to protect the vulnerable from abuse by those in power. But what seemed to be unaddressed was the fact that such behavior is also a crime. Before the scandals became widely known in 2002 few Catholic priests had been prosecuted; afterward many were, including some of the most notorious abusers. Now some dioceses have established zero-tolerance policies, including recognition that allegations of abuse should be turned over to law enforcement authorities for investigation and prosecution.

Sometimes legal and ethical duties conflict: For example, the ethical duty to maintain confidentiality—such as a reporter's promise to keep the identity of a source secret—and the legal duty to answer questions when testifying under oath in a trial or in a grand jury investigation. In 2005 the U.S. Supreme Court refused to consider an appellate ruling that journalists could not refuse to identify their sources to a grand jury investigating the Plame leak. As a result, a *New York Times* reporter, Judith Miller, went to jail rather than violate her promise—described by her and *The New York Times* as an ethical obligation—to protect the identity of her source.

> Some actions may be perfectly legal but also unethical.

Similarly, some actions may be perfectly legal but also unethical, such as representing two companies with conflicting interests. While such client relationships may violate ethical standards, unless there is a contractual prohibition against such a relationship the law is generally silent about them.

> It is common for people to confuse ethics with etiquette: what is polite.

It is also common for people to confuse ethics with etiquette: what is polite. For example, some people consider it impolite to criticize others. So they sometimes withhold criticism, or even tell a "white lie"—that is, an innocent untruth not intended to deceive, but to flatter—in order to avoid giving offense. While this kind of behavior is often seen to be admirable, the conflict between etiquette and ethics often comes into full focus when a desire to avoid offense leads to more than an innocent untruth, but to a full-blown lie—that is, a deliberate untruth intended to deceive. Often the duty to be truthful conflicts with the desire to be polite, and ethical people sometimes need to tell hard truths to others; failure to tell those hard truths may be seen as unethical. More significantly, because ethics refers to habitual behaviors, the default to etiquette over ethics can habituate someone to default to politeness over truthfulness, leading to inadvertent ethical lapses.

> Ethics is often confused with aesthetics: what is pleasurable.

Similarly, ethics is often confused with aesthetics: what is pleasurable. People say things that make them and others feel good, regardless of the underlying truthfulness of the statement. Or they avoid saying things that may be unpalatable or personally distasteful to them or to their audiences. Like etiquette, the desire to feel good and help others feel good is often admirable, but can lead to habitual behaviors that conflict with ethical duties.

Ethics as Habits

Aristotle noted that we are what we habitually do.

The English word "ethics" comes from the ancient Greek word that translates into the English word "habits." The word began to take on its current meaning when it was used by the Greek philosopher Aristotle (c. 384 to 322 BC) in his book *The Nichomachean Ethics*, which describes habitual behaviors that lead to happiness. He noted that we are what we habitually do.

Ethics consists of the behaviors that are habitually practiced by an individual and, collectively, by a group of individuals.

Over the years "ethics" has come to mean habitual behaviors that are appropriate in certain circumstances. So ethics consists of the behaviors that are habitually practiced by an individual and, collectively, by a group of individuals. As individuals form groups that serve particular purposes, they establish formal or informal codes of conduct to govern relations among themselves and between their group and other groups. Over time these codes of conduct describe socially-acceptable patterns of behaviors.

Ethics describes behaviors that are repeated over time and that therefore become unconscious.

It is useful to keep the word "habits" in mind when discussing ethics, because ethics describes behaviors that are repeated over time and that therefore become unconscious. As an ethical issue it is a matter of indifference whether an individual refuses to lie because of fear of getting caught or because of a strong commitment to morality. But as an individual becomes habituated over time to avoid lying, the original motive may be forgotten. Someone who initially refuses to lie because of fear of the consequences may, over time, become habituated to not lie—even when there are no likely negative consequences. In other words, the behavior has become habitual.

It can be risky to permit suspect behaviors, even when the reasons are defensible, because over time these suspect behaviors may become habits.

Similarly, it can be risky to permit suspect behaviors, even when the reasons are defensible, because over time these suspect behaviors may become habits: so someone who lies in certain circumstances may be habituated to lie in others, and it becomes more and more likely that such a person will lie as a first resort.

Codes of Ethics and Normative Standards of Behavior

Groups develop formal ethical rules to establish normative standards for behavior that can then become habitual among members.

One reason groups develop formal ethical rules is to establish normative standards for behavior that can then become habitual among members of the group. Such rules are an ordinary part of social interaction.

In the 1920s, Edward L. Bernays called for a code of ethics to govern the behavior of the emerging profession of public relations.

Over the years, and especially in the twentieth century, professional societies developed their own codes of professional behavior, establishing behaviors that are required, permitted, and forbidden among their members. So doctors in the U.S. are bound by the *Code of Medical Ethics* of the American Medical Association; lawyers by the *Code of Professional Responsibility* of the American Bar Association; accountants by the *Code of Professional Conduct* of the American Institute of Certified Public Accountants, and so forth.

In the 1920s, Edward L. Bernays, the first professional communicator to call himself a "public relations counselor," called for a code of ethics to govern the behavior of the emerging profession of public relations:

> The profession of public relations counsel is developing for itself an ethical code which compares favorably with that governing the legal and medical professions. In part, this code is forced upon the public relations counsel by the very conditions of his work. While recognizing, just as the lawyer does, that everyone has a right to present his case in its best light, he nevertheless refuses a client whom he believes to be dishonest, a product which he believes to be fraudulent, or a cause which he believes to be antisocial.[1]

In that very description of the choices a practitioner makes, Bernays previewed some of the ethical challenges facing public relations practitioners in the twenty-first century. Today the Public Relations Society of America's *Member Code of Ethics*, the International Association of Business Communicators' *Code of Ethics for Professional Communicators*, and the International Public Relations Association's *Code of Conduct*, set standards to which their member practitioners are expected to abide.

ETHICS AND PROFESSIONAL COMMUNICATION

Most professional communicators are not members of industry associations, and most associations do not have corporate members. So technically most professional communicators are not bound by such industry codes of conduct. Further, membership in these associations is voluntary and is not a requirement for most jobs in corporate and organizational communication. And the codes provide little in the way of enforcement. The maximum penalty for being found to have violated the code is removal from the association, an association that many communicators do not belong to in the first place. The enforcement is nothing like an attorney being disbarred for violating the legal profession's code of ethics, thereby losing his or her license to practice law. Some people argue that removal from a voluntary organization that doesn't affect employment is not a sufficient penalty to deter unethical behavior, and that therefore such codes are meaningless.

> Because the codes are normative, they provide standards that both members and non-members can use as guides for effective action.

But because the codes are normative, they provide standards that both members and non-members can use as guides for effective action. Clients and others can compare any given behavior to one of the codes to determine whether it is appropriate. In other words, regardless of the strength of the sanctions involved, the descriptions of normative behavior provide value by setting standards against which any individual's, group's, or company's behavior can be evaluated.

Indeed, the International Association of Business Communicators (IABC) "encourages the widest possible communication about its Code," publishes the code in several languages, and grants permission to any individual or organization to copy and incorporate all or part of its code into personal or corporate codes (with attribution to IABC).

As members and non-members of various professional associations adapt their behaviors to these groups' normative standards, and the behaviors become habitual, they establish even stronger norms. Violations of the code, even when committed by non-members who are subject to no disciplinary procedures, nevertheless can be recognized as inappropriate, and as aberrations from the professional practice of communication.[2]

International Association of Business Communicators' Code of Ethics for Professional Communicators

The International Association of Business Communicators' *Code of Ethics for Professional Communicators* offers three overarching rules:

* First, that members of IABC "engage only in communication that is not only legal but also ethical and sensitive to cultural values and beliefs."
* Second, that they "engage in truthful, accurate, and fair communication."
* And third, that they adhere to the articles of the *Code* itself.

The IABC *Code* itself consists of twelve normative statements, each describing the behavior of professional communicators. These include:

> Professional communicators disseminate accurate information and promptly correct any erroneous communication for which they might be responsible . . .
> Professional communicators give credit for unique expressions borrowed from others and identify sources and purposes of all information disseminated to the public . . .
> Professional communicators do not accept gifts or payments for professional services from anyone other than a client or employer.[3]

The complete *IABC Code of Ethics for Professional Communicators* may be found at http://www.iabc.com/members/joining/code.htm.

Public Relations Society of America Member Code of Ethics

After a significant ethics scandal in the early 1990s (see Case Study on Citizens for a Free Kuwait, page 76), the Public Relations Society of America (PRSA) came under sharp criticism. The Association was criticized for not taking a position in the public discussion of communication ethics during the scandal, and for having a code that was difficult to follow, not particularly helpful to individual practitioners, and out of date.

The PRSA's Board of Ethics and Professional Standards, which led the revision of the code in the late 1990s, recast the code to emphasize the standards that apply to the professional practice of public relations.[4] This Board focused on the fact that the most effective codes are normative, and can therefore serve as guides to the ethical practice of the craft as a whole, not just to the Association's members.

The new *Member Code of Ethics* was prepared by the PRSA Board of Ethics and Professional Standards, which consisted of nine senior public relations practitioners. They were assisted by the Ethics Resource Center, a Washington-based ethics consulting organization. The Ethics Board convened a series of discussions with members in 1998 and 1999, leading to the launch of the new Code in 2000.[5] In their introduction to the new *Code*, the authors note that "the primary obligation of membership in the Public Relations Society of America is the ethical practice of public relations," and observe that the new Code "is a way for each member of our society to daily reaffirm a commitment to ethical professional activities and decisions."[6]

Unlike the prior code (and unlike several others associations' codes, including IABC's) the new *PRSA Member Code* also includes examples of behaviors that would be considered unethical, providing more concrete guidance to members and others of what would be considered inappropriate behavior. It not only lists required and forbidden behaviors in the abstract; it demonstrates by example and analogy the kinds of behaviors that are inappropriate, making it more likely that proper behaviors will be habituated, that improper behaviors will be avoided, and that practitioners will find the Code useful as a guide to the real-world practice of professional communication.

- The *PRSA Member Code of Ethics* consists of three parts: *Values*, *Provisions*, and a *Pledge*: *Member Statement of Professional Values*. These values, each of which is defined with several bullet points, include Advocacy, Honesty, Expertise, Independence, Loyalty, and Fairness. They provide a conceptual framework for the ethical practice of public relations.
- *PRSA Code Provisions*. For each provision there is a plain English description, a statement of intent, guidelines, and examples of improper conduct.
- For example, the *Principle* Disclosure of Information is described as follows: "Open communication fosters informed decision making in a democratic society." Its *Intent* is described as "to build trust with the public by revealing all information needed for responsible decision making."
- The guidelines include:

  > Be honest and accurate in all communications. Act promptly to correct erroneous communications for which the member is responsible. Investigate the truthfulness and accuracy of information released on behalf of those represented. Reveal the sponsors for causes and interests represented.[7]

- The *Examples of Improper Conduct Under this Provision* section includes the following: "A member deceives the public by employing people to pose as volunteers to speak at public hearings."[8]

- *Pledge*, which each member signs, that affirms his or her commitment to, among other things, "conduct myself professionally, with truth, accuracy, fairness, and responsibility to the public."[9]

The complete PRSA Member Code of Ethics can be found at: http://www.prsa.org/_About/ethics/index.asp?ident=eth1.

International Public Relations Association Code of Conduct

The International Public Relations Association (IPRA) *Code of Conduct* is intended to serve as normative standards for communicators working in all countries and markets of the world. As a result, it needs to balance the practical realities of cultural, political, and legal differences in the environments in which professional communicators work. IPRA has updated its codes over the years, but always with an emphasis on honesty and integrity, and with reference to the United Nations *Universal Declaration of Human Rights*.

The most recent update, to create the IPRA *Code of Conduct*, was completed in 2011. It consolidated prior codes, and begins, as do the others, by recalling the 1948 UN *Universal Declaration of Human Rights*. And it notes that public relations contributes to the interests of all stakeholders and provides democratic representation to public authorities.

But the 2011 code also observes the new realities of the Internet, social networking, and social media. It notes that:

> channels of communication such as the Internet and other digital media, are channels where erroneous or misleading information may be widely disseminated and remain unchallenged, and therefore demand special attention from public relations practitioners to maintain trust and credibility.

It further calls upon practitioners to exercise particular diligence when using social media because of the potential for the technology to be easily abused:

> The Internet and other digital media demand special care with respect to the personal privacy of individuals, clients, employers and colleagues.

Indeed, in an interview with one of the authors the 2013 President of IPRA, Christophe Ginisty, noted that historically the IPRA codes were more concerned with top-down communication; the ways governments and large corporations distributed information to citizens and consumers. But political, social, technological, and economic changes have redefined the relationship of many citizens and consumers to large institutions. Today ordinary consumers and citizens have at their fingertips communication technology that once was the province of powerful institutions. As a result, companies, governments, and other individuals are now likely to be the subject of unethical and potentially harmful communication from other individuals. Mr. Ginisty notes, "Today brand hacking is a common phenomenon, and ethics needs to account for this new power dynamic. The IPRA *Code* recognizes that whether communicating on behalf of a large company or government or an activist group, PR people need to operate with integrity."[10]

After the brief introductory framework, the actual IPRA *Code*, in turn, is both short and straightforward, reprinted here in its entirety (spelling as in the original).

In the conduct of public relations practitioners shall:

1. Observance
Observe the principles of the UN Charter and the *Universal Declaration of Human Rights*;

2. Integrity
Act with honesty and integrity at all times so as to secure and retain the confidence of those with whom the practitioner comes into contact;

3. Dialogue
Seek to establish the moral, cultural and intellectual conditions for dialogue, and recognise the rights of all parties involved to state their case and express their views;

4. Transparency
Be open and transparent in declaring their name, organisation and the interest they represent;

5. Conflict
Avoid any professional conflicts of interest and to disclose such conflicts to affected parties when they occur;

6. Confidentiality
Honour confidential information provided to them;

7. Accuracy
Take all reasonable steps to ensure the truth and accuracy of all information provided;

8. Falsehood
Make every effort to not intentionally disseminate false or misleading information, exercise proper care to avoid doing so unintentionally and correct any such act promptly;

9. Deception
Not obtain information by deceptive or dishonest means;

10. Disclosure

Not create or use any organisation to serve an announced cause but which actually serves an undisclosed interest;

11. Profit

Not sell for profit to third parties copies of documents obtained from public authorities;

12. Remuneration

Whilst providing professional services, not accept any form of payment in connection with those services from anyone other than the principal;

13. Inducement

Neither directly nor indirectly offer nor give any financial or other inducement to public representatives or the media, or other stakeholders;

14. Influence

Neither propose nor undertake any action which would constitute an improper influence on public representatives, the media, or other stakeholders;

15. Competitors

Not intentionally injure the professional reputation of another practitioner;

16. Poaching

Not seek to secure another practitioner's client by deceptive means;

17. Employment

When employing personnel from public authorities or competitors take care to follow the rules and confidentiality requirements of those organisations;

18. Colleagues

Observe this *Code* with respect to fellow IPRA members and public relations practitioners worldwide.[11]

These three association codes of ethics describe, each in its own way, normative standards of behavior for professional communicators around the world.

They create a framework for understanding appropriate standards of conduct for all professional communicators.

More on the IPRA *Code of Conduct* and on IPRA can be found at http://www.ipra.org/about/ipra-codes

These three association codes of ethics describe, each in its own way, normative standards of behavior for professional communicators around the world. Although the specific provisions apply directly only to members of the respective organizations, they create a framework for understanding appropriate standards of conduct for all professional communicators. And although there are variations among the codes, they are generally consistent in broad overview and collectively serve as useful benchmarks against which to assess the typical ethical challenges that professional communicators face.

EXPERT PERSPECTIVES: ETHICS AND SOCIAL MEDIA

By Laurel Hart, Senior Advisor, Logos Consulting Group and Adjunct Instructor, New York University, MS in Public Relations and Corporate Communication

A CEO shamelessly tweeting under a pseudonym about himself, his company, and its competitors. A PR agency improperly editing its clients' entries on Wikipedia. A company crassly capitalizing on a national tragedy by linking its product promotion efforts to the tragedy on Facebook and Twitter. These are just a few examples of the kinds of unethical behavior that can occur in social media. While most companies participating in social media communicate ethically (just as most companies participating in other communication channels communicate ethically), every year there are numerous cases of organizations, individuals or agencies violating ethical boundaries of online behavior.

Ethical behavior within social media concerns what you do with your own content and what you do with others' content. The Word of Mouth Marketing Association (WOMMA) has developed a Code of Ethics and Standards of Conduct (http://www.womma.org/ethics/womma-code-of-ethics) that provides helpful guidance to everyone participating in social media, either on an individual basis or on behalf of an organization. The eight standards of conduct cover:

Standard 1—Disclosure of identity;
Standard 2—Disclosure of consideration or compensation received;
Standard 3—Disclosure of relationship;
Standard 4—Compliance with FTC Guides;
Standard 5—Genuine honesty in communication;
Standard 6—Respect for venue;
Standard 7—[No] Marketing with children and adolescents;
Standard 8—Compliance with media-specific rules.

There used to be an old adage that "On the Internet, nobody knows you're a dog." That simply is not true anymore (if it ever was). Because of the nature of social technologies, true identities (and behavior generally) can—and will—most often be discovered, and as any leader of a large organization should know, if you wouldn't be comfortable saying it on the record, it's best not to say it in the first place.

Regardless of individual codes, communication ethics fall into four categories:

1. Ethics inherent to communicating, usually involving truthfulness and transparency.

2. Ethics of running any kind of organization.
3. Ethics of representation.
4. Helping clients and employers behave ethically.

ETHICS OF COMMUNICATING

Effective communication starts with a climate of belief, and credibility is the strongest asset a professional communicator may have.

Ethics inherent to communicating involves behaviors one engages in that are intrinsic to the process of shaping public opinion by means of communication. Effective communication starts with a climate of belief, and credibility is the strongest asset a professional communicator may have.

CASE STUDY: NUCLEAR MELTDOWN AND CREDIBILITY

Audiences who believe they have been misled are less likely to believe a speaker in the future. Take, for example, the reaction of Japanese citizens in the aftermath of the 2011 nuclear meltdown following the earthquake and Tsunami that devastated much of Japan's east coast.

As early as 2002 Tokyo Electric Power Company (TEPCO) had a credibility problem. TEPCO is the largest non-government-owned electric utility company in the world. In 2002 TEPCO was found to have falsified nuclear safety data at least 200 times between 1977 and 2002.[12] TEPCO admitted to falsifying its records of nuclear inspections and hiding the facts for more than a decade.[13] Its chairman, president, and vice president stepped down in the aftermath,[14] and in 2003, 17 nuclear power plants were forced to shut down for safety inspections.[15]

According to *The Daily Yomiuri*, Japan's largest-circulation newspaper, the case came to light only after a U.S. employee of a subsidiary of General Electric Co., who inspected nuclear reactors together with TEPCO engineers, tipped off Japan's Ministry of International Trade and Industry (MITI), the predecessor of the present Economy, Trade and Industry Ministry. The *Yomiuri* also revealed that MITI itself had conspired with TEPCO to cover up the information later revealed by the GE whistleblower.[16]

When the 2011 Tsunami happened, compromising the safety of several TEPCO nuclear reactors at its Fukushima site, TEPCO's and the Japanese government's initial reaction was to offer reassurances that were not believed. As the world's attention was focused on the risk of meltdown at the reactors, Japan's ambassador to the United States appeared on CNN and told anchor Wolf Blitzer that there was no meltdown. But within minutes the ambassador was contradicted by the head of Japan's Nuclear and Industrial Safety agency, who told CNN that a meltdown actually "might be under way."[17]

Similarly, TEPCO officials continuously reassured people who lived close to the plant that they were not at risk of dangerous exposure to radiation leaks. Nuclear expert Arnie Gundersen of Fairewinds Energy Education said, "Tokyo Electric said, 'Don't worry be happy, everything is fine.' I don't believe that."[18] Similarly, Yukio Otsuka, a private school owner whose home was three miles from the plant, said, "I don't believe a word they say. I don't trust them. I don't believe it is possible."[19]

Most of the ethical questions relating to the practice of communication involve credibility in one way or another. The most significant issues of credibility involve truthfulness and falsity of communication, and disclosure of the client or cause on whose behalf a communication is being made.

> Most of the ethical questions relating to the practice of communication involve credibility in one way or another.

Some critics of professional communication assert that the very idea of public relations is itself unethical, and use words such as "propaganda" and "spin" to suggest that such activities are inherently misleading. Public relations critics John Stauber and Sheldon Rampton assert that the business of public relations represents a significant social problem. They claim that:

> Today's PR industry is related to democracy in the same way that prostitution is related to sex. When practiced voluntarily for love, both can exemplify human communication at its best. When they are bought and sold, however, they are transformed into something hidden and sordid.[20]

Stauber is executive director, and Rampton is research director, of the Center for Media and Democracy, which publishes *PR Watch*, dedicated to investigative reporting on the PR industry. In their 1995 book *Toxic Sludge is Good for You: Lies, Damn Lies and the Public Relations Industry*, Stauber and Rampton attribute sinister motive to the practice of public relations:

> Public relations exists to manufacture the necessary illusions that bridge the gap between the dream and reality of American society . . . If the PR industry were *only* based on "lies and damn lies," it might be easier to see through its deceptions. But PR's cunning half-truths and "spins" appeal to us and work on us because they come from us, from the constant plumbing of the social mind by surveys, opinion polls, focus groups, and information gathered as we apply for bank loans, purchase goods with credit cards, place birth announcements in newspapers, vote, and make phone calls.[21]

Stauber and Rampton particularly object to press releases, video news releases, and other techniques common to the practice of public relations that involve providing information to journalists for their consideration and publication.

While Stauber and Rampton acknowledge that not every instance of public relations practice is by itself illegitimate, they also argue that the craft is more often used in the service of illegitimate corporate gain:

> Citizens and individual PR practitioners can use ethical public relations techniques to right social wrongs, clean up the environment, promote minority rights, protect working people, and make communities better. But we consider it an illusion to imagine that PR is a "neutral" technology that can simply be adopted uncritically to achieve socially responsible ends.[22]

But a close look at many of the arguments used by Stauber, Rampton, and other critics shows them to be oversimplifications of the corporate communication process, to project to the entire profession the unethical behavior of a small number of people, to confuse criticism of PR with the practices of journalism, or to use PR as a foil in the service of a political agenda—in Stauber's and Rampton's case the argument that it benefits large corporations at the expense of ordinary people. Indeed, the introduction to *Toxic Sludge is Good for You*, by journalist Mark Dowie, lays out the political agenda of the book:

> A single public relations professional with access to the media, a basic understanding of mass psychology, and a fistful of dollars can unleash in society forces that make permanent winners out of otherwise-evident losers—whether they be products, politicians, corporations, or ideas. This is an awesome power we give to an industry that gravitates to wealth, offers surplus power and influence to those who need it least, and operates largely beyond public view.[23]

Stauber and Rampton attribute sinister motive to the practice of public relations. But much of their criticism seems to blend critique of the practice of corporate communications and public relations with criticism of journalists' reliance on PR's work product.

In particular, much of the criticism also seems to blend critique of the practice of corporate communications and public relations with criticism of journalists' reliance on PR's work product. Stauber and Rampton attribute sinister motive to the practice of public relations. But much of their criticism seems to blend critique of the practice of corporate communications and public relations with criticism of journalists' reliance on PR's work product.

Are Press Releases Unethical?

For example, some critics of public relations and corporate communication point to the tools used to communicate—especially press releases, video news releases, and related hand-outs that are provided to the news media—and suggest that these very tools are somehow sinister and misleading.

But most of the tools are neither. Press releases are corporate announcements written in the style of a newspaper story that a news organization may choose to use or not use. Some press releases are printed verbatim in newspapers; some are excerpted. Many press releases serve simply as a starting point from which a reporter will write his or her own story, often lifting language or quotes from the press release. Among the criticisms of press releases is the observation that quotes lifted from a release convey to the reader of the news story the impression that the reporter actually spoke to the person quoted. The suggestion is that using the quote misleads readers, giving a false impression that the reporter spoke with the newsmaker.

But a close review of such practices suggests that if there is an ethical issue, or a credibility issue, inherent in such practices, the ethical challenge is on the part of the news organization. News organizations are certainly free to ignore a press release, and many press releases are never printed in news media. News organizations are also free to supplement a release with their own reporting, including speaking with the person quoted in the release. They are also free to label the quote in such a way that lets a reader know that the quote came from a press release. Such formulations include "In a statement the company said . . ." or "In an announcement Mr. So-and-so said . . ."

> From a professional communicator's perspective, the ethical duty is to assure that the announcement genuinely represents the point of view of the client on whose behalf it is distributed; that the source of the information is clearly and accurately identified; and that there are no deliberate falsehoods in the text of the release.

From a professional communicator's perspective, the ethical duty is different: to assure that the announcement genuinely represents the point of view of the client on whose behalf it is distributed; that the source of the information is clearly and accurately identified; and that there are no deliberate falsehoods in the text of the release. So long as these ethical duties are met, the communication is generally considered ethical. All three professional association codes of ethics—IABC's, PRSA's, and IPRA's, require that all communication—including news releases and related materials—be truthful and that the source of the communication be clearly identified.

One of the counterarguments to the suggestion that press releases by their very nature are unethical (and that therefore they should not be used) is to note that often press releases are required by law and regulation. For example, under U.S. laws and regulations governing corporate disclosure in the securities markets (See Chapter 8, Investor Relations), companies whose stock is publicly traded are required to issue press releases to the media and investment community describing their financial performance and other significant news. In fact, a significant percentage of business news is the routine excerpting of such corporate press releases.

The same regulations that require press releases as a financial disclosure device also establish standards for accuracy and truthfulness of such communications. In general, these announcements may not be "materially misleading" or contain "material omissions"—that is, they must be accurate and complete. Releasing deliberately inaccurate or incomplete information may be considered securities fraud, and companies and individuals may be subject to civil or criminal penalties. Releasing information known by the communicator to be false or misleading is also a breach of ethics.

CASE STUDY: CHINA'S HIGH-SPEED TRAIN CRASH

When audiences are skeptical of official statements, in order to restore trust it sometimes takes very senior officials to punish those who lie.

Consider the Chinese government's reaction to its own initial missteps following a high-speed train crash in 2011. After two high-speed trains crashed on a viaduct in Wenzhou in southern China, killing 40 and injuring nearly 200 people, the government initially sought to downplay the accident, the deaths, and the causes of the crash.[24] But citizens responded, posting 26 million items on China's Weibo services, their equivalent of Twitter, and on other social media.[25] These included videos of the crash, of victims, of rescues, and even of a crane operator attempting to bury the rail cars.[26] The story became one of cover-up (both literal and figurative) and of dishonesty.

Six days after the crash, China's prime minister, Wen Jiabao, who had been in the hospital at the time of the crash, left the hospital and traveled to Wenzhou to take responsibility for the government's failed response to the crash.[27] He said:

> The public has had many questions regarding the cause and handling of the crash. I think that we should listen to the public and seriously address their questions and provide responsible answers . . . We want every step of the investigation to be open and transparent so that the public can supervise . . .
>
> I want to emphasize one point—our investigation must affirm our responsibility to the people, whether it was an equipment problem, a management problem or a production problem. We must get to the bottom of this. If there is any corruption exposed in the investigation, we will handle it according to the law, and the consequences will be severe. If we can do this we will not have failed the deceased, who lie in eternal rest.
>
> Whether we can handle the aftermath satisfactorily, the key is whether the people can get the truth. Therefore, the process of dealing with the aftermath, we should release information to the people in a timely and accurate manner.[28]

Several officials were fired in the aftermath, including the head of the Shanghai Railway Bureau, his deputy and the Bureau's Communist Party chief.[29]

Corrupting the Channels of Communication

One ethical concern facing professional communicators is the integrity of the channels of communication, particularly regarding the independence of news organizations and news commentators. The integrity of the communication process is impaired by, among other things, payments to reporters, so that their interest in providing objective coverage is or appears to be compromised. This includes providing bribes, inappropriate favors, hiring relatives, and otherwise mingling the reporter's private interests with those of a professional communicator's client or employer.

The PRSA *Member Code of Ethics* specifically calls for members to "maintain the integrity of relationships with the media, government officials, and the public."

In early 2005 *USA Today* reported that the prominent conservative commentator and columnist Armstrong Williams had received $240,000 from a public relations firm working for the U.S. Department of Education, to promote the Department's initiatives on Williams' television program.[30] A firestorm of controversy ensued. As a result of the disclosure, *Tribune Media Services*, which syndicated Williams' column, dropped the columnist, saying:

> Accepting compensation in any form from an entity that serves as the subject of his weekly newspaper columns creates, at the very least, the appearance of a conflict of interest. Under these circumstances, readers may well ask themselves if the views expressed in his columns are his own, or whether they have been purchased by a third party.[31]

The U.S. Department of Education initially defended its payments to Mr. Williams as legal, but after significant criticism the outgoing Secretary of Education, Rod Paige, said, "All of this has been reviewed and is legal. However, I am sorry that there are perceptions and allegations of ethical lapses."[32]

As the Williams controversy became public it was also learned that syndicated columnist Maggie Gallagher had promoted the Administration's "healthy marriage" initiative while receiving $21,500 from the U.S. Department of Health and Human Services.

At a press conference President George W. Bush was asked about the accumulation of scandals involving VNRs and payments to columnists. He replied, "All our Cabinet secretaries must realize that we will not be paying . . . commentators to advance our agenda. Our agenda ought to be able to stand on its own initiative."[33]

The PRSA's *Member Code of Ethics* offers guidance on less dramatic, but potentially equally challenging, ethical choices. In its *Examples of Inappropriate Conduct* under its *Free Flow of Information* provision, the *Code* offers two cases of inappropriate behavior: "A member representing a ski manufacturer gives a pair of expensive racing skis to a sports magazine columnist, to influence the columnist to write favorable articles about the product. A member entertains a government official beyond legal limits and/or in violation of government reporting requirements."[34]

The IPRA *Code of Conduct* also specifically requires that members "Neither directly nor indirectly offer nor give any financial or other inducement to public representatives or the media, or other stakeholders."[35]

Front Groups

Another challenge to the integrity of the communication process is the establishment of "front groups," or organizations that purport to have a certain, usually public purpose, but that in fact are acting on behalf of an undisclosed interest.

Citizens for a Free Kuwait (see Case Study, page 76)) is the most notorious example in recent memory, but is hardly the only such group. At the same time as the Kuwait story was in the news in the early 1990s, Greenpeace criticized a Washington PR firm for what it called a "phony citizens group," to lobby against increased fuel efficiency standards. The group, called "The Coalition for Vehicle Choice," was funded by the major automobile manufacturers.

Ironically, Edward L. Bernays, who in the 1920s called for a code of ethics for public relations, was a master of creating front groups. It all started in 1913 when Bernays, just out of college, was working at a medical magazine called *Medical Review of Reviews*. Bernays published a review of a play called *Damaged Goods*, which dealt with the effects of syphilis. The play violated social taboos against discussion of sexually-transmitted diseases. Bernays persuaded the Richard Bennett, a popular New York actor who wanted to produce the play, to let Bernays underwrite the production. According to his biographer, Bernays realized that in order to create interest in *Damaged Goods* Bernays needed:

> [To] transform the controversy into a cause, and recruit backers who already were public role models. The twenty-one year-old editor formed a Medical Review of Reviews Sociological Fund Committee, then attracted members with an artful appeal that played on Bennett's reputation as an artist as well as the worthiness of battling prudishness.[36]

Committee members included John D. Rockefeller, Jr., Mr. and Mrs. Franklin D. Roosevelt, and Mrs. William K. Vanderbilt, Sr. Rockefeller offered a typical endorsement: "The evils that spring from prostitution cannot be understood until frank discussion of them has been made possible."[37]

Despite weak reviews, *Damaged Goods* was a big success, and sold out in New York. It then went to Washington, where it was performed for Supreme Court justices, members of congress, and members of the Administration. Bernays' biographer says that using a third-party group of luminaries to lend credibility to a commercial or political cause became Bernays' preferred method of operating:

> This was the first time [Bernays] or anyone else had assembled such a distinguished front group. And its success ensured not only that he would use this technique repeatedly but also that it would continue to be employed today, when it takes a detective to unmask the interests behind such innocuous-sounding groups as the Safe Energy Communication Council (antinuclear), the Eagle Alliance (pronuclear), and the Coalition Against Regressive Taxation (trucking industry).[38]

In the 1940s Bernays was retained by Mack Trucks to help recover market share in freight hauling from railroads. He devised an extensive campaign to improve the quality of interstate highways to make shipping cargo by truck more feasible. And he created a number of front groups, including Trucking Information Service, the Trucking Service Bureau, and Better Living Through Increased Highway Transportation, which in turn created state chapters to run local campaigns to influence members of congress. Bernays was successful, and in 1950 Congress approved $556 million in new highway construction funds, and in 1952 increased the funding level to $652 million. The U.S. interstate highway system remains the living beneficiary of Bernays' campaign, which also set the standard for contemporary lobbying and political action committees.[39]

Front groups that purport to represent one interest but actually serve a hidden interest are violations of most ethical standards, which require disclosure of the interests on whose behalf communication is taking place

Today front groups that purport to represent one interest but actually serve a hidden interest are violations of most ethical standards, which require disclosure of the interests on whose behalf communication is taking place. PRSA's new *Member Code of Ethics* specifically requires identification of the ultimate beneficiary of any front groups. It requires that a member "reveal the sponsors for causes and interests represented." Its *Examples of Improper Conduct Under This Provision* includes this clause: "Front Groups: A member implements "grass roots" campaigns of letter-writing campaigns to legislators on behalf of undisclosed interest groups."[40]

Similarly, the IPRA *Code of Conduct* says that a member shall "Not create or use any organisation to serve an announced cause but which actually serves an undisclosed interest."[41]

ETHICS OF RUNNING AN ORGANIZATION

Professional communicators need also to abide by ethical standards that apply to any professional situations. These are ethical situations that any organization might face, involving mostly the interpersonal relationships between the organization and its employees, customers, business partners, and other companies.

Some of the particular ethical duties include the following:

Confidentiality

Professional communicators are often in a position to know things before the general public, and sometimes also to know information that should never be revealed because they include trade secrets, personal information about fellow employees, or other proprietary information.

Under U.S. securities law and regulations there are strict prohibitions about revealing "material non-public information" or to disclose selectively. So professional communicators are sometimes subjected to legal and regulatory requirements to keep secrets. (See Chapter 8 for more detail.)

Sometimes professional communicators are bound by contractual obligations to keep certain information confidential.

But even absent legal, regulatory, or contractual requirements, professional communicators may also be required to maintain confidences for ethical reasons. For example, the *PRSA Member Code of Conduct* has an entire provision on *Safeguarding Confidences*. The *Intent* of the principle is "to protect the privacy rights of clients, organizations, and individuals by safeguarding confidential information." The *Guidelines* require that members "safeguard the confidences and privacy rights of present, former, and prospective clients and employees. Protect privileged, confidential, or insider information gained from a client or organization." In *Examples of Improper Conduct Under This Provision* the *Code* notes "a member changes jobs, takes confidential information, and uses that information in the new position to the detriment of the former employer."[42]

Similarly, the IABC *Code of Ethics for Professional Communicators* contains two articles on the subject: "Professional communicators protect confidential information and . . . do not use confidential information gained as the result of professional activities for personal benefit."[43]

And the IPRA *Code of Conduct* says simply that members shall "Honour confidential information provided to them."

Conflicts of Interest

One of the persistent ethical challenges for professional communicators involves conflicts of interest. Sometimes the conflict is between the individual and his or her employer or client, such as when a professional communicator receives payment from an entity whose interest may be opposed to the communicator's employer or client.

The PRSA *Member Code of Ethics* has a provision on *Conflicts of Interests* that includes two guidelines on such personal/professional conflicts, saying that a member shall "act in the best interests of a client or employer, even subordinating the member's personal interests," and "avoid actions and circumstances that may appear to compromise good business judgment or create a conflict between personal and professional interests." The *Code* lists an *Example of Improper Conduct Under This Provision* the following: "The member fails to disclose that he or she has a strong financial interest in a client's chief competitor."[44]

Similarly, the IABC *Code of Ethics for Professional Communicators* contains an article that says "Professional communicators do not accept undisclosed gifts or payments for professional services from anyone other than a client or employer."[45]

Sometimes the conflict arises from a professional communicator having as clients two organizations whose interests are in conflict.

Note, however, that simply representing two competing companies does not necessarily result in a conflict of interest. For example, two competitors may have a common interest in legislation, and each could use the services of a government relations professional seeking to influence legislation that would benefit the clients' industry as a whole, and therefore both clients. Similarly, a communicator may represent two competing companies for different functions; for example, doing internal communications for client A, and government relations for client B.

Simply representing two competing companies does not necessarily create a conflict of interest. Many professional communicators have significant expertise in a particular indus-

Simply representing two competing companies does not necessarily create a conflict of interest.

try, and represent more than two companies who compete with each other. Some companies require exclusivity from their communication advisors, and usually pay a premium for that exclusivity. But others recognize that they ultimately benefit from an advisor with significant industry expertise.

One way to manage such multi-client relationships is full disclosure to all parties of the various relationships. The assumption is that there is no conflict if each party is aware of the various relationships.

The PRSA *Member Code of Ethics* requires members to "disclose promptly any existing or potential conflict of interest to affected clients or organizations," and to "encourage clients and customers to determine if a conflict exists after notifying all affected parties."[46]

Similarly, the IABC *Code of Ethics for Professional Communicators* says that professional communicators "do not represent conflicting or competing interests without written consent of those involved."[47]

And the IPRA *Code of Conduct* requires that members "Avoid any professional conflicts of interest and to disclose such conflicts to affected parties when they occur."[48]

In any event representing more than one company in a given industry, or representing competing companies, underscores the need for professional communicators to maintain strict confidentiality of client proprietary information, so as not to deliberately or inadvertently reveal to one company the business plans, strategies, staffing, sales volume, or similar sensitive data of another such company.

Ethics of Routine Business Relationships

Professional communicators are bound by the same ethical standards as other professionals, including fair treatment of customers, business partners, and employees. Routine business ethics challenges, such as accurate billing, paying employees for hours worked, providing safe workplaces, and adhering to legal and regulatory requirements apply to professional communicators as they do to employees in other industries.

Sometimes the ethical challenges of professional communicators in routine business matters cast the profession in a negative light. For example, at the same time in 2005 that the public relations industry was being criticized for VNRs and for paying columnists to support clients' policies, it was revealed that a public relations firm in Los Angeles had overbilled its client the City of Los Angeles and had also billed the City for work not performed. After an investigation the public relations firm, Fleishman-Hillard, agreed to a settlement with the City of Los Angeles valued at $5.7 million, and apologized to the citizens and city officials of Los Angeles,[49] and a Fleishman-Hillard executive pleaded guilty to fraud.[50]

In a similar ethics and legal crisis, two former senior executives of the advertising agency Ogilvy & Mather Worldwide were convicted in 2004 of ordering employees to alter time sheets, resulting in overbilling their client the U.S. Office of National Drug Control Policy. In 2005 both were sentenced to more than a year in prison and were fined. U.S. Federal District Judge Richard Berman further ordered the more senior executive, Shona Seifert, as part of her sentence, to write a code of ethics that could be used by the advertising industry to prevent such billing practices in the future.[51]

ETHICS OF REPRESENTATION

One area that provokes much discussion and disagreement is the question of representation; the suggestion that there may be something ethically suspect about working with certain clients or companies. Where should professional communicators draw the line? Are there whole categories of companies, industries, products, causes, and people that a professional communicator should refuse to help?

The PRSA *Member Code of Ethics* says that PR professionals "provide a voice in the marketplace of ideas, facts, and viewpoints to aid informed public debate," and that they "respect all opinions and support the right of free expression."[52] Some might interpret these statements of professional values as providing justification to representing all interests, however personally offensive, dishonest, distasteful, or ethically suspect those interests may be. Others suggest that just because all parties may be equally entitled to representation, there is no duty on any given practitioner to agree to work with any given client.

As Edward L. Bernays pointed out in 1928:

> While recognizing, just as the lawyer does, that everyone has a right to present his case in its best light, [a professional communicator] nevertheless refuses a client whom he believes to be dishonest, a product which he believes to be fraudulent, or a cause which he believes to be antisocial.[53]

Whether to work with a given client is often a matter of personal choice.

In practice many professional communicators, and the firms that hire them, understand that whether to work with a given client is often a matter of personal choice. The IABC *Code of Ethics for Professional Communicators* makes such a choice explicit: "Professional communicators refrain from taking part in any undertaking which the communicator considers to be unethical."[54] And the PRSA *Member Code of Ethics* does require that members "decline representation of clients or organizations that urge or require actions contrary to this Code."[55]

Such activities could include not just the ethics of communication and the ethics of running a business, but also the nature of the organization for which the communicator would work.

Among the industry categories that are often cited by practitioners as causing concern are:

- Tobacco companies.
- Individuals or companies accused or convicted of a crime.
- Companies that harm the environment.
- Companies that use animals in medical experiments.
- Foreign governments whose policies are thought to be repressive or contrary to a practitioner's national government's interests.
- The military, especially in time of war.
- Manufacturers of handguns or other weapons.
- Chemical companies.

- Pharmaceutical companies.
- Alcohol beverage companies.
- Causes that advocate policies contrary to a communicator's own values, religious beliefs, or political views.
- Companies with abusive workplace practices, or that employ child, prison, or slave labor.
- Companies based in countries with poor records of human rights, financial fraud, or political oppression.

The list could continue for quite a while, and some PR firms have affirmative policies specifying the industry sectors for which they will or will not work.

Some communicators differentiate between the company they work for and that company's parent. For example, in the U.S. for some time tobacco companies also owned food processing companies, and communicators who would never promote tobacco had no difficulty working for the food processors that were owned by tobacco companies. Others saw no difference between working for a benign division of a company they found objectionable and promoting the objectionable product, and avoided such companies altogether.

Sensitivities change over time. Edward L. Bernays, over the course of a long career, saw his own sensitivities change. In the 1920s and 1930s he was an ardent promoter of tobacco companies, and is credited with making it socially acceptable for women to smoke in public. Bernays' biographer, Larry Tye, notes that Bernays shifted his views as the science became clearer:

> When the surgeon general and other medical authorities released incontrovertible evidence of the dangers of smoking, Bernays used his talents of persuasion to help undo the addictions he'd help build. In 1964 he unveiled a bold and detailed plan to transform smoking into 'an antisocial action which no self-respecting person carries on in the presence of others.'[56]

Beyond categories such as industry sector or national policy, some representation choices concern the character of the individuals. Several PR firms routinely require prospective clients who are rumored to be involved in organized crime to pay for independent private investigations of their activities to validate the prospects' claims that they had been falsely accused.

One common concern about representation is helping governments rally public support for a war. In a CBS *60 Minutes* program about the Citizens for a Free Kuwait controversy (see Case Study on page 76), correspondent Morley Safer summed up this view: "The troubling part of the story is the belief by the public relations industry that, with enough access, enough money, and knowing which buttons to push, war can be marketed, just like soft drinks and toothpaste."[57]

A close look at the history of public relations, however, shows that mobilizing public opinion has been an integral part of the U.S. going to war (in every war except Vietnam, in which the U.S. government made only half-hearted efforts to mobilize public opinion). From Committees of Correspondence in the American Revolution, to war cries such as "Remember the Maine!" in the Spanish–American War, to the use of sophisticated public relations techniques and embedded journalists in the 2003–2011 War with Iraq, professional communicators have been active in most U.S. military operations. Edward L. Bernays himself practiced his craft on behalf of U.S. involvement in World War I and World War II.

Professional communicators who work with the military argue that there is nothing inherently suspect about working for a military operation, including during a war, but note that they continue to be bound by the usual ethical requirements, including the duty to communicate honestly and accurately. John R. MacArthur, who revealed the Citizens for a Free Kuwait controversy (see Case Study on page 76) and whose book examines ethical failings of both the news media and the public relations industry, notes that truth is often a casualty of war:

> In modern wars, exaggerated or manufactured enemy atrocities have frequently played an important part in the cause of boosting war fever at home . . . Slaughtered and mutilated Belgian babies were a tremendous propaganda triumph for the Allies [in World War I]. In retrospect, the success of these manufactured stories possessed ominous implications for future wars, especially the one to liberate Kuwait.[58]

> Every professional communicator, as part of his or her ethical development, needs to reflect on the kinds of companies, causes, people, and circumstances that cause ethical concern, and be ready to make decisions on whether to represent such causes or not.

Every professional communicator, as part of his or her ethical development, needs to reflect on the kinds of companies, causes, people, and circumstances that cause ethical concern, and be ready to make decisions on whether to represent such causes or not. The three criteria to consider in making such a decision are:

- Who is the client? Is there anything inherent in the client's identity that is objectionable—e.g., convicted felon, etc.?
- What does the client do? Is the client's industry sector objectionable—e.g., tobacco, firearms, etc.?
- What does the client want you to do? For example, is there a difference between marketing the client's product and helping it develop effective internal communications, or outreach to communities?

HELPING COMPANIES BEHAVE ETHICALLY

> Increasingly, corporate communication departments are seen as the conscience of a company, and play an important role in helping a company behave ethically.

The corporate scandals of the 2000s demonstrated that a company's ethical lapses can cause significant harm to reputation, operations, morale, customer demand, stock price, and in some cases even a company's survival. Often ethical slippage is a leading indicator—a kind of early warning—of legal problems. From Enron to Andersen to the Roman Catholic Church, ethical lapses that were apparent to insiders and observers were ignored by organizations' leaders, only to re-emerge in criminal conviction, civil penalties, and in Enron's and Andersen's cases, corporate death.

Increasingly, corporate communication departments are seen as the conscience of a company, and play an important role in helping a company behave ethically. Recognizing the relationship between ethical lapses and reputational harm, many companies now see commitment to ethics as an integral part of managing their reputation and preserving the value of the company's intangible assets.

On a more practical level, U.S. Federal Sentencing Guidelines, which set rules for punishment for corporate crimes, mandate that companies with strong ethics codes, training programs, and compliance procedures can be subjected to less severe penalties if they should be convicted of certain crimes.

Sometimes the professional communicator's ethics role is informal, helping the company navigate day-to-day communication decisions in an ethical way.

Sometimes the corporate communicator's ethics role is paired with the company's program of corporate social responsibility (see Chapter 12). And sometimes the corporate communicator's role is paired with the company's own code of ethics.

Some companies have robust ethics codes and training programs. For example, General Electric's Code, called *Integrity: The Spirit and Letter of Our Commitment*, runs for 35 pages. It starts with a single page GE Code of Conduct, which requires that GE people obey laws and regulations, be honest, fair and trustworthy, avoid conflicts of interest between work and personal affairs, foster an atmosphere of fair employment practices, strive to create a safe workplace and protect the environment, and sustain a culture in which ethical conduct is recognized.[59] The balance of the document provides extensive procedures for implementing the code.

Sometimes companies overhaul their codes following ethical lapses. For example, from 2002 to 2004 The Boeing Co. suffered reputational harm through a series of scandals involving the recruitment of Pentagon officials for senior positions in the company while these officials were still overseeing Boeing and other defense contractors for the government. Eventually Boeing's chief executive officer, Phil Condit, was forced to leave the company. He was replaced by retired vice chairman Harry Stonecipher, who promptly instituted a revised *Code of Conduct*. The new single-page *Code* includes the following sentence: "Employees will not engage in conduct or activity that may raise questions as to the company's honesty, impartiality, reputation, or otherwise cause embarrassment to the company."[60] It also requires that employees promptly report any unethical conduct.

Ironically, soon after implementing the *Code*, Mr. Stonecipher conducted a romantic affair with a female subordinate. A fellow employee, following the Code's requirements, reported his suspicions to the company's board, which promptly investigated. Mr. Stonecipher was fired for violating his own code.

Commentators noted that the Board's dismissal of their new CEO demonstrated that the *Code* worked and that the company took ethics seriously. The *Seattle Post-Intelligencer* quoted University of Washington business professor Jonathan Karpoff saying that Boeing reacted so dramatically to the CEO's affair because of its recent ethical challenges. "'Everyone's on pins and needles when it comes to manipulating the numbers, but now it's spreading out to all aspects of a firm's leadership—especially in light of the lapses Boeing has been involved in over the years,' Karpoff said." The newspaper also quoted Kirk Johnson, vice president at ethics consulting firm Integrity Interactive Corp., saying "This story demonstrates that ethics programs work, and that they do have teeth."[61]

Some companies' commitment to ethics is triggered by a series of ethical scandals that impair their ability to do business effectively. For example, in 2004 Japanese banking regulators revoked Citigroup Private Bank's license to operate in Japan. Citigroup's chief executive officer, Charles Prince, formally apologized to the regulators, including participating in a seven-second ceremonial bow. A photograph of Mr. Prince bowing before regulators appeared in newspapers around the world on October 26, 2004.

Citigroup's Japan problems were just the latest ethical challenge in a series of mishaps over several years. Citigroup was involved in financing Enron, WorldCom, and Parmalat, each of which was found to have committed financial fraud. Its European traders were implicated in a controversial trading strategy named "Dr. Evil," although the company was later cleared of wrongdoing in that strategy. And it had been implicated in scandals involving the independence of its research analysts.

In March, 2005, Mr. Prince announced a new ethics initiative, telling *The Wall Street Journal* that the project would consume "at least half his executive time and energy over the next several years." He told the newspaper, "This is job one. If I don't own this, I don't think it will succeed."[62] Mr. Prince specifically linked the ethics initiative to restoration of Citigroup's reputation, saying it was intended to make Citigroup the most respected financial-services company.

Mr. Prince recognized that even the best ethics code won't protect a company's reputation if the company's culture isn't responsive to ethical considerations and ethical responsibilities.

Indeed, Enron Corp., which has become synonymous with corporate corruption, had a 65-page ethics code that included all the usual requirements and prohibitions that highly respected companies' codes contain. These include four core values: Respect, Integrity, Communication, and Excellence.

An elaboration of the Respect value is particularly ironic, given Enron's ultimate demise: "We treat others as we would like to be treated ourselves. We do not tolerate abusive or disrespectful treatment. Ruthlessness, callousness, and arrogance don't belong here."[63]

An introductory letter to the Code from Kenneth L. Lay, chairman and chief executive officer of Enron, said:

> We want to be proud of Enron and to know that it enjoys a reputation for fairness and honesty and that it is respected. Gaining such respect is one aim of our advertising and public relations activities, but no matter how effective they may be, Enron's reputation depends on its people, on you and me. Let's keep that reputation high.[64]

The letter was dated July 1, 2000. Less than two years later Enron was out of business, brought down by a series of ethical and legal shortfalls.

Another company to go out of business in the wake of the Enron scandal was Enron's auditor, Arthur Andersen. The firm went out of business just six months after it emerged as inextricably linked to the Enron scandal, following its conviction for obstruction of justice. But a close look at the firm in the years before the scandal shows that the Enron entanglements were a symptom of a much larger problem, particularly an inattention to the ethical standards that had helped propel Andersen to the heights of respectability and profitability.

Barbara Ley Toffler, formerly a professor of ethics at the Harvard Business School, and presently a professor at Columbia University's Business School, ran Arthur Andersen's Ethics and Responsible Business Practices consulting group. After the firm's demise in 2002, she wrote a book diagnosing the root causes of the firm's collapse. She writes that:

> Arthur Andersen was a great and venerable American brand that had, over the course of the twentieth century, become a global symbol of strength and solidity . . . In my years working at Arthur Andersen, I came to believe that the white-shoed accounting firm known for its legions of trained, loyal, honest professionals—a place that once had the respect, envy, and admiration of everyone in Corporate America—had lost its way. The accountants and the consultants forgot what it meant to be accountable. The fall of Arthur Andersen, I believe, was no murder. It was a suicide, set in motion long before there was ever an indictment. Yet while the guilty verdict sealed Andersen's fate, by the time it came it was merely a formality, the last nail in a coffin whose grave had been primed for burial.[65]

Toffler says that her attempts to bring ethical problems to management's attention were rebuffed. She says that it was clear to her—and to anyone who chose to see—that Andersen's culture had shifted powerfully to a short-term focus on profitability at the expense of its core values of independence and client service, to what she termed "billing our brains out," regardless of the value delivered to the client, of unethical entanglements, or of suspect behavior. She describes a culture where every employee who had or might have anything to do with a client had to figure out a way to sell more services to clients, regardless of the client's need. "Some would call this client service—but in my experience it seemed to be more about raping the client than serving it."[66]

Toffler's business was advising clients on ethical business practice, not serving as an in-house ethics officer for her own firm. But internal ethical issues came to her attention, including a partner who she says had taken his and a client's daughters to a New York Yankees game in a limousine, which waited for the entire game, and then took them home. The partner directed that the expenses for the trip be billed to the client as an audit-related expense. She recounts:

> I could find no indication that ethics was ever talked about in any broad way at Arthur Andersen. When I brought up the subject of internal ethics, I was looked at as if I had teleported in from another world . . . The end result was the continual reinforcement of the idea that it was okay to play with numbers . . . The laxity of this approach would come back to haunt the Firm later: Billing Our Brains Out or compromising quality was what we all had to do to get ahead—or to keep up.[67]

According to Toffler, "there was simply too much similarity of thought, too much acceptance that the way thing were done was the best simply *'because that's the way we do it'* to see that this culture was turning on itself."[68]

One of the critical roles of a professional communicator is to serve as an early warning system, on the lookout for danger signs.

She concludes: "I believe strongly that the suicide of Arthur Andersen—and the assault on the investing public's trust—could have been avoided had people paid attention to the danger signs flashing everywhere in the late 1990s."[69]

One of the critical roles of a professional communicator is to serve as an early warning system, on the lookout for such danger signs. As the entity formally charged with protecting and advancing an organization's reputation, the corporate and organizational communication function needs to be fully engaged in discussions of all of an organization's reputational threats, including the implications of unethical behavior.

CASE STUDY: HILL & KNOWLTON AND CITIZENS FOR A FREE KUWAIT

The most significant communication ethics scandal of the last several decades concerned the PR firm Hill & Knowlton's work for its client, Citizens for a Free Kuwait (CFK). The scandal was triggered by publication of *Second Front: Censorship and Propaganda in the Gulf War*, by *Harper's Magazine* publisher John R. MacArthur in 1992. Much of the book focused on the U.S. government's management of the media in the 1991 Gulf War, and the media's acquiescence to the government's groundrules. But the revelations about ethically suspect behavior involving the PR firm and its client set off a firestorm of criticism against the firm and PR in general.

In August, 1990 Iraq invaded Kuwait. In the days that followed Hill & Knowlton undertook a major campaign to mobilize U.S. public opinion to defend Kuwait and go to war with Iraq. Hill & Knowlton was the largest and, by some accounts, the most powerful public relations firm in the world.

Working for an entity it described as "Citizens for a Free Kuwait" (CFK), Hill & Knowlton staged a number of public events that it said represented the interest of private Kuwaiti citizens in the U.S. and Canada. After the war MacArthur called into question the legitimacy of much of Hill & Knowlton's work, including the identity of CFK.

Although Hill & Knowlton insisted, both to MacArthur and to the CBS television news magazine *60 Minutes*, that its client was a group of concerned citizens and not the government of Kuwait, MacArthur concluded that Citizens for a Free Kuwait was a front group for the government:

> The "Citizens" part of the organization was a fiction, as was the pretense of being an ordinary nonprofit charity. After the war, when it grudgingly owned up to its true status, CFK reported to the Justice Department receipts of $17,861 from

seventy-eight individual U.S. and Canadian contributors, and $11,852,329 from the government of Kuwait.[70]

Jack O'Dwyer, editor of a leading public relations trade newsletter, characterized the veracity of Hill & Knowlton's claim by analogy: "If the manufacturer of a suit that was 99.85 percent cotton called it a wool suit because it was 0.15 percent wool, you'd expect the company to be arrested."[71]

The identity of Hill & Knowlton's client was just the starting point in a discussion of systematic ethical wrongdoing. MacArthur further suggested that Hill & Knowlton (H & K) was really doing the bidding of the White House. Craig Fuller, then head of the CFK account and Washington-based President of H & K, had previously served as chief of staff to then-Vice President George H.W. Bush. He left H & K when the scandal broke, and served as chair of President Bush's 1994 Republican National Convention.

What is the Congressional Human Rights Caucus? And Who is Nayirah?

One of the more serious criticisms of H & K's work involved what MacArthur described to *60 Minutes* as the Kuwaitis' and Administration's need for a "defining atrocity."[72] That defining atrocity concerned allegations that the invading Iraqi army had systematically pillaged hospitals in Kuwait, removing dozens (in some reports, hundreds) of premature babies from incubators, leaving them to die on the hospital floors. The most riveting account of the incubator story came from a fifteen year-old Kuwaiti girl identified only as Nayirah.

On October 10, 1990, Nayirah testified at a meeting of the Congressional Human Rights Caucus. Although it had the appearance of a full-fledged congressional hearing, in fact it was merely an informal gathering of like-minded members of Congress. MacArthur points out that:

> The Human Rights Caucus is not a committee of Congress and therefore it is unencumbered by the legal accoutre-ments that would make a witness hesitate before he or she lied . . . Lying under oath in front of a congressional commit-tee is a crime; lying from under the cover of anonymity to the caucus is merely public relations.[73]

The nature of the caucus and its relationship to H & K and CFK is a critical one. According to MacArthur, the co-chairs of the caucus, Congressman Tom Lantos (C-CA) and Congressman Edward Porter (R-IL), were also co-chairs of the Congressional Human Rights Foundation, whose rent-free offices were in H & K's Washington offices. After the caucus meeting at which Nayirah testified, the Congressional Human Rights Foundation, which had paid for travel and lodging for Congressmen Lantos and Porter, and for their wives, received a $50,000 contribution from CFK.[74]

At the caucus' October 10 meeting, Nayirah was introduced only as a fifteen year-old girl with first-hand experience of the events to which she was testifying. Her full identity was withheld, it was said, in order to protect her family in Kuwait from reprisals.

Nayirah, who had been coached by H & K and whose testimony was later included in H & K's press materials about the caucus meeting, told the caucus:

> While I was [at the al-Adan hospital] I saw the Iraqi solders come into the hospital with guns, and go into the room where 15 babies were in incubators. They took the incubators, and left the babies on the cold floor to die.[75]

Nayirah's story, distributed by H & K via video news releases, press releases, and other tools of the trade, was widely covered, and referred to often by President Bush and by members of the U.S. Senate and House of Representatives.

As the U.S. Senate debated a resolution authorizing the U.S. to go to war against Iraq, the babies-pulled-from-incubators story had become the war's defining atrocity. It was mentioned often by President Bush. More significantly, the war resolution passed the U.S. Senate on January 12, 1991 by a five-vote margin; six senators who voted for the resolution referred to the baby incubator story in justifying their vote. MacArthur argues:

> The significance of the baby incubator story in the larger prop-aganda campaign against Saddam Hussein and for the war option cannot be underestimated. Without it, the comparison of Hussein with Hitler loses its luster; to make the case effec-tively, one had to prove Hussein's utter depravity.[76]

After the war ended, MacArthur discovered that Nayirah was no ordinary refugee, and questioned whether her anonymity would have made any difference in protecting her family from reprisals: She was in fact a member of the Kuwaiti royal family, and the daughter of Kuwait's Ambassador to the United States (and, because CFK was a front group for the Kuwaiti government, the Ambassador was also H & K's client). He further discovered that five of the other six Kuwaitis who spoke at the U.N. used false identities. He says that H & K claimed that the fact that the witnesses used false identities had been revealed at the time, but he was unable to find any proof of this. He further notes that several of them were prominent Kuwaitis, whose identity would have been known in Kuwait, including the head of the Kuwaiti Red Crescent. MacArthur muses, "Why would a well-known public health official—even one working for the Kuwaiti government—need to hide his identity if not to mislead the media and human rights investigators and to make follow-up inquires more difficult?"[77]

After the war leading human rights organizations—including Amnesty International and Human Rights Watch—went to Kuwait to investigate reports of atrocities, and each concluded that the baby incubator atrocity had never taken place.

Aftermath and Backlash

MacArthur revealed his findings in a *New York Times* op-ed article on January 6, 1992, just before the one-year anniversary of the war. The article, based on his book, was the first salvo in what would be an escalating and nearly year-long scandal. Within weeks the criticism included an editorial in *The New York Times* called "Deception on Capitol Hill" and criticism of Hill & Knowlton—and of public relations in general—by *60 Minutes*, ABC *20/20*, *Newsweek*, the *Wall Street Journal*, and the *Washington Post*. *TV Guide*, with a circulation of more than 15 million, ran a story that accused Hill & Knowlton of "systematic manipulation of the news."[78]

Hill & Knowlton defended its work for CFK, and rebutted MacArthur's and the media's criticisms. Thomas E. Eidson, H & K's president and CEO in 1992, defended both the accuracy of Nayirah's testimony and the firm's insistence that it worked for a citizen's group and not for the government of Kuwait.[79]

In the aftermath of the CFK scandal, with H & K's and PR's integrity impeached, the firm became the subject of intense scrutiny about other clients it represented. Soon after the Kuwait story broke H & K was sued for "PR fraud" by creditors of its client, the disgraced Bank of Credit and Commerce International (BCCI), and its work against abortion for the U.S. bishops and for the Church of Scientology was criticized as well. It was also criticized for its work for governments of countries implicated in human rights abuses, including Turkey, Indonesia, and China. It suffered severe decline in staff morale, client defections, and ultimately turnover of most of the people at the top of the company, including nearly every senior person involved with the CFK business.

Inside PR magazine, which published a yearly report card on major public relations firms, assessed the damage to Hill & Knowlton in its July/August 1992 issue:

What was the greatest PR agency in the world has come to be regarded as a pariah by many prospective employees. Internally, morale is resurgent, but a reputation for petty politics and the controversies of the past two years make H&K in the '90s look about as attractive as Dow [Chemical] in the '70s . . . Crisis-plagued and battered in the media, new management faces an uphill battle.[80]

Hill & Knowlton's battering in the media served as a proxy for the public relations industry as a whole. Senior PR executives opined that employees of H & K had violate the PRSA *Code of Ethics*, but the PRSA was largely silent on the scandal, creating a vacuum of opinion and leaving the impression that H & K's behavior was acceptable and common PR practice. The PR profession was in crisis, but the industry association seemed paralyzed and either unable or unwilling to take a public stand on the scandal. The board of the PRSA met in New York in late January, but refused invitations to speak with the PR trade media.

The controversy severely damaged the reputation of Hill & Knowlton, of the public relations industry, and of the PRSA, which remained paradoxically silent about the scandal while its members, the media, and critics were calling for it to take a stand on the controversy. Six months after the scandal broke, the chair of the association's "PR for PR Committee" called the PRSA its "own worst enemy."[81]

Six years after the CFK scandal the PRSA began a complete overhaul of its ethics process. The PRSA's new Member Code of Ethics, ratified by the society's membership in October 2000, specifically addresses front groups. Its provision on *The Free Flow of Information* says that a member shall "reveal the sponsors for causes and interests represented." Its Examples of Improper Conduct Under This Provision includes a clause that specifically describes front groups purporting to represent one interest but secretly representing another interest.[82]

And today the PRSA has a mechanism for commenting on ethical issues, in the form of Practice Advisories, that provide standards on ethical issues in the news, and Practice Commentaries, that provide topical comment on ethical behavior.[83]

In the aftermath of the scandal PRSA saw defections from its own ranks, including this book's co-author Fred Garcia, who at the time was teaching a communication ethics workshop at New York University, and who resigned both from the PRSA and from a leadership position in the association's New York chapter because of the association's mishandling of the ethics issue and its failure to defend the profession.

Over the course of the mid-to-late 1990s Hill & Knowlton recovered, and is again a strong and respected firm. But it lost significant market share, momentum, and clout.

HISTORICAL PERSPECTIVES
ON COMMUNICATION ETHICS

The professional practice of public relations is not a twentieth-century invention. Neither are the ethical challenges facing it. Concern about the integrity of professional communication goes back much farther than 1923, when Edward L. Bernays was worried that people viewed it as some "vaguely defined evil, 'propaganda.'"[84]

In fact, professional communication emerged as a profession 2500 years ago. And it was criticized in much the same way it is now: Those who practiced it were said to care little for the truth.

A careful review of the critique of classical public relations can be helpful in pointing the way to solving the problem of communication ethics in the twenty-first century.

The historical antecedents of professional communication may be found in fourth-century BC Greece. While Plato never used the term "public relations," he had a deep awareness of the importance of crystallizing public opinion, and of the methods and proper uses of persuasion. Unlike Aristotle, whose *Rhetoric* provides a theoretical construction of oral persuasion, Plato (c. 427 to 346 BC) did not articulate a discrete theory of persuasive communication. But his *Gorgias* provides a sharp criticism of the practice of professional communication in his day, and his *Republic* articulates the appropriate method for shaping public opinion.

Classical Rhetoric

Classical Greece was an oral society. While today most communication is done in print, on television, or on the Internet, in Greece most public discourse was spoken.

But like today, in classical Athens public opinion determined matters both large and small, from whether to build city walls to the appointment of generals to sentences at criminal trials. And also like today, there was a growing demand for expert help to shape public opinion. To meet that demand, a new class of professional persuaders, called *rhetoricians*, emerged. They called their craft "rhetoric," which Aristotle later defined as "the faculty of discovering the possible means of persuasion in reference to any subject whatever."[85]

Aristotle differentiated this general persuasive nature of rhetoric from the specific natures of other pursuits:

> This is the function of no other of the arts, each of which is able to instruct and persuade in its own special subject; thus, medicine deals with health and sickness, geometry with the properties of magnitudes, arithmetic with number, and similarly with all the other arts or sciences. But Rhetoric, so to say, appears able to discover the means of persuasion in reference to any given subject.[86]

Rhetoric as a distinct practice emerged in the fifth century BC on the then-Greek island of Sicily. Citing a lost book of Aristotle, the Roman orator Cicero says that following a political upheaval, two enterprising Sicilians, Corax and Tisias, developed a method of instructing others how to argue persuasively, so as to recover property confiscated by the prior regime.[87] Corax, in addition to teaching clients how to argue persuasively and providing them with a set of rules for dealing with difficult questions, also wrote speeches for his clients to deliver in court, and was the author of the first handbook on rhetoric. His pupil Tisias, who also composed a handbook on rhetoric, later became tutor to the great Greek rhetoricians Gorgias, Isocrates, and Lysias.

Rhetoricians should not be confused with other distinguished Greeks who used persuasion as part of other pursuits. Statesmen such as Pericles were powerful speakers, but were primarily engaged in governing. Sophists such as Protagoras used techniques similar to those used by rhetoricians but claimed that their teaching instilled virtue in their pupils. Rhetoricians, on the other hand, were concerned neither with governing nor with instilling virtue. Rather, they provided communications services to those who paid for them. These services were remarkably similar to those offered by modern professional communicators. They included speechwriting, speaking on clients' behalf, and coaching clients how to argue their cases persuasively. This latter service included anticipating difficult questions and framing appropriate answers, similar to modern media training.

By Plato's day rhetoric as a distinct discipline was well established in Greece. The foremost rhetorician was Gorgias of Leontinium in Sicily, who is reputed to have lived 108 years (c. 483 to 375 BC). Gorgias' view of rhetoric differentiated it specifically from other persuasive pursuits such as governing and instilling virtue. Gorgias claimed that his only object was to foster persuasive skills on any subject whatever. Cicero, again citing a lost book of Aristotle, reports that Gorgias further encouraged speakers to exaggerate or extenuate, as the occasion might require.[88]

Plato's Critique

Plato wrote his *Gorgias* in about 387 BC and relates events said to have taken place when Gorgias was in his eighties and at the pinnacle of his influence, around 403 BC. The work, in dialogue form, pits the Platonic protagonist Socrates in argument with Gorgias and Gorgias' disciple Polus regarding the nature of rhetoric.

Socrates and Gorgias agree that, if it is anything, rhetoric is a form of persuasion. Gorgias defines it as

> the ability to persuade with speeches either the judges in the law courts or statesmen in the council-chamber of the commons in the Assembly or any audience at any other meeting that may be held on public affairs.[89]

He agrees with Socrates' further characterization:

> You say that Rhetoric is a producer of persuasion, and has therein its whole business and main consummation.[90]

Socrates begins his critique of rhetoric by securing Gorgias' acknowledgement of the difference between knowledge and belief. While knowledge can only be true, belief can be either true or false. Gorgias further agrees that rhetoric, as a persuasive medium, is not concerned with instilling knowledge:

Socrates: This rhetoric, it seems, is a producer of persuasion for belief, not for instruction in the matter of right and wrong.

Gorgias: Yes.

Socrates: And so the rhetorician's business is not to instruct a law court or other public meeting in matters of right and wrong, but only to make them believe.[91]

Gorgias asserts that the rhetorician will persuade the public on all matters, even when competing for public opinion against experts.

Socrates: Now, do you mean to make him carry conviction to the crowd on all subjects, not by teaching them, but by persuading?

Gorgias: Certainly, I do.

Socrates: You were saying just now, you know, that even in the matter of health the [rhetorician] will be more convincing than the doctor.

Gorgias: Yes, indeed, I was—meaning, to the crowd.

Socrates: And "to the crowd" means "to the ignorant"? For surely, to those who know, he will not be more convincing than the doctor.

Gorgias: You are right.

Socrates: And if he is to be more convincing than the doctor, he thus becomes more convincing than he who knows.

Gorgias: Certainly.

Socrates: But he who is not a doctor is surely without knowledge of that whereof the doctor has knowledge.

Gorgias: Clearly.

Socrates: So he who does not know will be more convincing to those who do not know than he who knows; supposing the [rhetorician] to be more convincing than the doctor. Is that, or something else, the consequence?

Gorgias: In this case it does follow.

Socrates: Then the case is the same in all the other arts for the [rhetorician] and his rhetoric: there is no need to know the truth of actual matters, but one merely needs to have discovered some device of persuasion which will make one appear to those who do not know to know better than those who know.[92]

Pressed by Gorgias and his disciple Polus to provide his own definition of the art of rhetoric, Socrates responds that it is not an art at all:

It seems to me, then, Gorgias, to be a pursuit that is not a matter of art, but showing a shrewd gallant spirit which has a natural bent with dealing with mankind, and I sum up its existence in the name of flattery.[93]

Asked to elaborate further, Socrates identifies rhetoric as a semblance of a branch of the art of politics.[94] By semblance, he means an unreal image or counterfeit: It uses the same techniques, and vocabulary, and claims to be directed toward the same end.

Socrates elaborates on the nature of such a semblance by analogy. Consider, for example, the health of the body. Maintenance of health, which Socrates calls gymnastic, has a semblance, self-adornment. While gymnastic is concerned with maintaining a body's health, self-adornment is concerned with the appearance of health. Gymnastic strives for a body that is robust and functioning at its best. Self-adornment, on the other hand, strives for a body that appears healthy, without regard to whether it actually is healthy.

Similarly, medicine is concerned with the restoration of health in an ill body. The doctor prescribes the proper foods, herbs, and beverages to be ingested to restore health. The semblance of medicine is cookery, which provides foods, herbs, and beverages that are pleasing to the body without regard to whether they will help restore health. Socrates summarizes:

> Cookery is flattery disguised as medicine; and in just the same manner self-adornment personates gymnastic: with its rascally, deceitful, ignoble, and illiberal nature it deceives men by forms and colors, polish and dress, so as to make them, in the effort of assuming an extraneous beauty, neglect the native sort that comes through gymnastic.[95]

Socrates asserts that rhetoric, as practiced by Gorgias and his followers, is a semblance of something else, which in this instance he calls justice. "As cookery is to medicine, so rhetoric is to justice."[96]

Socrates' specific objection to rhetoric, it must be noted, is that it is concerned merely with persuasion, without regard to whether those persuaded have received knowledge or merely belief, which may in turn be either true or false.

So, to state his objection more briefly, rhetoric is the semblance of justice because it is concerned with persuasion without regard to whether the beliefs it generates are true or false. We can construct a matrix for justice (see Table 2.1):

Table 2.1 Matrix for Justice

Justice	*True*	*False*
Beneficial	x	
Harmful	x	

Rhetoric, on the other hand, is concerned with what is beneficial to the persuader without regard to whether it is true or false. We can construct a matrix for rhetoric (see Table 2.2):

Table 2.2 Matrix for Rhetoric

Rhetoric	*True*	*False*
Beneficial	x	x
Harmful		

Notice that Plato's objection is not that rhetoric persuades by instilling beliefs that are necessarily false. In his analogy, cookery is perfectly capable of providing foods that could restore health; it is merely unconcerned with whether its foods restore health or not. Similarly, self-adornment is concerned with providing the body with the appearance of health, even when the body is already healthy. It is unconcerned with whether the body is or is not healthy.

The objectionable nature of Gorgias' rhetoric is its lack of concern whether its statements are true or false; it would be objectionable even if its statements turned out to be true.

Translating this into modern vocabulary, we can create a matrix that helps us understand the ethical use of professional communication: So a modern professional communicator can ground his or her professional judgment on the degree to which he or she promotes statements that are both true and beneficial to his or her client. As a general principle, a professional communicator does not promote statements that are harmful (with the possible exception of disclosure in the investment markets, which may require such communication). But an ethical communicator is concerned with whether his or her statement is true; an unethical communicator isn't necessarily one that deliberately promotes falsehoods, but someone who is unconcerned with whether a statement is true or false. We can construct a similar matrix to differentiate between ethical and unethical communication (see Tables 2.3 and 2.4):

Table 2.3 Ethical Communication

Ethical	*True*	*False*
Beneficial	x	
Harmful		

Ethical communication promotes statements that are both truthful and beneficial to a client.

Table 2.4 Unethical Communication

Unethical	*True*	*False*
Beneficial	x	x
Harmful		

Unethical communication is concerned with statements that are beneficial, without regard to whether those statements are true or false.

The ethical practice of professional communication is one where the professional communicator deliberately seeks to promote only true and beneficial statements, avoids false statements, and cares about the difference.

The ethical practice of public relations requires both a desire to behave ethically and an understanding of ethical issues in professional communication.

 ## ETHICAL COMMUNICATION BEST PRACTICES

The ethical practice of public relations requires both a desire to behave ethically and an understanding of ethical issues in professional communication. Here are some of the best practices:

- Understand the letter and spirit of the various industry association codes of ethics, both for communication professionals and for the industries on whose behalf you communicate.
- Recognize that codes of ethics are valuable because they establish normative standards of behavior that become habitual through repetition.
- Understand the difference between ethics, morality, legality, etiquette, and aesthetics.
- Know where you draw the line. Ultimately you need to know what behaviors are acceptable to you and which are unacceptable. If you think this through in advance you'll be better able to navigate ethical challenges when they present themselves.
- Identify likely inadvertent violations of ethics codes before they happen, and call attention to them. Don't argue just on the basis of morality, but on the basis of practical business issues, including the likelihood that the unethical behavior will be discovered, and the negative consequences to the organization if this should be the case.
- When in doubt, seek counsel of more experienced practitioners.

 ## RESOURCES FOR FURTHER STUDY

Council of Public Relations Firms

The Council of Public Relations Firms represents the business of public relations in the United States, and includes more than 100 public relations firms. The Council's members agree to abide by its *Code of Ethics* and *Statements of Principles*. Its overriding principles are that openness and transparency are not only in the public interest, but also necessary tools for meeting clients' objectives. Its website is http://www.prfirms.org/who/code.asp.

Ethics Resource Center

The Ethics Resource Center in Washington, D.C., is the oldest not-for-profit association in the United States devoted to organizational ethics. The ERC conducts research, including an extensive National Business Ethics Survey, and publishes a free monthly electronic newsletter, *Ethics Today Online*, http://www.ethics.org/today/et_subscribe.html.

The Center publishes a number of guides to ethical practice, including *Creating a Workable Company Code of Ethics: A Practical Guide to Identifying and Developing Organizational Standards*. The Center also sponsors character development and ethics courses for educational institutions and for corporate ethics officers. The Center advised the Public Relations Society of America in its overhaul of the PRSA Member Code of Ethics. The Ethics Resource Center can be found at http://www.ethics.org.

Global Business Standards Codex

This survey of business ethics standards around the world was conceived by several Harvard Business Schools scholars and described in detail in the *Harvard Business Review*. See *Harvard Business Review*, "Up to Code: Does Your Company's Conduct Meet World-Class Standards," by Lynn Paine, Rohit Deshpandé, Joshua M. Margolis, and Kim Eric Bettcher (December, 2005), page 122. Reprints can be ordered at http://www.hbr.org.

International Association of Business Communicators (IABC)

The IABC, based in San Francisco, has more than 13,000 members in more than 60 countries. It publishes guides to best practices, and offers professional development programs. The IABC can be found at http://www.iabc.com; its *Code of Ethics for Professional Communicators* can be found at http://www.iabc.com/about/code.htm.

International Public Relations Association (IPRA)

IPRA, based in Surrey, UK, is a membership organization of public relations professionals from nearly one hundred countries. IPRA has more than fifty years of experience in sharing and promoting professional development. IPRA has published several Codes and Charters seeking to provide an ethical framework for its members' professional activities. IPRA can be found at http://www.ipra.org; its various Codes and Charters can be found at http://ipra. org/aboutipra/aboutipra.htm.

Public Relations Society of America (PRSA)

The PRSA, based in New York City, is the world's largest organization of public relations professionals. It was founded in 1947 and as of 2006 had 20,000 members. The PRSA can be found at http://www.prsa.org. The PRSA's *Member Code of Ethics* can be found at http:// prsa. org/About/ethics/index.asp?ident=eth1.

▶ QUESTIONS FOR FURTHER DISCUSSION

1. What are the differences among morality, ethics, legality, aesthetics, and etiquette as they relate to any particular practice of corporate communication?

2. Codes of ethics are normative standards of behavior, and as such can be used by individuals or organizations who are not members of the organization that drafts the code. What are some of the other advantages of codes of ethics as normative standards of conduct?

3. Are print and video news releases, by their very nature, unethical?

4. How can a professional communicator resolve conflicting duties? For example, if asked a factual question by a reporter about a sensitive issue, the duty to keep confidences and the duty to be truthful may conflict. What are some ways to resolve the apparent conflict?

5. Is there a meaningful difference between public relations and propaganda?

▶ NOTES

1 Edward L. Bernays, *Propaganda*, with an introduction by Mark Crispin Miller (New York: IG Publishing, 1928 and 2005), p. 69.

2 "Enforcement and Communication of the IABC Code for Professional Communicators," p. 2 of *International Association of Business Communicators Code of Ethics for Professional Communicators*, www.iabc.com/members/joining/code.htm.

3 Ibid. www.iabc.com/members/joining/code.htm.

4 Interview with James E. Lukaszewski, APR, Fellow, PRSA, and member of PRSA Board of Ethics and Professional Standards, July 22, 2005.

5 Ibid.

6 "A Message from the PRSA Board of Ethics and Professional Standards," PRSA Member Code of Ethics (New York: PRSA, 2000), p. 6.

7 Ibid., p. 11.

8 Ibid.

9 Ibid.

10 Personal interview with Helio Fred Garcia in Sharm El Sheikh, Egypt, June 27, 2013.

11 Reprinted with permission, http://www.ipra.org/about/ipra-codes.

12 Terry Macalister, "Embattled Tepco Faces Its BP Moment over Japan Nuclear Disaster," *The Guardian*, March 19, 2011, http://www.guardian.co.uk/business/2011/mar/20/tepco-japan-nuclear-disaster-bp/.

13 Tim Shorrock, "TEPCO's Shady History," *Money Doesn't Talk, It Swears,* n.p., March 14, 2011, http://timshorrock.com/.

14 "Heavy Fallout from Japan Nuclear Scandal." CNN.com. N.p., September 2, 2002, http://archives.cnn.com/2002/BUSINESS/asia/09/02/japan.tepco/index.html?related.

15 Kuroda (Corporate Communications Dept.), Hiroyuki, *Lessons Learned from the TEPCO Nuclear Power Scandal*. Issue brief. n.p., March 25, 2004, http://www.tepco.co.jp/en/news/presen/pdf-1/040325-p-e.pdf.

16 "TEPCO, Credibility, and the Japanese Crisis: JapanFocus," *The Asia-Pacific Journal: Japan Focus*, n.p., March 16, 2011, http://www.japanfocus.org/events/view/52.

17 Shorrock, op. cit.

18 "Gundersen: I Don't Believe What Tepco Said—Some Indications of a Problem in Unit 1 at Fukushima Daiichi after Quake—Hydrogen Levels up Dramatically (VIDEO)." ENENews. N.p., December 10, 2012, http://enenews.com/gundersen-dont-believe-tepco-indications-problem-unit-1-fukushima-daiichi-hydrogen-levels-dramatically-video.

19 Ravi Nessman and Yuri Kageyama, "Japanese Government under Fire over Disaster Plan," usatoday.com, n.p., April 17, 2011. Web.

20 John Stauber and Sheldon Rampton, *Toxic Sludge is Good for You: Lies, Damn Lies and the Public Relations Industry* (Monroe: Common Courage Press, 1995), p. 14.

21 Ibid., pp. 203–4.

22 Ibid., pp. 205–6.

23 Ibid., p. 4.

24 Clifford Coonan, "China Blames Fatal Train Crash on 54 Officials," *The Independent*, Independent Digital News and Media, December 29, 2011, http://www.independent.co.uk/news/world/asia/china-blames-fatal-train-crash-on-54-officials-6282476.html.

25 Michael Wines and Sharon LaFraniere, "In Baring Facts of Train Crash, Blogs Erode China Censorship," *The New York Times*, July 28, 2011, http://www.nytimes.com/2011/07/29/world/asia/29china.html?pagewanted=all&_r=0.

26 "Bodies 'fall from Carriages' during China Train Crash Clean-up," *The Telegraph*, Telegraph Media Group Limited, July 25, 2011, http://www.telegraph.co.uk/news/worldnews/asia/china/8660485/Bodies-fall-from-carriages-during-China-train-crash-clean-up.html.

27 Tania Branigan, "Chinese Rail Crash: Premier Visits Site amid Mounting Anger," *The Guardian*, Guardian News and Media, July 28, 2011, http://www.guardian.co.uk/world/2011/jul/28/chinese-rail-crash-wen-jiabao.

28 *The New York Times* Beijing Bureau. "Press Conference of Premier Wen Jiabao," Speech, Press Conference of Premier Wen Jiabao, Wenzhou, China, July 28, 2011, *The New York Times*, July 28, 2011, http://graphics8.nytimes.com/packages/pdf/world/Wen-Transcript.pdf.

29 "China Fires Top Officials after Railway Crash Kills 35," *BBC News*, BBC, July 25, 2011, http://www.bbc.co.uk/news/business-14271163?print=true.

30 Greg Toppo, "Education Dept. Paid Commentator to Promote the Law," *USA Today*, January 7, 2005, at http://www.usatoday.com/news/washington/2005-01-06-williamswhitehouse_x.htm.

31 Statement by Tribune Media Services, published in *Poynter Forums*, *PoynterOnline*, by the Poynter Institute, http://poynter.org/forum/view_post.asp?id=8580.

32 Ben Feller, "Senators Probe Administration-Paid Journalist; Pundit Paid By Education Department Calls Move a 'Witchhunt'," Associated Press, January 13, 2005.

33 Howard Kurtz, "Propaganda Wars," Washington Post, January 27, 2005.

34 PRSA *Member Code Of Ethics*, p. 11.

35 IPRA *Code of Conduct*.

36 Larry Tye, *The Father of Spin: Edward L. Bernays and the Birth of Public Relations* (New York: Owl Books, 1998), p. 7.

37 Ibid.

38 Ibid.

39 Ibid., p. 58.

40 PRSA *Member Code of Ethics*, approved by the PRSA Assembly, October 2000, p. 13.

41 IPRA *Code of Conduct*.

42 PRSA *Member Code Of Ethics*, p. 14.

43 IABC *Code of Ethics for Professional Communicators*.

44 PRSA *Member Code Of Ethics*, p. 15.

45 IABC *Code of Ethics for Professional Communicators*, ibid.

46 PRSA *Member Code Of Ethics*, p. 15.

47 IABC *Code of Ethics for Professional Communicators*.

48 IPRA *Code of Conduct*.

49 Unattributed article, "Omnicom Unit Settles on Overbilling Suit," *The New York Times*, April 21, 2005, http://www.nytimes.com/2005/04/21/business/media/21addes.html. (Full disclosure: at the time of this writing co-author Helio Fred Garcia held shares of Omnicom Group, the parent company of Fleishman-Hillard.)

50 Ted Rohrlich and Ralph Frammolino, "PR Exec to Plead Guilty in Fraud; Steve Sugerman Will Cooperate in the Probe of Overbilling of DWP by Fleishman-Hillard," *Los Angeles Times*, June 10, 2005, www.latimes.com/news/local/la-me-fleishman10jun10,1,5463756.story?coll=lAlines-california.

51 Unattributed article, "Former Ogilvy Executives Sentenced for Overbilling," *The New York Times*, p. C5.

52 PRSA *Member Code of Ethics*, pp. 6 and 7.

53 Bernays, *Propaganda*.

54 IABC *Code of Ethics for Professional Communicators*.

55 PRSA *Member Code of Ethics*, p. 15.

56 Tye, *The Father of Spin*, p. 49.

57 CBS *60 Minutes*, January 19, 1992.

58 John R. MacArthur, *Second Front, Censorship and Propoganda in the Gulf War* (New York: Hill and Wang, 1992), pp. 51 and 53.

59 General Electric, *Integrity: The Spirit and Letter of Our Commitment*, www.ge.com.

60 *Boeing Code of Conduct*, January 26, 2004, www.boeing.com.

61 Dan Richman, "Analysis: Boeing Conduct Code Worked Properly, Expert Says," *Seattle Post-Intelligencer*, March 8, 2005, http://seattlepi.nwsource.com/business/214916_ethics08.html

62 Alan Murray, "Citigroup CEO Pursues Culture of Ethics," *The Wall Street Journal*, March 2, 2005, p. A2.

63 *Enron Corp. Code of Ethics*, July 2000, p. 4, www.thesmokinggun.com.

64 Ibid., p. 2.

65 Barbara Ley Toffler with Jennifer Reingold, *Final Accounting: Ambition, Greed, and the Fall of Arthur Andersen* (New York: Broadway Books, 2003), p. 7.

66 Ibid., p. 124.

67 Ibid., pp. 124–6.

68 Ibid., p. 60.

69 Ibid., p. 8.

70 MacArthur, *Second Front*, p. 49.

71 Jack O'Dwyer, "PR Opinion/Items" by Jack O'Dwyer, *Jack O'Dwyer's Newsletter*, January 22, 1992, p. 4.

72 CBS *60 Minutes*.

73 MacArthur, *Second Front*, p. 58.

74 Ibid., p. 61.

75 Ibid., p. 58.

76 Ibid., p. 68.

77 Ibid., p. 65.

78 As recounted in *O'Dwyer's PR Services Report*, vol. 6, no. 2, February, 1992, p. 1, and *Jack O'Dwyer's Newsletter*, February 26, 1992, p. 1.

79 On September 9, 1992 Fred Garcia contacted Hill & Knowlton about the CFK controversy and was referred to Thomas Ross, head of the media services group. Garcia told Ross that he was about to launch a communication ethics class at New York University; that he was assigning MacArthur's book, and that MacArthur would be a guest-speaker in the class. Garcia told Ross that in fairness to H & K, he wanted to give H & K the opportunity to tell its side of the story, and would make available time, either before, during, or after MacArthur's talk. Ross said he was not interested in debating MacArthur, whom he described as a self-defeating alarmist. Garcia reiterated that I was inviting H & K to speak before, during, or after MacArthur.

Ross said that H & K had probably spent too much time addressing MacArthur's views already, and would be reluctant to commit more resources to address the class. Garcia noted that he intended to continue to include MacArthur's allegations in his writing and teaching. H & K was invited to send documents outlining their point of view on the scandal. Ross said that H & K had been vindicated and declined to discuss the matter further. Source: Contemporaneous notes taken after phone call between Helio Fred Garcia and Thomas Ross, September 9, 1992

80 *Inside PR*, July/August, 1992, p. 30.

81 *O'Dwyer's PR Services Report*, vol. 6, no. 8, August, 1992, p. 1.

82 PRSA *Member Code of Ethics*, approved by the PRSA Assembly, October, 2000, p. 13.

83 Interview with James E. Lukaszewski, op. cit.

84 Edward L. Bernays, *Crystallizing Public Opinion* (New York: Boni and Liveright, 1923), p. 12.

85 Aristotle, *Rhetoric*, I, 2, 1, in *The "Art" of Rhetoric with English Translation* by John Henry Reese, vol., XXII of *Aristotle in Twenty Three Volumes*, Loeb Classical Library (Cambridge, MA: Harvard University Press, 1982), p. 15.

86 Ibid.

87 Cicero, *Brutus*, xxii, 46, in J.S. Watson (trans.), *Cicero on Oratory and Orators* (Carbondale and Edwardsville: Southern Illinois University Press, 1970), p. 273.

88 Ibid., p. 274.

89 Plato, *Gorgias*, 452e, in W.R.M. *Lamb, Lysis, Symposium, Gorgias with an English Translation*, vol. 3 of Plato in Twelve Volumes (Cambridge, MA: Harvard University Press, 1983), p. 279.

90 Ibid.

91 Ibid., 455a, p. 287.

92 Ibid, 458e–459c, pp. 299–301. Note: the translator alternates his translation of *ho rhetor* between "rhetorician" and "orator."" For the sake of consistency, we translate it as "rhetorician" three times in this quotation, and shall do so in all subsequent quotations.

93 Ibid, 463a, p. 313.
94 Ibid, 463d, p. 315.
95 Ibid, 465b, p. 319.
96 Ibid., 465c, p. 321.

3 MEDIA RELATIONS

By the authors and
Jennifer Hauser

*That we teach others how
to treat us is as true in press
relations as anywhere else.*

■ ■ ■

ENHANCING GLOBAL REPUTATION

Starbucks Coffee literally takes a "newsroom approach" to its media relations across its global network, which includes well-trained in-house teams and public relations agency support. A central team in Seattle works to align its global business priorities with its editorial calendar, which gets reviewed and refreshed on a weekly basis, based upon company news and the overall business and media environments. The Starbucks communications team takes this centralized approach to ensure all company stories can be amplified at the right time, with the right content, using the most appropriate mix of traditional, hybrid, social, and owned media.

Traditional and Hybrid Media

The Starbucks in-house communications teams structures itself to reflect the different media "beats," from national business to consumer lifestyle to ethical and environmental news. Each team develops tailored content and stories that contribute to a "master" editorial calendar based on upcoming company announcements, news and milestones. The communications team works across the company to develop the content and assets that will be used to bring these stories to life. Content pushed through the Media Clover Leaf comes in all forms, including photos, video, infographics and by-lined articles.

Social

Starbucks has the reputation as one of the most socially engaged brands online. With over 34 million fans on Facebook, the company is held as one of the highest-ranked brands using social media. Starbucks was an early adopter of Facebook and its high levels of engagement were established by combining opportunities to share content alongside impactful offers and promotions which rewarded the online community and encouraged more brand interaction. The company also has 3.5 million followers on Twitter, which has led it to be ranked as one of the top Twitter brands behind Samsung, ITunes and NASA. Starbucks has ignited other social media channels, including Instagram and YouTube, which encourage its customers and other stakeholders to connect and share their enthusiasm of and passion for the brand.

Owned

Starbucks has one of the world's largest customer loyalty initiatives through its "My Starbucks Rewards" programs. This owned channel provides opportunities for customers to pay with great convenience as well as creates ongoing moments for the company to communicate and connect with its customers. The program, which is estimated to reach 9 million members this year, has also gained significant momentum through mobile technology advances.

Most recently, Starbucks has refreshed its Twitter handle, @StarbucksNews, as a channel through which it can now engage its media following and influencers. This owned channel is used to alert media to upcoming Starbucks news and announcements, allowing for direct and real-time media engagement. This Twitter handle is also connected to a 24-hour media hotline and e-mail inquiry service that ensure every media inquiry is handled and directed in the fastest and most appropriate way for the company.

■ ■ ■

NEWS MEDIA

What each constituency believes and feels about an organization contributes to its reputation. But there is one group that influences every other constituency that matters to a

---

Media relations consists of all the ways an organization interacts with the news media. These include the ability to build long-term relationships with reporters whose area of responsibility, often called a "beat," includes covering the organization every day. Media relations also includes managing ad hoc contact with reporters who may be calling the company for the first and only time in their careers. Media relations includes the processes of seeking media coverage and responding to reporters' requests for interviews or information. And it includes developing procedures to measure, monitor and manage the contact between an organization's employees and reporters. In major organizations including most large companies, the media relations function has major responsibility for social media, which is ideal because social media channels are an increasingly powerful way for companies to communicate with stakeholders, as well as influence coverage with traditional news outlets.

company, a group that can affect the company's reputation quickly and profoundly: the news media.

Media relations is one of the core disciplines in public relations and corporate and organizational communication, and it is often one of the most visible and impactful. But it is also one of the most difficult for senior management to understand.

■ ■ ■

THE CASE FOR A CENTRALIZED MEDIA RELATIONS FUNCTION

An organization should not communicate through the news media until it knows what the facts are, and then only when the organization is prepared to disclose those facts. And it needs to communicate with a single voice.

> It is neither intuitive nor self-evident that an organization must have a strict policy governing which people can communicate with the media.

But to the outside world, it is neither intuitive nor self-evident that an organization must have a strict policy governing which people can communicate with the media about the organization, its activities, products, policies, and positions. Why should the researcher who conducted the breakthrough research for the organization not take the call from the reporter who is inquiring about that research? Why should the chief financial officer or senior accountant not take a phone call about the company's latest sales and earnings press release? Why should any employee not be permitted to express his or her opinion on what is happening at the company?

Outsiders, especially young journalists and young employees (sometimes, even including those in the communication department), tend to sense a conflict between forthright communication and managed communication, and they tend to believe that "open and forthright" means "tell everyone everything right away." Yet such a strategy would be irresponsible—in fact, anarchic. And in light of securities regulations, it could also present a company with legal liability and regulatory problems.

To an organization's constituencies, anyone from the organization who speaks about the organization is often seen to be speaking for the organization. But different people speak from different perspectives, using different vocabulary, and based on different levels of knowledge about an issue. The result can be confusion, inaccurate communication, and reputational harm.

When speaking with reporters, it is even more important for communication to be centralized. Reporters, especially when covering breaking news, are often less interested in understanding a complex issue than in harvesting quotes to bring a story to life. The way reporters use quotes is different from the way most constituencies use the information they receive. Speaking with a reporter without knowing how one's words are likely to be used can lead to what are often seen by the person quoted to be misquotes. But in our experience, most instances of a "misquote" are really accurate quotes based on people speaking imprecisely, with limited knowledge, or with little understanding that only one or two sentences—out of dozens or hundreds spoken—would be quoted. Good organizational practice dictates that only people who have been trained to speak effectively with reporters be authorized to do so.

One of the best examples of the consequences of uncoordinated press communication remains, three decades later, the nuclear accident at Three Mile Island, PA. The accident that occurred there on March 28, 1979, was the USA's first nuclear accident, and it provoked a torrent of press inquiries.[1] Within minutes, local journalists, including wire service reporters, were on the scene. They interviewed several employees of the Metropolitan Edison utility company who were not fully informed, were not communicating with each other, and were unfamiliar with the utility's plan for corrective action. As a result, the various employees related inconsistent information about what had happened and about what was being done in response. The result was confusion, fear, and the sense that the utility did not know what it was doing. The press coverage, which would have been negative in any case, was made much worse by the perception that the utility was unprepared for such a situation, and that the public was at greater risk than it actually was. What had begun as a manageable situation was turned into a communication disaster by the utility itself, acting in unwitting concert with local journalists, who in many cases had little understanding of science or science writing.

Even when reporters know a company or industry well, it is still important to limit their access to information and people in a company. For example, we have been struck over the years by how individual pharmaceutical researchers viewed the promise of a particular research project differently. If ten scientists were working on a new medicine, seven might think it held little promise, two might be cautiously optimistic, and one might think it was the next penicillin. Allowing reporters random access to any or all of the researchers would present a confusing picture of the therapeutic potential of a given medicine. While robust internal debate can be a good thing, the tendency of the media to oversimplify would lead such a story to be cast as confusion, disagreement, or internal strife, rather than the natural give-and-take of a scientific enterprise.

Unrestricted communication to the news media can cause more than just confusion. It can be irresponsible, and sometimes even illegal. For example, it would be both irresponsible and potentially a violation of securities laws and regulations for an executive to prematurely reveal to a reporter that the company is in negotiations on a potential merger. The very coverage of a merger negotiation would have an adverse impact on the negotiation itself, often limiting the flexibility of one side or the other. Similarly, the securities market's reaction to the news may affect the price of the various companies' stocks as investors buy or sell stock on the news, potentially affecting the economics of the merger. And the news would give competitors, and other potential merger partners, a heads up on what the organization was planning, often triggering reactions on the part of competitors, including a possible bidding war for the company that may be acquired. So premature disclosure could result in the derailment of a merger that appeared to be headed to a successful conclusion. Just as significant, merger discussions and other material information are subject to strict disclosure rules, and premature or selective disclosure of such negotiations could subject the company or individuals to civil or criminal liability.

Enlightened organizations establish clear guidelines on who can speak to reporters on what topics, maintain press logs for tracking who has spoken to whom, on what topics, what was said, what follow-up is required, and when a story is likely to appear.

ORGANIZING THE MEDIA RELATIONS FUNCTION

Media relations typically resides within a corporate communication function, but it can also reside in other corporate structures, including:

- Marketing
- Product divisions
- Regional offices
- Operating companies
- Investor relations (in the case of the financial media)

In large companies, there is often a breakdown of responsibility, with different people responsible for different kinds of media relations, including the following.

- Corporate media relations, for articles about the corporation as a whole, including governance issues, industry trends, senior leadership, sales and earnings, and issues affecting the entire corporation.
- Brand media relations, sometimes residing with a single person or team, often with a different person responsible for each brand category. These individuals focus on inquiries about, or stories featuring, individual brands. These can include the general interest consumer media (newspapers, magazines, television, electronic), or can include industry trade publications.
- Marketing public relations, focusing on initiating coverage of the company, its products, issues, and people. This function often is responsible for creating special events, promotional campaigns, and other opportunities to affirmatively and proactively show the company in a positive light.
- Financial media relations, usually coordinated carefully with the investor relations function, responsible for distributing news of interest to the investment community, and in fulfillment of a company's securities law disclosure requirements.
- Operating company/Regional media relations, often a distinct function in each geographic region or company, and often reporting to the management of the region, or the operating company, with a dotted-line reporting responsibility to corporate media relations.
- Digital departments, which can include the strategic management and operations of the company's website, social media channels, and sometimes blogger engagement, should be closely aligned with other communications functions.

Bloggers, like most journalists, are increasingly influential in today's news environment. In fact, many bloggers should be regarded as highly and managed as thoughtfully as traditional journalists. Popular bloggers can have substantial followings, with their readers able to comment in real-time on blogger stories. Reader comments propel the story forward, and generate more story interest. It's important to note that many traditional journalists have added blogs to their reporting responsibilities, given the continued importance of the blogosphere in news reporting. So, many companies are now putting blogger engagement in the hands of corporate communication leadership. For the sake of this chapter, we'll refer to both traditional reporters and bloggers as "journalists."

There are many other configurations of the media relations function. The most effective functions are those that fit the strategic and operational needs of their organizations. But to succeed, the function must be closely linked to the company's executive leadership team and integrated and well coordinated with all communications functions, regardless of the structure or reporting responsibilities. Many companies manage the coordination by having well-defined policies for who is responsible for which relationships with which kinds of media; who is responsible for handling inquiries on which topics, and the like. They also have frequent, often weekly conference calls with all media relations staff to assure up-to-date understanding of pending stories and developments, and to share insights, resources, or information.

Most companies also have clear policies directing all other employees to refer any press inquiries, on any topic, to certain people in the media relations department.

MEDIA RELATIONS AS A LIGHTNING ROD

It is important that communicators feel free to pass along to senior management negative comments and questions without fear that management will want to "kill the messenger."

Reporters who cover a company or industry speak constantly with industry observers, participants, critics, and supporters. They sometimes develop insights that are even deeper than a company's management may have at any given time. They can serve as an early warning system of trouble ahead. And they are often seen within a company to have an anticompany agenda or bias, even when that is not true.

Journalists will often know about problems in an organization early on. It is important that communicators feel free to pass along to senior management negative comments and questions without fear that management will want to "kill the messenger." And it is important for senior leadership to see these negative comments or questions as possible precursors of trouble ahead, not with the individual reporters but with the business performance or practices in question. In other words, communicators need beware of the Pushmi-pullyu syndrome (Chapter 1).

For example, several years before the accounting scandals about American business broke onto the front pages, several journalists openly questioned the accounting methodologies and inherent conflicts of interests that would bring down major companies in 2002. Similarly, many journalists questioned the independence of Wall Street research for several years before then-New York State Attorney General Elliot Spitzer and the Securities and Exchange Commission forced major Wall Street firms into a financial settlement and structural changes to ensure that analysts' opinions are in fact independent of the investment banking agendas of their employers.

At least one thing is certain from the communication post mortem of these business crises: Not enough corporate and organizational communicators listened early on, and few raised their voices internally against negative practices that were clearly wrong and often indefensible.

FIVE MODELS OF PUBLIC RELATIONS

In the seminal public relations text *Managing Public Relations*, James Grunig and Todd Hunt identified four models that generally guide the communication philosophy of practitioners.[2] We believe it can be helpful for public relations practitioners to examine their own communication philosophies to try to determine which model they generally follow. Although it can be helpful to look at these models in terms of communicating with various constituencies, the models can be especially helpful with media relations. The following definitions of the models, which have stood the test of time, are Grunig's and Hunt's; the commentaries are by Doorley and Garcia.

1. **Press Agent / Publicity Model.** The guiding principle here is to get favorable publicity—not to try to ensure accuracy and truthful reporting. *Commentary*: This model can place the goals of accuracy and truth in second place to publicity. While this model can produce good results for the client organization, at least over the short term, it can be bad for the various constituencies (for example, the media, customers, employees, and the community). The term "spinning," which came into vogue twenty years after this model was defined, is just another label for it. This is the approach that gives public relations a bad reputation.

2. **Public Information Model.** The focus here is on the communication of objective information, generally without regard to the self-interests of the organization or client for whom the PR person works. *Commentary*: In theory, the constituency wins. The client organization, often a government agency or nonprofit, can also win. But we would argue that public relations practitioners have a responsibility to advocate for the client, not just to disseminate information. And if the advocacy is up front—that's why organizations have letterheads!—then the advocacy is transparent and ethical.

3. **Two-Way Asymmetric Model.** The PR practitioner conducts research to determine the views of a particular constituency and then uses that information to help achieve the client's objectives. *Commentary*: The client organization can win, at least over the short term. But the constituency probably loses, and we would argue that this is a myopic and sometimes unethical approach.

4. **Two-Way Symmetric Model.** The PR practitioner conducts research to determine the views of a particular constituency and then uses that information to help achieve the objectives of both the client organization and the constituency. *Commentary*: This is the approach that will most often produce a win–win outcome. It can be useful in conflict resolution and in any public relations program. It can help address ethical questions,

including that of advocacy versus objectivity, by looking at the interests of both the client organization and its constituencies.

5.   **A Fifth Model: The Rise of the Media Clover Leaf.** A new communications model has been created in the public relations industry to illustrate how the media environment has evolved and expanded to include digital properties. Because there are four distinct, but related, types of media today, the model has been named the Media Clover Leaf to reflect our new media environment.

The Media Clover Leaf is comprised of Traditional, Hybrid, Social, and Owned media. In the first leaf, we have the traditional delivery vehicles of print or broadcast. In the second leaf, hybrid, are the dot.com versions of traditional media and media that is "born" digital like *The Huffington Post*. The third leaf, social, includes Facebook and Twitter feeds and YouTube channels. And, the fourth leaf, owned, includes the brand or company's websites and apps.

Sitting in the middle of the Media Clover Leaf is search, the new on-ramp to all forms of media, as well as content, which fuels "search rank" and paid amplification. Today's PR practitioner must work to stimulate coverage that creates motion across all of the different types of media.

MODERATING EXPECTATIONS

If the story turns out badly for the organization, the media relations person will usually take at least a small hit.

When a story turns out well for the organization, the people interviewed are seen to have done a good job, and they might pass along a brief compliment to the media relations person. If the editors are pleased with the story, the journalist might thank the media relations person as well.

On the other hand, if the story turns out badly for the organization, the media relations person will usually take at least a small hit, regardless of how the report arose or the accuracy of it. If the journalist's editors are unhappy with the report, the journalist is generally unhappy with the media relations person because of, for example, inadequate access.

To be effective, the media relations professional needs a supportive boss. If he or she does not have a superior who will absorb at least some of the criticism for the bad stories and take only some of the credit for the good ones, the media relations person might be able to survive for a while, but he or she cannot do the job well over the long term. It is impossible. Polish the résumé. It is time to leave.

The good news is that most heads of public affairs (or whatever function media relations reports into) have the honesty and courage required to support their people. Fortunately for us—John Doorley over the years at Roche and Merck, and co-author Fred Garcia at two corporations and a number of firms—most of our bosses fell into that category.

One challenge, an occupational hazard, is the tendency of some executives to assume that the media relations professional is an advocate for the news media. Sometimes this is framed as "being on the reporter's side"; sometimes as having "gone native" and caring more about maintaining relationships with reporters than protecting an organization's reputation. Most of the time such criticism misses the mark. The best media relations people are advocates in two directions: they need to clarify and focus the organization's viewpoint for reporters. But they also need to help management better understand what a reporter is up to and whether and why it is in the company's interests to engage with the reporter.

Nevertheless, it is extremely important that the media relations person take substantial responsibility for the news that appears. We have known press relations people who would say, "I don't write the news reports, you know." Our answer to them, assuming they were actively involved in cooperating with the journalist, was: If the article had turned out well, would you be saying the same thing?

One key to effectiveness in media relations is to manage the expectations that company executives have, both inflated expectations about positive news or the ability to avoid bad news, and negative expectations about a crisis. And it is usually best to put it in writing.

THE JOURNALIST AND THE SPOKESPERSON

In many ways reporters and company spokespeople are similar. They go to many of the same events and conferences, and share interviews with the same important people. They often have similar academic and professional backgrounds—in fact, many media relations professionals began their careers in journalism. Both address (talk or write about) the same subject matter. But their jobs are different. The journalist's job is to write stories that his readers or viewers want to read or watch. The media relations professional's job is to manage the company's engagement with the journalist in ways that ultimately benefit the company, or are, at minimum, fair. The two jobs are not mutually exclusive. In fact, each depends on the other for success. But the jobs are not the same.

So media relations people should try to build good working relationships with journalists, meaning that each party tries to understand and respect the perspective of the other. It means treating each other with dignity and honesty. It means that the media relations person needs to respect the timetable that reporters work under. But it does not mean that the timetable should be the sole driver of a company's response to an inquiry. It means that a spokesperson should deal forthrightly with the journalist, even when they disagree. But it does not mean acquiescing to every request or withholding criticism when it is deserved. And it sometimes means giving the other party the benefit of the doubt, as in the story about the misdirected fax that began this chapter.

Most important, building good relationships does not mean that the spokesperson and reporter should conspire with each other as if they were partners in a common enterprise. Often media relations people confuse good working relationships with friendships. While such relationships have much in common with friendships, they are not the same. In fact, friendships can complicate things, mostly by letting down

> Often media relations people confuse good working relationships with friendships.

the guard that is often necessary to prevent one party from taking undue advantage of the other.

So journalists and media relations people work on the same projects, but often with completely different perspectives. Journalists are sometimes skeptical and they often see media relations people as impediments. Media relations people sometimes fear the journalist's penchant for bad news or oversimplification. The secret of good media relations is to find the common goal and work toward it together: a timely, fair news report or feature that accomplishes what the reporter wants—a story people are interested in—and that also accomplishes what the spokesperson wants—a story that is fair, and more favorable or less negative than it would have been without his involvement.

CASE STUDY: RELATIONSHIPS MATTER

In the spring of 1998, an administrative assistant in Merck's Corporate Communications Department tried to fax an eighteen-page, confidential internal memorandum on the planned restructuring of the company's relationship with Astra, the Swedish pharmaceutical firm, to an outside investment banker counseling Merck. The machine jammed and she pushed what she thought was the "redial" button, but inadvertently sent the fax to *The Star Ledger*, New Jersey's largest newspaper. To her credit, she told her boss, John Doorley, immediately, and John knew he had to contact his boss, Ken Frazier, senior vice president and general counsel.

The restructuring of the joint venture that marketed Prilosec for the prevention and treatment of gastroesophageal reflux disease (GERD) was weeks from culmination, and premature disclosure would pose countless communication and regulatory problems, as well as trust issues with Astra. Ken agreed that John would contact Iris Taylor, a reporter at *The Ledger* with whom he had a long-standing, trusting relationship. Ms. Taylor retrieved the fax and returned it to John as requested, promising she would not read it. Although the eighteen pages were coded for confidentiality, a business reporter covering the pharmaceutical industry would have been able to unravel it. The deal, valued at over $3 billion when it was announced weeks later, could have collapsed.[3] It was saved because the Communication Group and other people at Merck, including two CEOs, had invested much time and effort over many years in building a good reputation with that reporter. The relationship meant more to her—and she believed to her newspaper—than an ill-gotten scoop. The company's investment in the relationship, often intangible and hard to quantify, paid off handsomely that day.

FEAR OF THE PRESS

We believe that many media relations people are not very good at their jobs, and that this is so because many of them are afraid of journalists. "Now, please don't quote me on that," is the constant refrain. It's much like a salesperson ending a call with: "Now please don't buy any." Is not the spokesperson who is afraid to speak an oxymoron?

> Is not the spokesperson who is afraid to speak an oxymoron?

Especially in large organizations, there is a danger that media relations people become mere order-takers, responding to press inquiries and helping provide journalists with information, but not necessarily working to change a journalist's perceptions of the organization. And especially in a large organization that receives many press calls daily, there is a tendency for media relations people to see their job as fielding inquiries—catching, rather than initiating coverage, pitching. Sometimes this is for good reason: because the volume of incoming calls is so high. But sometimes it is inertia or even fear that suppresses a media relations person's appetite for initiating discussions with reporters.

One reason fear develops in media relations people is the constant scrutiny and criticism within an organization of what is stated and not stated in press reports. Senior officials in organizations often react out of all proportion to the slightest problem in a news report. A mistake by the spokesperson is out there for the world to read, see or hear—colleagues, bosses, CEOs, family, friends, and neighbors. The spokesperson begins to doubt his or her ability to synthesize and express a view on behalf of the organization.

Yet the spokesperson is paid to convey certain facts and points of view. While there are times when one should speak "for background," or even "off the record," or indeed not at all, constant pleas for the journalist not to print or broadcast certain information give the journalist another reason to want to ignore the media relations person. After all, the journalist usually wants to speak with someone else in the organization anyway.

Often media relations people are afraid of the media because they are intimidated by the prestige of the institution. For a twenty-five-year-old, or even a forty-year-old, a call from a senior reporter at *The New York Times*, or from a producer at CBS's *60 Minutes* can cause panic or worse. When the stakes are so high, it is easy for media relations people, especially those who are not particularly confident in their own abilities or their stature in their organization, to worry that their own words may come back to haunt them.

Some journalists, especially those with the news organizations that specialize in sensationalist stories, play "Gotcha journalism," hovering over the interview subject like jackals. We have witnessed instances where executives said something they did not mean to say—statements the journalists knew to be inaccurate and unintended—and the journalists used the misstatements because they buttressed the story angle. And there are small number of journalists, like some people in other professions, are simply bad people who will cheat and lie, and they do that by deliberately misquoting someone, and sometimes by inventing quotes or stories outright. We suspect that journalists who have no qualms about such matters are cynics who believe that the people they interview (the rest of the world) are duplicitous and untrustworthy, and that the journalist's dishonesty is therefore necessary to get the truth out to the public. The press relations person has to begin a relationship with a journalist presuming trustworthiness, just as one should begin other relationships in life that way, both because trusting relationships are more productive as well as for the sake of one's own sanity and soul. If a particular journalist should be untrustworthy or unethical, it will become clear soon enough.

> A big part of the media relations person's job is to figure out what the journalist's perspective is.

A degree of anxiety can increase performance. It is reasonable and good to be anxious when dealing with journalists because they are human and make mistakes. They sometimes misunderstand what is said or they mistranscribe quotes. And today, in the ever-faster-paced media world, there are more and more opportunities for mistakes.

Another reason for having a healthy degree of anxiety about the press is that every journalist brings a perspective to an assignment. Some are better than others at being objective, but no one can wipe clean the slate of life's experiences, opinions, predilections, and prejudices. A big part of the media relations person's job is to figure out what the journalist's perspective is. If the perspective is favorable and accurate, reinforce it. If it is unfavorable, try to understand why, and then deal with the problems and issues.

> Spokespeople say things ranging from insensitive to inappropriate to dumb.

Still another reason for healthy anxiety is one's own inadequacies as a spokesperson. How many people can talk with absolute precision for, say, an entire hour? Can one swear, at the end of the interview, that he or she said "appraise" rather than "apprise" or, "Yes, I disagree" rather than, "No, I don't disagree"?

Spokespeople say things ranging from insensitive to inappropriate to dumb. We all do so in our personal discourse, out of carelessness, naivete or ignorance, sometimes even offending the very people we care most about. Media relations people can say things that are inaccurate or reveal information that should not be revealed. One of the biggest fears of public relations professionals in technology-based companies should be that they might unwittingly reveal something proprietary. The rule most companies follow is: If the information has been presented before a scientific forum published in a scientific journal, it is considered public. But of course few rules are that simple. Sometimes, for example, scientists present information at a sidebar session (a "poster" session) and not in front of the entire conference. Sometimes, a scientist overstates or understates a scientific development and that might not be easily apparent from the transcript.

Similarly, public relations people who work in the financial industry must be acutely aware that everything they say is subject to securities laws and regulations, and has the potential to move markets. Fear of civil and criminal liability has a tendency to focus one's mind, and to make one default to precision or to silence.

EXPERT PERSPECTIVES: LAUNCHING A PRODUCT THROUGH EFFECTIVE STORY-TELLING

By Michael Neuwirth, Senior PR Director, The Dannon Company

In anticipation of introducing the first probiotic yogurt that had a benefit beyond tasting good and its inherent nutritive value, the corporate communications team at the Dannon Company devised a media relations plan to ignite interest in the new product before its market introduction and demonstrate the product's unique benefit in a highly credible context. At the time in 2005, the term "functional food" was not well known but of interest to a few food companies and a few of the business journalists who followed them.

The PR team at Dannon realized that it had a very compelling story to tell, provided it could produce a consumer to attest to the new yogurt's benefit. In addition, they needed a trend forecaster to address Americans' rising interest in functional foods. While the team identified a consumer who had participated in a pre-market focus group and who was willing to publicly discuss her experience with Activia, journalists at several international news organizations were researched to identify who would have the greatest interest in the story. Ultimately the lead food business writer at *The New York Times* was identified as the best journalist, based on the reach and influence of the *Times* and her personal interest in food.

After contacting dozens of consumers who had participated in the pre-market focus groups, one agreed to publicly share her experience, which she did directly with the journalist. The consumer's experience became the lead of the story, emphasizing the credibility of the new yogurt and differentiating it based on its unique probiotic that helped with digestive health.

The resulting front-page *New York Times* article was key to creating the momentum Dannon needed for its largest new product launch in the company's history. The headline of the article, "Eating Your Way to Health," and an enormous photo of a cup of Activia dominated the cover of the *Times*' business section on December 28, 2005, two weeks before the first cup of Activia was shipped to food retailers. The article established Activia as emblem of a new trend in food, and the consumer testimonial was evidence that its promise was fulfilled. Activia proceeded to become the most successful food launch of the year, and one of the most popular foods of the decade.

THE PRESS' RIGHT TO KNOW

If a journalist does not ask a question in precisely the right words, yet the spokesperson knows what information the journalist is seeking, does the spokesperson have an obligation to give the desired information?

For example, a journalist phones the spokesperson for the publicly owned ABC Company and says: "I understand that Ms. X (a senior officer in the organization) has resigned." The fact is that, as the spokesperson knows, Ms. X will formally resign the next day, but has not done so yet. So the spokesperson answers: "No, that is not true." The journalist failed to phrase the question precisely or broadly enough, and the spokesperson took advantage of that. "Gotcha journalism" in reverse, one might say.

Did this spokesperson handle the matter well? The answer is that it depends on the circumstances. If Ms. X is in line to succeed the CEO, the resignation announcement could be considered "material," meaning that a shareholder or prospective shareholder might buy or sell stock on that information. The spokesperson could not prematurely acknowledge the resignation to that one journalist, because that would constitute selective disclosure and possibly violate securities laws or regulations. Similarly, securities laws prohibit statements that are "materially misleading." Saying, "It's not true that Ms. X has resigned," while technically true when spoken, may no longer be true when the newspaper is published. Such a statement could be seen to be materially misleading. A safer approach would be to avoid commenting on the resignation at all. The story about the resignation would still appear, but without the company's comment, one way or the other.

> To deny certain rumors but not others is implicitly to confirm the others.

Such considerations apply when journalists raise questions about rumored business development activities. If a journalist asks: "I understand that you have acquired XYZ company," and the spokesperson knows that the acquisition agreement, while expected soon, has not yet been reached, the spokesperson can answer "No." A better answer might be: "As a matter of policy, ABC company does not comment on rumors about our business (or organization)." This is a particularly effective response if used consistently. The spokesperson can explain to journalists (as well as securities analysts and others who inquire) the reason for the policy: To deny certain rumors but not others is implicitly to confirm the others. Of course when rumors rise to the level where they have a significant (for example, "material") effect on the organization, a denial or confirmation may have to be issued before the organization would otherwise plan to do so. But that should be a rare exception. Armed with a no-comment-on-rumors policy, the spokesperson need not even make the internal inquiries to determine the truth about the rumor. In fact, he or she should not delay in giving the response: "As a matter of policy, ABC does not comment on rumors."

While the press arguably has the right to ask any question, the press does not have the right to know everything. Reporters often assert that they are proxies for the public at large, and that "the public has a right to know." They often assume that such an argument is persuasive, and in fact sometimes inexperienced media relations people fall into the trap of assuming that the public has some such right. In fact, the public does not have a right to know everything reporters might choose to write about. While companies have disclosure obligations, those obligations are very clearly specified in securities regulations, as is the timing and manner of such disclosure. But there is a big difference between a company's duty to disclose certain kinds of information in a certain manner, and the public's or press' right to know whatever it wants to know.

The press does not have a right to know proprietary information; personal information; information that is not fully developed; or information that might threaten security.

Proprietary Information

Inventions must be patent protected before they can be discussed outside the organization. The trade secret is another valid way of keeping information confidential until the appropriate time for disclosure. If a journalist asks a question about a proprietary matter, it is perfectly acceptable to say, "The matter is proprietary, and we don't discuss proprietary information." The reporter does not have a right to know trade secrets or other appropriately confidential information.

Personal Information

Individuals have the right to protect information that is truly personal and none of the public's business. So, also, do individuals within organizations have the right to protect their personal information. Publicly traded organizations have a duty to disclose some private information about a small number of their senior-most executives (usually, their salary, bonus, and stock

> The interaction was a kind of dance, with each party knowing precisely what the other would do.

holdings). But for most employees their compensation, personnel files, and other work-related personal matters are not public, and should be protected.

When Fred was a spokesperson at a major investment bank in the 1980s, Wall Street compensation was a hot topic, and Fred would frequently be asked about particular executives' compensation. As a matter of policy the bank did not disclose compensation information except for the small number of executives required by law. Fred would often say something like, "As a matter of policy we don't comment on executive compensation." Often reporters would persist, asking to confirm ranges: "Does he make more than $10 million? Does he make less than $20 million?" Fred's reply would persistently be, "That's a question about compensation and we don't comment on employee compensation." With one *The Wall Street Journal Reporter,* Fred and the reporter had this type of exchange for every salary level from $1 million to $20 million, always with the same response, over a period of a half hour. The reporter later told Fred, "You can't blame me for trying to get you to crack. And besides, I had to be able to tell my editor that I had grilled you on every salary level." The interaction was a kind of dance, with each party knowing precisely what the other would do, but duty-bound to do the dance anyway.

Information That Is Not Fully Developed

Even "sure things" fall apart. The train may be moving smoothly along the tracks, but even the conductor does not know with certainty what may be lurking in the tunnel or around the corner. In any case, spokespeople should never acknowledge anything before the organization agrees to the timing. The reasons range from illegality (for example, selective disclosure) to certain unemployment for the spokesperson. And sometimes the premature disclosure of a pending event may prevent the event from happening at all.

Preparation can prevent such problems. If something new is brewing in an organization, the communications people should be brought in early so that the best response can be prepared for the announcement day, and another for the interim period.

Some situations are so difficult that a "no-comment" response or a euphemism is called for. The phrase "no comment" has become, through movies and television programs, a caricature of evasion. And the phrase itself is awkward. Because of the baggage the phrase carries, it can cast a negative impression with both the reporter and with those who read, view, or listen to the story. But there are ample ways of avoiding comment without using that two-word phrase. Among the possibilities are:

- "We don't discuss financial projections."
- "As a matter of policy we don't comment on (rumors/employee matters/investigations, etc.)."
- "It is proprietary."
- "We cannot reveal the identities of the victims until next of kin have been notified."

Even a "no comment" is always better than a lie. The U.S. Supreme Court has ruled that "no-comment statements" are the functional equivalent of silence. But it also ruled that denying a rumor that happened to be true was the functional equivalent of a lie, and held the offending company liable for the lie.

So as a rule, some form of "no-comment" statement, however phrased, is the less bad alternative between inappropriate disclosure of private information and lying.

Some form of no-comment statement is preferable to "was not available for comment," since a big part of the spokesperson's job is to be available.

"Let me check and get back to you" can be a useful response when the spokesperson is caught off guard or unaware. The problem with this response is that the spokesperson has to get back to the journalist, who will expect some enlightenment after an hour or two of grace. It is far better to be prepared with an immediate response.

If the journalist and the spokesperson have a good relationship, the spokesperson will often have to work hard to see that confidentiality concerns do not damage their relationship. For example, if a journalist is hot on the trail of breaking news for three days, and the spokesperson cannot reveal anything until the fourth day, the spokesperson might gain the necessary internal approvals to tell that journalist first on the fourth day or to give him or her a special interview opportunity at the right time.

Security Concerns

Spokespeople have a profound obligation—especially in this day and age—to protect the security of the organization and its people. Yet anecdotal research suggests that most corporations do not train their communication people to guard against lapses that could pose a security threat.

THE PRESS' PENCHANT FOR BAD NEWS

"Does the press have a penchant for bad news?" is a question much like the ones we used to ask as kids about the Pope being Catholic, and the bear doing something in the woods. The answer is yes, and nobody can credibly take another position. "If it bleeds, it leads," is the mantra of local television news directors.

Journalists can argue that their behavior reflects society's desires and the discussion can become arcane, but the answer is still yes—there is a penchant for negative news. Realizing that is important for two reasons:

First, if there is bad news brewing in your organization, the press will probably find out about it and report it, so why not generally address the matter up front? When patents are about to expire on a major product in a technology-based company, for example, the business press covers the matter early and thoroughly. The best way for a company to deal with this is to understand that patent expirations are important and legitimate stories, and be ready with the best answers to such questions as "what will happen to the company's profitability?" Similarly, management turmoil, weak sales, and other negative information will often find its way to reporters before the company is fully ready to discuss it.

Second, the penchant for bad news interferes with coverage of good news, if only because the newshole (that is, the total amount of space in any given print or broadcast story minus the space or time for advertisements) is only so big. The 1988 story of Merck's introduction and donation of Mectizan to prevent and treat river blindness in millions of people is literally one of the greatest stories in history. Yet it proved extremely difficult over the years to get coverage of the story (with some notable exceptions such as the cover story in *The New York Times Magazine* of January 8, 1989)[4]. Journalists would often say that people in the West are not interested in stories about people afflicted with river blindness who live mainly in developing countries in Africa. Yet all one has to do is note how prominent the coverage is of the bad news out of Africa about AIDS, wars, famines, and other horrors. Would not one think that the media would rush to cover the story of a pill (taken just once a year) that prevents or treats a parasitic disease that ravages entire populations, with blindness being only one of the symptoms? As if that were not enough to ensure coverage, the company that discovered and developed the medicine has committed to continuing to donate it to the millions of people who need it for as long as necessary.

After the 1974 resignation of President Richard M. Nixon in the wake of the Watergate scandal, there was an influx of young people into journalism. They were following the example of Carl Bernstein and Bob Woodward, whose dogged pursuit of a "third-rate burglary" resulted in the downfall of the most powerful person in the free world. Romanticized by the movie *All The President's Men*, journalism was seen as a vital mechanism for democratic accountability.

But the thrill of the chase often became the foremost concern of some journalists. In the late 1980s, Fred had lunch with the newly appointed reporter in charge of the investment banking beat at *The Wall Street Journal*. It was a time of turmoil in investment banking, punctuated by insider-trading scandals that served as the basis for the popular movie *Wall Street* with Charlie Sheen. *The Wall Street Journal* had recently won a Pulitzer Prize for its coverage of the scandals. The once-powerful firm Drexel Burnham Lambert ceased to exist, and its charismatic head of junk bonds, Mike Milken, was on his way to jail. During the lunch Fred innocently asked the reporter what his goal was in covering the industry. In all seriousness the reporter said, "My goal is to bring down a major investment bank before I'm thirty." Fred thought the reporter was joking, and asked him, "No, really, what's your goal for your beat?" The reporter, with a straight face, replied, "No, really. That's my goal." After several seconds of awkward silence, Fred asked, "Well, how old are you?" The reporter was twenty-eight, which gave him two years to accomplish his goal.

Sure enough, the reporter wrote story after story that proved to be both very damaging and untrue. Numerous attempts to change his behavior proved unsuccessful. After a while, the only course left was for the chairman of the bank to send a forceful letter to the publisher of *The Wall Street Journal*, describing in great detail the various violations of the *Journal's* own standards in the reporter's coverage. It worked. The reporter turned his attention to other firms.

While, in the aftermath of Watergate, journalism came to be seen as investigative, over the last three decades—and particularly with the advent of all-news-all-the-time cable news coverage—journalism has morphed into a kind of entertainment medium, with production values and story lines similar to the dramatic features offered on television entertainment programs. Whereas in the "early years" CBS's news division was not considered a profit center, it now has to justify its existence in terms of advertising dollars. The result can be positive: production values and fast-breaking news. But it can also be negative: ignoring important stories for the sake of interesting ones.

In the fall of 2004, just before the presidential election, Fred had the opportunity to speak with Walter Cronkite, the celebrated CBS news anchor from the 1960s and 70s. Cronkite was once considered the "most trusted man in America." Speaking about his own craft, Mr. Cronkite said that the competition from cable news, and the premium on conflict, had changed his profession in profound and disturbing ways, and deprived the audience of what it needed to make informed decisions about pressing issues.

THE GOOD NEWS ABOUT THE PRESS

Journalists are usually not in the profession for the money, and many of them could do better financially on the "other side," in public relations. They are journalists because they believe in what they are doing and take great pride in it. Most believe that theirs is a noble profession.

Many press relations people, as well as leaders from business, government, and other fields, become jaundiced about journalism. This book's co-authors always felt grateful for journalism, believing that the social, personal, and business freedoms we have could not endure without it. When our clients' story is not being properly reported, we tend to look, first, at the performance of the sender (ourselves) in the classic academic communication model, the message, the channel (in this case the journalist), and then at the other information or attitudes ("noise") that might be causing interference.

Noise

Sender → **Message** → **Channel** → **Receiver** → **Feedback**

Noise

Today, more than ever, journalists need public relations, media relations people. There are fewer journalists doing more work, so they have less time to report and build relationships. Today, more than ever, the media relations person who can be trusted is invaluable.

Of course there is one other piece of potentially good news about the press: They can get very excited about good news from time to time. But new inventions can be oversold, and breakthroughs in basic biomedical research can be headlined cures for cancer. Advice to media relations practitioners: Beware of the good hype as well as the bad. We cannot have it both ways.

PRESS RELATIONS: A COLLABORATIVE RELATIONSHIP

It is easy to think that journalists hold all the power in the relationship with companies and other organizations, but this is not necessarily the case.

> Journalists often ask the questions an organization hopes would not be asked.

Journalists often ask the questions an organization hopes would not be asked. They are pressing, even threatening: "You know, I am going to cover the story with or without your help, and I believe I already have what I need." The spokesperson feels powerless. The senior-most people in the organization brazenly prescribe responses from afar—"Just stick to the prepared response"—until they get calls from the journalist directly or are about to be interviewed. Then the brazenness collapses into what they would call anxiety but some might call fear.

"Power" often implies something underhanded or Machiavellian, so heads of communications and senior officers in organizations may want to call it "strength" or "influence." But the fact is that a person in a stressful relationship must not feel powerless. Companies and other organizations have the ability to shape the stories that appear about them, but they need to wield that influence responsibly and carefully.

We know of one case where an individual reporter who was grossly unfair to an organization was frozen out of that organization's public relations information chain. Sometimes—rarely—this is necessary, and the journalist may move on to another beat because of a lack of access. But there is a big difference between "black balling" one reporter versus the entire news medium. The most famous instance of the latter was Mobil Oil's 1984 declaration that it would henceforth not communicate in any way with *The Wall Street Journal*.[5]

Again, there is seldom a need to even consider such extreme remedies. But it is critically important for an organization and its spokespeople to realize that it is not powerless in the face of the awesome power of the press.

Day to day, the best way for spokespeople to leverage power is by managing access. Journalists have to go through the communications office to get to the senior officers, and managing access in a fair way will rebound to the credit of the entire organization.

Enduring power in media relations flows from relationships built on fairness, respect, and credibility. One of the keys to power in the relationship with journalists is to be very good at the media relations discipline, knowledgeable about your own industry, and well-versed on what journalists do and why.

EXPERT PERSPECTIVES: THE ART OF THE PITCH

By Raleigh Mayer, Principal of Raleigh Mayer Consulting

Successful pitching to reporters begins with a clear understanding of the outlet, its audience, and the utilization of appropriate tone, timing, and content.

A pitch is not:

- a high-pressure sales presentation
- press release text
- advertising copy
- a plea or solicitation
- a social conversation.

A pitch is:

- an invitation to cover a story
- a concise, compelling, and customized invitation to interview an expert, preview an event, report on a phenomenon or trend, test a product or service
- an idea for a compelling story, and a road map for how to get the story.

Successful pitching requires comprehensive knowledge of the targeted media, including:

- prior and current coverage of your industry
- style and bias of the outlet
- format of specific columns, departments, segments
- preferences and interests of individual journalists.

Successful pitching requires comprehensive knowledge of your story, including:

- answers to basic questions about the event, person, business, market
- how to bring the story to life for readers or viewers
- how to get access to others, including those who are not part of your organization.

Pitching on Paper

Lead with:

- question
- juxtaposition
- comparison
- observation
- riddle.

After lead:

- Support or expand on your claim, or who you are and why you are writing.
- Present relevant facts, statistics, or documentation.
- Name what you are asking or offering: interview, story, profile, attend event, and so forth.
- Conclude with a promise to follow-up.
- Keep to one page if possible.

Pitching by e-mail

- Make it compact.
- Put the lead in the subject line.
- Condense body copy to one or two paragraphs.
- Include contact information in signature.
- Do not send attachments unless asked.

Pitching by Phone

- Conduct it conversationally.
- Identify yourself clearly.
- Deliver the lead and let the reporter respond.
- Have prepared message points ready.
- Organize your desk so you can concentrate during call.
- Give up graciously if the reporter declines or defers pitch.
- Thank the reporter for considering it.

Pitching by Voicemail

- Be concise.
- Be prepared to leave pitch as voicemail message.
- Give compressed pitch—still powerful, but short.
- Leave your name and number at both beginning and end of message.
- Do not be careless in leaving message.

If Pitch is Declined

- Pitch different angle to same reporter.
- Pitch same angle to different desk of the same outlet (if relevant).
- Pitch new angle to another section.
- Pitch competing reporter at different outlet.

After the Story Appears

- Thank the reporter (a handwritten note has the most impact) but do not gush.
- Keep in contact with reporter.
- Update reporter of relevant developments, even if there is no immediate benefit to you.
- Deliver next pitch with same level of professionalism as the last one.

If there are errors:

- Let the reporter know, politely, of the errors.
- Do not confuse contrasting opinions with errors of fact.
- Contact editors only if you believe willful or harmful errors are not being taken seriously.

What Reporters Dislike

- Unprepared or unknowledgeable pitches.
- Pitches delivered too fast or in a convoluted manner.
- Pitches delivered on deadline.
- PR people who cannot answer basic questions or provide access to the right people.
- PR people who whine that the story was not as positive as they had hoped.
- PR people who call to follow up on a release without adding anything new.
- PR people who call to ask when/if story has appeared.
- Unsolicited e-mail attachments.
- Overly ornate or poorly designed press materials; including those with tiny typeface.

SUCCESS IN MEDIA RELATIONS

Everyone in media relations chants the same mantra: success in media relations depends upon building solid relationships with the press. Of course knowing it and doing it are two different things. How to do it? The formula is simple: success as a communicator will be in direct proportion to one's skills as a communicator, one's conviction, the quality of the product, position, or story one is selling to the press, and one's preparedness.

Communication Skills

Communication is one of those things that most people think they are good at. After all, it involves speaking, reading, and writing. Most people have been speaking from the first year or so after they were born, and learned to read and write in first grade.

But true communication skill requires more than just speaking, reading, and writing. It involves using those behaviors to influence the attitudes and behaviors of others. And like any other set of skills, it can become stale and fall into disuse. Effective communicators regularly upgrade their communication skills.

For example, this book's coauthors have both taken numerous writing courses and won writing awards, but we still work hard at improving our craft. Over the years, we would routinely invite writing instructors to hold workshops for our professional staffs, and we would participate ourselves.

Conviction

Journalists are like kids and puppy dogs: if you do not mean what you say, they can smell it. For example, we knew of a young woman in corporate communications for a healthcare company who intellectually accepted the need for animal research of investigational medicines. But she did not have a firm conviction that, while the best tools of science should be mobilized to minimize the number of animals used, some animal studies must be performed before an investigational medicine can be administered to a man, woman, or child. As a result, she was often ineffective in interviews on the topic. It was not a function of knowledge or understanding, but of being able to enthusiastically represent a position.

> Journalists are like kids and puppy dogs: if you do not mean what you say, they can smell it.

Eventually, her superior asked her not to take any more calls about animal research, assuring her that her career would not suffer. There were many other things she could do well, and there were also other people in the group who had enough conviction in the appropriateness of responsible animal testing of medicines to withstand a badgering from any reporter or activist and still hold firm.

Quality of Product or Story

If the thing you are selling to the press is not a page-one story, do not try to get coverage there. If your product or story is not what your organization says it is, the lie or omission will eventually be uncovered. Do not lie or exaggerate. Sounds easy, but it is not. Be willing to stand up in your organization and object to a story line that obscures, blurs, or distorts the truth. Let your uncompromising position be known within the organization—you will not have to blurt it out, because the opportunity to let people know how you feel will come.

Similarly, if you are trying to interest a reporter in a story, you need to package it in ways that get the reporter's attention and make it more likely that the reporter will become the story's champion. Reporters don't want to cover stories with the sole purpose of driving a company or brand's commercial success. The media wants to show the human interest angle or societal impact of the story. To quote one of the greatest television producers of our time, Don Hewitt of *60 Minutes*, "The flood is the event; Noah is the story."

For example, if a company hires more employees, what's the financial impact to the community? If a new product launches offering a unique benefit, how does this product impact a person's life? It's critical to frame the news in the context of human or societal impact. This often requires doing more research and thinking more broadly about the news coverage you are pursuing.

Preparedness

Be knowledgeable about the reporter and the media outlet you are pitching. Do your research. Know if a reporter has covered your industry and/or subject matter so you can reference it in your pitch and subsequent conversation. Also know your organization, and its products, services, and people. Otherwise, you are just an obstacle to the press. Unfortunately, too many media relations people think their job is simply to arrange interviews. There is a time to call upon the experts in your organization to grant interviews, but the communications people should be able to field a significant percentage of incoming calls and be well enough informed to approach a journalist with the basics of a story. If you know what you are talking about—that is, understand your industry, not only your company—and provide assets that enhance the story, journalists will begin to rely on you. When they start calling you for guidance on a story that does not directly involve your organization, you know you have accomplished something. If you have arranged for someone in your organization to be interviewed, make sure he or she is prepared.

CONTENT DEVELOPMENT

Companies and brands are increasingly thinking about themselves as media companies, in order to tell their own story their way, penetrate the Media Clover Leaf, engage their target audiences in real-time, and become "discoverable" online. As a result, communications teams are developing "content assets" to communicate specific messages and distribute through media channels.

Content assets can include photography, imagery, slide shows, short and long form videos, and "infographics," which are data visualizations of a specific subject matter. Given the content surplus, with over 100 hours of video uploaded to YouTube every minute, communications teams need to think about how to break through the content clutter by ensuring their content hits at the right time, to the right audience, and in the right channel.

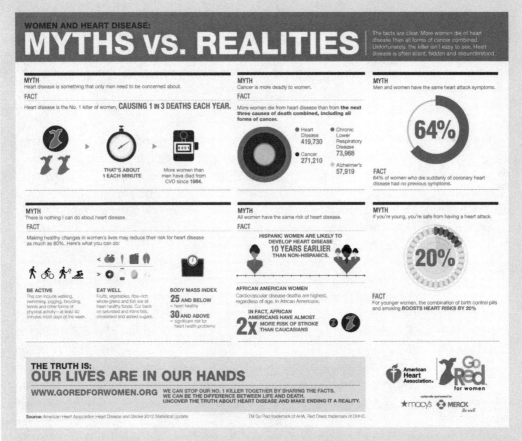

Figure 3.1 In 2012, the American Heart Association developed and distributed this infographic across the Media Clover Leaf to educate women that heart disease is the main killer of women and drive women to take control of their heart health. The infographic also positioned the American Heart Association as an industry leader and expert.

There's also an increasing trend for companies to "sponsor" content. Due to disruptions to advertising and subscription-based revenue streams, many publishers are now open to turning content that's created or curated by corporations into a new form of advertising. These are paid, not earned, contributed articles, infographics, videos, and more. These are ads that closely resemble journalist content and are often slotted in the news section, once-sacred ground. It's important to note that that no sponsored content should ever replace credible coverage by an independent, free press. The primary job for the PR professional remains to build and maintain trusted relationships with media and inform media coverage that's in the public interest.

EXPERT PERSPECTIVES: ALL CONTENT IS NOT EQUAL

By Bob DeFillippo, Chief Communications Officer, Prudential Financial, Inc.

No one disputes that integrating a public relations component into a marketing campaign can produce powerful results. Earned media has always been and will continue to be a highly effective marketing tool. That's because earned media is produced from objective reporting based on the merits of the information provided by a company and not the placement of a paid advertisement or advertorial.

Maintaining a bright line between advertising and editorial has always been essential in protecting the integrity of earned media.

But two compelling economic realities—the growing irrelevance of traditional advertising and the permanently broken media business model once dependent on that very advertising to deliver objective reporting—are blurring that line.

The "all content is equal" movement seems to be achieving unstoppable status, with marketers on one side and media sales representatives on the other, happily buying and selling editorial space without clearly identifying that content as branded or sponsored.

The ability of new digital media platforms to reach large numbers of consumers has also empowered marketers to see branded and sponsored content as an elegant way to circumvent the traditional methods to obtain earned media. After all, why bother relying on objective reporting to obtain a favorable story about your company, product, or service when you can simply go down the hall and pay someone in advertising to publish your story.

This blurring of the lines between paid and earned media has been neatly explained by the claim of authenticity. In other words, producing advertising content that has the look and feel of objective editorial content is OK as long as the content producer tells the truth.

Media buyers and their counterparts at news outlets argue that this practice is ethically sound as long as brands do not make a direct pitch to consumers in their (sponsored) articles. The argument goes that it isn't advertising if the content is about big issues that relate to thought leadership.

In other words, it is perfectly acceptable to sacrifice objective journalism on the altar of marketing as long as you call it thought leadership. Why bother taking the time to demonstrate with actions and facts that your leading thoughts deserve to be published on their merit when you can get published by simply writing a check?

Exhibiting more skepticism than ever before and rightfully so, most consumers can easily recognize the difference between earned and paid media. Ultimately, what's at stake is the public's trust—the very thing marketers covet.

Defenders of the branded content movement have adopted a convincing defense that social media requires companies to engage their customers directly. And, in fact, it is social media that has played a major part in blurring the lines between earned and paid media by creating a free-for-all of information.

However, as important and powerful as this new medium is, it doesn't mean we must abandon the principles that have been the underpinnings of the relationship between journalism and public relations by accepting branded content as equal to objective reporting.

Clearly, advertisers and the traditional media have a problem. Advertising is becoming irrelevant because consumers—largely as a result of social media—care less about what a company claims about its products and services, choosing instead to rely on the experiences of other consumers who do not have a vested interest in those products and services. Meanwhile, the traditional media business model, which was dependent on advertising revenue for its very existence, is disappearing because media executives apparently believe no one would be willing to pay for objective reporting.

The solution is to keep the line that separates advertising from objective reporting clear and bright. Use public relations as an effective tool in your marketing campaigns for social and traditional media by developing relationships with journalists and presenting information that helps them determine whether something is newsworthy or not. In other words, earn the coverage.

All content is not equal. If you need to pay to have content published on any platform—new or old media—it is advertising by definition. The principles that define the bright line separating earned from paid media are an important and sacred public trust that deserves to be protected. Public relations and marketing campaigns are doomed to fail once public trust is lost.

▶ BEST PRACTICES

1. Be quick (but not foolhardy).

Communication groups should have their own policy—for example, "return 90 percent of press calls/e-mails within one hour"—based on their resources and the demands of the press reporting on their organizations. But we do not subscribe to the often-stated PR principle to call every reporter back right away. First, it is not always possible. Second, some journalists—those who have not been fair or responsive to your organization—do not deserve a quick response. That we teach others how to treat us is as true in press relations as in anything else. But as a general rule, the earlier you can get back to a reporter the more influence you can have on the story. That is because the reporter, especially one on a breaking story, cannot wait for your response to write the story. He or she will write it whether you respond or not.

2. Know the media.

Understand the missions of the various print, broadcast, and digital media. *The Wall Street Journal* is not *The New York Times* and *The New York Times* is not the *Los Angeles Times* or *The Huffington Post*. Research! Know the consumer, professional, and trade media covering your industry. Understand those umbrella terms and use them correctly. Both coauthors read the *Columbia Journalism Review*, *The American Journalism Review*, and many first-person, behind-the-scenes accounts of life as a reporter. We require the same of our media relations students. Understanding what is important for reporters, the experience of being a reporter, and the pressures reporters face in doing their jobs every day is a critical part of being an effective media relations professional.

3. Know the reporters.

Of course you can only know a small number of journalists well. But media software offers media biographies. We cannot imagine arranging an interview for a senior executive or official without obtaining a journalist bio and recent news reports, features, or editorials. Research! Visit the journalists at the bureau or for lunch. Most spokespeople are not good at this, but doing so is tremendously important. A good time to ask to meet informally with a journalist is a few days after you have been helpful to him or her. It is also effective to call a journalist when he or she first begins covering your organization, and to go to lunch or grab a cup of coffee to get to know each other. Most journalists new to a beat are eager to make such contacts, and generally welcome such approaches. Once they are established it can be much harder to schedule such time with a reporter without having a story to discuss.

4. Have a plethora of standby statements.

Most companies know what is likely to become public prematurely. The most enlightened companies have standby statements ready to distribute on such topics well before a reporter calls. The statement should generally be ready for faxing or e-mailing to a reporter. One way to avoid questions on sensitive subjects is to say "we have a standby statement on that; should I e-mail it to you?" Invariably—literally—the answer will be yes, thank you, and goodbye. This avoids the possibility of misspeaking or of being misquoted, and the journalist has the precise words the organization wants to express.

5. Have a plethora of Qs and As.

If the spokesperson has days to prepare for a tough interview on a narrow subject and the journalist only has an hour or so, the spokesperson can anticipate every single, reasonable question. If the subject is broad—for example, growth prospects for a particular industry—the challenge becomes greater. But even then, the proposition is irrefutable: The more Qs and As the spokesperson has prepared, the greater the chances for success.

6. Media Coaching.

Speaking with reporters is different from speaking with other people, because they use your words differently than most people do. In particular, most conversations are private, unstructured, and informal, while interviews are always public, and should be formal and structured. Executives often behave with reporters the same way they behave with everyone else, and often with adverse consequences.

One way to prevent such negative outcomes is to prepare the executive not just on the subject matter to be discussed, but also on the skills necessary to communicate that content most effectively through the news media. The skills for effectiveness in print interviews are in some ways different from those necessary for television, radio, or the Internet.

One advantage of media coaching is that it is often videotaped—even training for print interviews. One reason for the taping is for the executive to see how he or she really comes across. It can be eye-opening, and much more effective than telling the executive how he or she did. Another advantage of media coaching is that it provides a safe setting to ask the executive difficult questions that would not be as acceptable in a rehearsal at the executive's desk.

Finally, the training provides a safe environment for an executive to fail—far better to fail in rehearsal than on CNN. The training can reveal how weak a particular response to a difficult question may be, and provide an opportunity to improve. It can reveal the gaps in information before the actual interview. Finally, media training can reveal character issues that would be catastrophic in a real interview. We have seen senior executives lie when pressed by a tough media trainer. Like a kid caught with his hand in the candy jar, a person armed with weak information tends to lie. It is far better to expose the lie and the weakness that triggered it in an exercise than with a reporter.

7. Have Visuals.

In today's media environment, a picture is better than a thousand words. The time we spend consuming information on screens expands while our collective attention spans shrink, so expect the media to cut text and use more visuals. Visuals are also more shareable across social media, and can include photography, video, infographics, and slide shows.

8. Recognize the influence of visuals on the print medium.

More media outlets are using video. *The Wall Street Journal* recently launched WSJ WorldStream (wjs.com/worldstream), a global publishing company for instant upload, short-form videos shot with smartphones by journalists. This example supports the

PR idea that we can no longer think of a story as just "print" or "broadcast." When creating a pitch, think about how the story will play across all devices, screens, and mediums. Offer reporters video assets, such as behind-the-scenes opportunities, that will make the story more enticing.

9. Do everything you can to build your organization's reputation.

The media relations person represents the organization as much as anyone and is in a position of great leverage in this regard.

10. Do not do anything that puts your organization's reputation at risk.

11. Make it interesting.

Given a choice between "interesting" and "informative," the journalist will choose "interesting" almost every time.

12. Never speak on background—unless you know what you are doing.

To most PR people and journalists, the phrase "on background" means that the information can be used, but cannot be attributed to or associated with the spokesperson or organization he or she represents. It is an indispensable part of an ongoing media relations program, and can be helpful in many cases—for example, when you are not sure of something but think the journalist should investigate, or when what you say might seem inappropriate in a news report quoting your organization. Make sure the journalist and you are working from precisely the same definition of terms, and that you explicitly note when you are "on background" and "off."

13. Never work with a reporter under "embargo"—unless you know what you are doing.

The rule should be: Do not issue a press release to a world of journalists and mark it "embargoed"—unless you actually want and expect someone to break the embargo. The embargo can be a useful tool, especially when the story is complicated and a journalist would need time to understand it, and when you have a mutually trusting relationship with the journalist. How can a publicly owned company issue a press release on a complicated matter after the New York Stock Exchange closes and expect it to be covered accurately on the evening news or in the morning papers? Make sure that the journalist and you have precisely the same understanding of what the agreement is. Make sure both parties understand exactly when the news can be released.

14. Never speak "off the record"—ever.

The term, at least to many in the media relations business, means that the information will never be reported. Fuhgeddaboudit!

15. Call every reporter back right away—Fuhgeddaboudit!

The golden rule taught in public relations courses is that a PR person must return a reporter's call as soon as possible, and in general that is a good rule to follow. The reason, of course, is that the journalist is usually under deadline. But there are exceptions, dictated by common sense.

Again, if a reporter has been unfair to the client or organization you represent, or if the reporter's news media often does a poor job, it does not make any sense to treat that person with the same degree of responsiveness you would the better reporters. Journalists talk, and it often becomes clear to one who feels mistreated by an organization he or she is covering that colleagues in the press do not feel that way. The light can go on. In any case, the PR person has power, as does the organization or client he or she represents, and it can and should be used.

16. Keep a media tracker.

There are two reasons. First, it can be circulated within your organization so that others know what you are doing with the press and so that PR people in the organization are not tripping over each other. Second, it will provide a record so that, in the future, you can reach out to all journalists who, for example, have inquired about a particular product or issue.

17. Have a "return-call policy."

It is a good idea to have a policy that says, for example, "we return 90 percent of all press calls within one hour." (Arrange lunch breaks and so forth accordingly.) Setting business objectives is as important in press relations as anywhere else.

18. Be available nights and weekends.

It is the deadline, stupid. There is no other way to run press relations. If there is more than one person in the press relations shop, spread the overtime work around. If you are the only one, make sure your superiors know what overtime work is required.

19. Correct every mistake in the press about your organization.

There are essentially three remedies: a letter to the editor; a correction notice for publication or broadcast; and a letter or call to the journalist to clarify the matter with him or her but not necessarily for publication or broadcast.

20. Get the journalist's agreement, when time permits, for review of quotations, before publication.

Especially if the matter discussed in the interview is complex, the journalist should agree to give the interviewee the opportunity to review quotes before publication. More journalism schools are adopting this position, and John cannot see the fairness or journalistic good of any other. On complicated stories, John's position is: No review of quotes, no interview.

21. Journalism support programs.

A great way of building relationships with the press is to fund programs that support good journalism. Of course this has to be a mutually productive but hands-off relationship. The benefits of a media relationship initiative will sometimes be hard to see, day to day, and some people in the organization might even think the initiative is counterproductive: "If you had not been reaching out to that reporter so often, he wouldn't now be all over us at a time when we don't need the attention." But over time, the relationship is beneficial in a number of ways. It provides a bridge for two-way interaction independent of any one story. It provides opportunities for executives and others to get to know reporters well, and vice versa. And, above all, it reflects the organization's honest desire for fair journalism.

22. A media relations person should always be working toward measurable results that support organizational objectives.

23. Codify rules of engagement for social media. (See Chapter 4.)

QUALITIES OF A GOOD MEDIA RELATIONS PERSON

The list is brief:

- Good communication instincts (some people are simply not communicative by nature and should not be in media relations).

- Good communication skills. The job interview can reveal much about speaking abilities.

- To assess writing ability, always give a writing test.

- Toughness and an ability to withstand criticism.

- Honesty.

- Good research skills.

- An ability to shine when under intense deadline pressure.

- Speed was always important. Today, given the 24/7 news cycle and the importance of social media, it is essential.

- Teamwork skills.

▶ RESOURCES FOR FURTHER STUDY

Cutlip, Scott M., Allen H. Center, and Glen M. Broom, *Effective Public Relations*, 9th edn, Pearson, Prentice Hall, Upper Saddle River, NJ, 2006.

Grunig, James E., and Todd Hunt, *Managing Public Relations*, Orlando, FL: Harcourt Brace Jovanovich, 1984.

Guth, David W. and Charles Marsh , *Public Relations: A Values-Driven Approach*, 5th edn, Needham Heights, MA: Allyn & Bacon, Inc., 2011.

Hiebert, Ray E. (ed.), *Public Relations Review: A Journal of Research and Comment*, Amsterdam: Elsevier.

Howard, Carole M. and Wilma K. Matthews, *On Deadline, Managing Media Relations*, 3rd edn, Prospect Heights, IL: Waveland PR Inc., 2000.

Schenkler, Irv and Tony Herrling, *Guide To Media Relations*, Upper Saddle River, NJ: Pearson, Prentice Hall, 2004.

Schmertz, Herb with William Novak, *Good-bye to the Low Profile*, Boston: Little, Brown, 1986.

▶ QUESTIONS FOR FURTHER DISCUSSION

1. Should media relations people proactively mention to journalists the reason the organization adheres to a centralized communication policy?

2. Do you think the Grunig-Hunt models of public relations apply today? Which one do you practice? Are you ethically committed to that model?

3. Does the press really have a right to ask anything at all?

4. Is there any reason PR people should not be as zealous about accuracy as the best journalists?

5. When the subject of the interview is technical, is it appropriate to ask the journalist before the interview to agree to clear the quotes before using them? What if the journalist will not agree?

▶ NOTES

1 James E. Grunig and Todd Hunt, *Managing Public Relations* (New York: Harcourt Brace Jovanovich, 1984), pp. 49, 399.

2 Ibid., p. 13.

3 Merck & Co. Inc. *Annual Report*, 2000, p. 22.

4 Erik Eckholm, "River Blindness: Conquering An Ancient Scourge," *The New York Times Magazine*, January 8, 1989.

5 Herb Schmertz with William Novak, *Good-bye to the Low Profile* (Boston: Little Brown and Company, 1986), p. 73.

4 SOCIAL MEDIA

By Laurel Hart

In times of change, learners inherit the earth.

– Eric Hoffer

■ ■ ■

SOCIAL MEDIA IN POLITICS

Before the 2008 primary season began, the generally acknowledged frontrunner for the Democratic nomination for President was Senator Hillary Clinton, the junior senator from New York State and spouse of former President Bill Clinton. People had heard of the even-more junior senator from Illinois, Senator Barack Obama, in part because of the rousing speech he gave at the 2004 Democratic Convention. But his reputation wasn't widely known, and many viewed his candidacy as the aspiration of an upstart, running before he'd put in his due time at a lower-level of the political ladder.

But building on the strength of the candidate himself and the campaign's traditional media outreach, the Obama campaign went on to conduct the most comprehensive, strategic, and well-executed use of grassroots organizing and social media for reputation building in a political campaign to date, and the junior senator from Illinois went on to become the 44th President of the United States.

The campaign was persistent in using social media to build and support the candidate's reputation in the minds of voters. Whether Democrat or Republican, both sides agreed that the Obama campaign was significantly better than Republican John McCain's campaign at harnessing the power of social media to drive support, action, donations, votes, and eventually victory, remapping the way a campaign communicates and interacts with supporters along the way. For example, in 2008 the Obama campaign created an online action site, MyBarackObama.com, to allow supporters to mobilize themselves, volunteer, and drive donations. The online platform combined social media, e-mail, text messaging and other technologies, and saw success on numerous levels, including 6.5 million donations totaling $500 million in online donations—an unprecedented amount of online fundraising for a political campaign, and success driven in part by the campaign's social media use. Obama also had official accounts on more than 15 different social media platforms during the campaign, with millions of supporters liking, following, and interacting with the campaign on those channels.

However, it was by all accounts a challenging first term for Obama, and his reputation took a hit.

But in the 2012 election, in a tight race with the Republican Party's nominee Mitt Romney, the Obama campaign used deep data analysis and channels such as social networking sites, Twitter, online videos, text messages and photo sharing sites to connect supporters with the candidate and, perhaps even more importantly, with each other.

Obama's 2008 and 2012 campaigns demonstrate how effectively leveraging social media can contribute to reputation management. The combination of an incumbent candidate, the Obama campaign's platform, and this multi-directional action and communication helped propel Obama to the White House for a second term. Social media offers evolving and necessary opportunities to influence stakeholders in politics, business, and beyond, and is crucial for managing reputations today.

■ ■ ■

WHAT IS SOCIAL MEDIA?

Social media is now a widespread part of how people and organizations communicate and participate online.

Social media has been called many things: new media (the name used in the first edition of this book), Web 2.0,[1] consumer-generated media, user-generated media, the live Web.[2] Social media is "often used to describe the collection of software that enables individuals and communities to gather, communicate, share, and in some cases collaborate or play."[3] Charlene Li and Josh Bernoff, in their book *Groundswell: Winning in a World Transformed by Social Technologies*, describe this as a "groundswell," "A social trend in which people use technologies to get the things they need from each other, rather than from traditional institutions like corporations."[4]

Social media is now a widespread part of how people and organizations communicate and participate online. Elements of social media have been around at least since the mid-1990s (and social elements of the Internet developed almost from the beginning of its invention), with sites like Blogger.com and other first generally available blog software services introduced in the late 1990s. Since then, the elements and channels of social media have evolved rapidly. Studies from the Pew Internet & American Life Project,[5] as well as research by countless others, have shown that, regardless of age, geography, gender, education or other demographic segment, social media is now an important and prevalent part of many people's daily lives in the United States and around the world.

We see this social media use by individuals manifest in all kinds of ways. From live reports of breaking news crises like the Boston Marathon bombings, to pop cultural events like the birth of the British Prince George, to sporting events like soccer's World Cup, to the collection of individually meaningful events in people's lives that get posted and shared by the billions every day, social media serves to both distribute and collaborate, inform and comment, observe and participate.

Because of the scale of social media today, organizations—no matter the sector, nonprofit or for-profit, small or large—must address social media as part of the reputation management matrix.

Part of the challenge in any text about social media is the pace of change. Individual platforms arrive and fade (or change shape and focus—just look at the evolution of Myspace over the past decade). Trends change. But because of the scale of social media today, organizations—no matter the sector, nonprofit or for-profit, small or large—must address social media as part of the reputation management matrix.

This chapter is written from the perspective of organizations (mostly corporate, with some nonprofit and governmental applications as well) and provides a broad overview, a glimpse of the many ways that organizations are interacting within social media, and some of the reputation management issues and reputational questions social media presents for organizations. There are many good online resources and books that cover these areas in greater depth and breadth, and many are listed throughout and at the end of the chapter. Our purpose here is to focus less on particular tools, tactics, or services, and more on the characteristics, strategies, and goals of social media as it relates to organizations' broader business goals and reputation management.

Social Media and Reputation Management

The first chapter of this book maintains that reputation can be measured and managed. In today's communication and media environment, social media must be part of reputation management. Social media can by no means be the only element of reputation management (good tweets alone shall not save you), but it's a critical element nonetheless. In part, that's why social media infuses every chapter of this book. And it's also why it's helpful to address some aspects of social media in more depth here, to consider the impact of these social media aspects on reputation management, and to discuss best practices in social media management for organizations.

The world of communication has changed dramatically over the last thirty years, first with personal computers, then cable news, then widespread Internet adoption, and more recently smartphones and mobile technology steadily accelerating and shifting the dynamics of public communication. Social media has been an important component of that shifting communication landscape since the mid-1990s. Social media impacts the way organizations communicate with people, and the way people communicate and connect with each other, be they employees, customers, partners, competitors, adversaries, advocates, the general public, members of the media, or others.

With social media, anyone (what Dan Gillmor calls "the former audience"[6]) can create and distribute content online, easily, quickly, often freely (or cheaply), and with little or no technical knowhow. With social media, people can connect with organizations and each other in ways that were

> With social media, people can connect with organizations and each other in ways that were limited or not possible before.

limited or not possible before—employees with the media, customers with employees, the general public with customers, and so on. With social media, many of the traditional barriers—between publics, between social media and so-called mainstream media—have become blurred. And finally, the combination of social media and search means that much of that content is available for all to see, not just days or months but often years after it was originally published. (See Chris Anderson's article *The Long Tail* for a more in-depth discussion of this phenomenon.[7])

In the seminal website and book *The Cluetrain Manifesto*, first posted online in 1999 and published as a book in 2000 (with a tenth anniversary edition in 2009) by Rick Levine, Christopher Locke, Doc Searls, and David Weinberger, the authors' first thesis states that "Markets are conversations."[8] Thesis six continues, "The Internet is enabling conversations among human beings that were simply not possible in the era of mass media."[9] In the years since the book's original publication, we've seen countless powerful examples of these networked conversations taking place in social media.

Social media does not replace most other forms of communication; it complements, expands and enriches those forms of communication. (Much as the Internet did not replace the telephone.) As Clay Shirky and others have noted, other forms of media now co-exist on the Internet as well, so that you can watch TV shows, listen to the radio, and make phone calls online. And as Shirky says, it's not just the "shiny new tools" of social media that make them interesting: "These tools don't get socially interesting until they get technologically boring. It isn't when the shiny new tools show up that their uses start permeating society, it's when everybody is able to take them for granted."[10]

> To be successful, an organization's social media activities must be coordinated with its larger business goals and strategy, as well as with its other communication efforts.

Successful social media use by organizations is also, in many ways, a continuation of the very best communication principles organizations have long aspired to or practiced. And to be successful, an organization's social media activities must be coordinated with its larger business goals and strategy, as well as with its other communication efforts. Social media is now ingrained in our culture and in the ways that people look to communicate with the organizations that matter to them in their lives, and so social media engagement is crucial to a company's reputation management activities.

Social Media Characteristics

There are some broad traits that characterize social media, many of which are ideals yet to be fully realized, but which organizations can aspire to in their participation within social media and which impact reputation management:

> Matching action to communication can help drive the development or sustainment of an authentic organization.

1. *Authenticity*

As "markets are conversations," people want organizations to communicate as they would in a conversation, in an authentic way. Spin, corporate talk, legalese, b.s., or bluster have never been good principles of communication, but in the era of social media, they have no place at all.

For many organizations, it can be a cultural shift to adopt a more conversational way of communicating. Authenticity can sometimes be conveyed through shifts in writing style. For example, organizations may use more personal pronouns and first-hand accounts in writing for social media than for other types of business communication. But perhaps even harder is that authenticity also requires a great degree of consistency between communication and action, and across communication channels and organizational functions. For example, if the communication or social media team says one thing while the customer service team is saying or doing something that appears to be completely at odds, it may leave the person on the receiving end feeling that the company is inauthentic. Matching action to communication can help drive the development or sustainment of an authentic organization.

In the study and report, "The Authentic Enterprise," the Arthur W. Page Society summarized this idea by saying, "In a word, authenticity will be the coin of the realm for successful corporations and for those who lead them." This is in part because a company's "actions and reputation, which used to be safe-guarded by a cadre of professionalized functions, are now the responsibility of everyone in the enterprise."[11]

But how does authenticity work in action? One example: The day after Thanksgiving, dubbed Black Friday, is typically one of the busiest shopping days of the year in the United States, and a day when most retailers are trying to sell as much product to as many people as possible. But beginning in 2011 and continuing in 2012 and 2013, outdoor clothing and gear company Patagonia caught many people by surprise by running an anti-Black Friday campaign urging people *not* to buy its products (and other products they don't need) and repair them instead. In 2013, the campaign highlighted a short film called "Worn Wear,"[12] used hashtags like #AntiBlackFriday and #BetterThanNew to drive awareness, and shared other related content across Tumblr, Facebook and other social media channels. From another company without Patagonia's long history of environmental stewardship, the campaign may have been met with cynicism. But because of Patagonia's history of recycling programs and environmentalism, the company's communication and actions were seen as authentic and worked jointly to bolster the company's reputation.

2. *Transparency*

Organizational involvement in social media is also characterized and driven by a desire by audiences for more transparency from organizations. The desire for transparency stems not just from the technology but also from some of the business problems of the last ten+ years, from Enron to AIG to Bernie Madoff. Trust in leaders and organizations fell dramatically in the wake of the Great Recession, but as the 2014 Edelman Trust Barometer found, "Business has recovered trust from the crisis period because it is seen as having made demonstrable strides in **transparency** [emphasis the author's], supply chain and product quality."[13] As this report notes, trust and reputation depend in part on increased transparency on the part of organizations.

Don Tapscott and David Ticoll, in *The Naked Corporation*, define transparency as, "*the accessibility of information to stakeholders of institutions, regarding matters that affect their interests* [accent theirs]."[14] They go on to say, "Corporations that are open perform better. Transparency is a new form of power, which pays off when harnessed. Rather than to be feared, transparency is becoming central to business success. Rather than to be unwillingly stripped, smart firms are choosing to be open."[15]

Transparency also relates to the generally public nature of the interactions that take place between organizations and people within social media. In the past, if a customer was dissatisfied with a product, they might write a letter or call the company directly, or tell a few people they knew. Now, those interactions are more likely to take place in the public square of social media for anyone to see, comment on, and spread even further. (See the sidebar on United Breaks Guitars in Chapter 11 for a vivid illustration of this phenomenon at work.) This also affects people within an organization: in the past, it may have been just the communications, public relations or customer service groups that witnessed those interactions or crises. Now, anyone at an organization can see the events unfold publicly, and can also share that information with their networks outside an organization's walls.

One caveat: Transparency does not override the kinds of information that organizations have always and must continue to be kept private and confidential (more on this later in this chapter).

3. *Decentralization of authority*

Social media is characterized by a decentralization of authority and by multi-directional and increasingly two-way conversations. (See Chapter 3 for more on the academic models of public relations.) Social media enables people to interact with and have the *potential* (but still infrequently the *promise*) to affect each other, an organization, a product, a cause, or government leaders. Instead of top-down, one-directional information dictated by the leaders of corporations, information has more opportunities to move from the bottom up, from the sides, and between different groups. However, many see the two-way symmetric model between organizations and people within social media as still an aspirational goal, yet to be fully realized.

> Social media is characterized by a decentralization of authority and by multi-directional and increasingly two-way conversations.

4. *Speed*

Speed is a defining element of social media and a characteristic that presents challenges for organizations in reputation management. The pace at which information is shared and propagated in social media is faster and broader than older forms of communication. In the event of a crisis, this can make it difficult for organizations to catch up, but a fast response can also help organizations mitigate the effects of an issue or crisis. On the positive side, speed can work in an organization's favor, as useful, relevant, interesting, or novel content is shared amongst networks, amplifying an organization's reach.

> Speed is a defining element of social media and a characteristic that presents challenges for organizations in reputation management.

Part of what drives the increase in speed in social media is the way in which information is networked, categorized (or tagged), and made searchable. The inter-connected pieces are easier to spread and share, and easier to find. Our networks online, not just in the social network sense, are part of the acceleration process.

5. *Collaboration*

Finally, collaboration is an inherent part of what defines social media—it is the building of relationships, not just the exchange of information. It is also an important part of how organizations are participating successfully in social media. Just as in other forms of communication, how an organization participates in social media depends on the audience and the general business goals but, generally speaking, the ones that have had the most success have approached social media as a collaborative medium that encourages commitment and sustainability.

> Collaboration is an inherent part of what defines social media.

Social Media Landscape

From social networks to blogs and Twitter, the landscape of social media has had only one constant—change. While (currently) dominant platforms like Facebook, YouTube and Twitter have emerged and matured with strong global footprints, there are still regional differences as well, with China and Russia being two notable examples of regions of the world with more distinct social media landscapes. In China, Weixin (or WeChat) and Sina Weibo are two of the most popular social media services, but the number of total Chinese social media companies and services is vast. In Russia, Vkontake (VK) and Odnoklassniki are the largest social media platforms. And globally, there are also countless numbers of smaller social media platforms and channels with passionate user groups. Organizations and communicators who are evaluating their strategic participation in social media should consider their audiences first (just as they would in other mediums), as important constituencies might reside online in lesser-known social media communities.

The landscape of social media participation for large organizations is also maturing. In 2012, Burson-Marsteller's "Global Social Media Check-Up" of the *Fortune* Global 100 companies found that 87 percent of those companies used at least one of Twitter, Facebook, YouTube, Google+, or Pinterest. In addition to steadily increasing participation within different social media platforms, the number of accounts per platform was also increasing. The study found that "growth in the volume of conversations on social media has encouraged companies to participate," and that corporations "are creating multiple accounts to target audiences by geography, topic or service."[16] This global growth in depth of participation also creates new kinds of complexities for social media management, with which organizations must grapple.

(For a helpful visualization of the social media landscape, see The Conversation Prism by Brian Solis and JESS3.[17])

ORGANIZATIONAL PARTICIPATION IN SOCIAL MEDIA

How an organization decides to participate in social media depends largely on its overall business and communication goals, and so each organization's approach will be different and should be tailored to its own needs. Social media is just one element of a larger communication picture and needs to fit coherently into the other actions and communication activities of the organization. To build and maintain reputation, social media activities must be in line with other efforts or there will be a disconnect, with the potential to cause audiences to lose trust.

While each organization is unique, there are some general categories of how companies are participating in social media.

1. *Community-building*

Perhaps the broadest way that companies are participating in social media is in engaging with and building online communities. For example, NASA has a robust social

Social networks can be powerful tools for organizations to build, foster, participate in, and grow communities.

media presence across multiple networks (by one count, "the agency has nearly 500 social media accounts"[18]), and has effectively used social media to unite the community of people interested in space and space exploration. From the first tweet from an astronaut in space—@Astro_TJ in 2010—to its active and passionate audiences on Facebook, Google+ and elsewhere, NASA's social media activities show a nuanced understanding of online communities, as well as the agency's role in nurturing and participating in those communities.

We often think of Facebook and other social networks as places to interact with our personal contacts, but these social networks can be powerful tools for corporations, nonprofits and other types of organizations to build, foster, participate in, and grow communities.

2. Customer service

For anyone who has spent thirty minutes on hold with a company's customer service phone line, only then to be transferred from one person to the next without anyone able to actually solve the problem, the notion of being able to go more directly to the source to get help can be very appealing. Particularly on Twitter, companies such as @JetBlue, @ComcastCares, and @Zappos_Service are using accounts to help customers directly. Twitter has become an important customer service channel for many companies to respond to customers' requests for help, problems, or concerns. The use of hashtags and generally public user profiles on Twitter can also help organizations identify potential customer service problems as they happen (or in near real time)—even when the tweets are not addressed specifically to the organization's Twitter account—and potentially staunch problems from spreading and evolving into larger crises.

The public nature of many social media platforms also allows customers to help other customers when something isn't working according to plan, and for companies to share news and updates about service problems with many customers at once.

Customer service is an area where people are hungry for a personal voice and personal expertise, and social media is one set of tools companies are using to try to change the sometimes broken dynamic of traditional customer service.

3. Market research and product development

Social media allows companies to go directly to their customers, potential customers, and a general audience to get immediate and direct feedback on products, services, advertisements or other offerings. Traditional market research—such as focus groups and more quantitative research methodologies such as randomized statistical sampling—are still absolutely critical, but social media can be a helpful complement to (but in general should not replace) other research methods. Social media can also be a helpful tool for organizations conducting competitive market research, by evaluating competitors' social media activities as well.

In addition, organizations are increasingly able to use more sophisticated data mining techniques to analyze large quantities of social media data. Just as Facebook,

Google and others analyze users' behavior and content to tailor the types of advertise-ments shown to them, so too can organizations use large scale data mining of social media to gain insights into business objectives and reputation management issues. (For more, see "Mining Social Media: A Brief Introduction."[19])

A number of companies are also using social media to ask customers and the gen-eral public to help them shape the future of the company and its products. Starbucks introduced the "MyStarbucksIdea" website in March 2008, which allows people to submit ideas that other people can then vote on and discuss.[20] Starbucks then posts items that are under consideration for implementation, and updates the site when new initiatives are launched. In the first year alone, 70,000 ideas were submitted, 94 were "put into action" and 25 were launched, and the site is still active and in use in 2014.[21] Dell, BestBuy and others have similar customer collaboration sites.

4. (Social) media relations

As mainstream media and social media have blended in the last decade, the line between "old media" and "new media" has become increasingly blurred. Today, the vast majority of mainstream media news organizations incorpo-rate social media elements into their online sites and activities, and many online-only sites have the clout and credibility of traditional news organizations. Many journalists today are also active on social media, providing organizations and the individ-uals who represent them another opportunity to connect with and understand the topics that are driving journalists' focus and writing. Many stories that once would have originated on main-stream media sites and then spread to social media now originate on social media and then are picked up by mainstream media. (For more information on the spread of news information online, see the research report, "Meme-tracking and the Dynamics of the News Cycle."[22])

> As mainstream media and social media have blended in the last decade, the line between "old media" and "new media" has become increasingly blurred.

There have also been countless powerful examples of breaking news updates on social media driving the news narrative (whether online or off), with first-hand accounts relayed through Twitter, YouTube or other social media channels (particularly with the aid of smartphones and mobile technology). From the Japanese earthquake, tsunami and Fukashima nuclear disaster, to the Arab Spring, individual updates on the ground have played significant roles in our understanding of breaking events around the world. (Edelman's "Media Clover Leaf" is a helpful illustration of how the types of media today interact and overlap in today's media environment.[23])

In this changing media environment, companies are also working to build rela-tionships with influential individuals, much as they have with influential journalists, working to find the right balance to participate in and add value to the discussion.

Additionally, corporations are sometimes using social media and their own websites as a force of media disintermediation, to talk directly with audiences and to tell their own stories in their own words, instead of relying on the mainstream media—or even influential members of social media—to do so.

Social media is also driving some evolution of the traditional press release and pitching process. In 2006, after a passionate discussion in the blogosphere about the state of the traditional press release, Todd Defren at Shift Communications introduced a template for a "social media release (SMR)."[24] Fast-forward to 2012, and Christopher Penn at Shift Communications said in a post introducing an updated approach to the social media release, **"the Social Media Press Release isn't relevant as a standalone press release** [emphasis his], because these days social media and earned media are one and the same. Gone are the days where you needed separate communications for someone who was in the mainstream media and someone who was a blogger . . . So what does the modern social media press release look like? Social is now embedded in it fully and wholly, and it's one and the same with your traditional press release."[25]

The dynamic of how information is pitched to journalists and online influencers has also been changing. In 2008, Peter Shankman created a service called HARO (Help a Reporter Out) that turns the traditional pitching process on its head. Instead of public relations people pitching journalists, HARO compiles requests from journalists for sources, and those requests are then distributed to a list of potential sources that are subscribers.

5. *Crisis management*

Social media can play roles both big and small during crises today, but social media almost universally plays *some* role, and so social media must be a part of organizations' crisis and reputation management plans.

Nearly every social media site or platform can be used by participants in some way to react to or further spread a crisis.

The form of stakeholder response to crises can take many shapes online: from Twitter hacktivists using accounts like @BPGlobalPR and @ATT_Fake_PR (allowed, with some guidelines, under Twitter's terms of service), to online petition and mobilizing sites like Change.org, to Pinterest boards like "Komen Can Kiss My Mammogram" documenting the Susan G. Komen crisis in 2012,[26] to Facebook groups organizing virtual events to cancel their Netflix accounts, nearly every social media site or platform can be used by participants in some way to react to or further spread a crisis.

Many organizations struggle to respond to the speed with which rumors or hoaxes can spread online, and just as with any type of information correction, it can be challenging for the correct information to spread as widely as the original misinformation.

And the necessity of social media response or participation isn't always driven by factors external to an organization. An accidental @KitchenAidUSA tweet in 2012 about the death of President Obama's grandmother was widely seen as offensive, but the company was able to remove the tweet and respond quickly and appropriately.[27] After the Boston Marathon bombings in 2013, the food website @Epicurious tweeted twice about breakfast items while linking them to the tragedy; the tweets were ultimately removed, but the company had to try twice to get its apologies right.[28] In addition, many organizations struggle to respond to the speed with which rumors or hoaxes can spread online, and just as with any type of information correction, it can be challenging for the correct information to spread as widely as the original misinformation.[29]

This scope and variety of social media interaction with crises requires organizations to be nimble, flexible, fast, and customizable in their social media efforts.

This scope and variety of social media interaction with crises requires organizations to be nimble, flexible, fast, and customizable in their social media efforts, something that can be difficult for organizations to do (particularly large, global and complex organizations).

A word of caution, though: social media (and communication) alone cannot fix larger business problems and, as stated earlier in this chapter, words must match actions to manage reputation and maintain trust. To prepare successfully, organizations need to incorporate social media into their larger crisis management plans; clear roles and responsibilities need to be delineated; and internal and external partners should practice their social media response to crises in advance. These preparatory elements form the core foundation to enable organizations to protect their reputations online during challenging times.

> Social media (and communication) alone cannot fix larger business problems; words must match actions to manage reputation and maintain trust.

(For a robust list of social media crisis examples from 2001–2011, see Jeremiah Owyang's post, "A Chronology of Brands that Got Punk'd by Social Media."[30])

6. *Employee engagement*

Finally, not all of the ways that companies are participating within social media are with external audiences. Using social media to transform internal communication is an important area of corporate social media adoption.

Intranets, or internal and closed networks within organizations, have been around for many years, appearing almost at the beginning of the adoption of the World Wide Web in the mid-1990s. But in the last decade, intranets have increasingly incorporated social media elements, and organizations that encourage internal social media use by individuals may be seeing a direct benefit in their reputation management activities.

> Organizations that encourage internal social media use by individuals may be seeing a direct benefit in their reputation management activities.

APCO Worldwide and Gagen MacDonald's 3rd Annual Employee Engagement Study looked at internal social media use at companies with at least 500 employees, and found that, among other results, "Employees at companies that do a good job with ISM [internal social media] are more likely to advocate to uphold their company's brand and reputation."[31]

Social Media in the Organizational Structure

With many different kinds of organizational involvement in social media, where does social media fit within the organizational structure? Social media elements in the enterprise are being incorporated not only by corporate communications and public relations departments, but also by human resources, marketing, information technology (IT), executive management, customer service, sales, and many other areas.

The Altimeter Group's 2013 report, "The Evolution of Social Business: Six Stages of Social Business Transformation," looked at how social media planning and execution was evolving within large enterprises, but also at "how companies organize their internal structure for social business." The 2013 survey found that there are multiple ways in which organizations structure their social media resources internally, but that today, the majority of large organizations use either a "Centralized" model, where "One department (like Corp Communications) manages all social activities," or a "Hub and Spoke" model, where "A cross-functional team sits in a centralized position and helps various nodes such as business units."[32]

SOCIAL MEDIA CHALLENGES FOR ORGANIZATIONS

Ethics

There are significant ethical issues that organizations must be mindful of when participating in social media, and violating these ethics can damage organizations' reputations. Most companies participating in social media communicate ethically, just as most companies participating in other communication channels communicate ethically. Unfortunately, however, there have been numerous cases of organizations, individuals, or agencies violating ethical boundaries of online behavior. For example, Whole Foods CEO John Mackey posted over one thousand messages under a pseudonym on a Yahoo! message board for more than seven years, on topics both trivial (his haircut) and germane (the merger of Whole Foods with a rival and other topics that had the potential to affect the price of Whole Foods stock). His identity was disclosed through legal proceedings regarding the merger of Whole Foods with Wild Oats.[33] This is one issue that often gets people and companies in trouble online—attempts to obscure identity and affiliation. There used to be an old adage that "On the Internet, nobody knows you're a dog." That simply is not true anymore (if it ever was).

> There used to be an old adage that "On the Internet, nobody knows you're a dog." That simply is not true anymore (if it ever was).

But disclosure is just one ethical challenge for organizations participating in social media. In this area, the Word of Mouth Marketing Association (WOMMA) has an illustrative Code of Ethics,[34] which includes eight standards of conduct, and the core values of trust, integrity, respect, honesty, responsibility, and privacy. In addition, the issue of disclosure also has legal ramifications, discussed later in this section.

Many organizations have also developed their own policies for employees who participate in social media, and the policies most often include ethical considerations. (See the "Social Media Policy Database" for specific policy examples.[35])

Legal

Earlier in this chapter, we talked about the ethics of disclosure, and how disclosure online also has a legal aspect. In 2009, the Federal Trade Commission (FTC) published its updated "Guides Concerning the Use of Endorsements and Testimonials in Advertising," which had last been updated in 1980. The changes "address endorsements by consumers, experts, organizations, and celebrities, as well as the disclosure of important connections between advertisers and endorsers." The updated

EXPERT PERSPECTIVES: SOCIAL MEDIA, ETHICS, AND REPUTATION MANAGEMENT: A BRIEF DISCUSSION

By Phil Gomes, Senior Vice President, Edelman; Co-Founder, CREWE (Corporate Representatives for Ethical Wikipedia Engagement); Founding Fellow, Society for New Communications Research

Broaching the topic of ethics and public relations tends to inspire one of two reactions. In one camp, folks might argue "What? Aren't ethics an *absolute?* Online or offline, public relations or not, what *difference* does it make?" Cruder, more cynical types may take the all-too-easy *Thank-You-For-Smoking*-Meets-*Wag-The-Dog* cheap shot like "Aren't 'ethics' and 'PR' a (*scoff*) *contradiction in terms?*"

I'll grant that, on some level, critics sitting in either camp *may* have a point, however, both camps are *also* equally wrong.

Let's address the latter camp first, simply on the basis of the sheer glibness of this well-worn canard. As anyone in the business will tell you, public relations has been mediocre at its *own* PR. In any case, I doubt that any such critic would want to be judged on the basis of the least or worst among *his or her* chosen line of work.

I strongly believe that PR people who don't engage in ethical practice won't last very long in the trade. Any level of moral flexibility that unscrupulous organizations might value in their public representative will be outweighed by that representative's exhausted, meager reserve of goodwill and near-permanently revoked license to operate among important audiences. Online communities will identify such practitioners as damage to be routed around.

Occasionally (thankfully not *too* often over the past almost two decades) I've had to deliver what I like to call my "Fear of God" talk to a client or prospect. In such cases, I'm approached by a company that thinks not in terms of "What's the right thing to do here?" but "What can I get away with?"

I've found that I can appeal to someone's natural desire to do the right thing 98 percent of the time—convincing them that what they are thinking of doing is against the mores of a community and will likely sour a relationship before it starts. After a moment's consideration, the company realizes that it was a bad idea after all and looks for ethical solutions that do right by all concerned.

For the remaining 2 percent, I know I can put the fear of God in them in terms of the indelible damage to their reputation that will occur when they inevitably get caught. As MTV veejay and podcasting pioneer Adam Curry once said, "There are no secrets. Only information you do not yet have."

Very rarely have I failed to convince a client or prospect of either one. One failure to do so resulted in walking away from a mid-six-figure contract issued by a consumer products company that wanted to, among other things, stuff e-commerce sites with fake reviews—positive for their products, negative for the competitions'. "After all," they reasoned, "we just *know* that all of our competitors are doing the same thing!" The company wasn't interested in alternative recommendations, so we weren't interested in working with them.

A friend once asked me, "Was that a tough choice to make?" I answered, *"What* choice?" Such companies *will* get caught and no amount of money is worth damaging your professional reputation or that of your client or employer.

So, what about the first camp described earlier, which wondered whether ethical questions differ online and offline?

Well, no less an ethics philosopher than the great Van Halen frontman David Lee Roth observed that rock music was little more than folk music delivered at very high velocity, "shot from guns." To him, simply the energy and speed applied was enough to justify the identification of an entirely new genre.

So, through that lens, are "ethics" necessarily different online and offline? Probably not. Lying, misrepresentation, subterfuge, theft . . . all of these are bad things online *and* in the so-called "real world." What *has* changed is that the consequences of engaging in unethical behavior achieve greater velocity and impact today than they did even just a few years ago. Even relatively minor infractions can be amplified and made very available to online search long after the fact, arguably *the* chief determinant today of what most of us call "reputation."

Some criminologists observe that recidivism rates decrease when the punishment from an authoritative source is known, certain and swift. Organizations are only now coming to the realization that the greatest such authority is not a government official or a marquee columnist from a major publication. Rather, this new authority is a connected public who can easily find perceived ethical affronts and, most powerfully, each other.

I sincerely hope that anyone interested or otherwise compelled enough to explore the concept of ethics and PR has a sophisticated view on the topic or is willing to attain one. This requires seeing past the obvious and exploring how companies can be viewed as credible participants, not simply interlopers, in the important and ongoing conversations taking place online. One can't presume to control these conversations, but a good communicator *can* credibly and ethically influence their outcome.

disclosure guidelines require bloggers ("or other 'word-of-mouth' marketers," regardless of social media channel or platform) to disclose "material connections."[36]

For example, "the post of a blogger who receives cash or in-kind payment to review a product is considered an endorsement. Thus, bloggers who make an endorsement must disclose the material connections they share with the seller of the product or service."[37] In 2013, the FTC published additional guidance in ".com Disclosures: How to Make Effective Disclosures in Digital Advertising."[38] The 2013 guidance includes helpful information on *how* to disclose, not just why disclosure is necessary. In the years since the updated guidelines were published, the FTC has reached non-monetary settlements with a number of companies, and the first monetary settlement (for $250,000) was reached in 2011.[39]

For organizations looking for help complying with these disclosure requirements, the FTC has used the mnemonic M.M.M.:

1. Mandate a disclosure policy that complies with the law;
2. Make sure people who work for you or with you know what the rules are; and
3. Monitor what they're doing on your behalf.[40]

There are legal issues other than disclosure to consider in social media as well. Earlier, we talked about how the idea of transparency in social media does not override legal issues and types of content that have always and must remain private and confidential. In *The Corporate Blogging Book*, Debbie Weil notes that legal risks for companies fall into two main areas: "stuff you don't want to reveal (trade secrets, financial information); [and] stuff you can get sued for (copyright, libel, privacy issues)."[41]

Libel laws in the United States also apply to social media, and its critical for communicators and the organizations they represent to understand how libel laws affect their online activities. Whether posted on Facebook, Twitter, Instagram, a blog, or other social media channel, individuals and organizations can be sued for defamatory comments. In a 2011 libel case, the singer Courtney Love paid a fashion designer $430,000 in an out-of-court settlement because of multiple online comments she'd made about the designer.[42]

International laws provide additional social media challenges. For example, in May 2014, the European Court of Justice ruled that Google had to remove particular data results about individuals when asked to do so by those individuals.

Highly regulated industries also have particular legal challenges in participating in social media. Some of the challenges include the following.

- Publicly listed companies cannot make forward-looking statements, discuss earnings or projections or disclose certain other kinds of financial information, including material information, unless done through the appropriate (non-selective) channels.
- Pharmaceutical companies have to consider legal and regulatory guidelines and requirements such as adverse-event reporting and off-label marketing.
- Insurance companies are governed by fifty-one separate regulatory bodies (in all fifty states and Puerto Rico), and cannot market specific products or services on a nationwide basis.
- Alcohol beverage companies must be careful not to market to individuals under the legal drinking age (which is twenty-one in the United States).

For employees, First Amendment laws most often do not protect free speech as it relates to their employment status, and violating legal guidelines in social media. Most employers are "at will" employers, and violating social media or communication legal guidelines can be an offense that can get a person fired without recourse. (In addition, employers in the U.S. and in many countries around the world can legally read and search employee e-mails, computer files and social media posts.)

At heart, the legal guidelines for social media boil down to areas that all employees should consider in any medium of communication and overlap in places with the ethical guidelines. Don't say things you wouldn't say face to face. Don't talk about confidential, proprietary, or forward-looking information. Be careful with copyrighted and trademarked material. Don't

Don't say things you wouldn't say face to face. Don't talk about confidential, proprietary, or forward-looking information. Be careful with copyrighted and trademarked material. Don't disguise your identity or affiliation. Don't use libelous, defamatory language. Don't reveal private information about your co-workers. In short, think before posting, tweeting or updating.

disguise your identity or affiliation. Don't use libelous, defamatory language. Don't reveal private information about your co-workers. In short, think before posting, tweeting or updating.

Bias

While social media has become increasingly ingrained in many people's daily lives in the United States (and in much of the world), there are issues of bias to consider, and organizations should be mindful of ways that potential bias may creep into their social media activities.

Ethan Zuckerman, of the Center for Civic Media at MIT, in writing about political discourse that can be extrapolated to corporate participation in social media, described "at least three filters in the voices we hear—access, language and bias."[43] Access to technology and social media is not universal, and access does not automatically correlate to knowing how to use the technology or social media channel. Think of the counter worker at a fast food establishment—how or when would he or she have access at work (both in terms of time and technology) to social media, or to the social media channels of the business? Taking this consideration into mind might mean altering elements of an organizations' communication strategy to reach the desired stakeholders.

Language is another consideration for organizations with multi-lingual audiences. An organization might ask itself, "Are certain kinds of communication only happening in English that should also be happening in another language?" Some kinds of social media are starting to incorporate translation ability into the channel itself, but this area is still developing. In addition, even if an organization is not generating social media content in other languages, it may be important for certain organizations to at least *monitor* content in other languages. Failure to do so may leave an organization's reputation at risk.

Bias might mean only following certain kinds of bloggers or other active social media participants to the exclusion of differing voices. While it's understandable (and generally encouraged) for organizations to link actively to others with views that support their own, that doesn't mean organizations can't or shouldn't listen to differing voices. The concept of "homophily" has been used to describe this phenomenon as it occurs online.[44] As Zuckerman wrote in another post on this subject, "Homophily" is a remarkably useful term, a compact word that succinctly expresses the idea that "birds of a feather flock together"—that you're likely to befriend, talk to, work with and share ideas with people who've got common ethnic, religious and economic background with you. . . . My argument, basically, is that it's possible to miss huge trends, changes and opportunities by talking solely to people who agree with you."[45] At their core, sites like Facebook and other social networks actively work to bring people of common backgrounds together. But while organizations may not be actively engaging with differing voices online, organizations can often benefit from listening to those voices.

In addition, it's important to note again that just because one social network— or any other social media channel—may be perceived to be more broadly popular, organizations should consider their specific goals and audience when developing a strategy for engagement and not neglect social media channels that may in fact be a better fit for their goals and audience.

Attacks and Campaigns

A major potential reputational issue for an organization is a targeted, coordinated attack or campaign within social media. In the face of such an attack, the key is to determine if the critic's position is based on a deficit, fault, or problem in the company, its leadership or its product(s)—basically, whether there is a basis in fact in the campaign, and thus, potentially room for improvement.

Perhaps the most famous example of a company that encountered a collective online outcry over its products and customer service was Dell. In June 2005, new media guru Jeff Jarvis first wrote on his blog, BuzzMachine.com, about his problems with the Dell products he owned and with the customer service he'd encountered, with a post called "Dell lies. Dell sucks."[46] The technical and customer service problems Jarvis detailed resonated with others. The outcry spread and became known as "Dell Hell." Followed by video of an exploding laptop (and subsequent recall) as well as falling earnings, it seemed that Dell's problems were practically insurmountable. The company also was not participating in the conversation that was happening about them in social media, and their absence in the face of the storm added more fuel to the fire.

Dell slowly worked to rebuild its reputation and regain the trust and support of the public and its customers through a combination of product and customer service adjustments, as well as through communication on its own blogs, outreach to others, and dialogue in social media channels. The company's worked paid off, and slightly over two years after the original "Dell Hell" post, Jarvis wrote a column that appeared in *BusinessWeek* titled, "Dell learns to listen," in which he said, "In the age of customers empowered by blogs and social media, Dell has leapt from worst to first."[47] But did you catch that timeframe? Two years. That's not a short amount of time for a company to be dealing with those kinds of widespread problems and complaints. While Dell has turned around, it took a tremendous amount of sustained work to make it happen. Dell now has a sophisticated and integrated social media presence that encompasses both external and internal audiences, all working to help build and reinforce its reputation.[48]

AIR FORCE WEB POSTING ASSESSMENT RESPONSE DIAGRAM

But what if the online attack is not necessarily based on an underlying problem or fact? The United States Air Force has developed a "Web Posting Response Assessment" (see Figure 4.1) that is a useful starting point for helping to analyze how, if and when to respond online.[49]

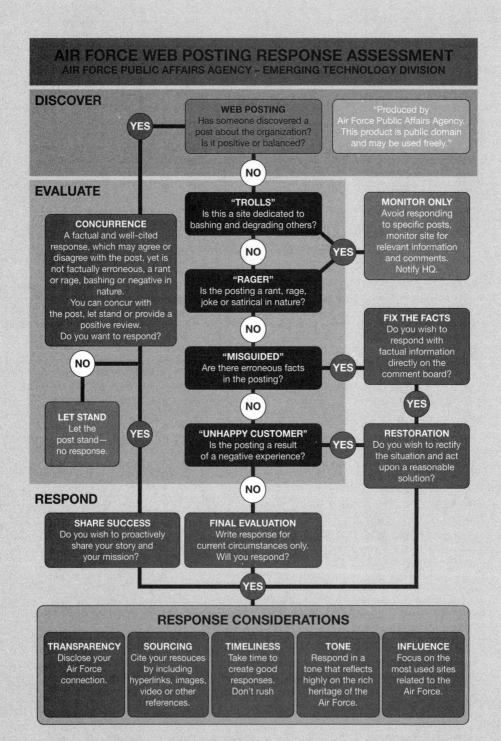

Figure 4.1 U.S. Air Force web posting response assessment

CASE STUDY: #SOCHIPROBLEMS: THE 2014 WINTER OLYMPICS

The news reports that surround the start of an Olympic Games are usually pretty predictable: inspirational stories about individual athletes; speculation about which country will come out on top of the medal count; debate about the amount of money the host country has spent in preparation for the Games; concerns about security and threat protection. Discussion of the state of restroom facilities and hotel rooms is not usually on the list.

But despite Russia spending $51 billion on the 2014 Winter Olympics in Sochi, the social media narrative at the start of the Olympics was dominated by reports of mishaps, inconveniences and more serious problems. A Twitter account, @SochiProblems, and hashtag #SochiProblems, quickly attracted attention and followers by aggregating visitors' frustrations and, within three days, the account had 178,000 followers, more than the official @Sochi2014 Winter Olympics Twitter account at the time. (More than 350,000 ended up following @SochiProblems over the course of the Games.) "In 24 hours alone, 26,000 tweets have been sent using the hashtag #SochiProblems."[50] And in the first days of the Games, the hashtag #SochiProblems "had been mentioned on social media platforms more than 'Team USA,' 'Putin' or 'opening ceremony.'"[51] In addition, there were countless broadcast and print media reports about the challenges in Sochi too.

Even when not using the specific hashtag #SochiProblems, reporters shared news about half-finished rooms and undrinkable water via social media. A reporter for the *Chicago Tribune*, Stacy St. Clair, tweeted: "My hotel has no water. If restored, the front desk says, 'do not use on your face because it contains something very dangerous.' #Sochi2014"[52] Her next tweet included a photo of yellow water in glasses: "Water restored, sorta. On the bright side, I now know what very dangerous face water looks like. #Sochi #unfiltered"[53]

Visitors, reporters and athletes posted information and photos of roving stray dogs in the streets, unfinished or barely finished hotel rooms, strange toilet configurations, double-booked or missing room reservations, locked fire doors, and all manner of non-working mechanical, electrical or plumbing parts in hotels, shops and other parts of the Olympic park. "My hotel room has no internet, no hot water, no curtains and no furniture. On the plus side, three of the four lights work. #Sochi2014," tweeted reporter Jian Ghomeshi.[54]

Even the International Olympic Committee's chief supervisor of the 2014 Olympics, Jean-Claude Killy, acknowledged that the organizers didn't realize the scope of the hotel construction difficulties until very close to the start of the Games. "We realized it too late," Killy said. "All the alarms went up in September . . . I made a special trip. I said, 'What do we need to do?' There is no way to organize a Games if you cannot accommodate people."[55]

The physical reality on the ground combined with this widespread social media narrative to damage the reputation of the 2014 Olympics, despite the fact that the athletic contests themselves went off relatively smoothly, and the biggest fear prior to the start of the Games in Sochi—a terrorist act or threat—did not come to pass. With the next Olympics scheduled to take place in Rio de Janeiro, Brazil, in 2016, time will tell if the organizers have learned the reputational lessons from Sochi.

▶ GENERAL BEST PRACTICES

1.   *Listen and monitor*

While there's certainly disagreement about some aspects of how organizations should participate in social media, most everyone would agree that the first step for

any individual or organization is to listen. In other words, just as you'd begin almost any type of communication planning with research, listen to people on blogs, on Twitter, on YouTube. Listen to what people are saying about you, your organization, your product or service, your competitors. Where are they talking? What are they saying? Who are they talking to and with? How do they expect you or the organization to respond or participate?

What are the risks of not listening?

But, you might say, that's a lot of conversations. There's no way I can follow all of that. It's too much information, coming too quickly, from too many people. First, there are tools and techniques to help manage the flow of information. And second, what are the risks of not listening?

These are just a few of the ways that can help manage the flow of information:

*   Create Google Alerts for all relevant search terms for you and/or your organization (brands, leaders, products and/or services, competitors).
*   Set up an RSS reader and subscribe to relevant content.
*   Use a desktop or mobile application for Twitter and other social networks to add greater flexibility for managing existing social media accounts, sorting, measuring, and following information.
*   Explore some of the sites where you can search the real-time Web (beyond simply Google), such as Social Mention and others.
*   As you get more advanced, you may want to consider whether you have a need for a paid social media monitoring service.

As you listen and explore, you'll begin to discover what topics or issues are most important to the people that matter to you. With time and by listening to the community, it will also help you determine the thought leaders and influential members of your network. And with time, you'll begin to see where there are opportunities to join—and potentially start or guide—the conversation.

2. *Plan and integrate*

Once you've done your research, then the more intensive planning should take place. Just like other forms of communication, organizational participation in social media should be strategically planned and integrated with the organization's broader business and communication goals. Remember the kinds of disconnect between actions and communication that we talked about earlier, and how it has the potential to hurt an organization's reputation and perception of authenticity? Planning and coherent integration of social media is a crucial best practice.

A few important questions to ask in your planning process include:

- How will your social media efforts tie to your larger business and communication goals and objectives?
- What communication efforts are already underway, and how can social media play a part?
- Who will lead, manage and update content shared online?
- How will you measure and integrate results?
- What potential risks can you identify and plan to mitigate in advance?

These are just a few of the questions that should be addressed, but developing a strategy for social media participation should come before implementing the actual tools or channels.

3. *Help your employees help themselves*

Develop a social media policy, and then educate and empower your employees. Organizations take different approaches to social media policies, but many of the guidance and rules that apply to other forms of communication also apply to social media. Private, confidential, proprietary, and other kinds of information still must be kept within the organization. But employees can also be the best ambassadors for an organization, and can be an organization's best asset for building and maintaining reputation online.

4. *Measure, and be prepared for the feedback*

Organizations also need to evaluate and measure social media activities, and make adjustments based on those results. In 2013, the Conclave, a coalition of industry associations and corporate representatives, released social media measurement standards addressing six key areas:

1. Content and Sourcing
2. Reach and Impressions
3. Engagement and Conversation

4.   Influence
5.   Opinion and Advocacy
6.   Impact and Value.[56]

The coalition included PR and social media agencies, major industry associations, such as the Council of PR Firms (CPRF), Public Relations Society of America (PRSA), the Institute for Public Relations (IPR), the International Association for the Measurement and Evaluation of Communications (AMEC), and others, as well as individuals from major corporations. The full standards document includes useful descriptions and applications of social media metrics, as well as completed examples.[57]

And it doesn't just end with measurement. Many times, an organization will get through the first few steps of social media engagement, but then won't know what to do or how to handle the feedback that is coming from online audiences. (And it can be particularly difficult for management within organizations to process or be able to respond to negative feedback.) You might ask the following kinds of questions:

- How will different departments work together to address feedback?
- Is the organization prepared to respond quickly?
- Is the organization able or willing to incorporate suggestions for improvement?

These are just a few to get started. What else might you ask?

5.   *Embrace opportunity*

Finally, social media can sometimes be scary and intimidating to people and organizations looking to expand their online efforts. Sometimes people feel like they're late to the party and don't know how to catch up. But there are many different kinds of opportunities within social media, and if you see the possibilities in terms of how it fits within your broader communication, business and reputation management goals, it just might seem a little less daunting. The technology, terms, and particular services will undoubtedly change, but the underlying cultural shifts will likely remain.

▶ RESOURCES FOR FURTHER STUDY

In addition to the resources and books cited throughout the chapter, here are some additional online resources for further study.

Altimeter Group's research reports, http://www.altimetergroup.com/research/reports
The Berkman Center for Internet and Society at Harvard University: http://cyber.law.harvard.edu/.
Common Craft's videos on social media, social networking and other technologies: http://www.commoncraft.com/videolist.
Edelman Trust Barometer: http://www.edelman.com/insights/intellectual-property/2014-edelman-trust-barometer/.

First Monday, an academic, open-access journal with extensive research papers on social
    media, http://firstmonday.org.
Mashable, http://mashable.com/.
Pew Research Center's Internet and American Life Project, http://www.pewinternet.org/.
The Poynter Institute's articles on social media, http://www.poynter.org/tag/social-media-2/.
PROpenMic, a "social network for public relations students, faculty and PR pros worldwide,"
    http://www.propenmic.org/.

▶ QUESTIONS FOR FURTHER DISCUSSION

1. How is social media changing the way that companies communicate? What
        hasn't changed?

2. What are some of the ethical challenges a company may face in social media, and
        how can a company alleviate those challenges?

3. How are mainstream media and social media interacting with each other, and
        how do you see that relationship continuing in the future?

4. How is social media affecting public relations?

5. What's different today about social media than when this chapter was written
        in 2014?

▶ NOTES

1 Tim O'Reilly. "What is Web 2.0: Design Patterns and Business Models for the Next
   Generation of Software," *O'Reilly*, September 30, 2005, http://oreilly.com/web2/archive/
   what-is-web-20.html.
2 Doc Searls, "Linux for Suits—The World Live Web," *Linux Journal,* October 31, 2005, http://
   www.linuxjournal.com/article/8549.
3 danah boyd, "Social Media is Here to Stay . . . Now What?", Microsoft Research Tech Fest,
   February 26, 2009 and Mass Tech Leadership Council, April 30, 2009, http://www.danah.
   org/papers/talks/MSRTechFest2009.html.
4 Charlene Li and Josh Bernoff, *Groundswell: Winning in a World Transformed by Social Technologies*
   (Cambridge, MA: Harvard Business Review Press, expanded and revised edition, 2011).
5 Pew Internet and American Life Project, http://www.pewinternet.org/.
6 Dan Gillmor, *We the Media: Grassroots Journalism By the People, For the People* (Sebastopol, CA:
   O'Reilly Media, 2004), p. 26.
7 Chris Anderson, "The Long Tail," *Wired,* October 2004, http://archive.wired.com/wired/
   archive/12.10/tail.html, and *The Long Tail: Why the Future of Business is Selling Less of More*
   (New York: Hyperion, 2006).
8 Rick Levine, Christopher Locke, Doc Searls and David Weinberger, *The Cluetrain Manifesto:
   10th Anniversary Edition* (New York: Basic Books, 2009), p. xiv.
9 Ibid, p. xiv.
10 Clay Shirky, "How Social Media Can Make History." *TED@State*, June 2009, http://www.
   ted.com/talks/clay_shirky_how_cellphones_twitter_facebook_can_make_history.

11 Arthur W. Page Society, "The Authentic Enterprise: An Arthur W. Page Society Report." 2007, http://www.awpagesociety.com/images/uploads/2007AuthenticEnterprise.pdf.

12 *Worn Wear: A Film About the Stories We Wear.* Patagonia, November 2013, http://www.youtube.com/watch?v=z20CjCim8DM.

13 Edelman, *2014 Edelman Trust Barometer Executive Summary.* http://www.edelman.com/insights/intellectual-property/2014-edelman-trust-barometer/about-trust/executive-summary/, p. 1.

14 Don Tapscott and David Ticoll, *The Naked Corporation: How the Age of Transparency Will Revolutionize Business* (New York: Free Press, 2003), p. xi.

15 Ibid, p. xii.

16 Burson-Marsteller, *Burson-Marsteller's Global Social Media Check-Up 2012.* http://www.burson-marsteller.com/Innovation_and_insights/Thought_Leadership/default_view.aspx?ID=99.

17 Brian Solis and JESS3, *The Conversation Prism,* http://www.conversationprism.com/.

18 Rick Mulready, "What NASA Can Teach You About Social-Media Marketing," *Entrepreneur,* July 30, 2013, http://www.entrepreneur.com/article/227603.

19 Pritam Gundecha and Huan Liu, "Mining Social Media: A Brief Introduction," *INFORMS TutORials in Operations Research,* vol. 9. INFORMS, Hanover, MD, 2012, pp. 1–17, http://www.public.asu.edu/~pgundech/book_chapter/smm.pdf.

20 Starbucks, *My Starbucks Idea,* http://mystarbucksidea.force.com/.

21 Starbucks, "Happy Birthday MSI!," *My Starbucks Idea,* March 19, 2009, http://blogs.starbucks.com/blogs/customer/archive/2009/03/19/happy-birthday-msi.aspx.

22 Jure Leskovec, Lars Backstrom and Jon Kleinberg. "Meme-tracking and the Dynamics of the News Cycle." *KDD '09 Proceedings of the 15th ACM SIGKDD international conference on Knowledge discovery and data mining,* June 28, 2009, pp. 497–506, http://www.cs.cornell.edu/home/kleinber/kdd09-quotes.pdf .

23 Edelman, *Cloverleaf,* http://www.edelman.com/who-we-are/about-edelman/the-details/cloverleaf/.

24 Shift Communications, *Social Media Press Release Template, Version 1.0,* http://www.shiftcomm.com/downloads/smprtemplate.pdf.

25 Christopher Penn, "Social Media Press Release 2.0," *Shift Communications,* December 20, 2012, http://www.shiftcomm.com/2012/12/social-media-press-release-2-0/.

26 Beth Kanter, "Komen Can Kiss My Mammagram: Documenting the pinklash," *Pinterest,* http://www.pinterest.com/kanter/komen-can-kiss-my-mammagram/.

27 Mark Memmott, "KitchenAid Apologizes for 'Offensive Tweet' About Obama's Grandmother." *NPR's The Two-Way,* October 4, 2012, http://www.npr.org/blogs/thetwo-way/2012/10/04/162293140/kitchenaid-apologizes-for-offensive-tweet-about-obamas-grandmother.

28 Lauren Indvik, "'Epicurious' Enrages Followers With Boston Bombings Tweets," *Mashable.* April 17, 2013, http://mashable.com/2013/04/17/epicurious-boston-bombings-tweets/.

29 Andrew Phelps, "Hacking For Truth, Whatever That Is: Ideas to fight misinformation," *Nieman Journalism Lab,* March 8, 2012, http://www.niemanlab.org/2012/03/hacking-for-truth-whatever-that-is-ideas-to-fight-misinformation/.

30 Jeremiah Owyang, "A Chronology of Brands that Got Punk'd by Social Media," *WebStrategist.com,* posted May 2, 2008, updated through 2011, http://www.web-strategist.com/blog/2008/05/02/a-chonology-of-brands-that-got-punkd-by-social-media/.

31 APCO Worldwide and Gagen MacDonald, "Unleashing the Power of Social Media Within Your Organziation," January 26, 2012, http://www.slideshare.net/apcoworldwide/unleashing-the-power-of-internal-social-media.

32 Charlene Li and Brian Solis, with Alan Webber and Jaimy Szymanski, "The Evolution of Social Business: Six Stages of Social Business Transformation," *Altimeter Group,* March 6, 2013, http://www.slideshare.net/Altimeter/the-evolution-of-social-business-six-stages-of-social-media-transformation. (In addition, Altimeter Group's research reports include additional information about the state of social media in large organizations today.)

33 Andrew Martin, "Whole Foods Executive Used Alias." *The New York Times,* July 12, 2007, http://www.nytimes.com/2007/07/12/business/12foods.html.

34 WOMMA (Word of Mouth Marketing Association), *"The WOMMA Code of Ethics,"* http://www.womma.org/ethics/womma-code-of-ethics.

35 Chris Boudreaux, "Social Media Policy Database," *Social Media Governance*, http://social mediagovernance.com/policies/.

36 Federal Trade Commission, "Guides Concerning the Use of Endorsements and Testimonials in Advertising Federal Acquisition Regulation; Final Rule," *Federal Register*, October 15, 2009, http://www.ftc.gov/sites/default/files/documents/federal_register_notices/guides-concerning-use-endorsements-and-testimonials-advertising-16-cfr-part-255/091015guidesconcerning testimonials.pdf.

37 Federal Trade Commission, "FTC Publishes Final Guides Governing Endorsements, Testimonials: Changes Affect Testimonial Advertisements, Bloggers, Celebrity Endorsements," *FTC.gov*, October 5, 2009, http://www.ftc.gov/news-events/press-releases/2009/10/ftc-publishes-final-guides-governing-endorsements-testimonials.

38 Federal Trade Commission, ".com Disclosures: How to Make Effective Disclosures in Digital Advertising," *FTC.gov*, March 12, 2013, http://www.ftc.gov/sites/default/files/attachments/press-releases/ftc-staff-revises-online-advertising-disclosure-guidelines/130312dotcomdisclosures.pdf.

39 Federal Trade Commission, "Firm to Pay FTC $250,000 to Settle Charges That It Used Misleading Online 'Consumer' and 'Independent' Reviews," *FTC.gov*, March 15, 2011, http://www.ftc.gov/news-events/press-releases/2011/03/firm-pay-ftc-250000-settle-charges-it-used-misleading-online.

40 Lesley Fair, "Using Social Media in Your Marketing? Staff Closing Letter is Worth a Read," *FTC Business Center Blog*, December 22, 2011, http://www.business.ftc.gov/blog/2011/12/using-social-media-your-marketing-staff-closing-letter-worth-read.

41 Weil, Debbie, *The Corporate Blogging Book.* New York: Penguin Group, 2006, p. 10.

42 Jennifer Preston, "Courtney Love Settles Twitter Defamation Case," *The New York Times,* March 4, 2011, http://artsbeat.blogs.nytimes.com/2011/03/04/courtney-love-settles-twitter-defamation-case/.

43 Ethan Zuckerman, "Activist Media and Selective Amplifiers," . . . *My Heart's in Accra,* July 7, 2009, http://www.ethanzuckerman.com/blog/2009/07/07/activist-media-and-selective-amplifiers/.

44 Ethan Zuckerman, "Homophily, Serendipity, Zenophobia." . . . *My Heart's in Accra,* April 25, 2009, http://www.ethanzuckerman.com/blog/2008/04/25/homophily-serendipity-xenophilia/.

45 Ibid.

46 Jeff Jarvis, "Dell Lies. Dell Sucks," *BuzzMachine,* June 21, 2005, http://www.buzzmachine.com/archives/2005_06_21.html.

47 Jeff Jarvis, "Dell Learns to Listen," *BloombergBusinessweek*, October 17, 2007, http://www.businessweek.com/stories/2007-10-17/dell-learns-to-listenbusinessweek-business-news-stock-market-and-financial-advice.

48 Jennifer Rooney, "In Dell Social-Media Journey, Lessons for Marketers About the Power of Listening," *Forbes*, September 25, 2012, http://www.forbes.com/sites/jenniferrooney/2012/09/25/in-dell-social-media-journey-lessons-for-marketers-about-the-power-of-listening/.

49 United States Air Force, Air Force Public Affairs Agency——Emerging Technology Division. "Air Force Web Posting Response Assessment." http://www.afpc.af.mil/shared/media/document/AFD-091210-037.pdf

50 David Nelson, Tweet, February 6, 2014, https://twitter.com/DavidNelsonNews/status/431393272871669760.

51 Sam Laird, "'Social Problems' a Twitter Hit as Olympic Schadenfreude Grows," *Mashable,* February 6, 2014, http://mashable.com/2014/02/06/sochi-problems-twitter/.

52 Stacy St. Clair, @StacyStClair Tweet, February 3, 2014, https://twitter.com/StacyStClair/status/430536725341798402.

53 Ibid., @StacyStClair Tweet, February 3, 2014, https://twitter.com/StacyStClair/status/430550673977913344.

54 Jian Ghomeshi, @JianGhomeshi Tweet, February 5, 2014, http://mashable.com/2014/02/06/sochi-problems-twitter/.

55 Matthew Futterman and Gregory L. White, "Sochi Olympics Official: We Realized Hotel Problems 'Too Late,'" *Wall Street Journal*, February 17, 2014, http://online.wsj.com/news/articles/SB10001424052702304899704579388882111244174.

56 The Conclave, "Complete Social Media Measurement Standards ," June 2013, http://www.smmstandards.com/wp-content/uploads/2012/06/Complete-standards-document2.pdf.

57 Ibid.

CHAPTER

5 ORGANIZATIONAL COMMUNICATION

By Jeff Grimshaw,
Tanya Mann, and
Lynne Viscio

The challenge: To align employees' hands, minds, and hearts with the organization's reputational interests.

■ ■ ■

ALIGNING HANDS, MINDS, HEARTS . . . AND SOULS

The day after the Congress of Cardinals elected him pontiff, Pope Francis realized he'd forgotten to check out of his hotel room. So he got on a bus with some other cardinals and they went back and he took care of the bill. Presumably the papacy comes with plenty of perks—and lots of people could have taken care of this for him. But he chose to do it himself.

When asked about this, he cited the obvious: He needed to settle his bill. But he also noted that he wanted to set an example for the cardinals and the bishops regarding how he would like to see them act.

Then, very shortly into his tenure, he fired the "Bishop of Bling," who spent $43 million not to promote the mission of the Catholic Church, but to build a palatial residence (including luxury bathtub and private gym). Since then, Pope Francis sacked four of the five cardinals who were responsible for directing the scandal-tainted Vatican Bank.

Meanwhile, he's spending significant time with the poor, sick, and disfigured. He's also posing for selfies with teenagers.

Clearly, this is a leader who knows very well how to create meaning and shape culture in the organization he leads. He follows the admonition of his namesake, St. Francis of Assisi, who said, "Preach the gospel at all times. If necessary, use words." But because the messages sent by Francis' actions are so powerful and consistent, people are tuning into his words as well. Attendance at Papal Audiences at St. Peter's Square has increased fourfold. There's even buzz about what topic he'll address in his next encyclical.

In the world of business, there are some senior leaders whose instincts for how to create meaning, shape culture, and align the organization are as good as Pope Francis'. But the vast majority can pull this off only with the support of a very strong and strategic communication function.

■ ■ ■

ALIGNING EMPLOYEES IS ESSENTIAL TO REPUTATION MANAGEMENT

In order to have a great reputation—and to sustain it—an organization needs to align its employees' behaviors and performance in support of business results and reputational interests.

> Strategic organizational communication: The process of aligning employees' "hands, minds, and hearts" with the organization's reputational interests—as a way to produce competitive advantage.

This isn't easy to do. Which is why many senior leaders complain about the support they get from their internal communication function—whether it's housed in Corporate Communications, HR, or somewhere else. They say that their current internal communication function isn't "strategic" enough—although these leaders usually aren't quite sure what a more strategic internal communication function would look like. They say the work that their internal communicators do is too often irrelevant to the advancement of their leadership agenda and the organization's long-term business and reputational interests.

At the same time, there are plenty of senior executives who are very happy with their internal communication function, because they see it playing an instrumental and indispensable role in the advancement of their leadership agenda and the organization's long-term business and reputational interests.

So what's the difference between the internal communication function that's irrelevant and the internal communication function that's indispensable? The answer, in our experience, is the adoption and execution of five best practices. Specifically, the best internal communicators:

1. **Don't just focus on producing great, creative *output*. They focus on helping leaders create *outcomes*.** They directly and measurably advance the leadership agenda by aligning hands, minds, and hearts in support of business results and reputational interests. Cool new communication products, events, and technologies, when used, are merely a means to an end. Never for their own sake.

2. **Successfully position themselves as trusted advisors to the leaders they serve.** This is important for a lot of reasons. One is that formal communication is a single channel (and arguably the weakest) via which organizations create and manage meaning and shape culture. Intentionally or not, leaders and organizations also continuously broadcast messages through their decisions and actions, through what they reward and recognize, through what they tolerate (or don't), and through how they show up informally. With trusted-advisor status, communicators can help leaders deliberately and consistently broadcast consistent messages across multiple frequencies.

3. **Recognize that they are competing for employees' attention in an increasingly crowded information marketplace.** As the influential social scientist Herbert Simon observed four decades ago, attention is a scarce resource, and therefore, "a wealth of information creates a poverty of attention."[1] If information peddled internally isn't reliable, relevant, and easy to engage and

process, we shouldn't be surprised when employees choose not to *pay* attention. Economists call this "rational ignorance." That's when consumers determine that the value of becoming informed about something isn't worth the time investment and energy costs involved. From that perspective, paying attention would be an irrational economic activity.

4. **Help leaders tell a consistent story and connect the dots.** Our brains are hardwired for stories. That's why information presented in a recognizable archetype form is more memorable and emotionally resonant to employees. The most common archetype is to the *quest*. So one of the easiest, most compelling ways to earn employees' attention is use a consistent storyline about "where we're going, how we're going to get there," and the role that each employee plays in reaching the destination.

5. **Equip employees for "moments of truth and trade-off."** In too many organizations, the guiding principles or values are just words on a poster or tchotchkes. The strongest internal communication functions promote the organization's long-term reputational interests by working with leaders to equip employees for situations where living the values competes with short-term profit or productivity or is otherwise inconvenient.

The rest of the chapter elaborates on these five best practices.

1. THE BEST INTERNAL COMMUNICATORS DON'T JUST FOCUS ON PRODUCING GREAT, CREATIVE OUTPUT; THEY FOCUS ON HELPING LEADERS CREATE OUTCOMES

Historically, leaders in large organizations have looked to the employee communication function to play a primarily tactical role, focused on delivering formal communication *products* "to specs." In this model, the employee communication department is an internal vendor. Communicators provide value and make names for themselves based on their writing, editing, event management, and production skills, as well as their proficiency in the latest communication tools and social media. What gets measured is attention ("How many people visited our news page on the intranet site last week?"), as opposed to actual behavior change ("Are we helping leaders align performance and behavior? And how much?").

The alternative—one that provides significantly more value—is to focus on out-*comes* before focusing on out*put*. To that end, we have, for many years, found it useful to equip our clients with a process we call Know/Feel/Do™. It's simple, but requires rigor and discipline to engage the leaders who are sponsoring a particular communication effort around a few questions:

• What's the business context? What results have you committed to produce?
• To produce these results, what audiences will you need to effectively inform, influence, align, and engage?

- As a result of the communication choices I help you to make and execute, what do we need each targeted audience to *know*? (In other words, what objective knowledge must they possess and understand?) What do we need them to *feel*? (In other words, what beliefs or emotions do we want to change or reinforce?) And then what do we want them to *do*? (In other words, how do we want them to act?)

And then the communicator strictly rationalizes the communication strategy and the investment of finite resources against those specific *know*, *feel*, and *do* outcomes.

As in any strategic endeavor, it's really about "starting with the end in mind." As some of our clients with military backgrounds have observed, the "Know / Feel / Do™" exercise is a way for leaders to equip communicators with "commander's intent" or "CI." As brothers Chip and Dan Heath describe in their bestseller *Made to Stick*, "CI is a crisp, plain-talk statement that appears at the top of every order, specifying . . . the end-state of an operation . . . when people know the desired destination, they're free to improvise, as needed, in arriving there."[2]

> In the Marine Corps, descriptions of CI often begin with the phrase: "Final result desired is . . ."

In the Marine Corps, descriptions of CI often begin with the phrase: "Final result desired is . . ." When soldiers—or in this case, communicators—know the desired outcome, they can stay focused on what's really important even in the heat of battle—and more effectively use their smarts, skills, and creativity to achieve desired results for their leaders.

A growing number of organizations have integrated "Know / Feel / Do™" into their annual strategic planning process, so that their entire employee communication and alignment strategy for the year is directly, explicitly, and measurably aligned with the senior leadership agenda. Lonnie Ross, who leads internal communication at DTE Energy, a Michigan-based Fortune 500 company, explains how it works there:

> During the summer and fall, our leaders go through a rigorous process to shape business strategy for the following year. The tail-end of that process is the perfect time to engage them around how we can help them align employees in support of the strategy they've just shaped. Our leaders know they can't successfully implement strategy all on their own. They'll need the support and discretionary energy of our 10,000 employees. So we really dig into the questions in a rigorous way: "What, as a result of our overall communication choices in the coming year, will we need our employees to know, and feel, and do . . . if we're going to achieve the business outcomes to which you've committed?"

In the course of that process, senior leaders might come up with fifty potential know, feel, and do goals to guide internal communication strategy for the coming year. "But we can't focus on 50 things," Ms. Ross says. "We can only focus on twelve to fifteen. And so we take our senior leaders through a prioritization process."

The prioritization process culminates when the CEO and the Executive Committee solidify the know, feel, and do goals for the coming year. "This year," Ross says, our senior leaders selected five "know" goals. For example, as a result of our overall communication efforts, we want employees to know how their work supports our aspiration to become the best-operated energy company in North America. Our senior leaders selected four "feel" goals. For example, as a result of our overall communication efforts, we want employees to feel able to contribute and make a difference. And our leaders selected four "do" goals. For example, we want employees to hold themselves and one another accountable for safety.

With the thirteen know, feel, and do goals for the coming year formalized by the Executive Committee, Ms. Ross and her team did three things:

- **First**, they used an employee survey to conduct a baseline measurement, "so everyone knows where we're starting from in our efforts to 'move the needle' on the Executive Committee's leadership agenda, as represented by the know, feel, and do goals, says Ross."
- **Second**, they developed an internal communication strategy for the coming year that is strictly rationalized against the Executive Committee's know, feel, and do goals. "Lots of people have great ideas. Maybe they've heard about something cool that another company is doing with their communication program. And we're always looking at emerging best practices. But if we can't make the case that this new communication product is the best way to move the needle on the leadership agenda here, this year, we're not going to do it. We are focused on putting our efforts on the things that represent our highest and best use as communicators. That means sometimes saying no, but only when we have a rationale for why we are saying no," Ross says.
- **Third**, Ms. Ross and her team partner with other functions in pursuit of a common set of goals. "We're not the only ones creating meaning in the organization," Ross acknowledges. "If we're going to move the needle on the leadership agenda, we've got to work arm-in-arm with HR, the Continuous Improvement function, the Organizational Effectiveness team, and others. The Executive Committee's know, feel, and do goals give us a common set of outcomes for which leadership is holding us all accountable. And so we're partnering more effectively than we did in the past."

Then, over the course of the year, DTE Energy measures progress against its Executive Committee's know, feel, and do goals every four months. "So we know where we've moving the needle, and where we aren't. That allows us to double down on the things that are working and, where needed, recalibrate our communication strategy throughout the year," Ross says.

> New to our process is looking at comparisons across business units. If we're strong in one area and weak in another, we look at opportunities to share what's working in one area and apply it more consistently across the enterprise. And we use statistical modeling to identify which "know" and "feel" levers give us our best opportunities to shape what employees "do."

Because in the final analysis, it's all about aligning employee behavior in pursuit of our strategy and our reputation with our customers, community, and shareholders.

Elevating internal communication as a strategic business process gives leaders a strong sense of ownership, Ross says. "They think really carefully about the communication objectives for the year. They're clear on how achieving the know, feel, and do outcomes enables their leadership agenda and the business results to which they've committed. So when the survey scores aren't as high as we'd like, leaders don't just ask what the communication team is doing to move the needle. They also ask, 'What do *we* need to do?'"

2. THE BEST INTERNAL COMMUNICATORS SUCCESSFULLY POSITION THEMSELVES AS TRUSTED ADVISORS TO THE LEADERS THEY SERVE

Why is this so important? With trusted-advisor status, internal communicators earn the jurisdiction with the leaders they support to:

- Ask questions
- Push back
- Coach

The jurisdiction to ask questions. It's hard to be a strategist if you can't ask questions to determine what outcomes a particular communication activity is intended to create. But many times senior leaders go to communicators having already identified what output they want the communicator to produce. ("Make a video of me talking about our growth strategy. Make it look like a video I saw at a conference I attended last month.") Calling a timeout to ask questions—"Okay, boss, before we shoot that video, let's talk about the 'know, feel, and do' outcomes we're trying to create"—slows down the process and can frustrate the executive. Trusted-advisor status provides the jurisdiction to call that strategic timeout and move beyond talented-tactician status. (Maybe delivering that video just as the leader envisions *is* the right call. Or maybe there's an even better option, given the leader's need to inform, influence, align, and engage his or her audience.)

The jurisdiction to push back. Leaders often make communication decisions that have unintended message effects. For example, we've worked with many leaders who employ a straightforward, "just the facts" communication style—until it comes time to announce a layoff. And then suddenly they feel the urge to wax poetic, using verbiage about this very difficult decision that they haven't used before. What we say is, "that new language will make you feel better—but it's not going to sound authentic or even relevant to the recipients of the message." The jurisdiction to push back makes it possible to suggest another way of producing targeted outcomes.

The jurisdiction to coach. This is the hardest jurisdiction to get and the most important. Here's why: Intentionally or unintentionally, leaders are constantly broadcasting messages to employees across five frequencies through: (1) their decisions and actions; (2) what they reward and recognize; (3) what they tolerate—or don't; (4) how they show up informally; and (5) formal communications.

A communicator whose jurisdiction extends only to providing counsel on the fifth frequency—very arguably the weakest of the five—can influence only a fraction of the means by which the leader is actually creating meaning and shaping culture. The impotence is sobering.

HOW LEADERS CREATE MEANING IN ORGANIZATIONS

Intentionally or unintentionally, leaders create meaning and culture in the organization through the signals they broadcast across five frequencies.

Their decisions and actions. Recall the quote attributed to St. Francis of Assisi, mentioned at the start of this chapter: "Preach the gospel at all times. And when necessary, use words." Adapted to organizations, the admonition becomes: "Promote our values or guiding principles at all times. And if necessary, use words." Employees pay close attention to what leaders *do.* Take Enron, for example. While CEO Ken Lay and COO Jeff Skilling were making glossy videos extolling respect and integrity as core values, their decisions and actions showed that what they really valued was anything that would make a lot of money.

What they reward and recognize. When Alan Mulally took the reins at Ford, he said he expected his leadership team to operate with transparency, honesty, and accountability. Fair enough, but that's not what Ford had previously rewarded. So when he held leadership meetings where he asked everyone to report on the status of their priorities, no one conceded any problems. How can that be possible, Mulally wondered, when we're losing billions of dollars? Finally, one executive, Mark Fields, spoke up to identify a problem with the transmissions in the new Ford Edge. Based on history, everyone else expected Fields to be fired on the spot. Instead, Mulally literally applauded. He rewarded what he wanted to see more of. Soon, other executives raised issues as well—and began collaborating on solutions. Ford's turnaround to profitability had begun. (And as of this writing, Fields is set to succeed Mulally as CEO.)

What they tolerate—or don't. We tell leaders: "You and your culture will be defined by what you tolerate." They recognize this at Vanguard, one of the world's largest investment management companies. And so if you are one of the firm's 12,500 employees, your leaders will make sure you know what's out of bounds. You learned it in your first week of work, possibly in a face-to-face setting with the CEO himself. Before he retired a few years ago, CEO Jack Brennan frequently showed up at "new crew orientation" to deliver a message.

"We make mistakes all the time," he'd tell them. "You can make mistakes at Vanguard. But you can never make an *ethical* mistake, period. You violate our sense of the right thing, and I am personally going to run you over in the parking lot." And then, with their full attention, he recited a list of boundaries. "Violate client confidentiality, and you're out. Accept a gift from a vendor, and you don't work here anymore."

"Of course," Mr. Brennan acknowledged later, "the 'run you over' bit is hyperbole. And HR hates that I say it. But I do it for a reason. Because it's effective."

Some CEOs might want to be remembered for something else, but one gets the feeling Mr. Brennan is perfectly happy with this kind of legacy. "It's important never to give ground," he said. "If we give ground, we create gray areas. There is no gray area."

And therein lies the payoff for employees . . . and for Vanguard: No gray area means employees waste little time and energy wondering and second-guessing what's really expected. As Brennan explains, "This isn't an easy place to work. But our uncompromising approach on ethical mistakes is part of what makes this an easy place *to come to work*. Because we are never going to put you in a compromising position."

Terry Mullen, a senior executive at Sun Life Financial is another leader who understands he's defining culture by what he tolerates. A few years ago, at a national sales conference, one of Mullen's top people made an inappropriate, off-color remark at the podium. "So we fired him," Mullen recalls. "He was shocked. He thought, 'I'm the top guy. They can't fire me.' But we did." Shortly after that, another top performer was caught cheating on his expenses. "And he was gone," Mullen says. "If you just say, 'Don't say inappropriate things,' and 'Don't cheat,' but don't do anything about it, no one will listen. The trick is, you have to follow through."

How they show up informally. Research shows that employees place more trust in leaders they feel they can connect to and engage with on a personal level. That's why it's important for leaders to consider, and be deliberate about, how they "show up" in informal settings—when the expectation is that they are unscripted and unrehearsed. This is where a lot of organizational meaning is created and where culture is shaped—intentionally or not. Informal, casual settings provide great opportunities for leaders to connect the dots for employees, ensuring they know their work contributes to the big picture. Informal settings provide a great opportunity to make folk heroes out of people and teams who are living the values and delivering results, by celebrating their efforts and accomplishments. And informal settings are a great opportunity for leaders to gather feedback, with questions like these:

✓ Where are you making progress? What are you proud of or feeling good about?
✓ Anyone I should be sure to recognize this week (for his or her hard work, living our values, progress, etc.)?
✓ What could be working better?
✓ Anything I need to know but probably don't?

Formal communications. Last, but still important, leaders create meaning through formal communications.

Great communication professionals know how these five frequencies combine to create meaning and shape culture. Great communicators *with trusted-advisor status* can help leaders broadcast more deliberate and consistent signals across all five frequencies—providing indispensable business value in the process.

Now that we've described why trusted-advisor status is so important, let's examine how a communicator gets it. Organizational design, role clarity, leader expectations, and organizational processes can make it easier or harder for a communicator to

Table 5.1 Attributes and Evaluations

Attribute	What leaders evaluate
Professional credibility	Quality of strategic thinking and counsel
Reliability	Execution of strategy and provision of tactical support
Integrity	Trustworthiness, whether the communicator "says what he or she means and means what he or she says"
Motives	Commitment to the advancement of the leader's agenda (even at a cost or inconvenience to the communicator)
Likability / chemistry	Whether it's easy and enjoyable to work with the communicator
Business acumen	The degree to which the communicator understands the business context
Organizational credibility and relationships	The degree to which the leader can benefit from the communicator's knowledge of the organization and participation in its informal networks
Problem solving	The communicator's ability to assess obstacles and develop solutions
Time management	The communicator's ability to prioritize and get things done
Energy management	The communicator's energy, perspective, and resilience (e.g., resistance to burnout)

negotiate optimal jurisdiction. After controlling for all of those things, the personal attributes of the communicator ultimately determine whether he or she will achieve trusted-advisor status. More specifically, trusted-advisor status is, in our experience, a function of perceived performance across ten attributes (see Table 5.1).

We've seen (and helped) many communicators earn their seat at the table (along with greater jurisdiction to ask questions, push back, and coach) by elevating their perceived performance across these dimensions.

EXPERT PERSPECTIVES: RUNNING COMMUNICATIONS AS A BUSINESS

By Paul Gennaro, senior vice president and chief communications officer, AECOM

My philosophy is to run Communications as a business. We exist to deliver communications excellence and customer delight. That requires actively managing all of our customer relationships. We see ourselves as having two types of customers:

1.   The *requesting* customers are the AECOM leaders who we support. We want them to recognize us as a strategic business partner providing expert communications counsel to educate motivate, inform, and influence their audiences. On the internal communications side, in particular, we want to enable a collaborative, connected, and highly engaged culture.

2.   The *receiving* customers are our 45,000 employees around the world. We want them to see us as a valued and trusted source of timely and credible business information.

To help manage our relationships with our first customer group, our *requesting* customers, we use customer relationship management (CRM) tools such as a quarterly survey where we ask just three questions.

*   **First**, we ask them to rate, on a 5-point scale, their satisfaction with a few of the key projects that our team delivered during the previous quarter.
*   **Second**, we ask them to rate how effectively our team has delivered for their business or functional area in the previous quarter.
*   **Third**, we ask them, in an open-ended item, to help us identify improvement opportunities.

Typically, about half of the leaders respond each quarter. I follow up by telephone with some of the rest. We use the data to continuously improve and increase the value that we deliver to our *requesting* customers. That creates trust and strengthens relationships. This, in turn, means our *requesting* customers are more receptive when we engage them with strategic questions and bring our ideas and potential strategies to the table.

For our *receiving* customers, we utilize an internal communications survey and focus group feedback to supplement real-time anecdotal comments that we solicit.

Our goal is to delight both customer groups and contribute to the success of the organization by executing strategies that enable the achievement of our business goals.

3. THE BEST INTERNAL COMMUNICATORS RECOGNIZE THAT THEY ARE COMPETING FOR EMPLOYEES' ATTENTION IN AN INCREASINGLY CROWDED INFORMATION MARKETPLACE

As social scientist Herbert Simon observed four decades ago, attention is a scarce resource. And therefore, he said, "a wealth of information creates a poverty of attention."[3] That "wealth" has exploded in recent years, with thousands of new information sources competing with leaders for their employees' attention. Research shows that many people are checking their devices more than 150 times per day.[4] According to Deloitte's 2014 Human Capital Trends Survey, 65 percent of executives rated the "overwhelmed employee" an "urgent" or "important" trend.

All of which raises the question: In a highly competitive and increasingly noisy and chaotic information marketplace, how do you get employees to *pay* attention? Below we'll suggest six answers.

Don't flood the marketplace. Leaders can't expect employees to pick out and pay attention to their genuinely important messages if they've flooded the informational marketplace with cheap imitations. But lots of organizations push out communications to their employees like a Soviet factory—uncoordinated, undisciplined, and without regard to the actual demand or need for what it's producing. This misguided activity often flows from good intentions: "We just did something. And communication is good. Ergo, let's communicate what we just did." In other cases, leaders make supply-side communication choices because it makes them feel good—for example, to show off all the important stuff they're doing—or just because they can (e.g., "We have a cool studio, so let's make some videos.").

> In any case, uncoordinated, undisciplined, supply-side communication choices—instead of producing "fully informed employees"—create an environment where employees just ignore most of the information delivered.

In any case, uncoordinated, undisciplined, supply-side communication choices—instead of producing "fully informed employees"—create an environment where employees just ignore most of the information delivered through formal channels while wondering what is really happening . . . and what they really ought to align with. This undermines leaders' ability to get their people engaged around efforts to promote the organization's long-term reputational interests. What's the alternative? Coordinated, disciplined, demand-driven communication practices. Moving from a bias of inclusion to a bias of exclusion. Recognizing that every message of secondary importance has the potential to diminish a message of primary importance—and therefore, deciding to keep it out of the organization's information marketplace.

One CEO who understands, perhaps better than most, the importance of demand-driven communication is GenPacific's Thanh Trinh. When he was a kid growing up outside Hanoi, most of the books in the local bookstore came from Moscow. To encourage reading, state-run publishers sent lots and lots of books and priced them very inexpensively. Thanh and his friends made frequent visits to the bookstore. "But not," he confesses, "because we were voracious readers." They found that they could buy stacks of subsidized books, remove the covers, and take them to the recycling center and turn a profit. "So the books were very valuable to us," Thanh recalls, "but not in the way intended."

The insights from that experience influences the way Thanh communicates with his employees today. "I run the company, so they always listen respectfully when I'm talking," he says. "But I always ask myself: 'Am I really giving them valuable information?'"

He's learned that what his employees appreciate most are conversations that address three questions: (1) "Who are we and how do we make money?"; (2) "How are we different from the competition, or how are we trying to be different from the competition?"; (3) "What do our customers really need, and how can we work together more effectively to address those needs." By focusing his leadership communication on the actual information demands in the system, Thanh earns their attention.

The same is true of Chris Franklin. He's a regional president at Aqua America, a water utility that serves 3 million people in 13 states from Maine to Texas. "I've watched a lot of utility managers walk into the garages and say 'I need more produc-tivity' and throw a bunch of swear words around, which is kind of fun and all," Chris told us, "but that's not what the employees there are looking for."

What they're looking for, he says, is the same kind of respectful communication that you would get in a management briefing. "Yes, you need to tailor your message to the audience," Chris says. "But those employees want to know how the company is performing on Wall Street, why the stock is down, what's happening with earnings, how they fit in, and how we are going to control operating expenses to make our budget." They want to know those things, he believes, because they want to contrib-ute. "And," he adds, "because they want to be smart about the company, like everyone else. When they are asked a question by a customer, friend, or family member, if they are 'in the know' about the company, they are a better ambassador for the company than anybody else in the organization." But most importantly, by addressing their information needs, Chris has the attention of his employees when it's crucial.

Deliver information through preferred information sources. In the vast majority of organi-zations, four-fifths of employees identify their immediate leader as their preferred information source. And yet too many organizations ineffectively equip managers and supervisors for this role. Others make the most of this important communica-tion asset by equipping front-line leaders with information that is both privileged and prioritized.

- *Privileged information.* Front-line leaders are almost always communicating with their employees. But if you're treating them as just information "pass-throughs," they're probably not communicating what you want them to. In our research of this important audience, they tell us they feel resentful, underutilized, and ill-informed when they're expected to simply "hit the forward button," or read information off a sheet of paper. They don't want to look like a parrot. What they do want is to look smart, relevant, and ready to translate higher-level mes-sages at the local level. They want to be prepared for the toughest questions their employees might ask. This means using all-leader meetings, skip-level meet-ings, structured cascade processes, and BS-free leader materials that explain the "why," not just the "what" we're doing. Additionally, it's valuable to provide a "single source of truth"—a place where leaders can pull information when they need it. In order to be useful, however, it must be updated and current, easy to navigate, and user-friendly.
- *Prioritized information.* In a crowded information marketplace, leaders struggle with information overload—even when they believe that all the information is valuable. The solution is to: (1) *streamline* communication so front-line leaders have fewer sources to monitor; (2) *filter* the information so leaders get more of "what's relevant to me," and less of the other stuff; and then (3) *prioritize* what you need and expect them to communicate. They'd rather you say "*This* com-munication is the priority this week" than to guess which one of fifteen messages is most important. To that end, we've helped organizations successfully put in place a governed process for pushing, on a regular cadence, a *finite* number of prioritized messages to front-line leaders (e.g., every two weeks there are only two corporate messages, two business unit messages, and two local messages the

company requires front-line leaders to deliver effectively). With clear and credible expectations in place, these companies then create positive consequences for the managers and supervisors who play their communication role effectively, and negative consequences for those who don't.

Use folklore as an information delivery device. Two defining characteristics of folklore are that it is remembered—and repeated. That makes organizational folklore an ideal format for transmitting meaning and competing for attention. The most reliable way for leaders and communicators to create successful folklore is to share success stories and make folk heroes of the people who are doing what's needed. At retailer AutoZone, "Extra Miler" stories describe how someone has gone the extra mile to take care of a customer. Whether it's at a local store or the annual meeting, every AutoZone get-together begins with one of these stories, which leaders are responsible for pulling from letters or other interactions with customers. The stories might involve, for example, keeping the store open late or driving a part to a customer's home. What's true at AutoZone is, in our experience, true in most other organizations as well: The best way to promote a principle or concept is to tell a story about other employees who are living or practicing it.

Provide an alternative to the rumor mill. In almost any organization, the toughest competition for employees' attention comes from the rumor mill. This is especially true in the midst of uncertainty. Unfortunately, this is when many leaders withdraw from the marketplace. But, according to Dave Watson, COO of the healthcare company MedeAnalytics, this is when it's best to give your people "the straight scoop."

He told us a story about working with a staff of engineers. With 400 people in the room, they were exploring some cost-cutting ideas, and the staff was unsettled and unsure about what was happening. One of the engineers working in desktop support asked: "Dave, are you going to outsource us?"

You could hear a pin drop.

Watson answered, "So you don't have to rely on rumors, here's what's happening: We have to take $50 million out of the organization and I am evaluating outsourcing as an option. I would not be performing my responsibilities to the organization if I did not. So yes, we're looking at it. I can't tell you that we made a decision, because we have not. And the best way for us to avoid an outsourcing scenario and remain employed, if that's the outcome that you want, is for us to cost-effectively deliver exceptional service to our clients. Otherwise, they will press for outsourcing."

Watson went on to discuss the opportunities he saw for delivering the service more effectively and more cheaply than a big outsourcing firm. He also laid out in close detail how management would be evaluating their efforts. He told us later that that he could feel the tension bleed out of the room. Although there was still uncertainty about the final outcome of their efforts, employees could see a logical process for working out the problem, proving their value to the company, and keeping their jobs. By speaking frankly, Watson had shown them that they had some control over the outcome—over their future—and he had provided them a road map for getting there.

Another best practice in this regard is to communicate probabilities.

Another best practice in this regard is to communicate probabilities. As introduced by T.J. and Sandar Larkin in their seminal work *Communicating Change*, communicating probabilities means equipping employees with the current thinking about what is definitely going to happen, what is probably going to happen, what is truly uncertain, what is probably not going to happen, and what is definitely not going to happen. To many leaders it sounds counter-intuitive to talk about what isn't certain. But it makes perfect sense from an economic perspective. In the midst of change, people in the organization want to reduce their uncertainty. So if leaders don't provide an alternative, employees will turn to the black market (the rumor mill) for information to fill that need. And when they're no longer paying attention to their organization's leadership, it's difficult to rally them around a call to action.

Here's an example of a probabilities fact sheet that one of our clients distributed to leaders in the organization (an example of providing them "privileged information," as described above). Leaders are, in turn, responsible for diffusing the information to employees. The client updates the fact sheet every few weeks as the situation changes and new information needs emerge.

WHAT CAN EMPLOYEES EXPECT?

As you know, we're undergoing significant change this year. While we don't know everything that's going to happen, if we hold back information until everything is certain, you'll never hear anything. So, based on current information, this is what we expect . . .

Will happen:

- Our organization will become smaller than it is now.
- Fewer local investment projects (due to greater investment in national initiatives).
- Demand for skillsets will change, with greater demand for integration skills.
- Skill assessment and development.
- We'll implement new practices, processes, and rigor to increase productivity and improve product quality.
- We'll recognize and reward top performers.
- We'll identify poor performers; they'll improve their performance or find work elsewhere.

Will *probably* happen:

- Further realignment of staff with other functional organizations.
- Further leadership and management changes as the changes unfold.

Is uncertain:

- How much smaller the organization will be than it is now . . . and when those changes will occur.
- Whether we'll need to ask a small number of employees to relocate.

Won't happen:

- Large-scale relocation.
- Off-shoring or outsourcing of our entire operation.

Current as of: October 29, 2013

Go organic. To make fun of the over-hyped messaging that so many organizations and consultants create, we invented the term P-NAFBI™, which is short for Proper Noun and Acronym-Free Business Initiative—a concept for which we sometimes seem to be the only advocates. Hopefully, we're not just entertaining ourselves with our tongue-in-cheek mockery. We're trying to make a point: In many organizations, the amount of attention employees will pay to any new thing that leaders introduce is inversely proportional to the amount of branding, new acronyms and jargon, esoteric and aspirational language (for example, the use of the verb "strive," which practically no one uses in day-to-day conversation), splash, and gloss associated with its rollout. In reality, low-hype, high-substance communication using organic language works best.

Another success story: At one client organization, the senior leader wrote a column each week on an important topic, which was posted to the intranet. The columns averaged between eight and ten paragraphs. As you'd expect, a senior leader chose the topic, but an executive speechwriter wrote the actual content. So it was always well-written and even reflected the leader's voice. But it's unlikely that many of the organization's 20,000 employees believed that their leader was sitting at his laptop banging out polished paragraphs every week. Which might help to explain the disappointing readership: Metrics showed that only 10 percent of employees clicked on the column each week.

We suggested that the leader switch to a blog, with shorter posts (one, maybe two, breezy, conversational paragraphs), a few times per week. Additionally, the leader made and posted short videos, most of them shot with his own iPad, in which he answered questions that employees sent him. Nothing slick. Nothing polished. Readership quickly quadrupled.

Stay on message. "The main thing is to keep the main thing the main thing," as the saying goes. That means all leaders have to use the same message . . . and stay on message over time. When Dr. Len Schlesinger, currently President of Babson College, was a C-suite executive at Limited Brands, he learned both how important and how hard this is to do. He trained as an academic and likes to play with words.

"Every time I used to talk about issues of strategy and positioning and stuff like that, I just used a little bit different phrasing," he says. "Because then it was more interesting to me. And I suddenly discovered that every time I used a little bit different phrasing, all of a sudden, people start saying, 'Oh my God, the strategy's changed again.'"

"I spent about a year screwing up the business by using a few different words every 6–8 weeks," Mr. Schlesinger jokes. "Then I realized: I better just shut up. I better use the same words all the way through." The lesson? "You've got to recognize it's not about just entertaining yourself—unfortunately!"

Schlesinger's experience is common. In fact, through our internal tracking studies in dozens of organizations, we discovered a few years ago a phenomenon we call the *puke point*. It refers to the point in time that leaders become so sick of staying on message (and hearing themselves repeat it) that they "want to lose their lunch." What's remarkable is that this point in time frequently coincides with an upswing in employee understanding of and engagement around the strategy. In other words, it's important for leaders to stay on message even after they're sick of doing so because that's the critical point in time that employees are just starting to truly "get it."

4. THE BEST INTERNAL COMMUNICATORS HELP LEADERS TELL A CONSISTENT STORY AND CONNECT THE DOTS

One of the most effective ways to compete for employees' attention is tell a consistent, compelling story that provides context for everything that is happening in the organization.

According to Janis Forman:

> It has long been known that storytelling is a powerful means of persuasion, although it may have been temporarily lost in our age of information overload in which strategic presentations are often little more than a data dump, a mind-numbing accumulation of facts, numbers, and models devoid of logical arrangement and interpretation. The Greeks, who introduced Western culture to the "art of persuasion" through Aristotle's book on rhetoric, knew . . . that storytelling can . . . create a sense of community among those who listen to the tale.
>
> Rather than the stuff of legend, "story" in this context means an argument for a particular vision of an organization's future.[5]

There are a variety of different story archetypes or narrative forms. But according to Christopher Booker, author of *The Seven Basic Plots*, "No type of story is more instantly recognizable to us than that of the quest." In a quest story, the protagonists aim to achieve something important or arrive at some important destination. And "whatever perils and diversions lie in wait on the way, the story is shaped by that one overriding imperative, and the story remains unresolved until the objective has been finally, triumphantly secured."

Sometimes leaders say: "Well, we have a strategy and a vision statement and a set of values. So we have the elements of a quest story already." And that's true. But the whole of a quest storyline is greater than the sum of its parts. Leaders need to pull it together into a narrative arc. If they're not consistently talking about the strategy as the means by which we work together to accelerate our progress toward our aspiration, with our values serving as rule of the road along the way, employees likely don't recognize the story form (consciously or unconsciously). Which means that these messages aren't as compelling as they could be.

Just to be clear, the organization doesn't need to tell employees that it has a "storyline," let alone one that is based on a quest archetype! The suggestion, rather, is to use compelling narrative form (e.g., "where we're going and how we're going to get there") to shape your high-level messaging—and then to reinforce the story and explicitly connect the dots for employees. In doing so, leaders and communicators have the ability to: (1) better equip employees to make decisions and take action; (2) make work more meaningful, and in the process elevate discretionary energy, commitment, and performance; and (3) rally people together in response to a challenge.

Shaping Decisions and Actions

Leading a quest toward a specific, consistent destination equips employees at all levels with criteria for making what otherwise might be tough decisions. Herb Kelleher, the legendary former CEO of Southwest Airlines, understood this well, as reflected in a story he related to political strategists James Carville and Paul Begala.[6]

> "I can teach you the secret to running this airline in thirty seconds. This is it: Southwest is the low-fare airline. Not a low-fare airline. We are THE low-fare airline. Once you understand that fact, you can make any decision about this company's future as well as I can."
>
> "Here's an example," Herb said. "Tracy from marketing comes into your office. She says her surveys indicate that the passengers might enjoy a light entrée on the Houston to Las Vegas flight. All we offer is peanuts, and she thinks a nice chicken Caesar salad would be popular. What do you say?"
>
> Paul stammered. So Herb told him: "You say, 'Tracy, will adding that chicken Caesar salad make us THE low-fare airline from Houston to Las Vegas? Because if it doesn't help us become the unchallenged low-fare airline, we're not serving any damn chicken salad.'"

Additionally, leading a quest toward a particular outcome (and consistently framing it that way) can get everyone focused on and talking about their role in producing strategic outcomes—instead of just tactical activities. "I don't care how many meetings you attend, how many emails you answer, how many committees you're on," says ADT senior executive Georgia Eddleman. "I care about what you're doing to get us closer to the *targeted end state*, whether that's improved quality, increased profit margins, reduced costs, or something else. That's what we're going to talk about, report, evaluate, and compensate. We'll connect it to every single level of the organization in a tangible way, every day."

Making work more meaningful

Kurt Schroeder, senior vice president of internal communication for Wells Fargo's Consumer Lending Group, finds inspiration in a quote from Antoine de Saint-

Exupéry: "If you want to build a ship, don't drum up people to collect wood and don't assign them tasks and work, but rather teach them to long for the endless immensity of the sea." That, Schroeder says, is what good internal communicators can help leaders to do.

"In our case," he says, "we want to enable the American Dream." And so his job is to help nearly 70,000 consumer-finance employees see how their work contributes to this quest. "For example," Schroeder says, "we don't just talk about how many billions in home mortgages we originated last quarter; we talk about how many millions of families we helped turn a house into a home. And we don't just talk about a 12 percent increase in auto originations; we talk about helping 50,000 additional people get to work. The role of my team is to bring the numbers to life and to find and retell stories from customers and employees that show how we are moving this cause forward."

Mr. Schroeder has found that "whether you are right out of college doing data entry, or a seventeen-year veteran, everyone wants to feel like they are doing something worthwhile. And that's serving customers in way that enables good things to happen in their lives. As you might imagine, our business involves a lot of paperwork. But when our team members think about their work, they don't just see forms, they see families. And that changes the way our people feel, which elevates their energy, commitment, and performance."

"Of course," he says, "this only works because our leaders' passion around this is so visible and authentic. You can't fake your way to real engagement." The other important factor, he says, is consistency. "This isn't our 2014 storyline. This is our story, period."

As Schroeder suggests, when work is meaningful, engagement goes up—which, in turn—has a positive impact on outcomes likes retention of high performers, focus, productivity and quality. In one of our client organizations, leadership has spent the last few years rallying employees around the quest to become the best-operated company in their industry. Statistical modeling shows that as employees become more and more committed to this aspiration, the more likely they are to continually find new and better ways to work, to provide great customer service, and to operate safely.

> Making work meaningful literally makes it more rewarding.

The payoff in employees' discretionary energy here makes perfect sense when you consider that making work meaningful literally makes it more rewarding. As researcher Kelly Lambert explains, "Our brains are programmed to derive a deep sense of satisfaction and pleasure when our physical effort produces something tangible, visible and—this fact is extremely important—meaningful in gaining the resources necessary for survival." She believes it's an evolutionary tool. "Our brains have been hardwired for this type of meaningful action since our ancestors were dressed in pelts," she says.[7]

Rallying the Organization in Response to Challenge

In response to an external threat or crisis, organizations and their employees can become panicked and paralyzed. Or they can be rallied, motivated, and aligned by a simple story form.

Carlos Nieva is Director of Services for Alcatel-Lucent in Spain. "Working for a multi-national company, we recognize that they can put their operations anywhere," he says. "And so I tell our people, 'Let's give the organization a reason to keep the doors open tomorrow. We have to earn that.'"

So the quest is to give the mother company a reason to keep your doors open? "Doesn't that scare people?" we asked. Maybe at first, Nieva says. But it connects people to a purpose. "It gives us a reason on a daily basis to bring all our brain power, all our ideas, all our enthusiasm—to bring everything to the table. Every day is a win—and everybody feels a part of that winning spirit."

Nieva shares an important reminder: The call to action needs to rally employees in response to an *external* threat. "I tell our people," he says, "that 'The enemy is outside. Never inside. Never inside.'" The greater the perception that there are internal winners and losers, the lower your likelihood of building and sustaining real energy behind your call to action.

For an example of leading a successful "quest to overcome adversity" on a global scale, one can look to McDonald's. In the mid- to late-1990s, McDonald's was seriously struggling for the first time in its long history. It experimented with a variety of new menu items, none of which seemed to catch on with the public. The executive leadership chose to pursue a strategy of opening more and more stores to try to add revenue with a bigger footprint, rather than improving what they were doing at their existing locations. But service and quality suffered as a result, and franchise owners were upset that the new locations were cannibalizing their own customer bases that they were already fighting to maintain.

In 2003, new CEO Jim Skinner and his team introduced the "Plan to Win." As they explained, "winning" meant attracting more customers more often, increasing loyalty, and becoming more profitable. That covered the "where we're going" part of the quest. How would they get there? They built a system-wide Plan to Win based on the "five P's": people, products, place, price, and promotion. And then they cascaded the Plan to Win, so that each team at each level everywhere around the globe created their own Plan to Win, all of which rolled up to support overall success.

"'The Plan to Win' galvanized us," a McDonald's executive told us. "It focused everyone on providing customers exactly what they expected." And it paid off. From 2004 to 2010, the company delivered an annual growth rate of 5 percent. Same-store sales increased every year in that period, and by 2011, the stock had returned more than 250 percent (compared to an average of 16 percent for the S&P 500). From 2008 through 2010, McDonald's was responsible for 90 percent of the sales growth of the U.S. fast-food and fast-casual industry.[8]

CASE STUDY: STICKING TOGETHER IN A QUEST FOR SURVIVAL

According to Christopher Book, author of The Seven Basic Plots, *"a distinct mark of the quest is the extent to which, more than in any other kind of story, the hero is not alone in his adventures." And therein lays the real power of the quest archetype in organizations: A means of rallying people to work together in pursuit of a common goal. In this particular case study, that goal was economic survival. The leader framed the situation in a way that produced both short-term and long-term advantages for the business and its employees.*

Severe Acute Respiratory Syndrome—more commonly known as SARS—hit Southeast Asia in 2003, infecting over 8,000 people, killing nearly 800. Very quickly, 80 percent of business travel and tourism to Vietnam evaporated.

At the Duxton Hotel in Ho Chi Minh City, the hotel manager faced some tough choices and spent a few days agonizing over what to do. Finally, he brought all of his employees together in the hotel's grand ballroom. "You all know about SARS and what it has done to our business," he said. "And you've seen other hotels in the city cutting jobs by 40 percent." Everyone nodded, prepared for the worst. Then he said, "I also understand that you still have your family to feed. I know what will happen if you don't have a job. So I have an idea." The manager then explained two options: The hotel could cut jobs by 40 percent . . . or everyone could take a 40 percent pay cut but no one would lose his or her job.

He allowed his employees to ask questions and discuss the options. Then he conducted a vote by secret ballot. Ninety-two percent of employees elected to reduce salaries so that everyone could stay—and fight together (under the leadership of a trusted manager) for their survival.

As one employee recalls, "From that day forward, things changed. Employees came to see each other as brothers and sisters. Before, there was a lot of fighting going on between different departments. But after the vote, everyone recognized that their fellow employees were protecting them and helping them keep their jobs."

That led to more than just camaraderie, however; it produced a sense of ownership and investment. Employees, who previously had just "punched the clock," for the first time, started coming up with ideas for how to cut costs. For example, because occupancy was only 20 to 30 percent, one staff member came up with the idea to close down the top floors. They turned off all the lights, shut off the water, and assigned just one person for the upkeep of those floors. They also stopped printing out reports for managers, and used email and other means instead. All together, they saved a billion Vietnamese dong on electricity, water, paper, and other small things. As one employee recalls, "The more we worked together, the more money we saved, and the more our morale grew."

And then something even better happened. When the World Health Organization declared Vietnam SARS-free, tourism started picking up again. Guests poured in, and all of a sudden, every hotel in Ho Chi Minh

City was up to full occupancy. For weeks, other hotels didn't have enough staff to meet guest demands and had to turn people away because they couldn't accommodate them. But at the Duxton, they had a full staff and could meet all their guests' needs. Other hotels had to go find new employees and then train them, which took at least three months' time before they were fully up and running again.

When those other hotels came to Duxton employees offering them more money to go work elsewhere, not a single Duxton employee left. "Because we had trust," one of them explained to us. "We knew that if SARS or another crisis struck again, the other hotels would throw us into the streets. But we believed that even if we got paid a little less, we'd be safe at the Duxton. So we stayed. We all stayed."

5. THE BEST INTERNAL COMMUNICATORS EQUIP EMPLOYEES FOR "MOMENTS OF TRUTH AND TRADE-OFF"

In a famous study[9] conducted at Princeton Theological Seminary, researchers recruited a group of young seminarians and prepared them to give a talk on the Parable of the Good Samaritan. In this parable, a traveler is robbed and beaten by thieves who leave him half-dead. A priest comes, sees the beaten traveler, and passes by.

Finally, a Samaritan arrives on the scene, bandages the man's wounds, and takes care of him at a nearby inn.

After the researchers prepared the seminarians to give a talk on the story and its implications, they sent the students off, one by one, to fulfill their assignment. Some were directed to move very quickly, and told, "You're a few minutes late. They were expecting you a few minutes ago." Members of the second, "medium hurry" group were told, "The assistant is ready. Please go right over." But there was no rush for the members of third group, who were told, "It will be a few minutes before they need you, but you as might as well head on over."

On the way to their assignment, each seminarian encountered a man on the sidewalk, slumped over, coughing and moaning. Unbeknownst to the seminarians, this man was a confederate—an actor who was part of the experiment.

Of the seminarians instructed to rush to their assignment to talk about the Parable of the Good Samaritan, only 10 percent stopped to help the man. The others walked past him . . . or over him. The seminarians in the second group, who'd been told merely to "go right over," fared better: Nearly half of them stopped to help the man . . . but the other half did not. Meanwhile, a majority of the seminarians in the third group, who weren't in any rush, stopped on their way to speaking about the Good Samaritan to act like one.[10]

What's true of many of the seminarians in this study is also true of many employees in the organizations where we've worked. They know what it means to do the right thing, at least in theory. In fact, just like the seminarians, they know it well enough that they can explain it to others. But when they encounter a "moment of truth and trade-off" where "doing the right thing" (a long-term interest) and completing an assigned task (or otherwise "getting results") or pursuing other immediate self-interests in a pressurized environment seems like mutually exclusive options, they choose the latter. And sometimes that's okay. But when employees put short-term needs ahead of long-term needs it very often leads to reputational risk. This is in fact *the* root cause of much reputational risk. And what's also true is that most organizations do a lousy job of preparing their employees for these pressurized moments of truth and trade-off.

Doing what most organizations do—simply communicating a list of values—doesn't cut it. The problem starts at the source: Pronouncements of "Our Values" often emerge from an executive retreat where a facilitator leads the senior team through the ritual of identifying the concepts with which they'd like to imagine themselves associated ("Commitment," "Fun," "Teamwork," etc.). But calling those things values cheapens the term. Values are what you stand for even when it's inconvenient and costs something, at least in the short run.

And so, in moments of truth and tradeoff, values posters and tchotchkes do little to help employees who need to distill a set of acceptable options and make a wise selection from among the alternatives. We do, however, prescribe several things that do work.

Engaging Employees Around the Gaps

The truth is that no organization lives its values or guiding principles 100 percent of the time. There are always gaps and room for improvement. But many leaders don't feel comfortable acknowledging that. Unfortunately, when employees see the inconsistency between how we operate and how we claim to operate, they dismiss the values as a source of practical guidance.

> It's counter-intuitive to many leaders, but the most effective way to communicate the values is to acknowledge that there are gaps.

It's counter-intuitive to many leaders, but the most effective way to communicate the values is to acknowledge that there are gaps and engage employees in conversations about what it will take to bring "what we say" and "what we do" into tighter alignment. One of the tactics we frequently prescribe for doing this is sending leaders out to talk to employees. In reality-based conversations with small groups of their people, leaders: (1) make the business case for the values (e.g., "The values guide how we show up with one another in pursuit of our long-term goals, so we all know the rules of the road and stay out of trouble"); (2) acknowledge there are gaps they want to help close; and (3) engage the employees around five questions for each of the organization's declared-for values:

1. How well are we currently living this value? (Use a 7-point scale, where 1 means "never see it" and 7 means "it's everywhere I look.")
2. What are examples of this value in action?
3. What are examples of violating this value?
4. What's getting in the way of living this value?
5. What's making it easy to live this value?

This exercise provides a powerful opportunity to catch small problems before they become big ones, clarify and amplify expectations, challenge employees' excuses, and identify how the leaders can more effectively align employee behavior with the organization's reputational interests. To a leadership team that cares about aligning words and actions, and has asserted a commitment to, say, "transparency," a comment such as, "I've never been penalized for keeping bad news to myself, but I get targeted every time I try to surface important risks" provides an unpleasant, but important, wake-up call. When leaders, in turn, take action on those issues, it sends a message that the values really are important. Which means that employees are more likely to make a values-driven decision when they encounter moments of truth and tradeoff.

Make the Tradeoff Order Explicit

Nguyen Toan runs the PetroVietnam unit that builds refineries and other technical installations. In recent years they've successfully completed twenty-six projects, with no failures. Toan says the secret of his success is that he communicates doggedly with his employees about values. "Our top three priorities," he says, "are safety, quality, and productivity."

Of course, building refineries is a dangerous, tricky business, and there is constant tension between these three values. So Mr. Toan also makes the order of importance clear. "We make sure that everyone understands that safety is the most important," he says. And it seems to be working. In the past seven years, Mr. Toan's team has logged nearly 10 million man-hours with only one accident—a broken leg. That's an impressive statistic in any industry, let alone in the refinery-building business.

"Then we have quality," Mr. Toan says. "At first, our quality was not very good and after construction, we'd have a lot of repairs and welding to go back and do. We'd spend a lot of time and money doing repairs afterward, delaying schedules. But we started providing incentives for better quality and we're seeing higher quality work emerge. But, back to safety: If someone is hurt in the process, the quality doesn't matter."

"Once we ensure that safety and quality are achieved, we value productivity," Mr. Toan says. "We don't push it too hard, though. Because the faster people work the less safety and less quality there will be."

Life is full of tradeoffs. Among the thousands of organizations that have communicated a list of stated values, many could provide more practical value to their employees if they did what Mr. Toan did: List the values in order of importance, equipping employees with a tool that actually helps them to evaluate tradeoffs from situation to situation and make more confident decisions about which alternative represents "the right thing to do."

Engaging Employees in Realistic, Scenario-based Discussions

When US Airways pilot Chesley "Sully" Sullenberger lost both engines shortly after takeoff from La Guardia in January 2009, he stayed cool and made the right call—to ditch the plane in the Hudson River—because he'd trained repeatedly for various crash scenarios. Even if the stakes aren't quite as high in most lines of work, realistic, scenario-based training is a great idea for leaders who want their employees to stay cool and make smart choices in moments of truth and tradeoff.

With our colleague Barry Mike, we've helped organizations create scenarios based on real-life situations that employees face. Then we help leaders prepare to hold face-to-face discussions with small groups of employees around these scenarios and the right thing to do in the situations described.

In some cases, there are actually "right" answers to the questions and the discussion provides an opportunity to talk about the application of specific compliance-related rules and procedures to actual sticky situations employees face. Here's an example of one such scenario and the associated discussion questions.

> *You and a vendor have developed a great working relationship during the course of a $2.5 million project. The contractor invites you to play golf and have lunch afterward, which you accept. On the way home, you realize you never saw a bill for either the golf or the lunch, which, as best as you can estimate, may have cost about $175.*

1. Did you just commit an act of non-compliance?
2. Why or why not?
3. What is the right thing to do?

Scenario-based discussions like these are a great way to bring the compliance manual to life and take away excuses about "gray areas." Such discussions let employees know unequivocally that the organization's compliance policies aren't like the admonition on the Q-Tip box to avoid inserting the product into the ear canal . . . a perfunctory message that for practical reasons people routinely ignore.

What's even more interesting are the scenarios that are less about compliance and more about reputational judgment—where there are typically no right or wrong answers from a regulatory or legal standpoint. Mr. Mike notes that clients "are often surprised at how much employees appreciate the opportunity to discuss the practical application of company values to what senior leaders may consider to be relatively mundane but realistic challenges."

> *Your boss emails you and asks you to print out a client document and deliver it to the client within the next hour. While printing the document, you notice many typos, spelling, and format errors. Upon reading the document for consistency, you find that it needs a lot of editing. Your boss has told the client that the document will be delivered within the hour, and the client is counting on it getting there on time. However, in order for you to read through the entire document and make the necessary edits, you will need at least two hours. What do you do?*

After outlining a scenario like this one, the leader then facilitates a group discussion around six questions we prescribe.

1. Which of our values should guide your decisions and actions in this situation?
2. Are there unwritten rules or precedents in our culture that would suggest how

to handle this situation, or one like it? If so, are those unwritten rules or precedents consistent with our values?

3. Would you be likely to seek input from others when deciding how to act? If so, who would you engage? How would you engage them? What would you say?
4. Would our values, and the way we apply them, differentiate us in a situation like this? In other words, would you expect us to handle this situation differently than a competitor?
5. What positive consequences, if any, would you expect to encounter as a result of making a values-driven decision in this situation?
6. What negative consequences, if any, would you expect to encounter as a result of making a values-driven decision in this situation? How would you manage them?

The discussions are enlightening for leaders and employees. Employees walk away with more practical clarity about what to do when they don't know what to do (and enhanced perceptions of the leader's credibility). And as a result of the opportunity to reinforce expectations, leaders come away with more confidence that employees will make smart decisions when it counts. Additionally, as a result of the opportunity to listen to candid input and discussion about challenges employees encounter, leaders typically come away from these conversations with good ideas about steps they can take to more effectively align employee behavior with long-term reputational interests.

THE RETURN OF "LONG-TERM GREEDY" AT GOLDMAN SACHS?

Reputational risk and damage is often the byproduct of short-term interests driving employee behavior and performance in moments and truth and tradeoff. Effective reputation management requires leaders to align employee behavior and performance with long-term interests, as the following case study illustrates.

Some politicians and pundits cite "greed" as the cause of the financial meltdown that began in 2008. But "greedy" is a subjective term—a disparaging descriptor of someone else's pursuit of his or her own self-interest. Amidst the handwringing, one shouldn't forget that self-interest is the basis of capitalism. Gordon Gekko, the Michael Douglas character in the movie *Wall Street* was right when he said: "Greed, for lack of a better word, is good. Greed is right, greed works."

Unless it's *short-term* greed. Short-term greed leads smart individuals to do collectively stupid things, which is a large part of what created the financial mess. Through their actions Wall Street CEOs, politicians, and regulators fostered a system that rewarded short-term risk-taking while putting in jeopardy the long-term health of the economy. Short-term greed isn't good and it isn't right and it doesn't work for long because it's not sustainable.

Which is why you won't be surprised when we reveal to you our all-time favorite declaration of corporate values. In the 1970s, Gus Levy, then managing partner at Goldman Sachs, was asked what made his firm so special. Levy responded, "we're greedy, but we're *long-term greedy*."[11]

And he meant it. Stories that demonstrated the "long-term greedy" ethos in action became part of the firm's folklore. After the stock market crashed in 1987, Goldman Sachs faced a $100 million loss—at the time 20 percent of the firm's earnings—on an underwriting deal to partially privatize British Petroleum. When some of the underwriters began looking for legal technicalities that would reduce their exposure, Goldman Sachs' managing partner at the time, John Weinburg, pushed back:

> Gentlemen, Goldman Sachs is going to do this [deal]. It is expensive and painful but we are going to do it. Because . . .those of you who decide not to do it . . . won't be underwriting a goat house. Not even an outhouse.

When the resulting loss chased other large firms out of the privatization business in Europe, Goldman Sachs picked up the slack and long-term greedy paid off. Similarly, Goldman Sachs left short-term money on the table when they refused to represent any company undertaking a hostile bid for another company. Threatened companies, in turn, took their business to Goldman Sachs,[12] which produced another win for long-term greedy. As the firm grew, this folklore helped employees navigate sticky situations: "We should do the right thing even if it hurts in the short-term, because at Goldman Sachs we're long-term greedy."

And for years, Goldman Sachs avoided the myopia from which most of its competitors suffered. Until it became like everybody else.

In the publicly traded firms on Wall Street (of which Goldman Sachs was one) "you were paid [in recent years] according (more or less) to your profits or fee generation, regardless of the outcome, down the road, of the deals you did or the loans you made or the assets you took on," according to *New Yorker* staff writer Nick Paumgarten. "You had an incentive to generate inflated or ephemeral gains, and, often little incentive not to."[13]

Inevitably, this led to trouble. Goldman Sachs' current CEO, Lloyd Blankfein, has acknowledged that "we participated in the market euphoria and failed to raise a responsible voice" in the lead-up to the financial crisis.[14] The collapse of long-term greedy required the firm to take a $10 billion government bailout. "We believe that repayment of the government's investment is a strong sign of progress and one measure of the ability to recover from the crisis," Blankfein said in a letter to Congressional leaders. "But real stability can return only if our industry accepts that certain practices were unhealthy and not in the long-term interests of individual institutions and the financial system, as a whole."

In other words, Mr. Blankfein wants to lead a return to "long-term greedy"—and he took steps to back up his words: For example, in May of 2009, Blankfein instituted new compensation practices. Some highlights:

- To avoid misaligning compensation and performance, the firm will use guaranteed employment contracts only in exceptional circumstances (for example, for new hires) and avoid multi-year guarantees entirely.
- The firm commits that cash compensation in a single year will never be so much as to overwhelm the value ascribed to longer term stock incentives that can only be realized through longer term responsible behavior.

- The firm will subject equity awards to vesting and other restrictions over an extended period of time. This allows for forfeiture or a "clawback" in the event that an employee's conduct or judgment results in a restatement of the firm's financial statements or other significant harm to the firm's business. The firm can also use the clawback in response to any individual misconduct that results in legal or reputational harm. And equity delivery schedules continue to apply after an individual has left the firm.
- The firm commits to evaluate an employee's outsized gain, just like an outsized loss, in the context of the cumulative record of that individual's risk judgments.

Of course, it would have been far better to have never forgotten Levy's maxim in the first place. According to another well-known saying at Goldman Sachs, "Our assets are our people, capital, and reputation. If any of these is ever diminished, the last is the most difficult to restore."

Portions of this chapter are excerpted with permission from *Leadership Without Excuses: How to Create Accountability and High Performance (Instead of Just Talking About It)* by Jeff Grimshaw and Gregg Baron, published by McGraw-Hill, 2010.

Know / Feel / Do™ and Five Frequencies™, concepts referenced in this chapter, are trademarks of MGStrategy.

▶ BEST PRACTICES IN ORGANIZATIONAL COMMUNICATION

1. Aligning and engaging employees in support of reputational interests must be—can only be—a leader-driven and leader-led activity. Indeed, in the organizations that most effectively promote alignment, the CEO is front-and-center on the topic.

2. For senior leadership to effectively "own it," they need the support of highly strategic communicators and trusted advisors to drive employee alignment with the organization's reputational interests.

3. The various functions that play a role in aligning employees with reputational interests (communication, legal, HR, advertising, customer service, etc.) actively integrate their alignment efforts.

4. It's impossible for an organization to align effectively its employees' behavior and performance until it has successfully won their attention in the crowded information marketplace. Cutting through the noise requires disciplined, demand-driven communication practices.

5. To align employee *behavior* with reputation.

6. Communicate interests . . .

- Communicate "bright lines and well-defined boundaries" . . . the things you can never do in pursuit of results or other self-interests . . . and then enforce those boundaries consistently.
- Communicate practical "rules of thumb" for managing moments of truth and tradeoff. These are more useful than a litany of esoteric concepts to employees who are trying to decide what to do when they don't know what to do.
- Equip employees for moments for truth and tradeoff with leader-led discussions about sticky scenarios that employees actually face.
- Engage employees in dialogue about the gaps between "what we say" and "what we do," amplifying expectations and taking away excuses in the process.

▶ RESOURCES FOR FURTHER STUDY

Amabile, T. and S. Kramer, *The Progress Principle: Using Small Wins to Ignite Joy, Engagement, and Creativity at Work*, Boston: Harvard Business Review Press, 2011.

Conniff, R., *Ape in the Corner Office: Understanding the Workplace Beast in All of Us*, New York: Crown Business, 2005.

Davenport, T., *Thinking for a Living: How to Get Better Performances and Results from Knowledge Workers*, Boston: Harvard Business Press, 2005.

Grimshaw, J, and G. Baron, *Leadership Without Excuses: How to Create Accountability and High Performance (Instead of Just Talking About It)*, New York: McGraw-Hill, 2010.

Heath, C. and D. Heath, *Made to Stick: Why Some Ideas Survive and Others Die*, New York: Random House, 2007.

Kersten, E.L., *The Art of Demotivation*, Austin: Despair, Inc., 2005.

Larkin, T. and S. Larkin, *Communicating Change: Winning Employee Support for New Business Goals*, New York: McGraw-Hill, 1994.

Maister, D.H., C.H. Green, and R.M. Galford, *The Trusted Advisor*, New York: The Free Press, 2001.

Stack, J., *The Great Game of Business*, New York: Broadway Business, 1994.

Weick, K.E. and K.M. Sutcliffe, *Managing the Unexpected: Resilient Performance in an Age of Uncertainty*, San Francisco: John Wiley & Sons, Inc., 2007.

Weinschenk, S., *How to Get People to Do Stuff: Master the Art and Science of Persuasion and Motivation,* United States of America: New Riders, 2013.

▶ QUESTIONS FOR FURTHER DISCUSSION

1. Is internal communication in your organization more out*come*-driven . . . or more out*put*-focused? To what extent do leaders perceive that the function plays in indispensable role in the advancement of their leadership agenda?

2. How effectively do the senior leaders in your organization "broadcast steady signals across five frequencies?" How much jurisdiction do communicators have to help them do this more effectively?

3. How effectively does your organization compete for employees' attention? What does it do well? What could be better? What is your most formidable competition in the information marketplace?

4. Does your organization have an overall storyline? Is it effectively communicated and reinforced? Why or why not?

5. What should professional communicators do when they know there's a sizable gap between "what we say" and "what we do?"

6. What is your reaction to the idea of "long-term greedy?" Why?

7. What are some sticky situations that employees in your organization frequently encounter?

8. How effectively does your organization prepare employees for these moments of truth and tradeoff?

▶ NOTES

1 H.A. Simon, "Designing Organizations for an Information-Rich World," in M. Greenberger (ed.) *Computers, Communication, and the Public Interest* (Baltimore: Johns Hopkins University Press, 1971), 40–1.

2 C. Heath and. D. Heath, *Made to Stick: Why Some Ideas Survive and Others Die* (New York: Random House, 2007), pp. 25–7.

3 Ibid.

4 Victoria Woollaston, "How Often Do You Check your Phone? The average person does it 110 times a DAY (and up to every 6 seconds in the evening)," *Mail Online*, October 8, 2013, http://www.dailymail.co.uk/sciencetech/article-2449632/How-check-phone-The-average-person-does-110-times-DAY-6-seconds-evening.html.

5 J. Forman, "When Stories Create an Organization," *Strategy + Business*, 1999, 15(2), 2–5.

6 J. Carville and P. Begala, *Buck Up, Suck Up . . . and Come Back When You Foul Up* (New York: Simon and Schuster, 2009).

7 K. Lambert, "Depressingly Easy," *Scientific American Mind*, August, 2008, 30–7.

8 All statistics from http://management.fortune.cnn.com/2011/08/23/why-mcdonalds-wins-in-any-economy/

9 J.M. Darley and C.D. Batson, "From Jerusalem to Jericho: A Study of Situational and Dispositional Variables in Helping Behavior," *Journal of Personality and Social Psychology*, 1973, 27, 100–108.

10 J.D. Hanson and D.G. Yosifon, "The Situation: An Introduction to the Situational Character, Critical Realism, Power Economics, and Deep Capture," *University of Pennsylvania Law Review*, 2003–2004, vol. 152, 129.

11 Lisa Endlich, *Goldman Sachs: Culture of Success* (New York: Touchstone, 1999), pp 18–19.

12 Ibid.

13 N. Paumgarten, "The Death of Kings," *The New Yorker*, May 18, 2009.

14 A.R. Sorkin, "Goldman regrets 'Market Euphoria' That Led to Crisis," *DealBook*, 2009. Retrieved on August 17, 2009, http://dealbook.blogs.nytimes.com/2009/06/16/goldman-regrets-market-euphoria-that-led-to-crisis/?ref=business.

6 GOVERNMENT RELATIONS

By Ed Ingle

Man is by nature a political animal.

– Aristotle

■ ■ ■

YOU SNOOZE, YOU LOSE

In March 1990, the Energy and Commerce Committee of the U.S. House of Representatives was holding a late night, closed-door session on proposed clean air legislation. Chairman John Dingell of Michigan—the longest-serving member of Congress in history—was presiding over the powerful committee.

It was near midnight and the negotiations had bogged down over a key issue—how to cost-effectively reduce emissions from power plants to address acid rain pollution in the Northeast. In particular, the discussion focused on how to divvy up the new emission allowances or "credits" among the nation's largest coal-burning utilities, primarily located in the Midwest. The proposed legislation capped emissions by allocating a fixed number of credits to the largest emitting plants. Each credit represented one ton of emissions. The more credits a utility received, the more it could legally pollute. As a result, the credits became a very valuable commodity.

On this particular evening, scores of utility lobbyists and their "hired guns" (i.e., lobbying consultants and lawyers) were huddled outside the closed-door session in the foyer of the Rayburn building. Every hour or so, members and committee staff would emerge from the hearing room only to be swarmed by the lobbyists hoping to make a last-minute case for more "credits" and to hear the latest results of the negotiations.

Bob Schule, former White House legislative aide to President Jimmy Carter and then partner in the Washington lobbying firm, Wexler, Reynolds, Fuller, Harrison and Schule,[1] was on hand with his colleague, Ed Ingle, then a twenty-nine-year-old associate and former program analyst at the Office of Management and Budget in the Reagan White House. Ingle had been with the Wexler firm for less than a year and was getting valuable on-the-job training on the lobbying trade. Schule and Ingle were representing Ohio Edison, a large Midwestern utility.[2] They were joined by Bob McWhorter, senior vice president of Ohio Edison, and Bob Giese, another lobbying consultant to Ohio Edison.

Some time after midnight, a corporate lobbyist from another large Midwestern utility, who had been sitting on the gray marble floor in the corner of the foyer, slumped over in exhaustion from the long day. His deep sleep caught the attention of many of those nearby—when suddenly Giese shouted out, "Quick, grab that guy's credits!" The foyer erupted with laughter and the startled corporate lobbyist was jarred from his sleep.

The life-long lesson for Ingle that night on Capitol Hill was this: only those companies who are present and engaged in the policy-making process in Washington will reap the benefits of their efforts. Those not present—or not paying attention—will pay the price of not having a sound corporate government relations function. In other words, "you snooze, you lose."

■ ■ ■

WHAT IS GOVERNMENT RELATIONS?

Few professions can point to the U.S. Constitution as the basis for their existence. Many are surprised to find that the lobbying profession is one of the few. In fact, you need only look as far as the First Amendment to see the eight words that serve as the basis for this vocation:

> Congress shall make no law respecting an establishment of religion, or prohibiting the free exercise thereof; or abridging the freedom of speech, or of the press, or the right of the people peaceably to assemble, and to *petition the Government for a redress of grievances.*[3]

Lobbying can take a variety of forms. Meeting with a member of Congress, a congressional staffer, or an executive branch official to influence public policy is a direct form of lobbying. Phone or written communications (e.g., via letter, e-mail, or fax) to these same decision makers are also regarded as direct lobbying.

However, lobbying can also be deployed indirectly. A "grassroots" campaign that encourages constituents of a given congressional district or state to write a letter, send an e-mail, post a message via social media, or make a phone call to a member of Congress or Senator can be an effective form of indirect lobbying.

Providing strategic counsel on political and policy matters to corporate executives is not lobbying, nor is managing the company's political action committee, but both can be important parts of an overall government relations function. Government relations is sometimes referred to as government affairs, and more broadly, public affairs. Regardless of the label, government relations

Few professions can point to the U.S. Constitution as the basis for their existence.

Lobbying: The practice of advocating one's policy position to government officials with the hope of influencing legislation, regulation, or other government action.

Government relations: A broader term that includes all forms of lobbying and non-lobbying activities that have the ultimate goal of influencing public policy.

is an important function within a corporation, and lobbying is at the heart of this function.

The lobby of the historic Willard Hotel on Pennsylvania Avenue in Washington, DC, is thought to be where the term "lobbyist" was first coined in the 1870s during President Ulysses Grant's administration. After a long day in the Oval Office, President Grant would frequently escape the pressures of the presidency with a brandy and a cigar in the Willard lobby, where he was approached by people seeking his ear on a given issue. Grant called these people "lobbyists."[4] The term subsequently became associated with individuals who seek out legislators in the lobby or hallway outside of a legislative chamber or meeting place.

Lobbyists can work for a corporation, trade association, law firm, lobbying consulting firm, interest group, or other organization. A lobbyist—particularly a corporate lobbyist—is sometimes referred to as a Washington representative or "Washington Rep" in lobbying parlance. Almost every business or political interest is represented by one or more lobbyists in our nation's capital—interests as varied as agriculture, transportation, energy, education, technology, healthcare, women's rights, abortion rights, gun owners, labor, snack food, florists, and pest management.

The first lobbying law was enacted by Congress in 1946, and required the registration of lobbyists, their employers, and their expenses. In 1995, Congress passed the Lobbying Disclosure Act (LDA), which expanded the definition of a lobbyist and greatly tightened reporting requirements. The LDA defines a lobbyist as any individual who is employed by an organization (or retained by a client) for services that include more than one lobbying contact, and who spends at least 20 percent of his or her time engaged in lobbying activities.[5]

Under the 1995 LDA, lobbyists and/or an organization were required to file semiannual reports disclosing the specific issues they work on, any interests by foreign agencies or businesses in their lobbying activities, and estimates of their lobbying expenses.

In the wake of the Jack Abramoff lobbying scandal of 2005–6, the lobbying profession came under even greater scrutiny. In 2007, Congress passed the Honest Leadership and Open Government Act (HLOGA), which substantially amended parts of the 1995 LDA. HLOGA further increased reporting requirements of lobbying activities and tightened restrictions on gifts and travel of Members of Congress and staff. For example, the frequency of lobbying activity and expense reporting was increased from seminannual to quarterly. And for the first time, HLOGA required registered lobbyists to disclose political contributions on a semiannual basis.

The role of lobbyists was also a popular topic during the 2008 Presidential campaign as evidenced by candidates like then-Senator Barack Obama, who promised to limit lobbyists' influence if elected. On his second day in office in January 2009, President Obama signed an Executive Order entitled, "Ethics Commitments by Executive Branch Personnel." The Executive Order placed additional gift restrictions on Presidential appointees, banned registered lobbyists from holding positions within the Executive Branch, and banned those who leave the Administration from lobbying the Executive Branch during the remainder of his presidency.

In March 2009, President Obama also issued a memorandum to federal agencies, laying out restrictions on lobbyist communications related to items funded by the

Table 6.1 Top Ten Corporate Lobbying Spenders (2012)

1	General Electric Co.	$21,120,000
2	Google Inc.	$18,220,000
3	Northrop Grumman Corp.	$17,540,000
4	AT&T	$17,460,000
5	Boeing Co.	$15,640,000
6	Southern Company	$15,580,000
7	Lockheed Martin	$15,347,350
8	Verizon Communications Inc.	$15,220,000
9	Comcast Corp.	$14,750,000
10	Royal Dutch Shell	$14,480,000

Source: Center for Responsive Politics

$787 billion economic stimulus legislation (American Recovery and Reinvestment Act) signed into law in February 2009.[6]

Despite the additional scrutiny on federal lobbying in recent years, the lobbying industry in Washington, DC is as big as ever. Total lobbying expenditures in 2012 were $3.3 billion – nearly double the amount reported in 2002 according to the Center for Responsive Politics. Although lobbying expenditures rose sharply from 2002 to 2008, reported expenditures have remained flat since 2008—probably more a function of the economy and corporate belt-tightening than added scrutiny.

However, new scrutiny and restrictions on lobbyists have resulted in fewer registrations since 2008. The number of lobbyist registrations has fallen from a high of 14,842 in 2007 to 12,411 in 2012, the lowest level since 2002. Some corporate, trade association, and union employees and executives, who might have otherwise registered in past years in an abundance of caution, are now choosing not to register to avoid the new restrictions and "lobbyist" label.

The top ten corporate lobbying spenders are shown in Table 6.1.

CASE FOR A CENTRALIZED GOVERNMENT RELATIONS FUNCTION

Similar to the case for a centralized media relations function covered in Chapter 3, it is critical for an organization to speak with one voice on all government relations matters.

> It is critical for an organization to speak with one voice on all government relations matters.

It is not uncommon for corporate executives to know a number of state and federal policymakers. In fact, these relationships can be quite beneficial to the company and generally should be encouraged. The company's government relations operation should inventory the relationships of its executives and midlevel managers, and seek to nurture them where possible. However, there is the potential for tremendous risk to the company's policy objectives if the communications with these political contacts are not closely monitored and coordinated by a central function.

At any given time, an organization or company may have numerous policy issues before Congress and the executive branch. Some of these issues may fall under the jurisdiction of the same congressional committees or executive branch officials. For instance, a large U.S. company with interests in trade policy may find itself working closely with the House Ways and Means Committee on a trade agreement before Congress. Meanwhile, the company's tax department may have an important tax issue before the same committee. If two parts of a company are talking to the same committee without coordinating through its government relations office, both policy objectives could suffer. Worse, the company risks being perceived by the committee as unorganized and unreliable, which may jeopardize the company's objectives on future policy matters.

> Companies like Microsoft have learned that a "Washington presence" is critical to its overall business.

Even very savvy and capable corporate executives and managers should not assume that they can navigate the rocky shoals of politics and policy formulation. What may seem a simple social media posting, phone call, letter, e-mail, or conversation at a social gathering with a government official should not be taken lightly. Government officials may be looking for an endorsement of their idea, legislative proposal, or policy initiative that could contradict other policy objectives of the company or alienate other industry allies.

It is worth noting that some organizations may question the need for a government relations function altogether. But companies like Microsoft have learned that a "Washington presence" is critical to its overall business, and that it pays to engage in the policy and political debate and to have experienced government relations professionals looking out for the company's welfare. Bottom line: a company or organization should integrate government relations into its business plan and ensure that its efforts are coordinated and strategic.

ORGANIZING THE GOVERNMENT RELATIONS FUNCTION

Government relations can reside within a number of broader functions within a corporation, including:

- Legal
- Communication or public relations
- Corporate affairs
- A business unit

The location of a government relations function is driven by a number of factors, such as how a company is regulated or potentially regulated by the federal government and the enforcement exposure of a company by regulatory agencies (e.g., Federal

Trade Commission, Environmental Protection Agency, Federal Communications Commission, or Food and Drug Administration). Oftentimes, a company that has heavy regulatory or enforcement exposure will locate government relations within the corporate legal department. However, in response to this same regulatory and enforcement exposure—and the likelihood of resulting communication challenges— it also is not uncommon for the government relations function to be located within the communication department.

In some companies, the government relations function falls under the corporate affairs (or public affairs) department. Corporate affairs can serve as a general catch-all for a number of functions, including government relations, communication, and community affairs. Government relations can also reside under a particular business unit of a corporation, especially in companies where that business unit may have its own unique exposure to regulatory and/or enforcement activity.

> Regardless where the government relations office resides, it is imperative that there be close coordination with the communication function.

Regardless where the government relations office resides, it is imperative that there be close coordination with the communication function, both proactively on the company's policy objectives, and reactively to unexpected circumstances as they arise.

The configuration of government relations offices within an organization also varies, and is often dictated by the types of issues a company faces, the size of the operation, and the management style of the head of government relations and the needs of his or her superiors. A corporate government relations function typically covers federal, state, and local affairs. Increasingly, larger companies with overseas operations and/or customers are adding international affairs coverage to their government relations functions. Most medium to large companies will have a government affairs office in Washington, DC, which will house the federal affairs operations, but may also include the state and international affairs functions. (State and international government affairs are covered later in this chapter.) Smaller companies will maintain a government affairs function at their corporate headquarters, which could include as few as one or two people.

A Washington government affairs office for a Fortune 100 company, for example, may include five to ten employees (although a few offices may have as many as twenty to forty employees if the company is heavily regulated or has diverse subsidiaries). The office will usually be led by a vice president, senior vice president, or managing director, who will report to the general counsel or top senior government affairs, communication, or corporate affairs executive back at headquarters. A VP or director of legislative affairs may oversee the office's lobbying activities on the Hill, and a VP or director of regulatory affairs may oversee executive branch lobbying.

Within these offices, you likely will find a combination of political and issue-specific lobbyists. For example, each lobbyist may manage a certain portfolio of issues that he or she will lobby on Capitol Hill and/or in the executive branch. Some offices may divide its lobbying portfolio by the two sides of the Hill and the executive branch; for example, a House lobbyist, Senate lobbyist, and executive branch lobbyist. Some may have a lobbyist for each political quadrant on the Hill, for example, a House Republican, House Democrat, Senate Republican, and House Democrat.

UNDERSTANDING THE KEY AUDIENCES

For any government relations office in Washington, there are two distinct audiences: Congress and the executive branch.

For any government relations office in Washington, there are two distinct audiences: Congress and the executive branch. Although they both consist of critical policymakers, these audiences could not be more different in many respects. Congress comprises Senators and House members elected every six or two years, respectively, whose number one goal generally is to get reelected.

The president, the White House, and the political appointees within the cabinet agencies also care about broad public sentiment, reelections (albeit limited to two four-year terms), and the congressional elections which dictate whether a president's party might control the House or Senate. However, they are less moved by the individual voter. As such, the dynamic of how they are lobbied is quite different. For example, one hundred individual voters writing letters to the Department of Health and Human Services about a Medicare provision will not demonstrably change how the HHS secretary will think about that issue. On the other hand, one hundred voters from the district back home writing to a congressman—particularly one who serves on the Ways and Means Health Subcommittee—may indeed have an impact on how that member views the issue and advocates for it in the Congress and with the administration.

Further, political appointees within the executive branch are a mere fraction of the overall federal workforce. While political appointees admittedly occupy the most senior positions within the administration, there are only about 3000 of them across the federal government among the millions of federal employees. A senior federal career employee is naturally interested in helping the president accomplish his agenda. But a career employee cares less about politics and more about implementing the laws Congress passes via regulation and administering the federal programs under his or her jurisdiction. Lastly, each agency is different, and how you approach a given agency or various officials within an agency should be tailored accordingly.

Capitol Hill is also made up of a wide variety of important audiences. There are one hundred Senators, four hundred thirty-five House Members, and over 15,000 congressional staff—all of whom are associated with various committees, leadership offices, caucuses, and working groups. A successful government relations function will advance its public policy interests by building and nurturing relationships with these key audiences:

- *House and Senate leadership*. It is important to know the members and their staffs who serve in leadership positions in both bodies and on both sides of the aisle. The leadership sets the agenda for each legislative body, and determines which issues get considered and how they ultimately get resolved.
- *House and Senate committees*. Most policy priorities of a company will likely fall under the jurisdiction of a handful of committees. These committees are responsible for holding hearings, drafting legislation, making modifications, reporting legislation out of committee to the full House or Senate, and reconciling the differences in House–Senate conference committees. It is imperative

that a company cultivate relationships and build allies with members and staff on these committees—both in the majority and minority.

- *Congressional caucuses.* There is a congressional caucus or working group on a myriad of policy issues, such as: intellectual property, agriculture, property rights, the Internet, Vietnam vets, wine, human rights, oil and gas, biotechnology, adoption, and China. These ad hoc groups are made up of members of Congress who have a personal, professional, or district-related interest with these issues. Members of these groups make great targets for building relationships around issues that are important to your company.

> At the end of the day, the elected officials most inclined to come to a company's aid when it needs help are the members of its home state delegation.

- *Home State Senators and Representatives.* At the end of the day, the elected officials most inclined to come to a company's aid when it needs help are the members of its home state delegation. A company with a big presence in a given state or district has one thing going for it: jobs. If a company does nothing else in Washington, it must make sure it keeps its own home district Congressman and its two Senators up to date on issues of importance, and cultivate them as champions for the company.

- *Congressional staff.* The congressional staff who support the 535 House and Senate members are a very important part of the legislative process and should be central to any government relations strategy. This includes the personal staff in each legislator's office, as well as the committee staff. The committee staff (e.g., counsel) and personal issue-specific staff (e.g., legislative assistant) help draft the bills and brief and advise the members. Time and care should be spent in working closely with congressional staff, understanding their value to the process, respecting their relationship and influence with the members, and by all means, not end-running them or blind-siding them along the way.

CASE STUDY: REPUTATION AND INTEGRITY—A BRYCE HARLOW PROFILE

One of Washington's most highly regarded corporate lobbyists was Bryce Harlow. During his forty-year career, Bryce Harlow served as a legislative aide to the House Armed Services Committee, senior legislative advisor to presidents Eisenhower and Nixon, and head of the first Washington government affairs office for Procter & Gamble from 1961 to 1978. In the foreword of the biography entitled *Bryce Harlow, Mr. Integrity*, Dr. Henry Kissinger wrote that Harlow "single-handedly created the entire modern advocacy industry."[7]

In June of 1981, about 250 of Bryce Harlow's friends and business colleagues gathered for a dinner in his honor. It was an event to mark not only his exceptional public and private service, but also his special contributions to the profession of corporate representation in Washington. The funds raised from the dinner became seed money for the Bryce Harlow Foundation, which was incorporated in 1982 as a non-profit organization. The foundation seeks to recognize and inspire gifted leaders, in both public and private sectors, who foster high ethical standards with regard to advocacy, and to "enhance the quality of professional advocacy and increase the understanding of its essential role in the development of sound public policy."

The Bryce Harlow Foundation has continued its annual awards dinners, and the proceeds help fund educational seminars on advocacy and ethics, as well as scholarships for graduate level students interested in pursuing careers in government relations.

Then Vice President Dick Cheney was the keynote speaker at the 2005 foundation awards dinner in Washington. In his remarks, the vice president commented on the man for whom the dinner was named: "Bryce passed away in 1987, but the foundation has carried on his legacy of service, integrity and patriotism in a way that would no doubt please him." The Vice President continued, "Every day in the West Wing, I work in the office that was once Bryce Harlow's office, and he is someone I think of often. For those of you who didn't get to meet Bryce, you should know that he wasn't a famous or a physically imposing man. He used to say that it's easy to keep a low profile when you're only 5 foot 4; but when it came to knowledge about this city and the understanding of the legislative process and personal integrity and wisdom, Bryce Harlow was a man of incredible stature."[8]

Harlow's own words, published by the foundation in 1984 regarding corporate representation in Washington, ring just as true today:

> Corporate representation is sometimes dangerous, often frustrating, and always time-consuming and difficult. It calls for an unceasing effort to educate and motivate current and potential allies—and to discourage and befuddle foes. It requires the coordination of personal visits, telephone calls, and letters from top management; the flexing of political muscle in the home districts of particularly recalcitrant members of Congress; the fine-tuning of press relations and advertising; and, throughout, a dogged determination to prevail. That may sound tedious and vexing and grim. But for the right person, corporate representation can also be fascinating, challenging, immensely satisfying, and—on balance, most of the time—fun.[9]

SETTING THE COMPANY'S GOVERNMENT RELATIONS AGENDA

How a company sets its government relations agenda differs from company to company depending on the issues, the corporate structure, and the various personalities involved. Nevertheless, there are common elements for successful agenda setting that should be taken into consideration.

Government affairs agenda setting should not be totally top-down nor should it be only bottom-up. For example, an agenda set solely by the government relations office, without input from senior management and the business units, may be out of step with the company's most important business objectives. Conversely, an agenda set solely by senior management and/or the business units, without input from the government relations office, may not take in to consideration the realities of the current public policy and political climate in Washington. As such, a company's government affairs agenda should be the result of a healthy collaboration between the government relations function, senior management, and affected business units.

> A company's government affairs agenda should be the result of a healthy collaboration between the government relations function, senior management, and affected business units.

The government relations office should drive and coordinate the agenda-setting exercise given its understanding of the public policy process. The agenda should be consistent with the overall business and communication objectives of the company and should be updated annually or as changing conditions may dictate. It should take into consideration the business cycle, key lines of business, and related policy and political issues.

The government affairs agenda must also be realistic. Moving an important legislative agenda item from a draft proposal to a bill and on to final enactment can take several years in most cases. It is better to focus attention and limited resources on a realistic number of policy objectives, rather than a long list of items that will never be realized. Once set, it is the charge of the government relations office to implement the agenda. This necessarily involves developing strategy, drafting briefing materials, talking points, and conducting and/or managing the lobbying activities.

SUCCESS AND EXPECTATIONS MANAGEMENT

One of the most difficult tasks of a corporate government relations function is managing expectations within the company. Many times, success in policy and political terms to a senior executive is very different from success to a government relations office.

Politics by its very nature is the practice of the art of compromise. And in compromise, the final result almost always ends up somewhere in the middle. No one side gets everything it wants. So where politics is involved, success is not achieving the perfect, but obtaining a legislative, regulatory, or public policy result that is as close to the company's objectives as possible.

Success from issue to issue may also vary considerably. Success many times is minimizing the damage of harmful legislation that is destined to pass. After the Enron and WorldCom scandals of 2001 and 2002, Congress sought to pass tough corporate governance legislation (Sarbanes-Oxley) and nothing short of an act of God was going to stop it. Therefore, success for a company during that debate was minimizing the damage of a regulatory overreach against a political backdrop that was clearly on the side of the public and not corporate interests.

On the other hand, obtaining a provision that expands the federal R&D tax credit to reduce the corporate tax burden for companies that invest heavily in research is undeniable success. But is it still success if the expanded tax credit is only approved for one year, despite the company's support for at least a three-year approval? If you are appropriately managing expectations, you bet it is. The benefits of a tax credit for one year are better than no credit at all, and the company can fight the good fight again next year to seek the tax credit's continuation.

ROLE OF THIRD-PARTY ADVOCACY

A trade association cannot substitute for a company's own government relations function.

Third-party advocacy has become an increasingly important tool for a company's overall government relations strategy. Medium and large companies should not only have a robust government relations operation, but they should also supplement their direct lobbying efforts through the effective use of third-party advocates. Third parties can include trade associations, coalitions, think tanks, and other interest groups which share the company's policy goals.

- *Trade associations.* Trade associations are formal organizations that generally represent companies from the same industry or "trade." Most companies are members of one or more trade associations that have a presence in Washington, DC, Trade associations can play a vital role in a lobbying campaign by speaking with one voice on a given issue—representing numerous companies and a large, combined employee base. A company could belong to an association as large and diverse as the National Association of Manufacturers (NAM), while also belonging to more trade-specific associations such as the Business Software Alliance (an association of software companies).

  Trade associations can supplement lobbying activities on an issue that is already being lobbied by individual companies, and they can also effectively serve as the sole lobbying voice in situations where companies may not wish to publicly lobby an issue. Nevertheless, a trade association cannot substitute for a company's own government relations function. On any given policy issue, a company may have unique positions on certain provisions that warrant the need for the company to lobby Congress and the executive branch in its own voice. This is a critical point that bears amplifying. Trade associations are vitally important and play a key role in a company's overall government relations function. However, companies should not rely totally on trade associations in Washington to meet their policy objectives.

- *Coalitions.* Unlike trade associations, coalitions are typically more ad hoc, are established around a certain policy issue, and usually cut across multiple industries. Whereas some coalitions are created under a more formal, long-term arrangement, most coalitions are set up as temporary, informal organizations that exist only for the purpose of achieving specific policy objectives—for example, passage of immigration reform legislation, healthcare reform, corporate tax reform, energy security legislation, and so forth.

  Member companies, and in some cases trade associations, finance coalition efforts. Those companies who pay more typically have more say over the day-to-day direction and priorities of the coalition. The funding may pay for full-time staff and/or outside government affairs consultants to manage the coalition. The coalition allows disparate companies and organizations to come together around a single cause to combine their voices for greater impact with Congress and the executive branch.

- *Think tanks.* Companies seeking to find other voices to support their views on a given policy issue may consider think tanks. A think tank is a collection of academic and government scholars, which may bring a particular political or philosophical bent to its writings and publications; for example, conservative, liberal, libertarian, or somewhere in between. They add credibility and a degree of objectivity to a debate. There are scores of think tanks in Washington. Smaller think tanks may focus on a narrow set of issues, such as defense policy, international affairs, or economic policy. Larger thinks tanks—such as the Brookings Institution, the American Enterprise Institute, and the Center for American Progress—support scholars who cover a wide range of issues. For example, if a particular scholar has written on the issue of energy security, a group of oil companies or its trade association may seek to cosponsor an energy-related symposium with the scholar/think tank to coincide with consideration of energy legislation before Congress.

- *Grassroots advocacy.* One of the most effective tools in a company's government relations tool box can be the use of third-party "grassroots" advocacy. Grassroots advocacy is an indirect form of lobbying in which constituents of a given congressional district or state are encouraged to write a letter, send an e-mail, post a social media message, or make a phone call to a member of Congress or Senator. "Grasstops" advocacy occurs when influential community leaders (e.g., local or state officials, business owners, and heads of local organizations) are targeted to communicate their feelings on an issue to their respective members of Congress, Senators, or executive branch officials.

  Companies, trade associations, and coalitions are also increasingly turning to social media tools to augment their grassroots campaigns. For example, many large companies now host their own public policy blogs. Micro-blog sites (e.g., Twitter) and social networking sites (e.g., Facebook) are also being utilized to generate support or opposition to various legislative proposals aimed at influencing the

> Companies, trade associations, and coalitions are also increasingly turning to social media tools to augment their grassroots campaigns.

White House and/or Congress. Ironically, the private sector is merely taking a page from President Obama's successful 2008 and 2012 campaigns, which so effectively demonstrated the grassroots power of these new social media tools.

Corporate America was not the first to use grassroots advocacy. In fact, it was the extensive use of grassroots activities by various interest groups, such as environmental organizations, senior citizens, small business, and human rights that led companies to recognize grassroots advocacy as not only an effective tool but a necessary one. The sheer numbers of lobbying contacts made possible by a successful grassroots campaign demonstrate to lawmakers that an issue is important to their constituents and worthy of consideration.

One final note, whether through third-parties or direct advocacy, the smart use of technology is key to any successful corporate government relations effort. Digital strategies (e.g., including social media and data analytics) are central to how today's top political campaigns run and how the Executive Branch and the Congress governs, so it is critical that companies fully embrace these tools in their own public affairs programs.

ROLE OF THE LOBBYING CONSULTANT

Companies increasingly view Washington as a more active player in their daily affairs.

A company's communication department routinely hires outside public relations consultants to supplement its work. Likewise, many companies will enlist external lobbying consultants to enhance its government relations activities and to expand its reach in Washington. In recent years, corporate America has been hiring outside lobbyists at a record clip based on a number of factors. First, companies increasingly view Washington as a more active player in their daily affairs. This is a product of the massive financial bailout and the economic stimulus legislation of 2008 and 2009, and a Democratic White House eager to address major reform efforts in healthcare, energy, climate change, taxation, and corporate governance.

Second, the number of lobbying consultants has increased given the declining cost of entry into the profession as a result of new communications technologies. In 1995, a successful lobbyist needed a downtown office, expensive office equipment and an assistant to type memos, answer the phone, and fax materials. Today, that same lobbyist can thrive with a virtual office via a handheld communications device or "smart phone" to screen calls, receive/send e-mails, use social media, view attachments, and surf the Internet—whether he or she is in the office, in a restaurant, in the car, or on the steps of the Capitol.

Third, during the same period, U.S. corporations have been under pressure to tighten their own payrolls given the challenging economic climate. It is no wonder that our nation's corporations have turned to a greater use of outside lobbying consultants to help them engage in Washington and take advantage of the opportunities. Since 1998, the top 20 lobbying firms combined (in terms of lobbying fees reported), brought in nearly $4 billion (see Table 6.2).

Table 6.2 Top 20 Lobbying Firms (in terms of fees reported from 1998 to mid-2013)

1	Patton Boggs LLP	$496,107,000
2	Akin Gump Strauss Hauer & Feld LLP	$400,045,000
3	Cassidy & Associates	$363,962,100
4	Van Scoyoc Associates	$312,958,000
5	Williams & Jensen	$226,334,000
6	Ernst & Young	$192,076,737
7	Holland & Knight	$179,989,544
8	Quinn Gillespie & Associates (now QGA)	$162,388,500
9	Brownstein, Hyatt, Farber	$159,325,000
10	Hogan & Hartson	$154,633,907
11	Podesta Group	$143,550,000
12	Barbour, Griffith & Rogers (now BGR Group)	$136,820,000
13	Greenberg Traurig	$136,308,249
14	Ogilvy Government Relations	$131,160,000
15	Alcalde & Fay	$129,810,660
16	Carmen Group	$123,975,000
17	Dutko Worldwide	$119,836,766
18	PMA Group	$115,930,578
19	Ferguson Group	$114,527,291
20	Wexler & Walker	$110,625,000

Source: Center for Responsive Politics

Who are these outside lobbying consultants? Some are former Senators, House members, and executive branch officials. Others are former congressional staff, White House staff, and agency staff. They may have their own one- or two-person consulting shops, or they may be part of a larger lobbying firm or law firm. Some law firms have a separate lobbying arm, composed of lawyers and non-lawyers, who handle the government relations work on behalf of clients. Other law firms have partners and associates, who may register as lobbyists and spend part of their time on government relations activities.

Lobbying firms focus exclusively on government relations services, such as: direct lobbying, strategic counseling, coalition building, grassroots activities, and government-related communication. These firms comprise lawyers, non-lawyers, and policy experts, most of whom have worked for Congress or the executive branch, or both.

Lobbying consultants help a company's overall government relations function in several important ways:

- *Intelligence gathering.* In Washington, as in Brussels and other capitals, information is power. The quicker you have a piece of information, the sooner you can act upon it, and your likelihood of success increases. Good consultants

> Outside consultants can clearly add depth and breadth to the company's thinking on addressing policy and political challenges and should be utilized early in a company's strategic process.

can greatly extend a company's "eyes and ears" capability to either help thwart bad policy or ferret out opportunities that would have otherwise gone unnoticed.

- *Strategic counsel*. There is frankly no substitute for hands-on experience when it comes to government relations. Outside consultants can clearly add depth and breadth to the company's thinking on addressing policy and political challenges and should be utilized early in a company's strategic process.
- *Direct lobbying*. Outside lobbying consultants can increase a company's "boots on the ground" capability where the tactical lobbying of members and/or staff is needed. Most important, outside consultants will invariably bring with them additional relationships with members of Congress, staff, and executive branch officials which can be leveraged on behalf of the company.
- *Communication*. Some government relations consultants can also effectively supplement a company's communication function in an effort to influence government officials on a given policy issue— both in Washington and in home district media outlets. Consultants can help with message development, drafting press releases, advertorials, op-eds, blogging, social media strategy, and arranging for media interviews.

A company's government affairs agenda, its priority issues, and the size of its consultant budget will obviously dictate how many outside consultants it may need. It is essential that the company's internal government relations function keep the consultants current on priority issues and engaged regularly—both strategically and tactically. The company should also conduct thorough, annual reviews of its consultants to determine whether the current consultants still map well to the priority issues and are still adding value.

Finally, a company should not only ensure that it follows the letter of the law and the rules that govern lobbying activities, but it should also insist that its outside consultants do the same.

ROLE OF POLITICAL CONTRIBUTIONS

Like it or not, it costs a lot of money to run a House or Senate campaign. Costs are driven by television and radio advertising buys, telemarketing, direct mail, staffing expenses, and political and media consultants. Campaign costs for a U.S. House seat in a contested race can easily exceed $1 million. Costs for running a U.S. Senate campaign can exceed $20 million. Short of major reform in the current political campaign system, these costs will continue to escalate.

Consequently, companies must decide how and whether to participate in the political contribution process. Since federal law prohibits corporate donations to candidates, the only legal option for a company is to establish a political action committee (PAC). Some companies question the need for a PAC, which is money raised through personal, voluntary donations from employees of a company or organization. However, many companies with a Washington presence today either have a PAC or are seriously considering it—particularly in light of the campaign finance law, the Bipartisan Campaign Reform Act (BCRA) of 2002.

BCRA's most notable achievement was ending the prior practice of corporate (and labor organization) contributions or "soft money" going to national party committees, such as the Republican National Committee, the Democratic National Committee, and the party campaign committees for the House and the Senate. Prior to BCRA, organizations and individuals could give large, unlimited soft money donations (e.g., $100,000 or $250,000) to these national party committees as long as the funds were not used to influence federal elections. However, concerns grew as the lines began to blur between the funding of "issue ads" from soft money and the ads' impact on federal political races. Under BCRA, no corporate or labor dollars can be given to these national committees (and individuals must comply with dollar limits). BCRA did preserve "hard money" contributions—personal and PAC donations going to federal candidates—which are subject to strict contribution limits.

A common misperception is that companies with PACs are able to "buy votes" of members of Congress through their donations. When you consider that donations from the largest corporate PACs are limited to $5,000 per election (i.e., primary election or general election), it is hard to believe that a Congressman, whose campaign will likely cost more than $1 million, will change his vote based on a $5,000 donation. And when you consider a Senate campaign that may cost $5 million, $10 million, or even $30 million, a $5,000 donation is clearly not a consequential amount. It is frankly this very reason why Congress and the Federal Election Commission continue to hold PACs out as a meaningful and effective way for individuals, companies, and interest groups to participate in the political process without fear of undue influence.

So if a company cannot expect its PAC to change a member of Congress' vote, then why have one at all? In today's political environment, where the costs of campaigns are so significant, a PAC demonstrates to a Senator or Congressman that the company respects the political process and realizes that it costs money to get reelected. A contribution will not change his or her vote, but it typically will give a company the opportunity to be heard on a priority issue. Most important, a PAC allows a company to support candidates who support its issues and interests.

> A PAC demonstrates to a Senator or Congressman that the company respects the political process.

With that said, a PAC is not a substitute for personal political contributions by corporate executives. In addition to supporting the PAC, executives should be willing to show support for key federal and state elected officials, particularly those who represent the district or state where the company is located and/or has significant facilities.

One should not confuse the use of a traditional PAC discussed above with the advent of so-called Super PACs. Super PACs, which are officially known as "independent expenditure-only committees," rose to prominence in the 2012 election cycle as a result of the 2010 *Citizens United* Supreme Court decision. That decision helped pave the way for corporations, non-profits, unions and individuals to contribute unlimited amounts of money to independent expenditure committees (which can run candidate-specific ads), as long as there is no direct coordination with a candidate's campaign or political party.[10]

Super PACs are regulated by the FEC and donations are publicly reported. As such, most corporations during the 2012 campaign chose not to contribute to Super PACs given the publicity around such contributions and potential for reputational risk. Super PACs played a major role in the 2012 Presidential elections, financed primarily by wealthy individuals on both the right and the left. These independent committees are likely to play an even bigger role in future election cycles, and corporations should continue to tread carefully in this area, while focusing attention on traditional PACs and individual contribution strategies.

STATE AND INTERNATIONAL GOVERNMENT RELATIONS

This chapter has focused primarily on how a corporation might approach the federal government relations function. Large companies are increasingly deploying state and international government affairs operations as part of their overall government relations activities. Many of the components covered in this chapter are also applicable to state and international government relations. However, it is important to note some unique aspects and the need for coordination across all activities.

State Government Relations

A presence in the state capital of a company's headquarters is an essential part of the overall government affairs function. State governments oversee a number of areas critical to most companies, such as education, transportation, communications, electricity, and tax issues. Local governments also play an important role on many of these issues. As such, corporate state and local government affairs representation is needed to oversee this function. Other professionals also may be situated around the country in state capitals, where the company may have a large employee base and/or a customer base. These representatives are there to monitor legislative activity that may impact the company and lobby state legislators, the governor's office, and agencies.

In light of increasing gridlock in Washington, many corporations are ramping up state government affairs activities. Companies are working with Governors and state legislators on policies and proposals, which seek to provide regulatory relief or business climate improvements in the absence of (or as the result of) federal legislation. State leaders are anxious to not only keep the jobs they have in their states, but find ways to attract new jobs from other states or overseas. Consequently, corporations are devoting more attention at the state level around tax, energy, and health care issues. Companies are also playing a more active role in engaging Governors and other state leaders on education issues that address skills needed for today's workforce.

Relationships developed with state and local officials can also pay dividends when an official decides to run for federal office. For example, it is common for a city mayor, state legislator, state attorney general, or governor to later run for Congress. As such, coordination between the state and federal teams is important—in terms of relationship building, political giving, grassroots advocacy, and legislative activity that may give rise to federal legislation.

International Government Relations

Many large companies have begun expanding their government affairs reach outside of the U.S. in foreign capitals such as Brussels (EU), Tokyo, Beijing, and Moscow. In the last decade, the rise in global competition has brought with it both increasing opportunities for U.S. companies and increasing regulatory action by foreign governments. Some American-based trade associations have staff and presence overseas and can provide some assistance to member companies. Yet, a company that relies

> Many large companies have begun expanding their government affairs reach outside of the U.S. in foreign capitals such as Brussels (EU), Tokyo, Beijing, and Moscow.

heavily on trade, foreign suppliers and markets, or personnel needs its own team of in-country government affairs professionals to engage in the policy and political process and build relationships with key officials. As in the United States, in-country government affairs consultants can also be retained to help supplement a company's own internal team by adding depth and breadth in response to changing conditions and shifts in a country's political leadership.

Each country and government is unique, requiring a tailored approach. Once again, close coordination between the United States and the international government affairs teams is critical. Policies that start in the United States may spread to foreign capitals or vice versa and must be closely monitored. And, in cases where foreign governments are taking U.S. companies to task through regulation and enforcement, U.S. government officials—and the pressures they can potentially bring via communications with their foreign counterparts—may serve to positively impact the outcome of these issues.

EXPERT PERSPECTIVES: AN INTERVIEW WITH KARAN BHATIA, VICE PRESIDENT FOR GLOBAL GOVERNMENT AFFAIRS AND POLICY, GENERAL ELECTRIC COMPANY

As head of GE's international law and policy group and a former international affairs expert with the U.S. Government, Karan Bhatia is regarded as one of the world's top international government relations specialists. In an interview from his Washington, DC office, Mr. Bhatia discussed GE's approach to global government relations.

Ingle: What is your role within the company?

Bhatia: I oversee GE's relations with governments outside of the United States. My team works with foreign governments on public policy issues that we consider important to the company's ability to operate effectively around the world. I also oversee our government relations activities with the U.S. Government on international and trade-related matters, including the Departments of State, Commerce and Treasury, the U.S. Trade Representative's office, and the White House's National Security Council.

Ingle: Who do you report to and how is your organization structured?

Bhatia: I report to the company's General Counsel and Senior Vice President, who reports to the CEO. We have a team of about eighty government relations professionals spread across twenty-five capitals around the globe, including Washington. We represent the company on cross-cutting international policy issues, such as trade, market access, environment, and technology and innovation, as well as sector-specific issues like energy, health care or transportation policy.

Ingle: Explain GE's approach to international government relations.

Bhatia: We have a very constructive approach to government relations. That is, we seek to build "trusted relationships" with governments around the world—to serve as a resource for policymakers, to help them assess the business consequences of policy change, to share practical experiences from other jurisdictions, and to brainstorm quietly about possible policy innovations. We remain in regular dialogue with policymakers, utilize various advocacy tools such as studies and white papers, and work with third parties, NGOs (non-government organizations), think tanks, and civil society groups as needed. We make it a point to work with governments at all levels—from the senior-most levels to the career ranks—matching them to the appropriate level of GE executive or representative.

Where possible, we try to employ country nationals to help manage our government affairs activities in the various capitals. We do not rely heavily on outside consultants in our international relations work; we feel it is usually more effective to speak directly to foreign government officials.

Ingle: GE is such a huge global company with over 300,000 employees worldwide. How do you coordinate your activities with other parts of the company?

Bhatia: It's a challenge. First and foremost, we coordinate very closely with our U.S. government relations colleagues in Washington, DC, given the natural synergies and shared objectives between our groups. Second, we work closely with GE's numerous business units to make sure our corporate-level and business-level activities are in sync. Third, we work closely with other functional departments within the company such as our corporate communications colleagues—collaborating on public affairs strategies, speeches, Congressional testimony, press statements, etc. In terms of coordination within my own organization, I am in weekly contact with each of our regional government relations leaders, and I also host a monthly global call with all regional government relations teams. We are also making increased use of online tools—issue trackers, internal web portals and online working groups.

Ingle: What are some of your biggest challenges?

Bhatia: Our constant challenge is to find a way to successfully make the leap to being a truly global company. We cannot escape the fact that we are an American-headquartered company—nor do we want to. We are what we are, and we are proud of that. However, our ultimate goal is to also be seen as a local company in any given country where we do business—a company that is a local employer and invests locally in the community.

American companies have been honing their federal government relations skills in Washington, DC for decades, but we are still only in the early stages of international government relations as a profession. And like in the U.S., the role of foreign governments and their impact on how we do business around the world is increasing—so we have our work cut out for us.

ETHICS IN LOBBYING

It takes twenty years to build a reputation and five minutes to ruin it.

– Warren Buffett

Adherence to sound ethical principles is vital to the lobbying profession, despite public perception to the contrary. The vast majority of registered lobbyists are decent and principled, and they realize that the fastest way to sink one's career is to cross the ethical line and, in doing so, implicate a government official. Just as the fate of Enron's executives serves as a reminder for all corporate executives as to the importance of strong ethical behavior, Jack Abramoff does the same for lobbyists.

The following is an excerpt from the "Code of Ethics" of the Association of Government Relations Professionals (AGRP). Established in 1979 as a non-profit organization, AGRP is the national professional association dedicated exclusively to lobbying. AGRP's mission is to enhance the development of professionalism, competence, and high ethical standards for advocates in the public policy arena.

Code of Ethics of the Association of Government Relations Professionals

ARTICLE I—HONESTY AND INTEGRITY

A lobbyist should conduct lobbying activities with honesty and integrity.

ARTICLE II—COMPLIANCE WITH APPLICABLE LAWS, REGULATIONS, AND RULES

A lobbyist should seek to comply fully with all laws, regulations, and rules applicable to the lobbyist.

ARTICLE III—PROFESSIONALISM

A lobbyist should conduct lobbying activities in a fair and professional manner.

ARTICLE IV—CONFLICTS OF INTEREST

A lobbyist should not continue or undertake representations that may create conflicts of interest without the informed consent of the client or potential client involved.

ARTICLE V—DUE DILIGENCE AND BEST EFFORTS

A lobbyist should vigorously and diligently advance and advocate the client's or employer's interests.

ARTICLE VI—COMPENSATION AND ENGAGEMENT TERMS

A lobbyist who is retained by a client should have a written agreement with the client regarding the terms and conditions for the lobbyist's services, including the amount of and basis for compensation.

ARTICLE VII—CONFIDENTIALITY

A lobbyist should maintain appropriate confidentiality of client or employer information.

ARTICLE VIII—PUBLIC EDUCATION

A lobbyist should seek to ensure better public understanding and appreciation of the nature, legitimacy, and necessity of lobbying in our democratic governmental process. This includes the First Amendment right to "petition the government for a redress of grievances."

ARTICLE IX—DUTY TO GOVERNMENT INSTITUTIONS

In addition to fulfilling duties and responsibilities to the client or employer, a lobbyist should exhibit proper respect for the governmental institutions before which the lobbyist represents and advocates clients' interests.[11]

▶ GOVERNMENT RELATIONS BEST PRACTICES

The following are eleven best practices that a corporate government relations professional should seek to employ to ensure the most favorable business and reputational outcomes:

1. *Shoot straight.* First and foremost, always tell the truth in all of your lobbying communication, oral and written. Nothing sinks your credibility faster than appearing to play fast and loose with the facts.

2. *Be consistent.* Do not tell one congressional office one thing and another office something else. By all means, you should customize your message to take into account your different audiences (e.g., a member of the Finance Committee versus a member of the Foreign Relations Committee). However, make sure the underlying facts of your advocacy stay consistent. Members and staff—on both sides of the aisle—routinely talk to one another and compare notes.

3. *Know your issues.* Do your homework before you meet with a government official. Have a clear outline of the key points you want to make, and be prepared to give your thirty-minute pitch in ten minutes if the member or staff starts the meeting late or has to leave the meeting early, which is quite common. Anticipate questions ahead of time, but never shoot from the hip on an answer if you are not sure of the facts. You should not hesitate to say, "I don't know, but I'll get back to you with the answer." Also familiarize yourself with the opposition's arguments and be prepared to address them.

4. *Know your audience.* As part of doing your homework, you want to know before you lobby a Congressman on an education issue that he was a former teacher (or his spouse is a teacher). Likewise, you want to know before you meet with a Senator on a tax issue that she pushed through a state tax measure (e.g., Internet tax), while in a previous capacity, that conflicts with your company's position.

5. *Know your "ask."* A government official will want to know why you are meeting with her and what you are "asking" her to do. For example, to a House staff person you might say, "We would like the Congresswoman to consider voting for H.R. 4545 when it comes up for a vote next week in the House." Keep your "asks" to a minimum, and make sure they are realistic. If you have several "asks" of a member or executive branch official, be prepared to prioritize them.

6. *Know your environment.* Beyond knowing your issue and your audience, you need to be aware of the broader political and policy environment at the time of your meeting. For example, your government relations strategy may call for the introduction of a bill by a friendly member of Congress the last week before the recess. You need to know that the Congressman during that same week might be preoccupied with fighting a base closure commission to keep a military base open in his home district, and your strategy should be modified accordingly.

7. *Offer solutions.* There is nothing that irritates a government official more than a lobbyist who complains about an issue, but proposes no solution to the problem. Be prepared to offer up an alternative that ideally helps the member accomplish her policy objective, while minimizing or eliminating any detrimental consequences to your company.

8. *Listen.* Effectively making your pitch is only half of the equation for a successful meeting. The other half is listening effectively. Listen carefully to what the lawmaker or official is saying. For instance, "We will take a look at your issue" is very different from, "I think we can work with you on this issue." Also, listen carefully to their questions and comments and make sure you are being responsive to their exact questions or concerns.

9. *Be adaptive.* The policy and political environment in Washington is fluid. Conditions can change without notice as a result of unfolding events that might have a direct or indirect effect on your issues. A new presidential initiative on healthcare announced in a State of the Union speech could undercut your own proposal that you had been lobbying on the Hill. In response, you will need to be able to regroup quickly and modify your strategy to reflect these changing conditions.

10. *Believe your own rhetoric.* Your lobbying strategy must be based on a sound policy argument. The world's greatest political maneuvers and strategies will not carry the day for a policy argument that does not hold water. Government officials will see through a hollow argument, particularly if you do not sound convinced yourself and are not enthusiastic about your message.

11. *Play by the rules (and then some).* Make it a priority to know the laws, regulations, and rules that affect you as a lobbyist—and live by them. Routinely consult an outside ethics, election law, or political legal counsel. And even if you are meeting the letter of the law, and if something does not feel right, do not do it. Always ask yourself: "Would I feel comfortable with my actions being reported on the front page of the *Washington Post, The New York Times* or my hometown newspaper?"

> Make it a priority to know the laws, regulations, and rules that affect you as a lobbyist—and live by them.

▶ RESOURCES FOR FURTHER STUDY

Publications

Andres, Gary, *Lobbying Reconsidered: Politics Under the Influence*, New York: Prentice Hall 2008.

Baran, Jan Witold, *The Election Law Primer for Corporations*, Chicago: American Bar Association, 2008.

Luneburg, William V., *The Lobbying Manual: A Complete Guide to Federal Lobbying Law and Practice*, Chicago: American Bar Association, 2009.

Thurber, James A., *Rivals for Power: Presidential-Congressional Relations*, Lanham, MA: Rowman & Littlefield, 2013.

Websites

The Center for Responsive Politics, http://www.opensecrets.org.

Library of Congress, Thomas, http://thomas.loc.gov.

Real Clear Politics, http://www.realclearpolitics.com.

The United States House of Representatives, http://www.house.gov/.

The United States Senate, http://www.senate.gov/.

The White House, http://www.white house.gov.

▶ QUESTIONS FOR FURTHER DISCUSSION

1. How significant is it to the practice of lobbying that the First Amendment expressly includes the right "to petition the government for a redress of grievances"?

2. What is the optimal relationship, if any, between the government relations and public relations functions?

3. Given the role of money in political campaigns, how important is it for a company to have a Political Action Committee (PAC) to make contributions to candidates?

4. With lobbying ethics coming under closer scrutiny, how can a company lobby effectively while preserving a reputation for integrity?

5. How important is coalition building in influencing government decision makers?

6. How has technology changed the way both individuals and corporations participate in the public policy-making process?

▶ NOTES

1 The lobbying firm formerly known as Wexler, Reynolds, Fuller, Harrison and Schule, founded in 1981, is now known as Wexler & Walker Public Policy Associates.
2 Ohio Edison is now part of the First Energy Corporation.
3 United States Constitution, First Amendment.
4 Website of Intercontinental Willard Hotel, http://www.washington.intercontinental.com.
5 United States House of Representatives, Office of the Clerk, http://lobbyingdisclosure. house.gov.
6 The White House, http://www.whitehouse.gov/the_press_office/Memorandum-for-the -Heads-of-Executive-Departments-and-Agencies-3-20-09/.
7 Bob Burke and Ralph Thompson, *Bryce Harlow, Mr. Integrity*, Oklahoma Heritage Association, 2000, Foreword by Dr. Henry Kissinger, p. 14.
8 Speech by Vice President Dick Cheney, given at Bryce Harlow Awards Dinner on March 16, 2005, in Washington, D.C., http://www.bryceharlow.org.
9 Bryce Harlow, "Corporate Representation," published by the Bryce Harlow Foundation, Washington, D.C., 1984, http://www.bryceharlow.org.
10 The Center for Public Integrity, http://www.publicintegrity.org.
11 "Code of Ethics," Association of Government Relations Professionals (AGRP), http:// grprofessionals.org.

7 COMMUNITY RELATIONS

*Good fences do not good
neighbors make.*
*— Paraphrase of
Robert Frost quote*

■ ■ ■

REVITALIZING A COMMUNITY

Uniontown, PA, may eventually be transformed from a place where many who drove down Main Street would roll up their windows to what will soon be a showplace, a catalyst for the renewal of Fayette County, among the poorest of Pennsylvania's sixty-seven counties. Since 2005, the town that almost died in the 1950s and 1960s with the coal mines and the birth of the strip malls, has been receiving a makeover of dramatic proportion: the State Theatre has been renovated and there are now cultural events held there; more than twenty store fronts have been repaired and reopened; three churches have been whitewashed, and the derelicts seem fewer. Local professionals who lived for years in the suburbs of Uniontown, seldom venturing downtown, now gather with town residents, as they would have in the 1950s.[1]

One man, with the all-American name of Joe Hardy, is a major force. He is the founder of 84 Lumber, the large, national building-supplies company named after the town of Eighty Four, some twenty miles from Uniontown. The company is adding about fifty stores each year, each about ten acres large, from Maryland to Nevada. He is starring in something that many long-term residents see as surreal, more like a movie than reality. And if it were a movie, the producers would somehow have to bring back Jimmy Stewart for the lead.

Mr. Hardy talked extensively about community involvement with John Doorley, coauthor of this book, who grew up in Uniontown, watching it thrive, almost die, and now being reborn. By the time Joe Hardy is finished remodeling Uniontown, he said, he will have spent at least $20 million of his own money.

The story of why Joe Hardy is rebuilding Uniontown (population 12,422), which is the county seat, is clearly an exceptional one in scope and dramatic effect. But it illustrates how and why organizations and their leaders should get involved in the community, for the benefit of both. His six principles of relationship building have made 84 Lumber the country's largest privately held building materials supplier to professional contractors; directed the way he built and runs Nemacolin Woodlands, one of America's best resorts, in the mountains overlooking Uniontown; and made him a very wealthy man. Mr. Hardy said that his principles guide his "philanthropy and community relations, just as they guide my personal and business relationships."[2]

In 2013, after years of lobbying, Joe Hardy, in partnership with Isle of Capri Inc., was finally able to realize one of his biggest dreams since opening Nemacolin in 1987: the opening of Lady Luck Casino. The $60 million resort casino opened on July 1, immediately bringing a new wave of excitement to Uniontown. "We have been welcomed with open arms into Fayette County," Virginia McDowell, President and CEO of Isle of Capri Inc., said.

The casino has over 600 slot machines and twenty-eight table games, boasts two restaurants, and is open 24 hours a day. The project has created 500 new jobs for casino workers with an additional 200 jobs to support the operation. "We are now the largest employer in Fayette County," Maggie Hardy-Magerko, Joe Hardy's daughter and President and CEO of Nemacolin, said.

Mr. Hardy doesn't seem to be slowing down. He will soon break ground on a 125-room hotel adjacent to the casino, providing a more affordable way for guests to enjoy the Nemacolin resort experience and will bring even more jobs to the area. "It will be Semicolon," Magerko quips.

It seems that few people know how to practice effective community relations as well as Joe Hardy: It is how he built his businesses, and helped a lot of people in the process. And while it can be said that he has a lot of money and can afford to do good things, it can also be said that he knows how to do them well. That is why the authors adopted the Hardy-centric architecture for this chapter.

■ ■ ■

Community Relations =

The strategic development of mutually beneficial relationships with targeted communities toward the long-term objective of building reputation and trust.

Reputation = Sum of Constituency Images
= Performance and Behavior + Communication
= Sum of Relationships

HARDY'S RELATIONSHIP-BUILDING PRINCIPLE #1: BE INVOLVED; BE COMMITTED

Joe Hardy:

> I was born on the other side of the tracks but my mother always told me I was special, like every parent should, really. And she taught me to get involved, to show up. So, over the years, no matter what I was doing in business, I always got involved, in politics and in the community. When it became clear to me that the three county commissioners could be of tremendous help in getting things done in Uniontown and Fayette County, I campaigned for and became a commissioner in 2004—the first time I ran for public office, and I was eighty-one. A few years ago, I participated in a policy conference at Carnegie Mellon University and was asked how one makes community programs work. I tried to tell them that it is not so complicated. It is just a matter of making up your mind to do something the community needs, something you have the ability to do, and then doing it as well as possible by working with people you trust.

In 1954, President Dwight Eisenhower encouraged business leaders to become more involved in politics and government, and that led to the formation of the Public Affairs Council, a Washington, DC-based association of corporate government relations and public affairs executives who lobby for various legislative and regulatory initiatives. Beginning in 1980, when he was elected to his first term, President Ronald Reagan made sharp cuts in federal funding for social programs. The initial cuts amounted to over $11 billion and they affected, in the first year, about 57 percent of voluntary agencies. President Reagan urged the business community to make up for the cuts by getting involved, not only with philanthropic contributions but with social service programs. Specifically, he urged businesses to double their contributions and to provide social services previously provided by federal funds.[3]

"Corporate contributions soared," writes Edmund M. Burke in *Corporate Community Relations: The Principle of the Neighbor of Choice*.[4] Burke, the founding director, in 1985, of The Boston College Center for Corporate Community Relations, explains that although corporate gifts to charity rose to $4.4 billion in 1985, they could not compensate for President Reagan's $33 billion cuts. Some argue that the corporate community relations programs that ensued were more productive than the federal give-away programs. In any case, the transition to a more privately funded community support system caused tremendous changes in corporate community relations philosophies, staffing, and funding. At the same time, the pressures on companies to increase their community support initiatives were compounded by rapid increases in the number of applications community service programs made to corporations.

Companies hired community relations specialists or redeployed staff. According to Burke, similar pressures in other countries in the 1980s resulted in major community relations initiatives by corporations in the United Kingdom, Japan, the Philippines, Australia, and elsewhere.[5]

Neighbor of Choice

The new community relations model—planned involvement that meets the needs of the community and company or organization—was a response to the realization that companies and other organizations situated in a community must obtain what Burke calls a "license to operate."[6] That metaphorical license is more difficult to obtain and retain than the licenses companies actually obtain from government or other regulatory agencies. It is issued based on the written and unwritten set of expectations between the organization and the community. For example, the community will provide certain services, such as roads and other infrastructure, and the organization will work within certain rules, abiding by standards that protect the overall community and its people.

> Companies that want to achieve favored status in the community can establish programs and practices that will tend to make them, over time, neighbors of choice.

Burke writes that the best way for an organization to obtain and retain a license to operate is to become a "neighbor of choice." Much like companies that try to become an employer of choice or a supplier of choice, companies that want to achieve favored status in the community can establish programs and practices that will tend to make them, over time, neighbors of choice. In other words, the organization will adopt community relations strategies geared toward establishing not just acceptance but real trust.

"The involvement of companies in communities has changed significantly since the 1970s," Burke writes. "It has shifted in response to changing community expectations from checkbook philanthropy to a principle about the way a company should behave in a community. Companies now need to act in ways that build community trust—to become neighbors of choice."[7]

HARDY'S RELATIONSHIP-BUILDING PRINCIPLE #2: BUILDING REPUTATION, ONE RELATIONSHIP AT A TIME, IS GOOD BUSINESS

Joe Hardy:

> I realize that reputation is a popular buzzword today in business, because of the scandals, I guess. But it's strange that companies and other organizations had to be shocked into realizing that everything in life is about relationships. And isn't it true that a person's or an organization's reputation is simply the sum of the relationships that person or organization has built? I am glad that the people of Fayette County are beginning to believe in themselves again, but the main reason for a company to be involved in the community is that it is good business. Don't get me wrong: I am not going to make money off our renovation of Uniontown; I could not sell that to our accountants, because we could not prove there will be adequate financial returns. But helping the people of Fayette County get back on their feet will help everybody (individuals and businesses) over

the long term. And besides, heck, if this was Montgomery County (one of Pennsylvania's wealthiest) it wouldn't be any fun.

In his seminal text, *Reputation*, Charles Fombrun, emeritus professor of the Stern School of Business at New York University, states that:

> The purpose of the typical community relations department is to convey a company's benevolence, corporate citizenship and social responsiveness. Key strategies range from pro bono activities and charitable contributions to relationship building with artistic, educational, and cultural institutions. In this way, companies integrate themselves into their local communities and surround their activities with a positive halo of goodwill.[8]

Three Reputation-Building Strategies

More specifically, Edmund Burke writes that there are three strategies organizations employ to build their reputations in the community into that of a neighbor of choice:

- Build sustainable and ongoing relationships with key individuals, groups, and organizations.
- Institute practices and procedures that anticipate and respond to community expectations, concerns, and issues.
- Focus the community support programs to build relationships, respond to community concerns, and strengthen the community's quality of life.[9]

Those three strategies are responsive to the needs of both the community and the organization. They help build the organization's reputation so that the organization can get along in the community day to day (as neighbors must); also, the strategies build reputational capital that can be drawn upon during the inevitable tough times, such as those accompanying plant accidents or layoffs.

Moreover, a good reputation benefits the company brand in immeasurable ways, including the ability to attract and retain business clients. One of the most popular (and respected) surveys of corporate reputation is *Fortune* magazine's annual Most Admired Companies survey and cover story. Inaugurated in 1984, one of the nine criteria is "social responsibility."

HARDY'S RELATIONSHIP-BUILDING PRINCIPLE #3: CHOOSE THE RIGHT PROJECTS; BE STRATEGIC

Joe Hardy:

> Nemacolin, which I purchased in 1987 and began renovating in 1988, is now a world-class resort. Guests from all over the world would often

want to go down into the valley and visit what they pictured as typical small-town America. Then they would be surprised at how rundown Uniontown was. I realized that much of the problem was physical, with dilapidated buildings and so on, and it became clear to me that I could make a difference in Uniontown by doing what had made me successful: building. I had built a successful business in building materials, and, over the years, I have cultivated many relationships with builders and contractors. I know who the good ones are, the ones I can trust to do a good job. So we renovated one building after another and tore down the ones that couldn't be fixed. I think that companies, like individuals, should contribute to their communities in ways that they are good at. People who have been fortunate usually want to give something back to the community, so they can take those skills that have made their companies successful and, well, use some imagination. Great things can happen.

To guide companies and other organizations in planning and implementing their community relations programs, Burke suggests an audit of the community's needs, strengths, and weaknesses, and an assessment of the organization with respect to its community relations plans and programs. Taking those two steps can make the difference between a community relations program that, however well intentioned, fails to meet the needs of the organization and the community, and a program that helps both.[10]

Community Audit

The community audit should be geared toward producing, first, factual information including a quantification, where possible, of the community's needs, along with an examination of the community's own resources. Other companies' community resources should also be identified in order to avoid duplication. Second, the audit should include qualitative information on such things as community attitudes toward the organization as well as the kinds of relationships people in the organization have already established in the community. Third, strategic information should be included in the audit concerning opportunities and threats to the organization in the community. For instance, is there a zoning restriction that could interfere with growth plans, or a pending environmental regulation that sets unrealistic goals? What can the organization do about the threats and opportunities?

Company Assessment

The company assessment is meant to give information that can guide its philanthropic, employee volunteerism, and community partnership programs. This information is just as important as the community audit in determining an organization's ad hoc and long-term community relations strategies and programs.

Identify the Communities

Another important aspect of strategic community relations is identifying the communities important to the organization. They include the fence line and site communities, as well as the employee community, the common-interest community, and the cyber-community. Of course organizations can only do so much, and must prioritize their community relations efforts, just as they do their business initiatives. But the point of a communities identification effort is to be sure that important communities are not being overlooked, which is to say that the communities that are the most proximal, the largest, or the loudest are not necessarily the most important.

The relationship between an organization and a community will be only as good as the two-way communication. A communication theory called General Systems Theory (see page 38) provides a framework for understanding that no constituency is an island, that communication flows between constituencies, whether it is orchestrated or accidental, and that there is no such thing as not communicating.

The Strategic Use of Corporate Philanthropy

Books have proliferated over recent years advocating the strategic use of corporate philanthropy: the targeted use of corporate philanthropy that takes advantage of the company's strengths and business interests for the benefit of certain social causes and charities. Two philanthropic marketing strategies have been employed with special effectiveness.

The American Express Company coined the term "cause-related marketing" to describe its 1983 program which encouraged use of the American Express credit card by having the company make contributions (one penny for each use of the card and one dollar for each new card issued) to the Statue of Liberty–Ellis Island Foundation.[11]

A second term, "social marketing," describes the adoption by a company of a program that clearly benefits society, while, over the long term, possibly benefiting the company. When First Alert was about to introduce its carbon monoxide detector for the home in 1992, the company learned that only 2 percent of potential customers knew that carbon monoxide leaks in the home could be a problem. The company held up on the introduction of the product and the paid advertising, while the PR people introduced a national (unpaid) carbon monoxide awareness program, consisting of briefings to health and science reporters in print and broadcast. Society benefited, with consumer awareness of the carbon monoxide threat soaring within months to 75 percent, as did the company from a timely, successful introduction of its product.[12]

HARDY'S RELATIONSHIP-BUILDING PRINCIPLE #4: KEEP MOVING AHEAD

Joe Hardy:

> Once I decided to lead a Uniontown renovation effort, I did all I could to do it right. People have commented on how workers are doing their work in downtown Uniontown in the rain, painting and sandblasting and so forth, as if there is some impossible deadline. Well, in the community, I think, just as in business, once you decide to do something you have to move ahead in a committed, planned fashion. You also have to realize that just about everything you want to do has been done, so why not take advantage of that? So I visited small towns that had been successfully rebuilt. It is good to know if something has been tried before you do it again. If it failed, why did it? If it worked, maybe you can put a twist on it, and do it a little better. I also worked with local politicians and with county and state leaders including Governor Rendell. Eddie and I have a good relationship, and I know he has a tough job. But he knows I am serious about Uniontown and Fayette County, and he knows I can be impatient. Uniontown is the county seat and it is important to help bring it back. But there are other towns in the county that need such help and I want the governor to know we are serious. We need his help and I think he trusts in our personal relationship. That can mean a lot moving forward.

Anyone who has worked in a community relations department has seen numerous good and effective projects abandoned, sometimes for good reasons such as budgetary, but other times because a new boss wants to institute his or her own programs. Organizations have to do a better job of requiring loyalty to the organization, the brand, and to the things the organization does well. An illustration of a company that has made and adhered to a long-term commitment to a particular, albeit distant, community is the story of Merck and the drug known as Mectizan (see the case study that follows).

CASE STUDY: A DEVELOPING-WORLD COMMUNITY

Almost alone in the history of corporate philanthropy in terms of human health benefits bestowed was Merck's decision, announced in 1987, that it would donate its new medicine Mectizan to as many people who needed it for as long as necessary, until river blindness (onchocerciasis) is eliminated as a public health problem. River blindness is endemic primarily to sub-Saharan Africa but also occurs in parts of Mexico, Central and South America, and the Middle East. The active ingredient in Mectizan, called ivermectin, was originally developed as a medicine for veterinary use. After studies indicated its effectiveness against onchocerciasis, a human formulation of the drug—now known as Mectizan—was developed. Seven years of clinical trials then resulted in the approval of Mectizan to treat onchocerciasis.

The disease has ravaged populations in tropical countries for centuries, causing, among other things, blindness. The parasite that causes the disease is spread by blackflies that bite people as often as thousands of times daily. In many African villages, more than half of the adult population would be blind as a result of the disease.

In most cases, treatment with just one oral dose of Mectizan annually will prevent the symptoms and halt the progression of the disease, including blindness, with few, if any, side effects. After much discussion within the company, then-chief executive P. Roy Vagelos, M.D., made an unprecedented decision: the company would give the drug to all who needed it, for as long as needed, for the treatment of onchocerciasis. *The New York Times'* Erik Eckholm wrote in a cover story in the paper's Sunday magazine on January 8, 1989, that: "In this case—the centuries-old torment of river blindness—developments have world health authorities cheering. In what will surely rank as one of the century's great medical triumphs, a dreadful scourge is coming under control."[13] Since then, on top of the costs needed to develop, manufacture, and donate Mectizan, the company has spent millions of dollars to help develop and support the distribution and administration infrastructure. President Jimmy Carter, whose Carter Center in Atlanta, GA, has worked with Merck on the distribution, praised the company lavishly: "I think Merck has set a standard of the highest possible quality. [The Mectizan Donation Program has] been one of the most remarkable and exciting and inspiring partnerships that I have ever witnessed."[14]

Dr. Vagelos knew that Merck, a global company, could not ignore the needs of millions of people in communities oceans away from the company's business center. A physician and renowned researcher, as well as one of America's most successful business leaders, he knew well that the parasite which infects a person's body produces intense itching that is believed to have caused many suicides, terrible skin disfigurement, and, after migrating to the eye, blindness. "The Merck community," he said in 1987, "does not end in New Jersey where we have our headquarters, in Washington or Brussels where we get our new drug approvals, or even in the Western World where we sell most of our medicines. We discover, develop and market important new medicines and, wherever we can make a difference, we must do all that we can."[15]

Together with other initiatives such as spraying to kill the blackflies, Mectizan has made a tremendous contribution. In 2005, the company

contributed Mectizan for more than 70 million people: 45 million people with river blindness and another 25 million patients with lymphatic
filariasis (elephantiasis), another disease prevented by the medicine. By
2010 Merck was donating Mectizan to treat about 100 million people a
year in Africa alone.[16]

HARDY'S RELATIONSHIP-BUILDING PRINCIPLE #5: EMBRACE DIVERSITY

Joe Hardy:

I know that diversity is also a buzzword today and it can be used in a forced
kind of way, as if government regulations and so forth are involved. But
I mean it in a very positive way. On the global front, it is good business
to embrace diversity. If something can be made in India for a fraction of
the cost, businesses are going to do that. But the market that evolves in
India can then be good for businesses and people in this country. In any
case, globalization is here to stay. In the local community, just as is the case
internationally, diversity means to me that we can respect people who may
look, speak, or think in a different way. People in Western Pennsylvania
have certain expressions, such as "youns" (plural of you), but don't let
that fool you. They are as smart as anyone. And even though people here
have had reason in the past to be discouraged, they can be motivated by
opportunity. For example, a large number of our employees at Nemacolin
are compensated not just with a salary but with performance-based incentives as well. Many of our employees at Nemacolin Resort are Fayette
County residents, and most of them had never worked in a hotel. But
we give them great training and they respond by helping us build what is
already one of the country's best resorts, right here in Fayette County. And
that means our Nemacolin workers can go on to any other hotel if they
wish—the famous Greenbrier in West Virginia, for instance—because the
management there wants our people. That's all good of course for everyone; even when we lose good people, it all works out is the way I look at it.
So building a hotel or a new 84 Lumber Store is doing something great for
a community, and if we can then go ahead and help people in Uniontown
get back on their feet, that is something extra. It all depends on people, on
relationships. My daughter, Maggie Hardy-Magerko, understands that;
she is a very good judge of people, and that is why she is president of 84
Lumber. I myself phone many friends and acquaintances each day (sometimes seventy-five, no kidding!) just to wish them a happy birthday, and
these are people from all walks of life. It's all about judging character and

building relationships over the years. That's how to get things done. That's a pretty good way to live one's life, too, I think.

A CEO can be incredibly important to the planning and implementation of a community relations program. Similarly, the head of any organization, for example the president of a university, can get involved directly in the community, with impressive, long-term benefits for the organization and the community (see the sidebar below on Wake Forest University's program of building relationships with various communities, local and beyond.)

Ambassadors to the Community

The success of any community relations program will in the long run depend on buy-in and support from people throughout the organization. "People in communities do not make relationships with companies," Edmund Burke writes, "but with people in companies and organizations." He identifies CEOs, facilities managers, and employees as all being important in an organization's community relations program. It is they who know the culture, the unique needs and capabilities of the community in which they live and work. "Employees are the bulk users of community services and programs," he continues. "Consequently, employee evaluations of needs and services in a community constitute valuable information for planning. They are also excellent sources of information on community attitudes toward the company."[17]

A survey of human resource executives by The Conference Board showed that a company's reputation was the third most important factor influencing people to become employees of particular organizations.

A survey of human resource executives by The Conference Board showed that a company's reputation was the third most important factor influencing people to become employees of particular organizations. (Only career development opportunities and compensation outranked reputation.) A study by the University of Missouri showed that a company's corporate social performance is positively related to its reputation and attractiveness as an employer.[18]

EXPERT PERSPECTIVES: WAKE FOREST UNIVERSITY: THE PATH TO BECOMING A NATIONAL UNIVERSITY

By Sandra Combs Boyette, Senior advisor to the president, Wake Forest University

In 1956, Wake Forest College did what few institutions have done in recent history: the school moved from its home of 122 years, near Raleigh, NC, to a brand-new custom-designed campus in Winston-Salem. The move was initiated by the Z. Smith Reynolds and Mary Reynolds Babcock Foundations, as well as civic leaders in the industrial

Piedmont city, located one hundred and twenty miles west of the picturesque town of Wake Forest.

The "new" campus was, in many ways, a reflection of the "old": Old Virginia brick Georgian buildings; fledgling magnolia trees; and a faculty/staff residential community contiguous to the grounds. A few miles from downtown, the campus was somewhat of a town unto itself in its beautiful new environment. Although college employees interacted with the city—joining Rotary clubs, participating in Winston-Salem's rich arts life—financial and industrial executives remained the key civic leaders.

In 1967, the college became a university with a growing reputation for academic excellence; but town and gown had not yet formed any serious bonds.

By 1983 when Wake Forest's trustees selected Dr. Thomas K. Hearn Jr. as the twelfth president, Winston-Salem was headquarters to several Fortune 500 companies and a number of other corporate giants—RJR Industries, Hanes textiles, Piedmont Airlines, Wachovia Corporation, and AT&T's North Carolina Works among them. The city's economy was thriving. As the former senior vice president for nonmedical affairs at the University of Alabama–Birmingham, Hearn had been active in Birmingham's civic and economic life, and he had great national ambitions for Wake Forest.

With the encouragement of trustees and administrators, Hearn began almost immediately to take Wake Forest into the local community. Early in his tenure, he led the United Way Campaign and established its first Leadership Circle. He founded Leadership Winston-Salem, to train and network local leaders, a step that proved invaluable less than a decade into his tenure. He encouraged Wake Forest faculty and administrators to serve nonprofit organizations in the city. He championed the growth of volunteer programs for Wake Forest students, citing the university's motto—Pro Humanitate—as the imperative.

At the same time, Hearn was taking steps that further elevated Wake Forest's national visibility as a leading academic institution, including a change in the relationship with the Baptist Convention of North Carolina, giving the university's trustees full autonomy. The college and university rankings began to proliferate at that time, too. Wake Forest held its number one spot among regional colleges and universities for several years, until it moved into the national research university category, where it remains in the top 10 percent.

A successful capital campaign—the school's largest ever—more than doubled building space, and applications increased rapidly. The Plan for the Class of 2000, initiated in 1995, created first-year seminars and added forty professors to the college faculty to preserve the advantages of small class size. Wake Forest led the nation in the introduction of technology as a tool of the liberal arts experience when students began receiving IBM ThinkPads, included as a benefit of tuition. From the mid-1980s until the conclusion of Hearn's tenure in 2005, nine undergraduates were selected as Rhodes Scholars. Further, the university added a residential program in Vienna, complementing its two longstanding programs in London and Venice, and today, half of Wake Forest's undergraduates study abroad prior to graduation. The university's progress resonated positively in its "new" hometown.

By the time Wake Forest hosted its first presidential debate in 1988 (and another in 2000), city leaders were supportive partners in the effort, recognizing the boost it would be for Winston-Salem as well as the university.

But also in the late 1980s, the city's economic fortunes began to turn. Mergers and acquisitions moved corporate headquarters to distant cities. The now-famous leveraged buyout of RJR Industries rattled the confidence of even the most optimistic of the city's movers and shakers. Suddenly, Wake Forest, with its growing medical center and the associated healthcare enterprises, was the city's largest employer. Dr. Hearn became instrumental in leading the fight to reshape Winston-Salem's economy and rebuild its self-image.

Ultimately, he chaired Winston-Salem Business, an organization established to recruit new companies to the area. Later, Hearn became chair of another new organization, Idealliance. Working with this group of corporate and education executives and focusing on biotechnology as the key to economic health, he and others— including Wake Forest's senior vice president for health affairs, Dr. Richard Dean and Winston-Salem State University Chancellor Dr. Harold Martin—committed to the establishment of the Piedmont Triad Research Park. A twenty-five year plan is transforming two hundred acres of the city's industrial topography to a downtown biotech park housing several departments of the Wake Forest School of Medicine and a number of biotech companies, some of which had their beginning in the university's research laboratories.

Concurrently, city leaders—many of whom were alumni of Leadership Winston-Salem, the program founded by Hearn— began an effort to revitalize the downtown area. A blighted area of warehouses and on-again-off-again retail shops has become a burgeoning, attractive arts district. Lofts and condominiums in former office and warehouse space are beginning to attract more residents downtown, with the expectation that eventually, biotech park employees and graduate students living there will keep the area vibrant.

One could argue that Wake Forest's rise in academe gave the university the credibility it needed to become an integral component of the city and region. One could also argue that the move to Winston-Salem opened new opportunity for a larger constituency to support the university's national ambitions. Both arguments have merit. It is certain that good things happened to the university and the city because of a president willing to take on daunting community issues while moving his institution to national academic prominence.

Dr. Thomas K. Hearn, Jr. died in August 2008 and is deeply missed by his colleagues at Wake Forest.

HARDY'S RELATIONSHIP-BUILDING PRINCIPLE #6: WHEN THINGS GO WRONG, MAKE THEM RIGHT AS FAST AS YOU CAN

Joe Hardy:

> Things will sometimes go wrong. It is a fact of life, business, and community relations. Successful people make lots of mistakes. They just know how to admit and fix them fast.

Walmart has been trying for years to build a store in one of New York City's five boroughs. Each time, small but PR-savvy citizen groups were able to block the behemoth, raising concerns about everything from traffic to alleged exploitive and unsafe workplace practices.

Recently the company lost a battle to build a store in Queens, and was beginning a new initiative in Staten Island. Immediately, some resident groups mobilized against having a store in that borough, even though many of them admit frequenting Walmarts in New Jersey. The company began a corporate advertising program to build support among Staten Island residents for a new store. As of late 2013, there is no Walmart in any of the five boroughs of New York City.

In founder Sam Walton's day, Walmart was admired as a company that knew how to do everything right, including employee and community relations. How much of the problem now is with the substance of Walmart's policies and actions, versus its communications, is unclear. But what is clear is that the Pushmi-pullyu syndrome of a two-headed organization (Chapter 1) applies here. In order for the company to overcome its community relations problems, it will have to behave and communicate in one way—a way that represents a marked improvement over recent times.

▶ BEST PRACTICES

Here are some of the things forward-thinking companies and other organizations do to build enduring community relationships.

1. Adhere to Hardy's six relationship-building principles.

2. Conduct a company assessment and community audit of the most important communities.

3. Learn from others: Celebrating major milestones, whether it is a centennial of service, a decade, or a year, is something that cuts across all industries and organizations. Research what has worked well for others before developing your plan.

4. Do a few things well: There are lots of ideas for special events and programs and the challenge is always deciding what not to do. Focus on a few things rather than many.

5. It is about the customers—not us. Find ways to involve and honor customers. The focus on economic development addressed a pressing community and customer need, while playing to the company's strengths.

6. Strengthen local partnership. Use a centennial, for example as a reason to educate customers and communities about longstanding company priorities (for example, philanthropy, volunteerism, service, operational successes). Explore the potential for new community opportunities, particularly where the needs of the customers, the community, and the organization intersect.

7. Recognize and involve employees and retirees. Employees and retirees personify the organization's values through their accomplishments at work, at home, and in their communities. Find ways to say "thank you" for their support and community involvement.

8. Regional and national visibility for a college or university reflect well on its home city. (See the sidebar on page 219.) Timely editorials in the local news, commenting on the school's achievements, can only serve to build the town and the relationship, and position the president as a community leader.

9. Local government officials need to be cultivated by universities and not-for-profits, just as prospective donors are. Regular meetings with them to discuss an organization's plans—capital improvements, neighborhood initiatives, large public events—foster trust and can help avoid conflicts.

10. Ensuring that the company's or school's president leads some purely community activities—a United Way campaign, an arts festival, a leadership training initiative—can exemplify the institution's willingness to "give back" to the community. Despite all the other demands on a president's or CEO's time, early in his or her tenure is a good time for such an activity to set the right tone.

11. Evaluate the number of events at the company, school, or other organization to consider ways that they can be expanded. Publish a regular calendar in the local newspaper as a reminder of the cultural opportunities that the company or school offers to the community. Be certain that the president or CEO when possible welcomes audiences at a number of these events.

12. A company or other organization that is going to spend money on a community relations program or on a particular philanthropic program should set aside a percentage of the funds for communication. It is not just for publicity's sake but rather to ensure that the program will work and endure.

▶ RESOURCES FOR FURTHER STUDY

Burke, Edmund M., *Corporate Community Relations: The Principle of the Neighbor of Choice*, Westport, CT: Praeger, 1999.

Burke, Edmund M., *Managing A Company in An Activist World: The Leadership Challenge of Corporate Citizenship*, Westport, CT: Praeger, 2005.

Center for Corporate Citizenship at Boston College, http://www.bcccc.net.

Grayson, David and Adrian Hodges, *Everybody's Business: Managing Risks and Opportunities in Today's Global Society*, New York: DK Publishing, 2002.

The Merck MECTIZAN® Donation Program, http://www.mectizan.com.

Sagawa, Shirley and Eli Segal, *Common Interest, Common Good*, Boston: Harvard Business School Press, 2000.

Weeden, Curt, *Corporate Social Investing: The Breakthrough Strategy for Giving and Getting Corporate Contributions*, San Francisco: Berrett-Koehler, 1998.

▶ QUESTIONS FOR FURTHER DISCUSSION

1. Are there global implications to the Uniontown story?

2. Joe Hardy has almost single-handedly been able to start rebuilding Uniontown, PA. If one man can accomplish that, why can large companies or multicompany organizations not rebuild some of our large, decaying cities?

3. How many companies base their community relations programs on community audits or company assessments? Does yours?

4. Could Wake Forest University have achieved its national reputation for academic excellence without an outreach into communities beyond the traditionally academic ones?

▶ NOTES

1 Walter "Buzz" Storey, "Uniontown and Fayette County: Another Look," *Herald–Standard* (Uniontown Newspapers, 2001).
2 John Doorley interviews with Mr. Joe Hardy on May 11 and May 25, 2005, and March 8, 2014.
3 Edmund M. Burke, *Corporate Community Relations: The Principle of the Neighbor of Choice* (Westport, CT: Praeger, 1999), 15–16.
4 Ibid., p. 16.
5 Ibid., pp. 17–18.
6 Ibid., p. 10.
7 Ibid., p. 28.
8 Charles J. Fombrun, *Reputation: Realizing Value from the Corporate Image* (Boston: Harvard Business School Press, 1996), 195.
9 Burke, *Corporate Community Relations*, p. 25.
10 Ibid., pp. 47–50.
11 Ibid., p. 19.
12 David W. Guth and Charles Marsh, *Public Relations: A Values-Driven Approach* (Needham Heights, MA: Allyn & Bacon, 2000), 424–7.
13 Erik Eckholm, "River Blindness, Conquering An Ancient Scourge," *The New York Times Magazine*, January 8, 1989.
14 2005 Merck Corporate Responsibility Report.
15 John Doorley's old notes verified by Dr. Vagelos in November 2005.
16 Facts via e-mail from Ken Gustavsen, Merck's manager of global product donations, February 1, 2006.
17 Burke, *Corporate Community Relations*, p. 54.
18 Ibid., 21–3.

8 INVESTOR RELATIONS

By the authors with
Eugene L. Donati

On Wall Street bulls make money and bears make money, but pigs get slaughtered.

■■■

OVERCOMING BARRIERS AND OUTPERFORMING THE MARKET? PRICELESS!

MasterCard stands as one of the great success stories of Wall Street, in terms of total investment return to its shareholders. A savvy investor who plunked down $1,000 for MasterCard shares at the company's initial public offering (IPO) in May 2006 would find those same shares worth more than $19,000 in mid-2014. MasterCard's performance beats the historic investment returns over the same period for many other investor darlings, including Google and Apple.

But MasterCard's success was not its predestiny. In fact, the company had a difficult time gaining investor favor at first. MasterCard, founded in 1966 and held as a private company by a consortium of U.S. commercial banks, passed its first forty years as a non-profit appendage to its owners. Its work was to provide the worldwide electronic 'switch' behind bank credit card operations, but not the credit cards themselves, which each of the owner-banks issued.

MasterCard's investor relations team faced three daunting challenges at the IPO:

1. The idea that MasterCard's core "switch" was an undistinguished commodity business under significant pricing challenge from the company's actual customers.
2. The vision that MasterCard believed itself to be a financial institution, although it was not (it was owned by financial institutions but MasterCard itself is a technology company of global reach).
3. The lack of a clear, compelling narrative that distinguished MasterCard to its potential investors as a state-of-the-art technology company.

MasterCard's senior management hired the best investor relations (IR) professionals it could find. The new IR team completed three tasks simultaneously prior to and after the IPO. First, it gathered and integrated information potential investors needed and wanted to hear, both in a wholly accurate way and in accord with disclosure law and regulation. Second, it communicated this information through a valid, convincing narrative that made clear the MasterCard investment story. Third, along with other groups within the company, it helped install a significant cultural shift within MasterCard, so that all employees understood its new regulatory requirements as a public company and, as important, that they understood, accepted, and spoke the MasterCard story.

The work paid off. The tangible results of investor relations are seen in MasterCard's nineteen-fold increased stock price, its continued growth and its sterling reputation. The way a public company engages Wall Street is not particularly esoteric or difficult. But it is intentional. A company's investor relations program employs many of the traditional tools of the trade, including investor targeting, presentations at brokerage conferences, road shows, analyst and investor meetings, facility tours and day-to-day contact with the Street. It also works hand-in-hand with public relations, government relations, and human resources others within the company to ensure consistent, cogent communication.

■ ■ ■

WHAT IS INVESTOR RELATIONS?

Investor relations (IR) is the subset of public relations and corporate communication that deals with a company's relationship with the investment community. Both current investors (who own a corporation's stocks and bonds) and potential investors (who might be persuaded to own these stocks and bonds) make up the primary audiences for investor relations.

> Investor relations is the subset of public relations and corporate communication that deals with a company's relationship with the investment community.

IR is most often employed by companies whose shares are held and traded by the public. Privately owned companies may also use IR in circumstances such as when they have bonds trading on the public markets or when they are owned by a dispersed group of private shareholders.

> IR is the most heavily regulated of communication disciplines.

IR is unique among communications disciplines in that real people make or lose real money every day, based on information, utterances, or omissions from a corporate IR department. Since IR mistakes can cost real people real money, IR is the most heavily regulated of communication disciplines. Laws, government regulations, and stock exchange regulations each dictate how IR is conducted and when. As a result, IR has exacting procedures and deadlines. In the U.S., IR practitioners are subject to significant civil and criminal liability if they violate certain principles.

> IR has exacting procedures and deadlines. In the United States, IR practitioners are subject to significant civil and criminal liability if they violate certain principles.

The demands of investors and regulators make investor relations among the most stimulating and academically rigorous of all communication disciplines. IR requires knowledge of communication, finance, law, accounting, and marketing. In general, IR practitioners are well compensated compared to other communications professionals with similar experience and responsibility. IR practitioners may become trusted advisors within corporations and participate at the highest levels of corporate strategy.

> IR requires knowledge of communication, finance, law, accounting, and marketing.

Corporate leadership has only recently come to acknowledge the strategic importance of IR. From its establishment as a distinct discipline in the 1960s until the mid-1990s, IR was seen as tactical, peripheral to strategic corporate decision-making. Since the mid-1990s, IR has matured into a strategic element of business operation. The reasons are many. For instance, the demand for reliable data about corporations grew as individuals increasingly held stocks, mutual funds, and retirement funds. The Internet erased barriers to information flow, giving Main Street investors access to financial information reserved previously for Wall Street. Further, CEOs are now often judged by how well their companies' stock performs. So CEOs are now much keener on what IR can do. And key to the evolution of IR as a strategic discipline are the many corporate scandals that have compelled more complete, integrated, timely, and thoughtful corporate financial disclosure. Without robust financial disclosure and transparency, a corporation now risks severe damage to its reputation and ability to do business.

Today, especially in the U.S. and Canada, IR is viewed as a financial function with an essential overlay of communication practice and theory. It is now common for the head of IR to report to the CFO, interact closely with the CEO, and make presentations to the board of directors. IR generally takes part in the corporation's strategic processes to a greater degree than corporate communication professionals without IR responsibilities.

THE GOALS AND ROLES OF INVESTOR RELATIONS

The first goal of investor relations is to ensure that a company's securities, that is, its stocks and bonds, are fairly and fully valued in the marketplace.

The first goal of investor relations is to ensure that a company's securities, that is, its stocks and bonds, are fairly and fully valued in the marketplace. "Fairly and fully valued" means that the price of a company's securities closely reflects both the present value and the potential value of the company. Given that a stock's price is set by the market based on demand for that stock, investor relations involves maintaining demand. IR does this by ensuring investors have access to accurate, timely information about the company so they can appraise the attractiveness of the company's stock relative to other investment opportunities.

IR's second goal is to help fulfill corporations' affirmative disclosure obligations under securities law and government regulation.

IR's second goal is to help fulfill corporations' affirmative disclosure obligations under securities law and government regulation. These are described in detail later in this chapter. Stock exchanges also have their own disclosure requirements, and IR is responsible for helping companies fulfill these disclosure requirements too.

A third goal of IR is to create competitive advantage.

A third goal of IR is to create competitive advantage. Just as a company tries to create competitive advantage for its products and services in the consumer marketplace, IR works to create competitive advantage for a company's securities in the investment marketplace. To do this, IR uses the same communication tools as other public relations functions and often coordinates closely with those functions, including media relations, internal communications (especially when employees, either directly, or through unions or pension plans, own stock), and sometimes advertising.

A BRIEF INTRODUCTION TO THE FINANCIAL MARKETS AND INVESTMENT

IR is primarily concerned with communication to the financial markets. Financial markets are physical or virtual places where those who have surplus money (capital) come together with those who need money. In theory, financial markets operate so that capital flows to its most beneficial and lucrative use, defined

> IR is primarily concerned with communication to the financial markets.

as where surplus money earns the greatest return relative to risk. In practice, inefficiencies of human actions and communication almost guarantee that capital may not reach its best use. IR supports the goal that capital reach its best use by working to eliminate inefficiencies in information and data among market participants and observers.

A business generally needs money for two purposes: to fund operations or to fund growth opportunities, such as building new factories. When a business needs money, it can turn to several sources. For instance, it can generate cash from internal operations by increasing productivity (and thus earnings) or by closing inefficient operations. A business also can borrow money from a bank. Sometimes a business prefers to ask the general public to become investors and provide the necessary money. A business does this through the financial markets, by issuing bonds ("debt securities"), which in essence are tiny, discrete simultaneous loans from large numbers of investors, or by issuing stocks ("equity securities"), which in essence are tiny, discrete portions of ownership, that is, "shares" of ownership in the company itself, to many investors simultaneously. These bonds or stocks collectively are called "securities" because the supplier of capital (the investor) has secured legal standing and claim on the corporation's assets in certain circumstances.

Those who have surplus money are investors. Financial markets move money from investors to entities that issue securities, in exchange for a promise to repay the money under specified future conditions.

Debt Securities

Because financial news tends to focus more on stocks than on bonds, it is tempting to assume that stocks are where the action is. But in the U.S. the debt securities markets are significantly larger, both in dollar terms and in number of issuers.

A debt security is a promise. In exchange for borrowing the investors' money (the "principal"), corporations or governments (the "issuers") promise to pay a previously determined return ("interest"), at a stated frequency, for a certain time period. Thus when investors receive debt securities, they gain an income stream for a certain period. Gaining this steady income is why investors invest. Investors in debt securities generally know what their income stream will be, so debt securities are also known as fixed-income securities. When a debt security matures, issuers give back the principal. From the issuer's perspective, the issuer is "renting" the principal.

Debt securities are classified by the time to maturity from its initial offering, that is, the time until the principal has to be paid back. Corporate debt that matures in five years or more from its initial offering is called a "bond," corporate "notes" mature in one to five years, "commercial paper" matures in less than one year. Each of these types of debt has its advantages to an issuer. For instance, commercial paper often funds a corporation's working capital needs to keep operations flowing smoothly.

Equity Securities

Whereas debt securities are essentially loans, equity securities represent actual ownership in a corporation. Equity securities differ from debt in that the money provided by investor is provided permanently to the corporation, that is, the money never has to be paid back. But for this permanent money, investors get a permanent share of ownership in the corporation. Equity securities are commonly referred to as shares, or stocks, for this reason. If the corporation does very well, the investors stand to do very well too. Shareholders gain both from the appreciation in value of a company's stock as set by the stock market and, sometimes, from dividend payments, which are profits paid to shareholders from time to time from excess corporate cash. But shareholders also run substantial risks, too, and are the first to lose their money if a corporation goes bankrupt. Dividends are distributed on a pro rata basis; that is, each share is entitled to an equal portion of the profits. In the U.S., dividends are customarily paid quarterly, in the United Kingdom, semiannually.

> Whereas debt securities are essentially loans, equity securities represent actual ownership in a corporation.

> The stock exchanges exist, in part, to allow investors to find other investors who are willing to buy their shares of ownership.

Even though shares in themselves are permanent at-risk capital, sometimes investors want out, understandably. The stock exchanges exist, in part, to allow investors to find other investors who are willing to buy their shares of ownership. These transactions often occur on well-established, well-regulated stock exchanges, such as the New York Stock Exchange (NYSE). New York, Tokyo and London are home to the world's largest stock exchanges. Shanghai, Toronto, Frankfurt, Sao Paulo, Hong Kong, Singapore, Seoul, Dubai, Sydney and Mumbai also host important markets. Most stock exchanges today exist only electronically and have no physical location or trading floor. The NASDAQ stock exchange in New York is a notable example. Even the NYSE is rapidly moving away from its trading floor operations. In January 2006, 86 percent of the NYSE's volume occurred on its trading floor. In 2014 about 82 percent is done electronically.

> Even the NYSE is rapidly moving away from its trading floor operations. In January 2006, 86 percent of the NYSE's volume occurred on its trading floor. In 2014 about 82 percent is done electronically.

What Does "Public Company" Mean?

Some words used in IR have specialized, specific meanings that are non-intuitive and even contrary to usage in everyday English. For example, in the securities markets "public" and "private" carry meanings which derive from the description of whether a company's stock is generally available to any buyer, or whether ownership is restricted to a few. A public company is a business whose stock is available for sale to any member of the general public. A private company is a business whose ownership is restricted by law to present owners and those who may buy its stock by invitation only, directly from the company or from one of its private owners. There is no public market in a private company's stock.

What differences do such distinctions make? By definition, since private companies have no stocks or bonds publicly available for sale, they are not subject to the disclosure obligations required of public companies by law. Privately held companies are not required to disclose their finances, profits, strategies, successes, or failures, and generally they do not. Conversely, public companies are required to make full, timely, and accurate disclosures of information a reasonable observer might believe reflects on the value of that company's securities. Investor relations is the communications skill set that companies use to meet these disclosure requirements and to relay material corporate information to all reasonable public observers so they can make reasonable investment decisions concerning the company.

The Role of Shareholders in a Public Company

Shareholder-owners manage a corporation's goals and risk through the system of corporate governance. Under this system, shareholders have two rights: the right to select individuals to represent their interests who in turn to direct the CEO and other senior managers on what to do, and the right to have access to a steady, accurate stream of information about the company and its actions. In other words, shareholders elect Directors, who assemble as the Board of Directors, whose only duty in the U.S. is to represent shareholders' interests, in accordance with the law. Directors have a fiduciary duty, or duty of good faith, to serve shareholder interests.

> Shareholders elect Directors, who assemble as the Board of Directors, whose only duty in the U.S. is to represent shareholders' interests, in accordance with the law. Directors have a fiduciary duty, or duty of good faith, to serve shareholder interests.

As owners, shareholders are entitled to participate in important corporate decisions. To do this, shareholders are entitled to vote their shares on a one share, one vote basis for the election of Directors, under the concept of shareholder democracy. Shareholders vote at meetings which generally take place once per year (annual meetings), but special-purpose meetings can be called any time under procedures set out in the corporation's bylaws. At annual meetings, shareholders decide issues including appointment of the company's independent auditors, election of Directors and other issues properly brought before the meeting.

> Shareholders have the right to access certain information about the company.

Also as owners, shareholders have the right to access certain information about the company. Some information is available from the company's proxy statement and formal filings with regulators, described below. A key job for IR is providing the rest of the information that current or prospective investors need to make informed governance and investment decisions. The concept of the level playing field means that all investors and potential investors must have access to all available pertinent information at the same time. Ensuring that this happens is one of the cornerstones of IR practice. Regardless of how many shares a holder owns, all shareholders and the

CASE STUDY: STARBUCKS 2014 ANNUAL MEETING

Every public company in the U.S. (with a very few exceptions) is required to hold a general meeting of its shareholders at least once a year, to give these shareholders—who are actually the owners of the company—the ability to decide major corporate issues.

At a typical annual meeting, shareholders elect directors to represent them, select the outside auditor to keep them informed, and advise on pay packages for the senior executives who run the company on the shareholders' behalf. Annual meetings themselves often become nothing more than a dry, formulaic and legalistic proceeding, sparsely attended by shareholders.

However, smart companies now realize that their annual meeting also is an excellent platform to communicate broadly with their most important stakeholders—their owners/shareholders. Take Starbucks, for instance, which pioneered the dual use of the annual meeting as the required legal platform *and* an exciting opportunity to tell its story.

In its 2014 Annual Meeting, for instance, Starbucks Chief Executive Officer Howard Schultz gave an impassioned plea that challenged business leaders globally to redefine the role and responsibilities of for-profit companies. Shultz highlighted Starbucks' own commitment to its owners, employees and communities through its record of "performance through the lens of humanity," as the company's news release headlined it. Oprah Winfrey then joined Schultz on stage as a surprise guest for an engaging discussion tied to Oprah's own "Steep Your Soul" website and Starbucks' launch of Teavana Oprah Chai beverage.

The entire production for Starbucks' Annual Meeting included state-of-the-art staging and lighting, video, live music, and engaging conversation, all to package copious and relevant information for shareholders in a way that has made the Starbucks' Annual Meeting, held each March in Seattle, one of the hottest tickets in town.

entire investment market are entitled to equal and simultaneous access to information about the company, which brings up the two key concepts of investor relations and corporate communications: disclosure and materiality.

DISCLOSURE AND MATERIALITY

The cornerstone of a successful IR practice is the provision simultaneously of all available pertinent information to current and potential investors. This begs the questions: Is all information pertinent? If not, how does one decide whether information is pertinent? And if it is, when and how must that information be disclosed?

Public companies have an affirmative obligation under the law to keep all investor and potential investors informed on matters that they might deem important. First, note the audience: all investors and all potential investors. A fundamental principle of investor relations is that no issuer gives one market participant an informational advantage over others, as noted earlier. Since nearly every person can and does participate in the market (through ownership of mutual funds or retirement accounts, for instance), IR is much broader than a conversation with Wall Street. A variety of initiatives over the last ten years reinforced this mandate for information parity—sometimes in the jargon called a level playing field—aided significantly by the ease, speed and ubiquity of Internet-based communications. Selective disclosure—telling only some investors important corporate news before other investors—is a violation of U.S. securities law and regulation.

> The cornerstone of a successful IR practice is the provision simultaneously of all available pertinent information to current and potential investors.

Two related concepts—disclosure and materiality—determine information flow to current and potential investors.

> Two related concepts—disclosure and materiality—determine information flow to current and potential investors.

Disclosure is the distribution of information, positive and negative, by a company, voluntarily, or to be in compliance with laws and regulations. Disclosure concerns whether and when pertinent information should be released. A series of discrete rules and procedures spells out the scope, content, format, timing, certification, signatories, and other items on communication of this information.

> Disclosure is the distribution of information, positive and negative, by a company, voluntarily, or to be in compliance with laws and regulations.

There are two types of disclosure, formal and informal.

Formal Disclosure

Formal disclosure requires that specific financial and business information be filed in a highly structured way with government regulators on a regular basis. The Securities and Exchange Commission (SEC), the U.S. government's main market regulator, provides standardized forms for formal disclosure; the three key forms that communication professionals should know are the Form 10-K, the Form 10-Q, and the Form 8-K.

> Formal disclosure requires that specific financial and business information be filed in a highly structured way with government regulators on a regular basis.

The Form 10-K is a detailed report filed annually on the corporation's ("issuer's") financial results, business, management and prospects. An outside accounting firm audits the 10-K prior to its release and the SEC then reviews the 10-K in detail.

The Form 10-Q is released by an issuer after the ends of the first, second and third fiscal quarters and is a scaled-down version of the 10-K. The SEC reviews the 10-Q but the document is not audited by outside firms.

The Form 8-K is a filed by the issuer on an as-needed basis, when the issuer needs to announce certain significant changes in the company, such as new management, change of auditors, or any other critical information the issuer feels the public should know.

Formal disclosure includes two other documents for which there are not SEC forms. These are the proxy materials for the shareholders' annual meeting and the company's annual report to shareholders.

The proxy statement is material made available or distributed to each shareholder in advance of a company's annual meeting, the required yearly gathering of a company's shareholders to review performance and take major decisions through a one share, one vote election. Large corporations may have tens of millions of shares outstanding (and thus tens of millions potential votes) held by tens of thousands of shareholders. Because it is unlikely every shareholder can attend the meeting, a proxy method was developed so all shareholders can vote regardless of whether they attend in person.

A proxy is an authorization to vote a shareholder's securities. Typically, a company's senior managers ask permission to be the substitute elector and shareholders generally grant permission routinely. Thus management often enters the meeting with enough votes in hand to control all decisions; the annual meeting becomes a pro forma. But increasingly, shareholders are withholding their proxies from management or giving them to dissident shareholders who challenge management on key decisions. Such a situation falls into the category of shareholder activism in which shareholders, as owners of the company, force decisions contrary to those of company management, who are the owners' agents. Recent proxy fights have occurred over issues including limiting executive compensation and directing a company's public policy initiatives in human rights and the environment. Proxy materials are usually made available to shareholders 30 to 45 days before a scheduled meeting. The SEC reviews and approves all proxy material before distribution.

Finally, formal disclosure includes the annual report to shareholders. Unlike the Form 10-K filed with the SEC, the annual report to shareholders is a "free writing," which does not need preclearance by the SEC. Nonetheless, there is significant legal liability for material omission or misstatement in the annual report. Commonly, corporations use the annual report as a corporate marketing brochure and include the technical financial and operating information in the back; the front becomes a high-quality stylized brochure with essays, pictures, and art. The IR department or the corporate communication department is charged with writing and designing the overall annual report to shareholders. Companies traditionally devote time and attention in creating the front part of the annual report. But a significant number of companies are de-emphasizing the hard-copy annual report to shareholders as digital media take primacy.

Informal Disclosure

Informal disclosure involves communication directly to the market that is free form and distributed through a variety of channels. It is not mediated by regulators. Informal disclosure can include press releases, meeting presentations, speeches, tours of manufacturing plants, blogs and so forth. Much, but not all, communication by an IR practitioner is considered to be informal disclosure.

It is vital to note that a corporation is not obligated to distribute any and all information about itself. At one extreme, a voluminous dump of unstructured data from a corporation would be virtually useless for the market. At the other extreme, corporation have a right to keep much proprietary information private. For instance, Coca-Cola can keep its beverage formulas secret, no matter how important it is to the company's profits, and thus its stock price. A corporation is obligated to release only pertinent information that is material, and then only under certain circumstances.

It can be said all corporation information is divided into two types: material information and non-material information. The U.S. Supreme Court defined material information:

> A fact will be considered "material" if there is a substantial likelihood that a reasonable investor would consider it important in reaching his investment decision—that is, the investor would attach actual significance to the information in making his deliberations.[1]

A corporation has a free hand to deal with non-material information as it sees fit. Business-as-usual information such as internal memos, advertisements, day-to-day media relations and marketing materials are generally not considered material and therefore not subject to restrictions on dissemination. But what "actual significance" makes information material? Congress, the SEC, and the courts have deliberately left this definition vague, allowing each issuer to make this determination based on the situation at hand. Issues of disclosure and materiality are exceptionally nuanced in day-to-day practice. IR and public relations professionals often must seek and defer to the specific advice of their legal counsel.

The Issue of Fraud

The U.S. Supreme Court also has affirmed what is known as the *fraud-on-the-market-theory*, which says that misleading statements affect the price of securities in the market as a whole and defraud purchasers or sellers, even if they did not rely directly on the misstatements. Material omissions of information or materially misleading statements distort the price of a company's stock. If performed deliberately, such material omission or misstatement could be considered fraud.

The significance of fraud-on-the-market theory is that a company's disclosure obligations apply to a much larger universe than its investors, as noted earlier. The company has a duty to the market as a whole and can be sued for improper disclosure

---

It is vital to note that a corporation is not obligated to distribute any and all information about itself.

A corporation is obligated to release only pertinent information that is material, and then only under certain circumstances.

A fact will be considered "material" if there is a substantial likelihood that a reasonable investor would consider it important in reaching his investment decision—that is, the investor would attach actual significance to the information in making his deliberations.

The *fraud-on-the-market-theory* says that misleading statements affect the price of securities in the market as a whole and defraud purchasers or sellers, even if they did not rely directly on the misstatements

The significance of fraud-on-the-market theory is that a company's disclosure obligations apply to a much larger universe than its investors.

even by people who never heard or saw the disclosure, because improper disclosure would have had an impact on the market as a whole. In the U.S. a company and its officers, directors, and IR professionals are governed by the anti-fraud provisions of the SEC. In its entirety, SEC Rule 10b-5 reads:

> It shall be unlawful for any person, directly or indirectly, by the use of any means or instrumentality of interstate commerce, or of the mails, or of any facility of any national exchange,
>
> (a) To employ any device, scheme, or artifice to defraud,
> (b) To make any untrue statement of a material fact or to omit to state a material fact necessary in order to make the statements made, in light of the circumstances under which they were made, not misleading,
> (c) To engage in any act, practice, or course of business which operates or would operate as a fraud or deceit upon any person, in connection with the purchase or sale of a security.[2]

> In the U.S., the SEC has ruled that IR professionals can be subject to civil or criminal liability if they knew or should have known that the information transmitted was materially misleading or a material omission

The rule does not specify particular content of communication that constitutes fraud. When a person or company commits a material omission or discloses something materially misleading, that action operates as a deceit in the securities market.

In the U.S., the SEC has ruled that IR professionals can be subject to civil or criminal liability if they knew or should have known that the information transmitted was materially misleading or a material omission:

> Although the SEC does not regard public relations firms to be the guarantors of the information they gather for distribution, such firms should not view themselves as mere publicists or communicators of information with no attendant responsibility whatsoever for the content of such information. Indeed, these firms must be aware of their obligation not to disseminate information concerning their clients which they know or have reason to know is materially false or misleading. The obligation is particularly crucial with respect to corporate financial statements, which are one of the primary sources of information available to guide the decisions of investors. In distributing financial information, public relations firms must take special care to ensure that the information which they have received is presented fairly, accurately, and completely. Public relations firms' dissemination of information concerning their clients which they know or should have reason to know is materially false or misleading, in connection with the purchase or sale of securities of such clients, may render them liable for violations of the federal securities laws.[3]

Regulation

To review, disclosure is related to whether and when information must be disclosed and materiality is related to what information must be disclosed. The final question becomes, who is in charge to see this happens?

Securities markets are regulated by an overlapping set of state, provincial, federal, and trans-national governmental agencies. In addition, with several exceptions, each stock exchange worldwide has a layer of private regulation pertaining to any security trading on the particular exchange. Such private regulators are termed self-regulatory organizations (SROs) and carry considerable clout in determining standards and methods listing and trading a stock.

The SEC in Washington, DC, is the chief governmental regulator in the U.S.. In Canada, responsibility is held at provincial level with the Ontario Securities Commission taking the lead. The Financial Conduct Authority is the U.K.'s regulator that regulates financial firms and mandates corporate disclosure. The principal SRO in the U.S. is the Financial Industry Regulatory Authority (FINRA), which oversees most activities on the NYSE and all on NASDAQ.

Over the last two decades technology has enabled capital to move virtually anywhere on the globe instantaneously. Such capabilities led to calls from investors, listed companies, and various national governments for greater regulatory harmonization and creation of a common, precise, legal framework for securities regulation and accounting standards. As it currently stands, a company listing its stock in London and New York needs to follow three sets of regulations and three sets of accounting standards that are at times contradictory. The current situation adds expense for public companies and is said to cause unnecessary rigidity in global capital flows.

The Financial Standards Accounting Board (FASB) sets accounting standards in the U.S. These accounting standards collectively are called "Generally Accepted Accounting Principles," or more simply GAAP. Most of rest of the world has its general accounting standards called "International Financial Reporting Standards," or IFRS for short. There is a longstanding effort to harmonize GAAP and IFRS, but much work remains.

> Disclosure is related to whether and when information must be disclosed and materiality is related to what information must be disclosed.

Recent Disclosure Regulation

Over the last fifteen years in the U.S., a variety of initiatives have gone into effect designed to enhance transparency, level the informational playing field, speed the availability of corporate data, and improve corporate governance.

One key initiative to understand is SEC *Regulation Fair Disclosure*, which became effective in October 2000. Regulation Fair Disclosure (or Reg. FD) generally prohibits disclosure of material information selectively by a corporation to analysts, or others. Prior to Reg. FD, it was common IR practice to hold special closed-door meetings for selected investors and analysts and to limit or forbid general investors' participation in management conference calls,

> Regulation Fair Disclosure generally prohibits disclosure of material information selectively by a corporation to analysts, or others.

and so forth. Even though stock prices could gyrate wildly during these sessions as the privileged few took advantage of insider status to make a few bucks, the principle was that "sophisticated" information discussed in these venues exceeded that needed by the average market participant. The potential for abuse was obvious.

Under Reg. FD, corporate officers are permitted to conduct closed meetings with certain analysts or investors, but material information may not be disclosed unless it is also made available to the entire market simultaneously through other channels. If new information is blurted out by accident—for instance, by a carelessly speaking CEO—the corporation has an affirmative duty to notify the entire market of that information "promptly." The SEC has interpreted the regulation to mean in no event more than twenty-four hours later or by the beginning of the next day's trading session, whichever comes first.

INFORMATION INTERMEDIARIES: SECURITIES ANALYSTS

When making investment decisions, investors frequently depend on the advice of specialized investment professionals known as analysts.

When making investment decisions, investors frequently depend on the advice of specialized investment professionals known as analysts. Analysts are experts in specific industries, market sectors, or trends. They are trained in specific academic disciplines, have had intensive financial training, and many are certified as Chartered Financial Analysts or its equivalent.

Securities analysts typically advise investors on issues ranging from asset allocation to promising industry sector opportunities, to recommendations on specific companies. Analysts can cover entire markets, specific geographic regions, entire sectors of the economy, or particular industries or companies. Some cover stocks, some bonds. But analysts all help investors to make informed investment decisions.

Analysts can cover entire markets, specific geographic regions, entire sectors of the economy, or particular industries or companies. Some cover stocks, some bonds. But analysts all help investors to make informed investment decisions.

Securities analysts can be divided into two classes, depending on the analysts' goals: sell-side analysts and buy-side analysts.

Sell-side analysts are employed by brokerage firms and make recommendations to the firms' customers. They are called "sell-side" analysts because their advice is intended to result in a sale of shares by the brokerage firm to its customers. The research is provided to customers free of charge; the firm is compensated by the commissions it generates from the sale or from profits from the sale of shares the firm may own and sell directly to customers.

Sell-side analysts are employed by brokerage firms and make recommendations to the firms' customers.

The primary work of sell-side analysts is predicting a company's financial performance and therefore the likely profits it will generate. Based on this educated guess, analysts advise investors to buy, hold, or sell their shares. Much quantitative work goes into an analyst's projection of earnings, stock price, and buy/hold/sell recommendations. Analysts work to find any opportunity to better understand companies they cover. They meet with management, call the company's IR professionals, interview customers or suppliers, and review publicly available company information, including those disclosures managed by IR.

Sell-side analysts' work is published in the form of reports on individual companies and industries. It is distributed to clients of their brokerage firms and is sometimes available on the Internet or other sources. Analysts also brief brokers at their firms about their recommendations so brokers can share those recommendations with their customers.

Buy-side analysts also make predictions about stock performance. But they are employed directly by large investors, known as institutional investors, which include mutual funds, insurance companies, trust companies, pension funds, and other organizations. They are called "buy-side" analysts because their firms buy and hold securities for long-term gain. Buy-side analysts make "in house" recommendations only to their own company's portfolio managers. Buy-side analysts review much of the same information and also the recommendations of sell-side analysts before making their own recommendations.

Much disclosure is directed to buy-side and sell-side analysts because they have significant influence over the investment process. Much time of IR and company management is spent working with, meeting with, and attempting to influence analysts positively. Conference calls held after release of material information are intended to give these analysts timely access to company management's perspective on this news and to provide them the opportunity to ask questions. IR professionals also spend considerable time on the phone and in email with analysts answering technical questions, arranging meetings, and otherwise helping analysts understand the company

> Buy-side analysts also make predictions about stock performance. But they are employed directly by large investors, known as institutional investors, which include mutual funds, insurance companies, trust companies, pension funds, and other organizations.

> Buy-side analysts make "in house" recommendations only to their own company's portfolio managers.

INFORMATION INTERMEDIARIES: THE FINANCIAL MEDIA

Analysts, the markets, investors and potential investors rely on the financial news media, both traditional and digital, for additional key information about a company or industry. Traditional media has been augmented, and in many ways replaced, by the growing role of digital media. The financial media as a whole has great freedom of action, greater legal protections, and sometime more resources to pursue corporate information than do investors. Journalists frequently are among the first to discern trends and discover change within a corporation or industry, and it is therefore important for investors making investment decisions to pay attention to the press. Given the leading role media plays in investment decision making, investor relations and corporate media relations naturally focus considerable time and energy attempting to inform and generate accurate and positive commentary for a corporation, its management, and its prospects.

Traditional Financial Media

Because of the breaking-news nature of their reporting, wire services play an integral part in the system of corporate disclosure. Key among these services for financial news are Reuters, Bloomberg News and Dow Jones Newswires, each of which run various real-time web-based newsfeeds, desktop analytics, and coded feeds into automated trading systems. Each service also maintains extensive archives of news and market data for subscribers.

Daily newspapers with global significance in financial news include *The Wall Street Journal*, *The New York Times*, the *Financial Times*, *Les Echos* in French, *Handelsblatt* in German, and the *Nihon Keizai Shimbun* in Japanese. Regional newspapers with heavy financial news content include the *Financial Post* and the *Globe and Mail*, both of Toronto; Australia's *Financial Review*, *Il Sole 24 Horas* from Milan, Germany's *Frankfurter Allgemeine Zeitung*, the *Asahi Shimbun* from Tokyo, the *South China Morning Post* in Hong Kong and the *Straits Times* from Singapore. Local newspapers, especially those writing from a company's headquarters city, can be exceptionally influential in financial news.

Broadcast media remains important for the financial markets. Bloomberg News and Reuters each run audio and video news divisions separate from their wire services. CNBC, Bloomberg TV and Fox Business hold leading places in U.S. for cablecast business news.

Other classes of media hold sway over financial markets and investment. Periodic business and investment magazines such as *Bloomberg Businessweek*, *Forbes*, and *Barron's* still maintain important readership, although influence is waning. Trade publications—for example, *American Banker* in finance, AMM (*American Metal Market*) for the metals industry, *Variety* for entertainment, and WWD (*Women's Wear Daily*) in apparel—specialize in single-industry coverage that can surpass investment insight and expertise in the general media.

Digital Financial Media

Finally, online newsrooms, digital newsletters and blogs originating from traditional media outlets increasingly drive financial news and stock market activity. Subscriber based and no charge online news services, such as *The Business Insider* increasingly are gaining readership. News aggregators such as *Yahoo! Finance*, and *Google finance* have a large following, especially among smaller investors.

Financial blogs are a powerful force in investment markets. These specialized media can tout sometimes seemingly esoteric investment theories, obscure happenings, or shadowy market prognostications. Some aggregators and blogs have devoted readerships and can move markets and specific stocks with amazing speed.

The New York Times' DealBook[4] and the *Financial Times' FT Alphaville*[5] each are read globally for market commentary news and insight. Both also offer push editions by email each business morning to subscribers. *The Wall Street Journal* competes with its *MoneyBeat*[6] blog, but its main digital workhorses are *MarketWatch*[7] and its related *Financial News*.[8] Reuters' entry is *breakingviews.com*.[9]

Many traditional media outlets also now provide RSS feeds of breaking and posted news stories, which are delivered passively to subscribers' desktops and continually updated.

The rise of digital media also allows for individual experts and pundits to build global readerships at low cost. The *Abnormal Returns, Marc to Market,* and *Deus Ex Macchiato* are several of the more colorful, influential blogs on finance noted by the *Financial Times* in its blogroll.[10]

▶ BEST PRACTICES

Reputation Management: Disclosing More than Required by Law

It is important to note the system of corporate disclosure currently in place is a floor, not a ceiling. It is what is required as a necessary fact of doing business as a public company in the US. But such disclosure is generally not sufficient to establish and maintain long-term investor appetite for company securities. Corporations are permitted to engage in far more disclosure than the minimum requirements, and many do.

For example, there is no requirement that companies speak to individual securities analysts or to groups of analysts. But most companies do. Except for the annual meeting in most States, there is no requirement for companies to meet with or speak directly with their own shareholders. But most companies stay in constant touch with their shareholders and with the analysts who influence them.

In conclusion, companies that disclose more information more frequently than required often establish a competitive advantage for their securities and simultaneously ensure investors are sufficiently comfortable to buy or hold their shares.

Effective management of investor relations can help enhance a company's reputation among its investors and other key constituencies. Among the best practices are:

1. Ground all IR activities in the corporate and financial goals of the company: IR is an integral, not incidental, part of corporate strategy and management.

2. Coordinate closely with the CFO, media relations, and, if employees own significant shares, with employee relations.

3. Coordinate closely with the accountants and lawyers on all formal disclosure, especially regulatory filings.

4. Do more than what is required: Make it easy for investors to access information that has been disclosed, including via the company's website.

▶ RESOURCES FOR FURTHER STUDY

National Investor Relations Institute

The National Investor Relations Institute (NIRI) is the professional society for investor relations professionals in the United States. It offers a number of publications, seminars, and programs to enhance IR professionals' practice. http://www.niri.org.

Publications

Berman, Karen and Joe Knight, *Financial Intelligence: A Manager's Guide to Knowing What the Numbers Really Mean*, Boston: Harvard Business School Press, 2006.

Bowen, William G., *The Board: An Insider's Guide for Directors and Trustees*, New York: W.W. Norton & Co., 2008.

Buffett, Mary and David Clark, *Warren Buffet and the Interpretation of Financial Statements: The Search for the Company with a Durable Competitive Advantage.* New York: Scribners., 2008.

Ho, Karen Zouwen, *Liquidated: An Ethnography of Wall Street*, Durham, NC: Duke University Press, 2009.

Investor Relations Magazine. http://www.irmag.com.

Levinson, Marc, *Guide to the Financial Markets*, Princeton, NJ: Bloomberg Press, 2006 (4th edn).

Starkman, Dan, *The Watchdog That Didn't Bark: The Financial Crisis and the Disappearance of Investigative Journalism*, New York: Columbia University Press, 2014.

▶ QUESTIONS FOR FURTHER DISCUSSION

1. Is it more important to be an expert in finance or to be an expert in your company's business (e.g., an engineer in a technology company) to be an effective IR practitioner?

2. What is the optimal relationship between the IR function and the media relations function?

3. Why is an IR person subject to different legal standards (e.g., subject to civil and possibly criminal action if he or she conveys false information) than other communication professionals?

4. How should an IR person balance the desire to position the company as positively as possible with the requirements regarding formal and informal disclosure of material information?

5. When employees own a significant percentage of a company's stock, how should an IR person optimally coordinate with employee communications?

▶ NOTES

1 *TSC Industries v. Northway, Inc*. 426 U.S. 438 (1976).
2 General Rules II Under the Securities and Exchange Act of 1934, 17CFR 240.10b5.
3 Securities and Exchange Commission. Release 34-21138, July 12, 1984.
4 http://dealbook.nytimes.com.
5 http://ftalphaville.ft.com/.
6 http://blogs.wsj.com/moneybeat/.
7 http://www.marketwatch.com/.
8 http://www.efinancialnews.com/.
9 http://www.breakingviews.com/.
10 http://ftalphaville.ft.com/all-links/.

9 INTEGRATED COMMUNICATION: EVERYTHING COMMUNICATES

By Tim P. McMahon, Ph.D. Clinical Associate Professor, Heider College of Business/Principal, McMahon Marketing LLC

In this new world, collaboration trumps control; engagement tops trumpeting; and communities outlast audiences.

▶ Sidebar: Switzerland's MS *Tûranor Planetsolar*, the Largest Solar Boat in the World, and the **Deepwater** Expedition Showcase the Practical Applications of Solar in Cities Around the World

▶ Summing it All Up: Best Practices

▶ Resources for Further Study

▶ Questions for Further Discussion

■ ■ ■

COMMUNICATION LESSONS FROM THE BUFFETT BEACH PARTY

Like Warren Buffett I was born and make my living in Omaha, Nebraska. That's about where the similarities end. However, due to this proximity I have enjoyed a pretty good vantage point of the phenomenon we now call the Oracle of Omaha. Dare I say, while he claims to have a unique gift to grow capital, he is also a masterful communicator, as well. For example, he opened his 2013 pilgrimage to Omaha (known as the Berkshire Hathaway Annual Meeting held in an arena with more than 35,000 in attendance) by making his first official tweet (@WarrenBuffett): "Warren is in the house." Within hours old Warren had more than 350,000 followers, and he was following 0. This is a cogent example of Integrated Communication.

Those five words—crafted in the vernacular of socially hip netizens—may be as apt as the first words of telegraph developer–inventor Samuel F.B. Morse who tapped out: "What hath God wrought." To use his word, Buffett "intrinsically" exemplifies Integrated Communication in his personal brand as well as any public figure or company in the world through shrewd, consistent, and efficacious use of multiple communication disciplines ranging from public speaking to public relations to financial communications to social media and whatever might come along. To Buffett, effective communication is about getting the content right, then channeling it appropriately to effectively connect with constituents.

Effective Integrated Communication is about the deft weaving of strategic persuasion, public opinion, and human imagination to achieve social coherence and organizational resolve toward matters of mutual importance. Moreover, it can have enormous impact on the value of a brand—product, firm or individual. Citing Buffett again, who could forget his brand-enhancing testimony in 1991 before the U.S. House Subcommittee on Telecommunications and Finance in response to the Salomon Brothers Scandal: "Lose money for the firm, and I will be understanding; lose a shred of reputation for the firm, and I will be ruthless." That statement, embedded with core Buffett values, has firmly ensconced him as a paragon of ethical practice, and it has generated immense value for more than twenty-five years.

■■■

> **Integrated Communication (IC) =**
>
> A dynamic communication practice embracing two-way, systematic communication activities across the organization inside and out and not just the marketing plan, and in so doing aligns **brand** with **reputation** inside and outside the organization.

OVERVIEW: THE MULTIDISCIPLINARY CHALLENGE

The Buffett vignette at the start of this chapter represents the value of understanding the concept that everything communicates. The current state of communication is ubiquitous. Public relations firm Waggener Edstrom considered this new environment a *communications cataclysm*: an "outbreak of new communication channels [have] gone from feeding people's hunger for information and connectedness to overwhelming their ability to absorb information, data and points of connection."[1] The new media landscape surfaces moments of truth for communicators. Today, anyone can grab the mic by generating relevant content that engages others on Facebook, Twitter, Vine, Instagram, YouTube, or what have you. When a message is relevant, it resonates and digitally populates social space on Twitter, Facebook, LinkedIn, or any of the thousands of communities online today.

Relevance is important because the web is a democratic voting machine. Content—whether it be words, music, videos, recipes, photos, or anything that may be digitally reproduced—is more susceptible to voting than editing. Don't get me wrong, editors exist too; but they have new identities as bloggers, curators, and re-tweeters. Participants hold the power. In other words, anyone who effectively carves a niche of followers through engagement effectively elevates their status and expands their power on the web to that of trusted source, or evangelist. The followers are the currency.

Social Media guru Eric Schwartzman[2] points to two digitally enabled activities—search and share—that are keys to success. In traditional, "old school" media, the task was on finding prospective customers. Today, the challenge is to have them find you. This new digital world makes this possible because it is searchable (you can be discovered through search) and shareable (when individuals advance you or your firm with others on Pinterest, Instagram, Twitter, etc.). In this new world, collaboration trumps control; engagement tops trumpeting; and communities outlast audiences.

Communicators whose task it is to generate support for organizational initiatives—whether that is selling products, garnering support for an idea, or pitching new possibilities—must demonstrate trustworthiness through transparency, honesty, and authenticity. Likes, Shares, Retweets, and Pins are all a means to measure a firm's relevance with key publics and markets.

This new environment provides a framework for leveraging powerful two-way, symmetric communication that generates trust in the organization and that opens the door to develop clarity of its purpose among critical constituencies—employees, customers, regulators, shareholders—any and all individuals who may have a role in advancing or denying the firm's agenda. Further, now more than ever Integrated Communication is more layered and nuanced demanding greater command of related disciplines.

Now, in its third edition, this chapter continues to expand on the importance of adopting a multi-disciplinary perspective toward accomplishing organizational objectives. That is, we must ask, if communication plays the key role everyone claims it does, *what really communicates*? We have learned it is not simply formal messaging, but leadership, culture, systems, and context that matter. Finally, the "cataclysmic" change in the way the world communicates has accelerated the convergence of *reputation* and *brand*—once considered separate are now inextricably connected.

THE CONVERGENCE OF BRAND AND REPUTATION

If there is one overpowering message to take from the brave, new world of communication, it is that our constituents will begin to assess our firm based on its authenticity, transparency, and relevance. Brand guru Mike Moser wrote: "The first step to having a cohesive brand is to have a cohesive company."[3] Today, brands extend past the characteristics of the product into its deeper DNA. Further, they are strengthened by consistency.

People now engage with a brand because they align with its deeper values. Brand is about "relevancy and differentiation (with respect to the customer) and *reputation* is about legitimacy (of the organization with respect to a wide range of stakeholder groups)."[4] These functions may report to different people on the inside, but the public makes no distinction. The evolving view takes into account that people are not discreet units to be labeled and targeted. Rather, they are participants in interactive communication who may wear many hats (e.g. shareholders, employees, suppliers, evangelists, and social activists). That is why we suggest creating effective communication today is not about managing it is about leading.

Marketers have learned that to sustain a value proposition, a firm must not only integrate the marketing communication of the offer it makes to customers, but must also integrate all of its functional activities that deliver the peripheral intangibles of the product experience. So, the goal is to integrate all aspects of the experience a customer may have with a product, whether it is a good, a service, or both.

Frederick Reichheld asserted that firms must ask the ultimate question: will my customers enthusiastically recommend my company/brand? His thesis is that "loyalty initiates a series of economic effects that cascade through the business system."[5] Ten years of research supported the idea that strong profits and healthy growth stem from a firm's ability to develop customer *promoters* while reducing customer *detractors*. This challenge surpasses the focus or ability of the marketing function alone, or pure product innovation. That is because products are vulnerable to copycats. It is relatively easy to reverse engineer a product innovation, it is much more difficult to knock off a firm's well-adapted culture. As Edgar Schein claimed: culture is the way we do things around here. By definition, he said, culture is always "striving toward patterning and integration."[6] People have a need to make sense out of their worlds and seek stability. The leader must recognize the relationship between a firm's mission and goals. Further, members must strike a balance between recognizing the changing demands of the external environment and the adaptive capacity of the internal integration. They are inextricably linked. That is why the role of leadership is so important; it is the lever that coalesces a cohesive culture. After all, "a group cannot accomplish tasks, survive, and grow if it cannot manage it internal relationships."[7] It all starts on the inside.

The "Leadership" of Communication

Joseph Rost wrote: "Leadership is an influence relationship among leaders and followers who intend real changes reflecting their mutual purposes."[8] To create effective, two-way, symmetric communication is to create leadership that reflects people's need to make sense, to be purposeful, and to nurture a strong, well-adapted culture that aligns brand and reputation inside and out.

Management researcher Charles Fombrun wrote: "Companies develop winning reputations by both creating and projecting a set of skills that their constituents recognize as unique."[9] In marketing parlance, it is called *positioning*, and firms that clearly present a differential advantage, or bundle of benefits the customers value and believe they cannot get anywhere else achieve it, and enjoy a competitive advantage.[10] In building both reputation and brand, it is the ongoing conversation about the firm—inside and out—that is aligning perception and reality. As adman Moser said, the first step to a cohesive company is having a cohesive brand.

STRATEGY IN THE BRAVE NEW WORLD

Echo Research CEO Sandra McLeod concluded that "successful public relations needs to be as much about listening and being influenced, as influencing and guiding, in order to support organizations in this increasingly technologically connected and fragmented world."[11] For years there has been a tendency to view the communications function as outbound and dependent on reaching the target audience with the right corporate message, rather than two-way and interdependent on creating dialogue and collaboration. This mistaken, one-way perspective has held true for both public relations and advertising, though PR practitioners were much quicker to recognize the eroding credibility of traditional unilateral messaging.

The dawning of the democratization of media has radically altered the rules of communication and marketing. PR has emerged as the more effective tool of influence in an over-communicated world. Effective persuasion is predicated on a two-way, symmetrical relationship-building model.[12] In this model, any attempt to control or cut off information, or demonstrate over-influence will create corresponding resistance. Similarly, entering the conversation with meaningful contributions, balanced by advocacy and inquiry creates trust, collaboration, and leads to the desired outcome for the firm and its many constituents as outlined in the firm's strategic plan.

By embracing the unique perspectives of customers and prospects through the give-and-take of a transparent conversation, marketers and communicators are able to more clearly understand compelling motivations, and simultaneously test, refine, and engage customers in real-life propositions. It is truly social construction where the constructs of reality about a brand, product, or service and how we categorize such, are challenged and affirmed through a public vetting of competing perspectives.

One of the critical roles of communication is to distribute leadership throughout the organization "because the solutions to our collective challenges must come from many places, with people developing micro-adaptations to all the different micro-environments."[13] This demands a new kind of communication leadership that involves the entire organization in setting direction, obtaining commitment, and facing adaptive challenges that develop along the way.[14] In its landmark study *The Authentic Enterprise*, the Arthur W. Page Society found that the chief communication officer (CCO) must develop leadership in: "(1) defining and instilling company values, (2) building and managing multiple stakeholder relationships, (3) enabling the enterprise with 'new media' skills and tools, and (4) building and managing trust in all its dimensions."[15] This requires expanding individual and organizational knowledge, vigorously confronting reality, and creating safety to members taking legitimate bold action.

Communication is now flat—easily accessible by all—and the true source of trust for most people is "a person like themselves or a peer," identified as an emerging reality in 2006 by Edelman's Trust Barometer.[16] In the 2013 version of the report, Edelman's top leader, Richard Edelman, proclaimed that bottom-up influence driven by online social communities demands that "Smart institutions will use vertical one-way communications while continually participating in the ongoing horizontal conversation"[17] to earn trust and perspective by demonstrating decisive one-way communication balanced with an active, open role in the conversation.

The multilogue—where participation is inclusive and transparent—has challenged marketer's ability to set the agenda. That is because there is a new dimension of reality testing. Edelman's advice to have a compelling message is necessary as it always has been. However, the transparency delivered by social media favors collaboration over control. So, an organization must indeed control its messaging, but it must jump in the stream of conversation and take an active role in forging a socially constructed reality through dialogue.

Most recently, IBM Chief Communication Officer and Page Society official John Iwata, advanced these findings in his comments on a Society monograph called *Building Belief: A New Model for Activating Corporate Character and Authentic Advocacy* (2012):

> No longer is mass communication the only way to reach people; no longer do an influential few control the world's communications channels; no longer can messages intended for one audience be walled off from those intended for others. Instead, we are all living through profound changes in the way businesses and people interact. This is the defining phenomenon of our time.[18]

In his video message, Iwata called on communication leaders to address this new environment by defining organizational beliefs, values, mission, and purpose; and more importantly, by finding a way to stimulate an active organizational response. Iwata called on communication professionals to not simply deliver the message, but to cause their internal constituents to embrace it and "activate the character" inherent in their firms. Iwata is pointing unmistakably at the expanding role of Integrated Communication, not just to supplant marketing efforts, but also to coalesce organizational resolve with respect to achieving the firm's broader strategic purpose.

THE ROLE OF MARKETING: GET AND KEEP CUSTOMERS

The primary task of marketing is to identify what is valued and deliver it to the target market that values it the most. For our purposes, *Integrated Communication* (IC) represents a process that helps create, capture, and sustain value.

In his seminal book on marketing, Theodore Levitt explained, "The purpose of a business is to create and keep a customer."[19] Michael Porter pointed to value creation as the condition for customer development and retention: "[V]alue is what buyers are willing to pay, and superior value stems from offering lower prices than competitors for equivalent benefits or providing unique benefits that more than offset a higher price."[20] Management guru Peter Drucker wrote that "any business enterprise has two—and only these two—basic functions: marketing and innovation."[21] These three nuggets provide foundational elements for what must be accomplished to sustain and grow the business enterprise, supported by disciplined communication.

Marketing is a "broad general management responsibility, not just a function delegated to specialists."[22] The primary task of marketing is to identify what is valued and deliver it to the target market that values it the most. For our purposes, *Integrated Communication* (IC) represents a process that helps create, capture, and sustain value. When developing a niche or a product, the degree of customization depends on identifying the needs of specific segments of consumers and assessing the firm's ability to meet them. This challenge is best met by gathering input from multiple constituencies (e.g. employees, customers, consumers, suppliers). Today, marketers have discovered the web to be a mechanism for accomplishing product development and market identification by analyzing web content and engagement patterns.

Hunter Public Relations developed five simple steps to utilize the web to inform marketing decisions: (1) Develop Keywords—the words your customers use to discuss your product; (2) Identify Chatter—monitor conversations (based on keywords) on Twitter, Facebook, Pinterest, etc.; (3) Review Share of Voice—by quantifying the presence of you and your competitors on the web; (4) Analyze Engagement—through content analysis, asking what, when and where your customers are discussing your product; and (5) Establish a Set of Benchmark—by challenging your internal and agency social media experts to establish a set of benchmarks that align your brand with what successful engagement looks like on the Web.

Marketers sharpen the proposition by moving from large mass markets to smaller segments, and web offers a rich vantage point. Web metrics are transparent and a traffic count (or number of views) is often affixed to the entry. A consumer shooting his own video review of a product exemplifies how the web enables anyone to have a say in the position of the brand. The web has become a treasure trove of User Generated Content (UGC) where participants dish up photos, videos, tweet, pins, or elaborate mash-ups where, once uploaded, it is subject to review of its relevance and importance. Most every site uses some sort of algorithm that calculates interest in an item (through Likes, Retweets, or similar measures) thereby elevating the visibility of that specific item.

UGC has disrupted the traditional channels (e.g. newspapers, television networks) by which we have traditionally learned of the world. There is no better example of this alternate path to public visibility than the three young ladies kidnapped and held for ten years in Cleveland. They chose a direct means to thank the public who came forward with money, prayers, and well-wishing during their time of need. Rather than call a press conference they made a video and uploaded it onto YouTube. Within days, millions of views were tallied. More importantly, mainstream media (TV, Newspapers and Websites) picked up the clip and aired it on their own channels, reaching tens of millions more people. UGC has become a phenomenon.

Consider Korean singer Psy, whose YouTube video *Gangnam Style* generated more than a billion views and earned him well over a million dollars from viewings alone (YouTube pays a royalty to high volume videos), and also launched him as a mainstream star. These are but two examples of the power of UGC in shaping cultural trends and thinking that are totally in the hands of the developer of the content.

By recognizing the power and observing web content, marketers can better understand two key positioning questions: (1) Who are the potential customers?; and (2) Does the product fit their needs? That is because what was once only obtainable through focus groups or other social science tools can often be obtained free of charge simply through disciplined observation or online engagement with target customers. By answering these questions marketers more accurately articulate market segments and determine which they are best able to serve. The process is abbreviated as STP: segmentation, targeting, and positioning. If a firm can solve its positioning problem, it can address its marketing mix. With shrewd use of the web, marketers can often accomplish both all the while creating early adopters of the ensuing product.

Marketers refer to the Four Ps (product, place, promotion, and price) as the marketing mix. Product involves the package of benefits for customers. Place refers to the channel, or how the product reaches customers. Promotion is about communication and how marketers create buzz. Consumers adopt brands that embody their values. Price is how marketers capture value and is dependent to a large degree on the other three Ps.

One of the best characterizations of brand comes from Dave Sutton and Tom Klein: "Like a person, a brand has individual values, physical features, personality, and character. Like a story, a brand has characters, setting, and a plot. Like a friend, a brand offers a personal relationship, one that—in the best-case scenario—evolves as you do."[23]

Customer relationship management (CRM), an area where communications may make an extraordinary contribution, is

> "Like a person, a brand has individual values, physical features, personality, and character. Like a story, a brand has characters, setting, and a plot. Like a friend, a brand offers a personal relationship, one that—in the best-case scenario—evolves as you do."

about developing and managing a long-term relationship between the company and its customers The objective is to sustain loyalty. Without dialogue with customers about changing needs, the relationship weakens and a firm loses its ability to accurately assess components of value until it is too late and a competitive challenge arises.

Southwest Airlines has a couple of million Facebook followers and about 1.3 million Twitter followers, a trailblazer in developing social media capabilities. The airline maintains an ongoing dialogue on these platforms and in one case reversed a marketing decision to move to assigned seating because their social media followers overwhelmingly reaffirmed group seating is why they preferred Southwest.

In business-to-business (B2B) environments, marketers must understand the quantity and nature of relationships on additional levels. In his revealing book on selling, Neil Rackham wrote: "As the size of the decision grows, more people become involved. Your success may often depend not just on how well *you* sell, but on how well the people in the account sell to each other."[24] Cohesive corporate communication promotes understanding among employees as to exactly how the company adds value. Rackham discovered the challenge of selling is getting people to sell themselves. Salespeople should not be selling as much as they should be walking the prospect through the buying process.

THE ROLE OF COMMUNICATION: MOVE PEOPLE TO DESIRED ACTION

Much of what has been discussed recognizes that organizational success depends on the will of people, their adaptability, and their ability to effectively deal with reality. Preeminent PR researcher James Grunig explained that "with the two-way symmetrical model [of public relations] practitioners use research and dialogue to bring about symbiotic changes in ideas, attitudes, and behaviors of both the organization and publics."[25] In this model, advocacy is balanced with inquiry to form skills of honest investigation.[26] This is facilitated through dialogue and straightforward communication. In the practice of Integrated Communication, *values* must first be understood, then shared, and then they will guide decision-making.

In a two-way world, where a *mommy blogger* dispatching 140-character Twitter-rants can call into question a firm's marketing efforts, it is not enough to have a vision. What is important is to be adaptive and engaged. Leaders must understand that a plan is based on today's best guess and may be disrupted. Without organizational self-awareness and shared values, members up and down the line will struggle for a coherent and sincere response.

When the Ford Motor Company constructed its launch plan for its Fiesta, a model that had enjoyed success in Europe and South America, it "tapped 100 top bloggers and gave them a Fiesta for six months. The catch: Once a month, they are required to upload a video on YouTube about the car, and they are encouraged to talk—no holds barred—about the Fiesta on their blogs, Facebook and Twitter."[27] Ford's social media head Scott Monty emphasized the bloggers are free to say what they want—a critical rule to be observed in the social media space. The web detests censorship and avoids it like the plague.

How firms act, react, and interact forges perception of the brand as acting responsibly with its publics' best interests at heart. Being open to honest dialogue demonstrates a sincere effort to get to the best outcome for all involved. This is walking the talk, a critical authenticity test for brands.

> Being open to honest dialogue demonstrates a sincere effort to get to the best outcome for all involved. This is walking the talk, a critical authenticity test for brands.

Ronald Reagan's cautionary phrase, "trust, but verify" is increasingly embedded in a communicator's solemn responsibility to a firm. The stakes are simply too high to guess on message accuracy, its desired effect, or its return on investment (ROI). It is imperative that CCOs devise a reliable and accessible set of measures. That begins with understanding what is to be measured.

Outputs, *outtakes*, and *outcomes* are three measures that must be properly evaluated. Outputs measure the ability to disseminate a message. Outtakes measure how a message is received and understood. Outcomes measure the behavioral change that results from communication. Third-party providers are available to help in each area. Accurate measurement here permits communicators to isolate communication problems. The ultimate measurement answers the question: will your constituents (customers, employees, investors, etc.) enthusiastically recommend the firm to others.

THE INTEGRATED COMMUNICATION HOOK® MODEL

The metaphor of a hook is not new and has been associated with a lure to catch fish, something to hang things on, or a means to get attention like a repeated musical refrain. The IC Hook® Model (see Figure 9.1) illustrates the parallel roles of communications and marketing. It is a framework to organize and manage the work of *Integrated Communication*. The four quadrants of the chart serve as a roadmap describing the activities that make IC powerful, measurable, and valued.

COMMUNICATION TOOLBOX

Here are some of the tools communication professionals commonly use in Integrated Communication to achieve an objective, create meaning, counter resistance, or simply move closer to a desired outcome.

Effective Persuasion

Organizational behavior professor Jay Conger pointed to four essential steps in effective persuasion: (1) establish credibility; (2) frame your goals in a way that identifies common ground

> In the workplace, credibility grows out of expertise and relationships.

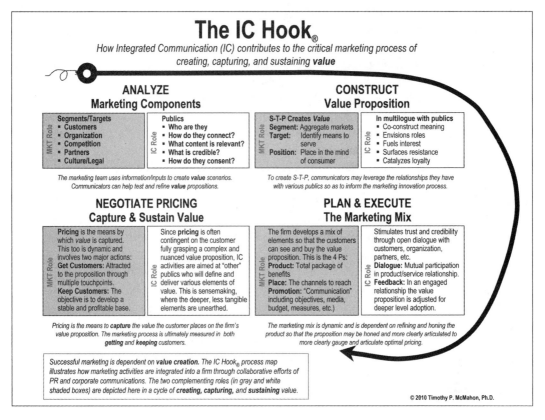

Figure 9.1 The IC Hook®, a map for plotting communication to marketing

with your audience (positioning); (3) reinforce your position by using vivid language and compelling evidence; and (4) connect emotionally with your audience.[28] Conger noted research suggesting that most managers strongly overestimate their credibility. In the workplace, credibility grows out of expertise and relationships. Expertise is shown by repeatedly demonstrating competence. Relationships develop when people see others as trustworthy and having their best interests at heart.

Meaning = empowerment

Language is the sum and substance of meaning making within a group. "The individual mind (thought, experience) does not thus originate meaning, create language, or discover the nature of the world."[29] People use language to relate to each other in a given environment and to define their reality.

In this manner, communication is about mining shared meaning, and it leads to the most elusive commodity in organizations: empowerment. Quinn and Spreitzer discovered two forms of empowerment: organic and mechanistic. They found the organic is "less predictable but more likely to create conditions where members have integrated their own values with values held by the larger organization."[30] Mechanistic is top-down and tends to be delegated, specific, and more dependent on compliance. This form, while effective in certain circumstances, did not engage employees as wholly. The researchers remarked that one group they studied "feared empowerment would create 'loose cannons,' a fear more imagined than empirically observed. When the people of a firm are connected through values, they can be organizational advocates as powerful as cannons.

Connecting the Dots

Knowing how to harness organizational will is the lynchpin in addressing organizational challenges. Individual will is tied to clarity and purpose. If the members of an organization know what they bring to the party, have the information that tells them if they are bringing it, and are subsequently recognized and rewarded for doing it . . . the individual and the organization win.

On the other hand, when people are confused and uninformed they are most likely a drag on the whole operation. Jim Shaffer wrote: "They are a drag on productivity . . . on quality and service. . . . they cause costs to rise . . . [and cause] everything to move slower while they're trying to figure to what to do."[31] The fact is confused and uninformed people don't want to be a drag. But, due to a lack of leadership, they have little choice. Shaffer advised leaders to connect the dots: "linking people and what they do to the business and its strategy, vision, and goals"[32]

Metaphors

Lakoff and Johnson explained that a metaphor creates coherence allowing people to understand something by relating it to what they know.[33] Amid a controversy regarding contributions, Richard Nixon demonstrated a keen understanding of how metaphor can be used to recoup credibility. While running for vice president on the ticket with Dwight Eisenhower, he referred to his wife as wearing a Republican cloth coat, to rustle a positive conservative notion held by his audience. No furs or leather for this second lady to be! TV cameras showed Pat Nixon wearing the coat on TV, but the candidate created the metaphor by calling it out verbally. His speech proved that even uncharismatic speakers can use powerful words to shape perception. The speech generated an enormous amount of pro-Nixon mail, and he and Eisenhower went on to victory.

Framing

"People respond to the meanings they have for words and events rather than to the words and events themselves."[34] Framing is the tool used to create appeal in the minds of the audience. It uses words that are most important to gaining approval on issues. Targeting is crucial to successful framing—just as Nixon reached out to Republicans with his cloth coat message.

Bridging gaps

Nirmalya Kumar brought this time-tested concept into sharp focus when he wrote: "Three mutually reinforcing changes are enabling faster and more coherent

Effective Integrated
Communication drives the
process, creating meaning
and understanding for all
employees.

coordination of customer value creating activities within organizations."[35] Organizations are moving from functions to processes, from hierarchies to teams, and from transactions to partnerships. These changes stem from the need to better serve customers in a world where an abundance of choices and channels has overheated the environment.

The challenge in creating value in today's marketplace is not simply about creating a product or service. It also requires the ability to deliver it on demand through coordinated teams of multi-talented employees who organize around the customer. Effective Integrated Communication drives the process, creating meaning and understanding for all employees.

Storytelling

Stories help people understand how beliefs translate to behaviors. One such story repeated frequently at Southwest Airlines is about a flight attendant popping out of the overhead luggage bin. At Southwest, this story has become a symbol of company spirit. At headquarters, the walls display company history, values and culture. It is not uncommon for a newcomer to be shown a wall display that reflects one of the company values. Culture is a powerful thing built upon effective communication.

Corporate Branding

"The first step to having a cohesive brand is to have a cohesive company."[36] Brand concept begins with an easy-to-understand promise. The popular bug killer, Raid®, for example, uses "Kills bugs dead" as its advertising slogan. A product brand, with its features, functions, and benefits, is usually easier to promote than a corporate brand. That's especially the case when a corporation is a holding company that owns many brands. Corporate identity begins with a clear understanding of corporate values.

Does Virgin® mean records? Maybe it once did when the name stood over the door of a single record store – but not today. The firm's iconic Times Square store closed in 2009, but, Richard Branson created an organization that marches to the beat of a different drummer with a set of values different from its competitors and this intangible is what endures. One of the distinct values of Virgin is "irreverence." It gives Virgin brand leverage because a significant number of customers identify with the unconventional image Virgin brings to businesses including airline and train travel, cell phones cards. Few companies today are executing integrated marketing better than Red Bull (see Figure 9.2).

The "gives you wings" people have excelled at events to distinguish the brand from the rest of the pack. What's more they employ a distinctive presence locally with their young and energetic representatives tooling around in their Red Bull rides with the can on top! The result for Red Bull has been a tight relationship between the beverage and its devotees with 2012 worldwide sales topping $6.5 billion. Co-owner Dietrich Mateschitz "eschews bureaucracy and famously rejected the recommendations of a market research

Figure 9.2 The Long Jump—Red Bull has wings!

Source: Camera Press/Ria Novosti/Redux

report which advised to him to not even try to launch an energy drink. He relied on his gut-feel instead and spent one year changing the formulation of the drink from the original Thai version and another two years fine-tuning its marketing and communications strategy."[37] This is fundamental structuring that accomplished one of the most durable and disruptive challenges in marketing: spawning a new category, the energy drink. The whole world watched live and several million times more on YouTube.

Vision, Values, and Purpose

A vision provides reference points for decision-making, and it motivates individuals to be a part of something greater than they could accomplish alone. More than ever, the vision is clarified from the bottom-up, and when that happens, it is truly empowering. It can set organization apart from all others –the desired outcome of Integrated Communication.

> A vision provides reference points for decision-making, and it motivates individuals to be a part of something greater than they could accomplish alone.

During my tenure at ConAgra Foods, one of our sales representatives visited a very large retail buyer who complained that his customers needed a complete dinner that was inexpensive, easy-to-make and gave the impression of something special for the family. The sales rep took the challenge back to the culinary team who came up with a hot casserole prepared in the time it took to change out of work clothes and set the table. Because the product was baked, the house would be filled with a fresh-from-the-oven aroma, a user-valued benefit. Banquet® Homestyle Bakes became a smash hit generating hundreds of millions of dollars in its first year, and it redefined the home meal solutions category. When the company and its customers share the vision, value-creation soon follows.

New Corporate Presence

A new corporate presence has emerged as organizations bring their identities to life through corporate social responsibility and corporate social engagement.

Marketing communications executive Carol Cone pioneered a discipline of communications called Cause Branding®, also known as cause-related marketing. It helps companies and nonprofits integrate values and social issues into brand equity and organizational identity.

Cone seized on two findings in her study of ConAgra Foods' social responsibility issues. First, employees were highly concerned about leveraging their expertise in sourcing, producing and distributing food to benefit society. Second, a U.S. Department of Agriculture statistic pointed to 12 million American kids who go hungry each year. Studies show that hunger is a root cause for many of the problems young people face today, from concentrating in school to conduct after school. ConAgra Foods launched *Feeding Children Better*, a multi-year commitment to help eliminate childhood hunger in America. This demonstrated corporate marketing in action—bridging the gap between customer need and organizational capability. The company warmly embraces the program more than a decade later.

Few firms have mastered the art of relationship building better than Southwest Airlines. It begins on the inside. Its internal newsletter, *LUV Lines*, sparks dialogue about company news and information. In their book about the company, Kevin and Jackie Freiberg wrote: "This dialogue almost always results in a better understanding of the implications of the information and its relevance to what people do."[38] When a front-line employee has a firm grasp on the issues, it has a seemingly magical effect on customer satisfaction because that so rarely happens elsewhere.

Responsibility also spurs corporate social presence. Smart, the largest telecom in the Philippines recognized a growing problem that has presented itself the world over. Textbooks have become too heavy and burdensome for school children to lug around. They arrive at school tired and bear long-term injury as a result of the stress on their growing bodies. In developed countries, tablets and robust e-readers provided a solution to this problem. However, in developing countries the cost of even the most economical devices was out of the question. The firm, working with textbook companies, devised a way to create 160-character lessons and embed them in the inbox of thousands of surplus SIM cards that could be readily used in analog phones, abundant and inexpensive in the Philippines. The program has worked beyond expectations and the esteem of the firm has risen dramatically in its home country and the world over, especially after being awarded a Gold Lyon at the 2013 Cannes Awards for Creativity.

For the program, Smart reworked its tagline from "Making text light and easy" to "Making text*books* light and easy," a clever modification that stuck nicely in the minds of consumers. The result was a 50 percent reduction in the weight of school children's backpacks, 95 percent attendance and 90 percent test scores. While not an ad, this action connected with people and inured to the positive reputation of Smart, and the power of its brand.

GMR Marketing, a pioneer in creating corporate and brand presence, uses the tagline, *The way to live marketing!* According to its web site, "Live Marketing is the engagement and stimulation of the senses in a uniquely personal brand experience."

A cold Pepsi at a summer concert or the aroma and sizzle of a Johnsonville bratwurst at a state fair are among the experiences GMR captures for its clients. GMR created a series of lifestyle, value-oriented connections to bring ConAgra Foods to life. This led Joe Gibbs, three-time Super Bowl winning coach and two-time NASCAR Cup champion team owner, to represent ConAgra Foods' many brands at a Walmart meeting. Gibbs embodied the values of the company: honest, competitive, family-oriented, and committed to winning. In addition, the red and white #20 NASCAR Bush Series car carried the ConAgra Foods logo on its hood and displayed thirty company brands on various other parts of the car. A die cast scale model was created and distributed to customers, employees and suppliers. Walmart employees and customers also were put in touch with the Joe Gibbs Racing Team at events across the country and by personal customer visits by Coach Gibbs.

> *Activation* is the term used to describe the way a sponsorship becomes Live Marketing.

Once called sponsorships, these connections extend beyond just famous names. *Activation* is the term used to describe the way a sponsorship becomes Live Marketing. For example, ConAgra Foods built a mobile kitchen pulled by a big rig that crisscrossed the country with samples of many ConAgra Foods products. Big Hungry, as the truck was called, even made a special trip to lower Manhattan in 2001 to serve Thanksgiving meals—Butterball turkeys and all the trimmings—to 9/11 rescue and recovery workers. This event was put together by hundreds of employee volunteers throughout the company who wanted to pay tribute to the thousands of firefighters, police, and rescue workers at Ground Zero. Traditional advertising also is often tied into these marketing efforts, including the messages below that appeared in *The Wall Street Journal*.

CASE STUDY: SWITZERLAND'S MS *TÛRANOR PLANETSOLAR*, THE WORLD'S LARGEST SOLAR BOAT, AND THE *DEEPWATER* EXPEDITION SHOWCASE THE PRACTICAL APPLICATIONS OF SOLAR IN CITIES AROUND THE WORLD

By Katja Schroeder

Countries too have reputations and the principles for managing national reputation are the same as for managing corporate reputation: Perform, behave and communicate well. Determine which stakeholder groups are most influential and learn what drives their views of the country. This case focuses on sustainability, an important driver of national reputation.

The Consulate General of Switzerland in New York (see Figure 9.3) partnered with Expedition PR to create excitement about the arrival of the MS *Tûranor PlanetSolar*, the world's largest solar boat, in New York, slated for mid-June 2013. The task was to leverage the boat's stopover in New York, a city that boasts a growing tech community and promotes sustainability, to highlight Switzerland's contributions to scientific

Schweizerische Eidgenossenschaft
Confédération suisse
Confederazione Svizzera
Confederaziun svizra

Consulate General of Switzerland in New York

Figure 9.3

research, technology innovation and sustainability. Onboard PlanetSolar was the *Deepwater* expedition, a team of scientists from the University of Geneva. The researchers were collecting data along the Gulf Stream to analyze changes in ocean currents and climate change. Due to tropical storm Andrea, the actual arrival date of PlanetSolar in New York was delayed and ultimately shortened the boat's stay in NYC. The team worked together to maximize the crew's limited time to meet with key influencers and increase the visibility for the PlanetSolar mission and Switzerland's leadership position in innovation and sustainability.

Strategy and Program

The team executed a PR strategy that segmented the program in three phases:

- **Anticipate:** Prior to the boat's arrival in New York, the team started reaching out to reporters covering sustainability, innovation and transportation to alert them about PlanetSolar's stop-overs in the United States as part of its world tour. The team used news announcements about setting the *world speed record for transatlantic crossing by a solar vessel* and *the start of the DeepWater expedition* in Miami to start the conversation about the Swiss boat's mission for solar energy.

  News about the boat's itinerary was shared via social media, and media reports were reposted via Twitter and Facebook. Prior to the arrival the Swiss Consulate hosted a Solar Quiz on Facebook contest. Each week, the Consulate posted a question related to Switzerland's solar industry and innovation; correct answers automatically entered a drawing for a ticket for the VIP reception.

  As the exact date of the press conference could not be determined due to the bad weather conditions, the team alerted NYC-based news, local, business, sustainability and maritime media about an upcoming press event on the PlanetSolar boat ahead of time, keeping the final date fluid until it could be confirmed two days prior to the arrival. The exact boat's docking time was communicated to TV stations and wires the day before the arrival.

- **Celebrate:** During the PlanetSolar stop-over in New York, the team organized the following activities with key influencers:

  - *VIP Reception*. Shortly after the boat docked, the Consulate General of Switzerland in New York hosted a Welcome Reception for the PlanetSolar and *Deepwater* expedition team, attended by the diplomatic circle, academic institutions, analysts and representatives of the New York clean tech community. Some of them tweeted their pictures from the boat during and after the event, spreading the word about PlanetSolar's stay in NYC to their followers.

  - *Press Conference and Interviews*. The next day, New York City's Sustainability Officer welcomed the crew together with the Swiss Consulate at the press conference. Twenty-nine TV, print and wire reporters and foreign media correspondents attended the event and talked to the PlanetSolar crew and the scientists of the University of Geneva and—most importantly toured the boat with its impressive "sundeck" that features two tennis courts of solar panels. To extend the reach beyond New York, the team issued a news announcement entitled "The Switzerland's MS *Tûranor PlanetSolar*, the World's Largest Solar Boat, Arrives in New York City" to a nationwide media list, which obtained more than 1200 reads.

  - *General public*. The boat's sheer presence at the marina created interest among passersby. Also, people who had read about the boat or seen it on Facebook took the opportunity to see it up close. As the boat was not available for tour, the Consulate General of Switzerland had prepared a brochure to educate the general public about Swiss solar projects, which was distributed together with a *PlanetSolar* flyer.

  - *Insights*—PlanetSolar *up close*. To get more in-depth coverage and features about the boat's mission, the team scheduled one-on-one-meetings with print, radio and TV media after the official press event, including U.S. and foreign media. Especially TV and radio reporters, including Bloomberg TV, TechCrunch TV, and WNBC The Takeaway, could take b-roll and sounds on and around the boat. Eight reporters from five publications were given the unique opportunity to take a Liberty Island Harbor cruise on the *PlanetSolar* before the boat departed to Boston. During the tour, they could interview the Captain and the research team on board, giving them unique footage for their reporting. Through a helicopter photo and video shoot, participants also obtained aerial pictures for their reporting following the tour.

Outcome

The MS *Tûranor PlanetSolar* was greeted with fanfare and excitement by New Yorkers at the marina. Al Jazeera and NBC News covered the boat's arrival. AFP pictures of *PlanetSolar* approaching New York with the Swiss flag on top of the boat were published in slideshows by newspapers around the world, including *The Economic Times* (India), *The Hindu* (India), *The Guardian* (UK), *Los Tiempos* (Bolivia), *The Wall Street Journal* (US), *Metro NYC* (US), *Arab World*, and *The Local* (Switzerland). Forty percent of the articles published included a AFP picture; 28 percent of the articles included AFP content.

More than forty-four reporters attended the media event and visited the boat for interviews. News coverage appeared in more than eighty-eight publications worldwide, including *The New York Times*, *National Geographic*, *Bloomberg TV*, *Huffington Post UK*, *International Business Times*, *The Boston Globe*, *WNYC*, *CleanTechnica*, *Mother Jones*, *Sustainable Mobility*, *Weather Channel*, *Huffington Post*, *Inhabitat*, and *Phys.Org*; 53 percent of the coverage appeared in foreign media, i.e. *NZZ*, *RTS*, *Le Temps*, *Die Welt* (Germany), *Le Figaro* (France) and *La Presse* (Canada).

A media content analysis for the key message penetration showed that 73 percent of the coverage mentioned Switzerland; 88 percent of coverage had images of *PlanetSolar*, 60 percent of which visibly showed the Swiss flag; 23 percent had mention of the Swiss Consulate; 69 percent mentioned the University of Geneva.

The boat's stay in New York received global attention on social outlets. Stories by reporters with large a social media following, i.e. Inhabitat and Verge, received numerous re-tweets.

▶ SUMMING IT ALL UP: BEST PRACTICES

The best approach to best practices is to develop measurement standards that help track and evaluate activities. Here are two sources that appeared on the Institute for Public Relations website. The first is a work in progress called Proposed Interim Standards for Metrics in Traditional Media Analysis.[39] This is an enlightening read that discusses standards under consideration for adoption, including: (1) How to Calculate Impressions; (2) What Counts as a Media "Hit"; (3) How to Calculate Tone or Sentiment; (4) Options for Assessing Quality Measures; and (5) Advertising Value Equivalency (AVEs) Should Not be Used as a Measure of Media. What follows is a well-considered approach to social media measurement, also from the Institute's website.

**The Eight Step Social Media Measurement Process: A Step-by-Step Approach
– Angela Jeffrey**[40]

1. Identify organizational and departmental goals.

2. Research stakeholders for each and prioritize.

3. Set specific objectives for each prioritized stakeholder group.

4. Set social media Key Performance Indicators (KPIs) against each stakeholder objective.

5. Choose tools and benchmark (using the AMEC Matrix).

- Public relations activity
- Intermediary effects
- Target audience effects

6. Analyze the results and compare with costs.

7. Present to management.

8. Measure continuously and improve performance.

▶ RESOURCES FOR FURTHER STUDY

Arthur W. Page Society, The Authentic Enterprise, 2007, retrieved from http://www. awpagesociety.com/site/members/page_society_releases_the_authentic_enterprise.

Arthur W. Page Society, *Building Belief: A New Model for Activating Corporate Character and Authentic Advocacy*, 2012, retrieved from http://www.awpagesociety.com/insights/ building-belief/.

Conger, J.A., "The Necessary Art of Persuasion," 1998, *Harvard Business Review 76*(3), 84–96.

Creevey, D. "'A Person Like Me' Now Most Credible Spokesperson for Companies; Trust in Employees Significantly Higher Than in CEOs, Edelman Trust Barometer Finds," January 23, 2006, retrieved July 4, 2009 from http://www.edelman.com/news/show-one.asp?id=102.

Deetz, S.A., S.J. Tracy, and J.L. Simpson, *Leading Organizations Through Transition,* Thousand Oaks, CA: Sage Publications, Inc, 2000.

Drath, W.F., *The Deep Blue Sea: Rethinking the Source of Leadership*, San Francisco: Jossey-Bass, 2001.

Drucker, P.F., *The Practice of Management,* New York: Harper Business, 1993 (original work published in 1954).

Eisenmann, M., D. Geddes, K. Paine, R. Pestana, F. Walton, and M. Weiner, "Proposed Interim Standards For Metrics in Traditional Media Analysis, 2012, retrieved July 11, 2013, from http://www.insti-tuteforpr.org/topics/proposed-interim-standards-for-metrics-in-traditional-media-analysis/.

Ettenson, R. and J. Knowles, "Don't Confuse Reputation With Brand," *MIT Sloan Management Review, 40*(2), 19–21, 2008.

Edelman, R., The 2013 Edelman Trust Barometer, 2006, retrieved July 9, 2013, from http://edelmaneditions.com/wp-content/uploads/2010/12/edelman-trust-barometer-2006.pdf.

Edelman, R., The 2013 Edelman Trust Barometer, 2013, retrieved June 1, 2013, from http://www.scribd.com/fullscreen/121501475?access_key=key-1ao9w09me9qq9h66m0d2.

Fombrun, C., *Reputation: Realizing Value from the Corporate Image,* Boston: Harvard Business School Press, 1996.

Freiberg, K. and J. Freiberg, *Nuts! Southwest Airlines' Crazy Recipe for Business and Personal Success,* Austin, TX: Bard Books, 1996.

Gergen, K.J. and M. Gergen, *Social Construction: Entering the Dialogue*, Chagrin Falls, OH: Taos Institute, 2004.

Grunig, J.E., "Two-way Symmetrical Public Relations: Past, Present, and Future," in R. Heath (Ed.), *Handbook of Public Relations* (pp. 11–30), Thousand Oaks, CA: Sage, 2001.

Hayes, R.B., "Public Relations and Collaboration: The Role of Public Relations and Communications Supporting Collaboration in a Complex, Converging world," 2008, retrieved July 11, 2009, http://www.lulu.com/content/paperback-book/public-relations-and-collaboration/4602019.

Heifetz, R., A. Grashow, and M. Linsky, *The Practices of Adaptive* Leadership, Boston: Harvard University Business Press, 2009.

Jeffery, A., "The Eight Step Social Media Measurement Process: A Step-by-step Approach," 2013, retrieved July 11, 2013 from http://www.instituteforpr.org/iprwp/wp-content/uploads/Social-Media-Measurement-Paper-Jeffrey-6-4-13.pdf.

Kumar, N., *Marketing as Strategy*, Boston: Harvard Business Press, 2004.

Lakoff, G.M. and M. Johnson, *Metaphors We Live By*, Chicago: University of Chicago Press, 2003.

Levitt, T., *The Marketing Imagination*, New York: Free Press, 1983.

Moser, M., *United We Brand*, Boston: Harvard Business School Press, 2003.

Pangarkar, N. and M. Agarwal, "The Wind Behind Red Bull's Wings," *Forbes Asia*, June 24, 2013, retrieved July 10, 2013 from http://www.forbes.com/sites/forbesasia/2013/06/24/the-wind-behind-red-bulls-wings/.

Porter, M.E., *Competitive Advantage: Creating and Sustaining Superior Performance* (Rev. edn), New York: Free Press, 1998 (original work published 1985).

Quinn, R. and G. Spreitzer, "The Road to Empowerment: Seven Questions Every Leader Should Consider," autumn 1997, *Organizational Dynamics, 37–49.

Rackham, N., *SPIN Selling*, New York: McGraw Hill, 1988.

Reichheld, F., *The Loyalty Effect*, Boston: Harvard Business School Publishing, 1996.

Rost, J.C., *Leadership for the 21st Century*, Westport, CT: Praeger, 1993.

Schein, E.H., *Organizational Culture and Leadership* (4th edn), San Francisco: Jossey-Bass, 2010.

Senge, P.M., *The Fifth Discipline: The Art and Practice of the Learning Organization* (Rev. edn), New York: Currency Doubleday, 2006.

Shaffer, J., *The Leadership* Solution, New York: McGraw-Hill, 2000.

Silk, A.J., *What is Marketing?* Boston: Harvard Business School Press, 2006.

Stacks, D.W., Best Practices in Public Relations Research, 2002, retrieved from Institute for Public Relations website: http://www.instituteforpr.org/research

Sutton, D. and T. Klein, *Enterprise Marketing Management: The New Science of Marketing*, Hoboken, NJ: John Wiley & Sons, Inc, 2003.

Swartz, J., "More Marketers Sign on to Social Media," August 28, 2009, *USA Today*, pp. B1–2.

Schwartzman, E., Social Media Bootcamp, 2013, slide retrieved July 8, 2013 at http://www. linkedin.com/profile/view?id=3016595&locale=en_US&trk=tyah .

Waggener Edstrom, "Thriving During a Communications Cataclysm," 2009, retrieved June 16, 2009 from http://waggeneredstrom.com/influence/influence-manifesto/default.aspx.

▶ QUESTIONS FOR FURTHER DISCUSSION

1. *Integrated Marketing Communication* (IMC) focuses on selling the product and building customer relationships through marketing and public relations, whereas Integrated Communication (IC) places greater emphasis on the growing importance of an organization's relationships that create its identity, image, and reputation. The argument is that brand is about differentiation and reputation is about legitimacy. What is the importance of this distinction?

2. What is the importance of a strong, well-aligned organizational identity and life to the vitality of the firm's identity, image, and reputation; and to the execution of its corporate strategy?

3. What role does the expanding influence of social media have on the effectiveness and role of Integrated Communication?

4. Why does the concept of a "multilogue" make more sense than that of a "dialogue" in the current landscape of communication?

5. Does a firm need to "break the rules" of top-down communication to engage its multiple constituents effectively?

6. Can you think of an example of where cause marketing failed to engage its constituents? If so, what caused the disconnection?

7. How does the idea of two-way communication challenge the principle that corporate communications is about articulating a firm's corporate strategy?

▶ NOTES

1 Waggener Edstrom, "Thriving during a Communication Cataclysm." retrieved June 16, 2009 from http://waggeneredstrom.com/influence/influence-manifesto/default.aspx, p. 2.

2 E. Schwartzman, Social Media Bootcamp, slide retrieved July 8, 2013 from http://www. linkedin.com/profile/view?id=3016595&locale=en_US&trk=tyah.

3 M. Moser, *United We Brand* (Boston: Harvard Business School Press, 2003), p. 15.

4 R. Ettenson and J. Knowles, "Don't Confuse Reputation with Brand," *MIT Sloan Management Review*, vol. 40, no. 2 (2008), pp. 19–21, p. 19.

5   F. Reichheld, *The Loyalty Effect* (Boston: Harvard Business School Publishing, 1996), p. 19.

6   E.H. Schein, *Organizational Culture and Leadership* (4th edn) (San Francisco: Jossey-Bass, 2010), p. 16.

7   Ibid., p. 93.

8   J.C. Rost, *Leadership for the 21st Century* (Westport, CT: Praeger, 1993), p. 102.

9   C. Fombrun, *Reputation: Realizing Value from the Corporate Image* (Boston: Harvard Business School Press, 1996), p. 9.

10 A.J. Silk, *What is Marketing?* (Boston: Harvard Business School Press, 2006), p. 89.

11 R.B. Hayes, *Public Relations and Collaboration: The Role of Public Relations and Communications Supporting Collaboration in a Complex, Converging World* (2008), retrieved July 11, 2009, http://www.lulu.com/content/paperback-book/public-relations-and-collaboration/4602019, p. 15.

12 J.E. Grunig, "Two-way Symmetrical Public Relations: Past, Present, and Future," in R. Heath (ed.), *Handbook of Public Relations* (Thousand Oaks, CA: Sage, 2001), pp. 11–30.

13 R. Heifetz, A. Grashow, and M. Linsky, *The Practices of Adaptive Leadership* (Boston: Harvard University Business Press, 2009) p. 3.

14 W.F. Drath, *The Deep Blue Sea: Rethinking the Source of Leadership* (San Francisco: Jossey-Bass, 2001), p. 18.

15 Arthur W. Page Society, "The Authentic Enterprise" (2007), http://www.awpagesociety.com/site/members/page_society_releases_the_authentic_enterprise, p. 7.

16 D. Creevey, "'A Person Like Me' Now Most Credible Spokesperson for Companies; Trust in Employees Significantly Higher Than in CEOs, Edelman Trust Barometer Finds," retrieved July 4, 2009 from http://www.edelman.com/news/showone.asp?id=102.

17 R. Edelman, The 2013 Edelman Trust Barometer, 2013, retrieved June 1, 2013, from http://www.scribd.com/fullscreen/121501475?access_key=key-1ao9w09me9qq9h66m0d2, p. 1.

18 Arthur W. Page Society, *Building Belief: A New Model for Activating Corporate Character and Authentic Advocacy*, 2012, retrieved from http://www.awpagesociety.com/insights/building-belief/.

19 T. Levitt, *The Marketing Imagination* (New York: Free Press, 1983), p. 7.

20 M.E. Porter, *Competitive Advantage: Creating and Sustaining Superior Performance* (rev. ed.) (New York: Free Press, 1998 [original work published 1985]), p. 3.

21 P.F. Drucker, *The Practice of Management* (New York: Harper Business, 1993 [original work published in 1954]), p. 35.

22 A.J. Silk, *What is Marketing?* (Boston: Harvard Business School Press, 2006), p. vii.

23 D. Sutton and T. Klein, *Enterprise Marketing Management: The New Science of Marketing* (Hoboken, NJ: John Wiley & Sons, Inc., 2003), p. 23.

24 N. Rackham, *SPIN Selling* (New York: McGraw Hill, 1988), p. 85.

25 Grunig, "Two-way Symmetrical Public Relations."

26 P.M. Senge, *The Fifth Discipline: The Art and Practice of the Learning Organization* (rev. ed.) (New York: Currency Doubleday, 2006), pp. 183–6.

27 J. Swartz, "More Marketers Sign on to Social Media," *USA Today*, August 28, 2009, pp. B1–2.

28 J.A. Conger, "The Necessary Art of Persuasion," *Harvard Business Review*, vol. 76, no. 3 (1998), p. 87.

29 K.J. Gergen and M. Gergen, *Social Construction: Entering the Dialogue* (Chagrin Falls, OH: Taos Institute, 2004), p. 48.

30 R. Quinn and G. Spreitzer, "The Road to Empowerment: Seven Questions Every Leader Should Consider, autumn 1997, *Organizational Dynamics*, p. 37.

31 J. Shaffer, *The Leadership Solution* (New York: McGraw-Hill, 2000), p. 3.

32 Ibid.

33 G. Lakoff and M. Johnson, *Metaphors We Live By* (Chicago: University of Chicago Press, 2003), pp. 3–6.

34 S.A. Deetz, S.J. Tracy, and J.L. Simpson, *Leading Organizations Through Transition,* (Thousand Oaks, CA: Sage Publications, Inc., 2000), p. 67.

35 N. Kumar, *Marketing as Strategy* (Boston: Harvard Business Press, 2004), p. 6.

36 Moser, *United We Brand*, p. 15.

37 N. Pangarkar and M. Agarwal, "The Wind Behind Red Bull's Wings," *Forbes* Asia, June 24, 2013, retrieved July 10, 2013 from http://www.forbes.com/sites/forbesasia/2013/06/24/the-wind-behind-red-bulls-wings/.

38 K. Freiberg and J. Freiberg, *Nuts! Southwest Airlines' Crazy Recipe for Business and Personal Success* (Austin, TX: Bard Books, 1996), p. 125.

39 M. Eisenmann, D. Geddes, K. Paine, R. Pestana, F. Walton, and M. Weiner. "Proposed Interim Standards for Metrics in Traditional Media Analysis." Retrieved July 11, 2013, from http://www.instituteforpr.org/topics/proposed-interim-standards-for-metrics-in-traditional-media-analysis/

40 A. Jeffrey, "The Eight Step Social Media Measurement Process: A Step-by-Step Approach," retrieved July 11, 2013 from http://www.instituteforpr.org/wp-content/uploads/Social-Media-Measurement-Paper-Jeffrey-6-4-13.pdf.

10 ISSUES MANAGEMENT

*Plan for what is difficult when
it is most easy,
do what is great while it is
small.
The most difficult things in the
world must be done
while they are still easy, the
greatest things
in the world must be done
while they are still small.*
*– The Tao-te Ching, or
The Way and Its Power
By Lao Tzu (604–581 BC)*

■ ■ ■

NEUTRALIZING CHALLENGES BEFORE THEY BECOME CRISES

As consumer electronics became ubiquitous in American homes, a growing but underappreciated danger arose: The tendency of young children to swallow the small, coin-shaped lithium batteries that power many devices. In the United States, more than 3,500 cases of swallowed batteries are reported to poison control centers each year. And the number of cases involving a fatality increased by 400 percent between 2005 and 2010.[1]

Children often put foreign objects in their mouths, and sometimes even swallow them. But lithium batteries present a particular health concern: saliva activates an electrical current that can cause severe burns in the esophagus.

This safety issue presented a threat to the battery industry. Left unaddressed, there was a risk of significant numbers of young children being harmed. That, in turn, could lead to public outcry, to regulatory or legislative activity, and to reputational harm to companies that produced the batteries.

Faced with a growing public safety problem, industry leader Energizer developed an issue management campaign, with help from the public relations firm FleishmanHillard, that sought to raise awareness of the safety issue among parents. It also became the first battery maker to voluntarily change its packaging to comply with U.S. Consumer Product Safety Commission standards.[2]

In partnership with Safe Kids Worldwide, FleishmanHillard and Energizer developed "The Battery Controlled" campaign that engaged more than 200 local and community partners. The campaign included education about the risk that coin-shaped batteries pose to young children, helped parents understand how to prevent those batteries coming into children's reach, and signs to look for that might indicate that a child had swallowed a battery, as well as steps to take immediately if they so suspected.

At the beginning of the initiative, research showed that only 28 percent of parents of small children were aware of the safety issues. Through traditional and social media and community outreach, the campaign reached more than 220 million people in the first year. And after one year its research showed that more than 66 percent of parents of young children were aware of the safety issues.[3]

For their work, FleishmanHillard and Energizer won a 2013 Silver Anvil—a top award for public relations—in the Issue Management category from the Public Relations Society of America. But more important, they improved public safety in the United States. And by taking the initiative both to educate parents and to change their packaging to make batteries less likely to get into children's hands, they avoided significant reputational harm—for Energizer and for the entire battery industry.

■ ■ ■

ISSUE MANAGEMENT OVERVIEW

Issue management is a corporate process that helps organizations identify challenges in the business environment — both internal and external — before they become crises and mobilizes corporate resources to help protect the company from the harm to reputation, operations, and financial condition that the issue may provoke. Issue management is a subset of risk management, but the risks it deals with are public visibility and reputational harm.

> Issue management is a corporate process that helps organizations identify challenges in the business environment before they become crises.

Enlightened companies have formal issue management processes, at both the enterprise-wide level and in individual business units or geographically defined operations. Sometimes the corporate communication department runs the function, but often the function is run from the legal, quality assurance, government relations, or risk management departments. Wherever issue management may reside in an organization, typically it is an inter-disciplinary function involving multiple corporate perspectives and several communication functions.

> Wherever issue management may reside in an organization, typically it is an inter-disciplinary function.

There is often meaningful overlap among issue management, government relations, public relations, law, and other corporate functions. And there is a strong relationship between issue management and crisis management: issue management can be seen as a subset of crisis management that anticipates and manages long-duration crises that are chronic, in order to anticipate and mitigate harm before the issue explodes into a full-blown crisis. Or as some have said: "Manage the issue so that you won't have to manage a crisis."

> Manage the issue so that you won't have to manage a crisis.

Establishing the Issue Management Function

A formal issue management function involves establishing a multi-disciplinary issue management team consisting of all major business function

> Every company's issue management structure should align with its business operations, marketplace realities, and leadership styles.

Every company's issue management structure should align with its business operations, marketplace realities, and leadership styles. But as a general principle, the most effective issue management structures have several elements in common. They adapt these elements to their unique circumstances and needs.

Figure 10.1 shows a typical issue management structure. The elements of such a structure are:

1. *Governance.* There needs to be some senior body to whom the standing issue management team reports. That governance structure is responsible for review and approval of major recommendations and plans; identification and assignment of resources to manage issues; and supervision of the work of the issue management team.

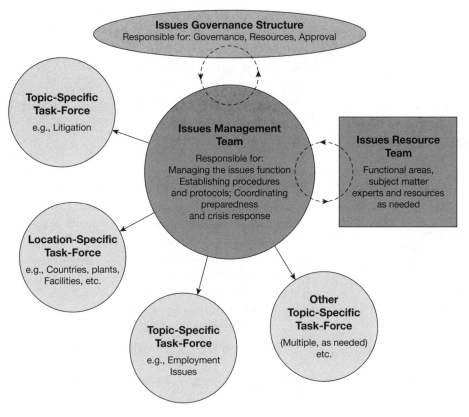

Figure 10. 1 Typical issue management structure

2. *Issue management team.* This is a standing group of people who represent core functional areas across the organization (e.g., legal, manufacturing, human resources, public relations, marketing/advertising, sales, security, administration, information technology, etc.). It meets on a set schedule, and also whenever a pressing or breaking issue warrants. The duties of the issue management team include:

    - Establishing procedures for consistent assessment of issues, planning for managing the issues, and communicating about events or decisions regarding those issues.
    - Serving as eyes and ears within the company and among stakeholders outside the company.
    - Developing an issues agenda and working through that agenda in a systematic fashion.
    - Naming individual issue champions to have authority to develop plans and documents on particular issues, to then be reviewed by the entire team. Each issue champion heads a topic-specific task force (see below).
    - Serving as a central clearing house for any issue that may threaten the company's reputation.

That governance structure is responsible for review and approval of major recommendations.

Issue management team: a standing group of people who represent core functional areas across the organization.

- Managing the approval process for communications about any particular issue.

The issues resource team serves as a group of pre-designated experts in particular functional areas who can be harnessed by either the issue management team or by the topic-specific task forces as needed.

3. *Topic-specific task forces*. Topic-specific task forces are groups of employees tasked with developing understanding of a particular issue or set of issues. The task forces are typically led by a member of the issue management team who has been designated the issue champion for that task force. The task forces can be assigned on based on geography, on functional area, on kind of threat (e.g., litigation), or by any other criteria that the issue management team determines. Each task force reports to the issue management team.

Initial tasks for the issues management team include identifying issues that matter to the company.

4. *Issues resource team*. The issues resource team serves as a group of pre-designated experts in particular functional areas who can be harnessed by either the issues management team or by the topic-specific task forces as needed. They may include lawyers, communicators, IT professionals, administrative personnel, or members of particular business units. They are not a standing structure, but rather a group of individuals who may be brought into particular issues as needed.

Initial tasks for the issues management team include indentifying issues that matter to the comnpany. Typical issues include:

- Possible legislative activity impacting the company, its competitors, its products, its pricing, or its marketplace.
- Regulatory events and changes to the business climate. For example, between 2001 and 2005 there were significant changes in the regulatory climate in the United States for the public accounting, investment banking, pharmaceuticals, and insurance industries. After the 2008 financial crisis, there was a new round of legislative and regulatory activity affecting companies in a broad range of industries.
- Changes in social trends that make previously accepted practices unacceptable. After nationally televised U.S. Senate hearings on the 1991 nomination of Clarence Thomas to the U.S. Supreme Court made the issue of sexual harassment highly visible, workplace standards for many companies were revised. In the wake of US legislatures and courts ruling that gay couples can be legally married in several US states, companies have had to reexamine their own benefits policies and employment practices, both to assure that they are in compliance with the law in each state, and so that they can continue to attract and retain talent.
- Competitors' activities, both positive and negative. For example, in 2004 Marsh Inc., an insurance brokerage, mutual fund, and consulting organization, suffered a series of setbacks in the wake of investigations by New York State Attorney General Elliot Spitzer. This called into question the integrity and soundness of many other insurance companies, and the insurance industry as a whole was cast in a negative light. So all U.S. insurance companies were under a cloud.

- Lawsuits, including class action lawsuits where a large number of people claim to have been harmed by a company's products or business practices.
- Product quality and safety issues, especially issues that require the recall of defective products or put customers' lives, health, safety, or financial condition at risk.
- Internal problems, such as the need to re-state earnings or change accounting treatment of previously disclosed earnings.
- Activities by groups with specific agendas.

Prioritizing Issues

Once an issue is identified, it is important to understand how significant it is and what corporate resources will be needed to manage the issue effectively.

> Once an issue is identified, it is important to understand how significant it is and what corporate resources will be needed to manage the issue effectively.

The two critical factors in assessing the importance of an issue are: likelihood—how likely is it that this issue will play out to the company's disadvantage; and magnitude—if it does play out to our disadvantage, how significant could the harm be?

Any given issue can be measured on a magnitude/probability matrix, as shown in Figure 10.2.

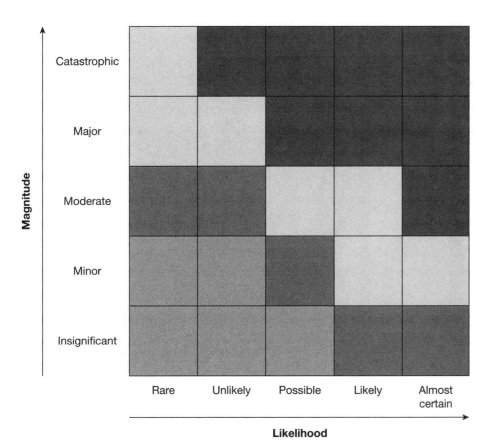

Figure 10.2 Magnitude/probability matrix (single issues)

High likelihood/high magnitude issues would get primary attention.

The farther up and to the right on the chart, the more compelling the issue. The upper right contains issues with high magnitude and high likelihood; the upper left, issues with low likelihood and high magnitude; the lower right, high likelihood and low magnitude, and the lower left for issues where both magnitude and likelihood are low.

Single issues can be plotted on this matrix, which functions as a tool to allocate resources and management attention to a given issue. High likelihood/high magnitude issues would get primary attention. Various scenarios of how an issue might play out can also be plotted on the matrix to help give a sense of the relative resources required to manage an issue in dynamic circumstances. Multiple issues, represented in Figure 10.3 with individual letters, can be plotted to help the issues management team prioritize its work based on the relative magnitude/probability of each issue.

For each issue identified, the issues management team would next develop a plan to analyze it, allocate resources to influence events to lessen its impact, and engage stakeholders in support.

If an issues management team considered a range of issues plotted on the chart below, it would focus most of its attention and resources on the two issues in the upper right portion, issues g and d. Second, it would appraise the single issue with high likelihood but low magnitude, a, and the two issues with moderate

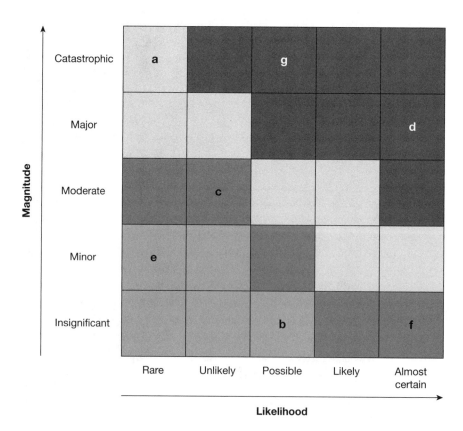

Figure 10.3 Magnitude/probability matrix (multiple issues)

magnitude/probability or high probability but low magnitude, c and f. The two issues where both magnitude and probability are low, e and b, would be put on a watch list and periodically reviewed.

For each issue identified, the issues management team would next develop a plan to analyze it, allocate resources to influence events to lessen its impact, and engage stakeholders in support.

Issues Management Planning Process

In general terms, the planning process for issue management is similar to the public relations process described by Hunt and Grunig and others.[4]

Typical steps are as follows:

Formula For Issues Management Success

Research/Risk Assessment + Planning Action +
Communication + Evaluation = Crisis Avoidance

THREE FIRST STEPS

- Establish a mechanism (e.g., regularly scheduled meetings, ongoing research, periodic discussion with key stakeholders) to identify potential issues crises before they occur.
- Prepare background documents and analysis. The longer the document, the more important the executive summary.
- Empower the communications team to advocate with lawyers, business heads, and company members who might not see the connections between discrete issues and the business interests of the enterprise.

DEVELOP AN ACTION PLAN

- Develop an issues management and communication plan with objectives, strategies, tactics, messages, budgets, timelines and an evaluation mechanism.

ENLIST OR ADAPT THE CURRENT COMMUNICATIONS PROGRAM

- Aggressively manage the communication program.

EVALUATE AND REVIEW

- Periodically assess results.

CASE STUDY: ESTABLISHING AN ISSUES MANAGEMENT FUNCTION

In early 2000 one of the largest financial services companies in the United States faced a significant business challenge. It had recently lost a major lawsuit, had some serious regulatory setbacks, and was on the receiving end of wave after wave of negative scrutiny, from regulators to customers to the news media to its own employees. It was the subject of major class-action lawsuits and also of major investigative reports on prominent television investigative news programs. And as challenges arose the company suffered meaningful self-inflicted harm.

Because it didn't have a mechanism to prioritize and coordinate communication around the many challenges it faced, different parts of the company took it upon themselves to communicate—but in ways that were inconsistent with what other parts of the company did. It also let many challenges go unaddressed, giving its adversaries the upper hand. It needed two different kinds of help. First, immediate crisis response capacity (see Chapter 11). But more important, it needed to take a holistic view of the issues it faced, the resources it deployed, the stakeholders who mattered, and the ways those issues were managed.

As a first step the company created a standing issues management team, drawing two representatives each from the major business functions (law, communication, sales, administration, human resources, business development) and one each from ancillary functions (research, operations, compliance, security). The team was charged with coordinating the issues management function across the enterprise, and all other business areas were told to stop attempting to manage issues ad hoc. That issues management team then was trained in the use of the Issues Management Template presented here, and also in best practices in communicating internally and externally. In the first year the issues management team met daily for several hours. In the course of the year, it identified and began to manage 153 discrete issues of varying degrees of complexity and significance. In that year it successfully resolved dozens of outstanding difficult issues.

Over time, as the issues management team became better at managing issues, and as the company stopped suffering self-inflicted harm, adversaries became less aggressive in pursuing their own advantage at the company's expense. And as members of the issues management team rotated off the team and were replaced by others, the business units became populated with issues-sensitive executives who could identify challenges early and refer them to the issues management team for consideration.

In 2014 that company's issues management team is still in operation— after more than ten turnovers of team members—and the company has seen significant improvement in its competitive position. And it has gone from one of the least capable to one of the most capable companies in issues management in the financial sector. The keys were discipline, perseverance, and continuous learning.[5]

DEVELOPING AN ISSUES MANAGEMENT PLAN

The starting point of an issues management plan is an analysis that identifies both the problem to be solved and the organization's ability to provide meaningful impact on the issue. Effective analysis attempts to develop understanding of the external environment and the company's internal state, as well as ways the company might adapt operations, practices, procedures, or structure. In other words, the analysis is intended to develop both situational awareness and self-awareness.

> The starting point of an issues management plan is an analysis that identifies both the problem to be solved and the organization's ability to provide meaningful impact on the issue.

All too often companies focus on understanding and trying to manage external issues without acknowledging the internal realities of the company. Issues management then becomes ineffective because the company is constrained throughout the process by internal obstacles such as lack of buy-in or sufficient resources. Over 2000 years ago the Chinese philosopher–warrior Sun Tzu identified the need for both situational awareness and self-awareness in navigating through perilous times. He wrote:

> If you know others and know yourself, you will not be imperiled in a hundred battles; if you do not know others but know yourself, you win one and you lose one; if you do not know others and do not know yourself, you will be imperiled in every single battle.[6]

This chapter describes an approach to issues management planning that has been field-tested by dozens of companies and organizations from Fortune-25-size financial firms and small not-for-profit advocacy groups; publicly-traded companies and private concerns; and by U.S. corporations and companies based abroad. It has been applied to issues that threatened a company's survival, and to minor bumps that merely caused embarrassment; to issues that were planned for and expected well in advance, and to those that arose suddenly and became public quickly. The planning process allowed these companies to respond effectively, quickly, and definitively and to protect their reputations, operations, and financial conditions.

The plan should consist of two key sections:

- An analysis identifies the issue, event, or potential crisis and assesses the scope and likelihood of operational or reputational damage. The analysis section names the problem

> The plan prescribes the steps to take to protect the company from operational harm and protect or restore the company's reputation.

and elucidates how it is likely to affect the organization and stakeholder groups which matter to the organization.

• The plan prescribes the steps to take to protect the company from operational harm and protect or restore the company's reputation. Bear in mind that drafting the plan—the proposed solution—without a clear understanding of the problem can be highly counterproductive. It is possible to craft at least an outline of an analysis quickly. An analysis can catalyze an entire management team into a common understanding of the problem and of the ramifications if the issue remains unaddressed.

The issues management analysis and plan may be written in complete sentences or paragraphs, in bullet points, in presentation slide format, or in any other medium that works for the company in question. The style of the written document is less important than the quality of the thinking and the level of engagement by management in the issues raised in the plan.

"Issue" Versus "Event"

Below is a quick summary of the Issues Management Analysis and Planning Template, followed by a detailed description of each element. Note the template is similar to the actions mandated in handling crisis communications. The major difference is that an "issue" is more typically a situation played out over a period of time instead of a singular event.

Introducing the Template

The **Issues Management Analysis and Planning Template** provides a structured way to think about solutions to a problem.

The **Issues Management Analysis and Planning Template** provides a structured way to think about solutions to a problem. It provides an ordered, outlined overview of a basic, viable, and strategic issue-management approach. It is a predictable, goal-oriented process which clarifies actions and messages in support of business goals.

Issue Management Analysis and Planning Template

Issue Analysis

• Threat assessment
• Magnitude
• Likelihood
• Define affected stakeholders
• Research additional information

ISSUE MANAGEMENT PLAN

Business decisions/actions

- Business objectives
- Issues management strategies
- Actions to take (tactics)
- Staffing
- Logistics
- Budget

Communications plan

- Communication objectives
- Communication strategies
- Target audience(s)
- External
- Internal
- Tactics
- Targeted messages
- Documents
- Logistic
- Success criteria

WHAT THE ELEMENTS OF THE ISSUES MANAGEMENT ANALYSIS AND PLANNING TEMPLATE MEAN

Issue Analysis

Issue analysis is descriptive: It answers the question "what?" It addresses what happened, and what could happen if the issue is not handled properly. It helps to establish both self-awareness and situational awareness.

Issue analysis is descriptive: It answers the question "what?" It addresses what happened, and what could happen if the issue is not handled properly. It helps to establish both self-awareness and situational awareness.

This establishes the context in which an issue is to be understood and the challenges it presents. It leads management toward a response action plan and communication plan calibrated to the magnitude and likelihood of the event or threat. The analysis is intended to provide management, internal and external staff, and other company employees with a common understanding of the nature of the threat and the possible consequences. The subsequent action plan should be crafted to neutralize damage resulting from the threat identified in the analysis.

The key elements of the analysis follow.

The analysis begins by naming the problem: It presents a clear description of the threat and the various ways it could play out.

Threat Assessment

The analysis begins by naming the problem: It presents a clear description of the threat and the various ways it could play out. There are many kinds of threat:

- A negative event within the company, such as termination of key employees, discovery of malfeasance, abrupt departure of key leaders, filing a lawsuit, or the verdict in a lawsuit.
- A negative event outside the company but directed at it, such as litigation, a competitor's triumph, or legislative or regulatory activity.
- A routine business process or decision that risks being misunderstood or will be the subject of opposition.
- An accepted business practice that becomes controversial because the political, social, or business environment has changed.
- An event or change in the business environment that affects the company's competitiveness, financial stability, or operations. These could include natural disasters, new legislation, acts of terrorism, or similar issues not directed at the company but from which the company suffers collateral damage.

In addition to naming the threat, the analysis should address why the threat is something to be managed:

- What is the likely impact on the company, its stakeholders, and its operational and financial health?
- What is the likelihood that the issue, left unmanaged, will cause harm?
- What is the likelihood the company can minimize or prevent that harm?
- What is the likelihood the company will make matters worse?

SAMPLE THREAT ASSESSMENT: AN EMBEZZLEMENT

The threat assessment should assess the specific business processes, business relationships, and elements of the business environment that might be affected. For example, a company discovering employee embezzlement might identify the following as areas of concern:

- Reasons existing control structures did not detect the embezzlement earlier
- Facilitation by or participation of other employees
- Vulnerability of other areas (financial reporting, physical property theft, accuracy of pre-employment data, etc.)
- History of similar events
- Advisability of involving law enforcement
- The need to dismiss the employee; and what to say internally upon the employee's dismissal

- Desirability of investigating via internal or external legal and accounting resources
- Likelihood of news of the embezzlement leaking
- Advisability of proactive disclosure of discovery and steps taken to identify scope and prevent recurrence
- Materiality of the dollar amount and the need to disclose into the financial markets
- Connections between the embezzlement and seemingly unrelated problems that might become public in the same timeframe
- The probability that competitors, adversaries, activists, regulators, or others may use the event to agitate against or embarrass the company

In addition to the business processes, relationships, and environmental challenges, the threat assessment should also identify the likely visibility that the threat represents, either left to itself or if mishandled, including visibility in the news media and likely public comment by investors, adversaries, regulators, legislators, ratings agencies, securities analysts, employees, and others.

To the degree that the issue is caused or may be inflamed by an adversary, the threat assessment should also anticipate the adversary's likely plan of attack and its next moves.

Alternative Scenarios

It may also be useful for the threat assessment to include a number of possible scenarios, particularly when the threat is outside the control of the company. For example, if a regulatory investigation is underway, there may be several scenarios including:

> It may also be useful for the threat assessment to include a number of possible scenarios, particularly when the threat is outside the control of the company.

- The investigation concludes that there was no malfeasance on the part of the company or its officers
- The investigation concludes that there was malfeasance on the part of a single or limited number of employees of the company
- The investigation concludes that malfeasance was widespread and endemic within the company.

Similarly, in the case of a pending verdict in litigation, the scenarios could include:

- The company has a major victory
- The company has a major defeat
- An ambiguous verdict that finds for us in some elements of the case, but against us in others
- The company settles on favorable terms that are publicly disclosable.
- The company settles on confidential terms

For each scenario, there would be a corresponding list of considerations, including an assessment of the likely response to each outcome among those who matter to the company, and the company's and adversary's likely next steps (appeal, settlement discussion, initiation of new litigation, etc.).

Magnitude Analysis

The magnitude analysis assesses the threat's relative impact on the company's reputation and operations.

The magnitude analysis assesses the threat's relative impact on the company's reputation and operations. If the threat could play out according to several scenarios, the reputational and operational impact of each scenario should be assessed. This assessment involves the same process as was described above, in the discussion of prioritizing various issues.

Likelihood Analysis

The likelihood analysis assesses the relative probability that any particular event will take place and will cause operational or reputational damage.

The likelihood analysis assesses the relative certainty or probability that any particular event will take place and will cause operational or reputational damage. As with the magnitude analysis, the likelihood analysis should take account of different scenarios.

The likelihood/magnitude matrix described earlier in this chapter should be used to plot the relative impact of an issue or set of scenarios.

Affected Stakeholders

The stakeholder analysis creates an inventory of the groups likely to be most affected by the issue and their likely attitudinal or behavioral predispositions. These stakeholders could include internal groups such as employees, specific internal functions or departments, or affiliated groups who function as internal resources, such as contractors, brokers, or an independent sales force; or external groups such as regulators, customers, investors, allies, or adversaries.

For each stakeholder group named, the analysis should inventory what is known about the group and how it is likely to interpret the issue in question:

*   Which people and groups matter in this situation?
*   Which will influence, be influenced by, or form expectations about the outcome of this issue or event?
*   What do we know about them?
*   What else do we need to know about them?
*   What would reasonable members of those groups appropriately expect a responsible company to do in such a situation?

What Additional Information Is Required?

The analysis should also identify additional specific information that needs to be obtained in order to either fully assess the threat or to begin the planning process. It also identifies the internal and external resource persons who need to be consulted or involved in the planning process.

THE ISSUE MANAGEMENT PLAN

Once the issue or event has been analyzed, the issue management plan can be constructed. Whereas the issue analysis was descriptive, the issue management plan is prescriptive: it prescribes a course of action to deal with the situation as presented in the analysis. Not all of the following categories may apply in every case. However, each category should be considered for each issue, event, or crisis, and the decision not to include one or more categories in any particular written plan should be made based on the issue in question.

At the very least, every plan should include business objectives, issues management strategies, actions to take, communication objectives, communication strategies, messages, and tactics.

> Whereas the issue analysis was descriptive, the issue management plan is prescriptive: it prescribes a course of action to deal with the situation as presented in the analysis.

> At the very least, every plan should include business objectives, issues management strategies, actions to take, communication objectives, communication strategies, messages, and tactics.

Business Objectives

Business objectives describe what will be or what ought to be if the company's management of the issue is effective.

These objectives define the business goals that the actions and communications will accomplish. They are formulated as desired outcomes: the resulting status or change in the business environment that action and communication is intended to create. For example, business goals could include the ones listed below:

> Business objectives *define the business goals that the actions and communications will accomplish*.

- Maintain market share despite a product recall or pricing pressures
- Prevent regulators from taking action against the company in the wake of discovering problems
- Prevent proposed legislation from restricting a company's ability to operated in its marketplace profitably
- Sustain productivity during a management shakeup
- Protect the company's independence in an environment of consolidation
- Preserve the ability to raise capital in the wake of a financial scandal
- Avoid involuntary bankruptcy

Issue Management Strategies

The issue management strategies describe how the business objectives will be achieved. They delineate the conceptual frameworks which a company will use to organize its energies and deploy its resources to influence the business environment and protect the company's operations and reputation, and to remedy any damage. They further describe ways the problems identified in the analysis will be fixed.

> The issue management strategies describe how the business objectives will be achieved.

Strategies are not actions to take. It is easy to confuse the two, and the difference between strategies and actions to take (tactics) is described in greater detail in the following text. In general terms, though, strategies will be the constant processes to be employed using many changing tactics.

> Strategies are not actions to take. It is easy to confuse the two.

Actions to Take (Tactics)

Actions to take describes the specific business decisions that need to be made or steps that need to be taken. These are the tactics to implement in order to reduce vulnerabilities, mitigate harm, or to restore trust or confidence quickly. The actions could be changes to an operating process, convening of a team of people designated to handle the company's response to a crisis, articulation of steps to take to reach various stakeholder groups, or any other concrete step. For the plan to work well, the actions to take should each put into operation at least one of the issue management strategies. An action that does not derive from one of the issue management strategies is likely to be counterproductive in at least three ways: first, it may not help solve the problem and could even make it worse; second, it expends resources that could otherwise be directed to solving the problem; and third, the misguided action makes management believe that it is taking effective steps to solve the problem.

The Actions to Take section could also include a menu of possible actions to be considered under various scenarios, as well as timelines of events known or expected to take place in the future, or targets for certain company-initiated activities to take place. The timetable may prescribe regularly scheduled meetings or conference calls for the core team, its advisors, and management to review progress and facilitate decision-making.

Secure Area

Depending on the scope and duration of an issue, a company may consider establishing a secure room or suite of rooms (known informally as a "war room" or "operations center") to serve as a location for the issues management team to work. Such a facility usually has restricted access and robust technological capability including phone lines, conference call capability, secure computers, printers, fax, and copiers, plus cable television, presentation slide projection

> A company may consider establishing a secure room or suite of rooms (known informally as a "war room" or "operations center").

capability, and a shredder. Much of the work product generated by the team can be produced in the room, and meetings of the core team can take place there, which will reduce distraction and curiosity in normal operating areas of the company and diminish the flow of rumors.

THE DIFFERENCE BETWEEN ISSUE MANAGEMENT STRATEGIES AND TACTICS (ACTIONS TO TAKE)

It is easy but counterproductive to confuse strategies and tactics. The two must be kept clear and distinct. The tactics serve the strategies, which in turn serve the business objectives.

Issue management strategies describe in conceptual terms how the objectives will be accomplished. The strategies are unlikely to change as the crisis unfolds. But the actions to take—the tactics—are likely to change. Multiple actions can support a single strategy. And as the circumstances evolve, some actions may be discontinued and others begun, all in the service of a single strategy.

For example, a **strategy** could be: *Identify the scope and severity of an embezzlement*. For that single strategy there could be a number of actions to consider. These could include the following.

- Retain a forensic accountant to review the books and determine whether other funds were stolen, as well as how the embezzlement took place
- Retain an outside law firm to conduct a thorough investigation
- Review whether there were any other instances of dishonesty by the employee, including expense reports, prior employment and educational data, vendor relationships, and the like
- Cooperate with law enforcement authorities investigating the criminal elements of the embezzlement

These actions are not mutually exclusive, but all or part could be conducted simultaneously or in sequence. New tactics may arise as the issue unfolds, as the company learns more about the embezzlement, and as the stakeholders who matter to the company react to the crisis and to the company's initial responses. All proposed tactics should be compared to the strategies to determine whether each possible tactic serves an existing strategy. No tactic should be embraced unless it demonstrably supports at least one strategy. And the totality of tactics need to demonstrably support the totality of the strategies. If there is a strategy that is not supported by at least one tactic, the tactics list is not sufficiently developed.

If it becomes difficult to differentiate between strategies and tactics, a simple rule of thumb could help: **Strategies are conceptual; tactics are tangible**. You can assign a precise cost or date for the tactics, whereas the strategies transcend such tangible precision. In the embezzlement example above, the strategy is to identify the scope and severity of an embezzlement. However tempting, it is difficult to assign a particular cost or date to that strategy. The tactics, on the other hand, are more concrete. The first tactic is to retain a forensic accountant to review the books. This is tangible. You can point to a particular accountant to be hired for a particular fee to deliver a report on a particular date. The other tactics are similarly concrete, and each could be quantified if necessary.

Staffing

The issues management plan should designate the team or teams who will work on issue day-to-day. Most plans identify a core team that is accountable for results. That team is often empowered to prepare the plan for management review and approval, and to implement the plan once approved.

Some plans identify both the core team and a governing group of managers to whom the core team will report and who can facilitate the allocation of resources quickly.

The plan should also identify other resources, both internal and external, that the team can draw upon or who may be asked to join the core team. These can include legal counsel, accounting or investment banking counsel, crisis communication counsel, operations, security, human resources, and other functional experts who can contribute based on the company's needs and the specifics of the issue.

Part of organizing the core team is developing a complete and up-to-date working group list of all the people involved in the issue. This should include names, titles, assistants' names, and all relevant addresses, phone, mobile phone, e-mail, and other contact information.

The staffing section of the plan may also describe the frequency of core team or management team meetings, conference calls, and other contact, as well as an expedited process for review and approval of documents.

Logistics

The logistics section of the plan, which is optional, identifies the operational details that need to be addressed for the plan to work. The logistics section covers everything from who will be responsible for what work product, to the number of desks, printers, photocopiers, phone lines, etc., that will be required for the secure "war room," to ensuring access to the building after hours, to making certain that teams working late are fed and have transportation home at night or a place to sleep.

The logistics section of the plan can range from a single piece of paper to a large three-ring binder to a computerized database. This helps the core team or its leaders understand how to operationalize the tactics they recommend and the day-to-day procedures of the crisis team.

Budget

The budget section is also optional, and addresses the costs of managing the issue, including the retention of outside experts, out-of-pocket expenses, and remediation of the underlying issue, including possible costs of litigation, medical care, reconstruction of facilities, etc.

Very often cost is the least important consideration in a managing an issue. But it is useful to have some accountability and predictability in cost; at the very least to have a mechanism to assure that resources are properly allocated and to understand the consequences of assigning additional resources to a crisis. But in general terms, responses are not driven by a budget, and certainly should not be held up while a budget is being developed and approved.

Communication Planning

Because most issues are or could become public, and because much damage to a company's operations and reputation is based on public reaction and criticism of the company, each issue management plan should include a communication section.

> Because most issues are or could become public, and because much damage to a company's operations and reputation is based on public reaction and criticism of the company, each issue management plan should include a communication section.

The communication section is intended to support the business strategies and actions to take. It should be written following the establishment of the business strategies and specification of the actions to take. Because speed is sometimes a factor in issues management, it may not be necessary to wait until the logistics and budget sections are fully completed before beginning communication planning. Ideally, the communications plan should be written as an integral part of the issues management plan.

Communication Objectives

Communication objectives answer the "conceptual what" questions. What will be the end result of our communications efforts, effectively implemented? Objectives describe desired outcomes, not the processes by which these outcomes will be accomplished. Communication objectives answer these questions:

> Communication objectives describe the attitudes, emotions, or behaviors to be exhibited by your stakeholders.

- What do we want those who matter to us to think, feel, know, and do?
- What are the changes we seek in what they think, what they feel, what they know, and what they do?

Business objectives describe the desired change in the business environment; communication objectives describe the attitudes, emotions, or behaviors to be exhibited by your stakeholders as result of your communication program. Communications objectives could include:

- Changes in knowledge, awareness, understanding, support, or feelings
- Steps we expect our audiences to take, such as approving a course of action, supporting a point of view, or trying a new product
- Neutralizing or minimizing the impact of negative visibility on audiences' thinking.

For example, if a business objective is to maintain the company's stock price, the communication objective may be to maintain investor confidence in the company's management team and prospects for future success.

Communication Strategies

Communication strategies are ways in which the communication goals will be achieved. Communication strategies answer the "conceptual how" questions. In broad overview, how will the communication objectives be accomplished? Once we know what we want our stakeholders to think, feel, know, and do, the communication strategies answer these questions:

• How do we get them to think, feel, know, and do those things?
• What are the ways we can organize our audience engagements to get them to think, feel, know, and do those things?

The communication strategies provide the broad game plan for all communication activities.

As with business strategies and actions to take, it is common to confuse communication strategies, which answer "conceptual how" questions, with communication tactics, which answer "operational how" questions. The difference between business strategies, communication strategies, and communication tactics is critical.

The communication strategies provide conceptual frameworks for accomplishing the communications objectives. They provide the broad game plan for all communication activities. For example:

• A business objective could be: *Maintain the company's stock price.*
• A communication objective to support the business objective may be: *Maintain investor confidence in the company's management team and prospects for future success.*
• A communication strategy to support that communication objective may be: *Keep analysts and investors aware of progress being made to solve problems.*
• Among the many communication tactics to support that communication strategy could be:

    • Send an e-mail to all analysts with an update.
    • Hold a conference call with analysts and investors.
    • Post regular updates on the website.
    • Be prepared to field inquiries from analysts and investors.
    • Conduct an interview with a financial newspaper that is read by investors.

Audiences

The audiences section lists the stakeholders to whom the communications will be directed.

The audiences section lists the stakeholders to whom the communications will be directed. While not every communication plan needs an audience section, it provides a reality check in the form of an inventory of the groups who matter and to whom communications will be directed.

The audience inventory, in turn, informs the balance of the plan. In general, the tactics section ought to include at least one mechanism for reaching each audience, either directly or indirectly.

It is common for audiences to be prioritized in a number of ways. A typical prioritization order is:

- Internal: Board of Directors, all employees, departmental, regional, or specific-level employees; senior management, etc.
- External: Current shareholders; the market as a whole; governments, academics, activists, etc.

It's also common to differentiate ultimate audiences, those you ultimately want to reach and who matter directly to the success of the organization, and indirect or influencer audiences, who are not necessarily your stakeholders but through whom you reach your stakeholders. Examples include:

- Ultimate audiences: employees, shareholders, regulators, the general public
- Influencer audiences: Media, investment analysts, academics, consumer advocates, etc.

ULTIMATE AUDIENCE/INFLUENCER AUDIENCE

A stakeholder that in some circumstances is an ultimate audience in other circumstances be an influencer audience. For example, if we are seeking initial analyst coverage of our stock, analysts are an ultimate audience. However, if we wish to persuade shareholders to accept a point of view, we may consider the analyst to be an intermediary audience, to whom we communicate in order for the analyst to then communicate our message to shareholders.

The list of audiences in the plan may or may not be identical to the list of affected stakeholders in the analysis portion of the template. The difference is the following: For purposes of analysis it is useful to identify those stakeholders who are affected by the issue in question. However, not every affected stakeholder group would necessarily be an audience of communication. Similarly, some audiences (e.g., the media) may not be an affected stakeholder group, but may be instrumental in reaching an affected stakeholder group (such as customers) to whom direct communication will not be attempted.

Messages

Messages are the critical thoughts we wish the audiences to internalize; the core themes we wish to reinforce in all communications.

The word "message" has many possible meanings, but for the purposes of developing an issues management plan, it should be understood to mean what you want those stakeholder who matter to the company to think, feel, know, or do—and what you need to say in order for those groups to think, feel, know, and do those things. As a general rule, the messages can be determined by focusing on

> Messages are the critical thoughts we wish the audiences to internalize; the core themes we wish to reinforce in all communications.

the communications objectives: the desired attitudinal, emotional, or behavioral outcomes among ultimate audiences.

One way to determine the messages is to undertake the following process.

1. Assume your ultimate audiences. What do you want them to know, think, or feel about either the company or the issue in question? What is the strongest credible thing you can say that, if believed, will cause them to know, think, or feel this way? This becomes your first message.
2. Assume that your audience has fully internalized the first message. What is the second thing you want them to know, think, or feel about either the company or the issue in question? This becomes your second message.
3. Assume that your audience has fully internalized the first two messages. What is the third thing you want them to know, think, or feel about either the company or the issue in question? This becomes your third message. As a general principle, three messages are the maximum you can expect any audience to internalize.

These three sentences become the three topic sentences that drive all substantive communication about the issue. Just as tactics may change but strategies usually will not, the factual support to a particular message may change as the crisis unfolds, but the message usually will not. And different support statements may be used with different audiences, or with the same audience at different times, while the message remains unchanged.

Using Core Messages

The three core messages stand by themselves, and should be included in each communication the company makes regarding the issue: These three messages become the quote in the press release; they become the topic sentence in employee meetings; they become the outline of presentations to the investment community; they become the three themes in letters to regulators or to customers; they serve as hyperlinks on the company's website, driving a visitor deeper into the supporting detail of each. The three messages need to be repeated every time the company communicates about the issue, requiring a very high tolerance for repetition.

The ability to consistently articulate the top three things a company wants its stakeholders to know is a critical attribute of leadership, and essential to effective management of issues. General Electric's CEO Jeff Immelt, has said, "Every leader needs to clearly explain the top three things the organization is doing. If you can't, you're not leading well."[7]

It is only at this point in the planning process that attention should turn to the tactics. Paradoxically, most companies reflexively default to tactics as a first resort: "We need to hold a press conference . . ." or "We need to send out a press release . . ." This is the rookie's mistake in issues management and crisis avoidance. It is impulsive, unthoughtful activity, and it is often both self-indulgent and self-destructive. But once the plan is in place, a

Paradoxically, most companies reflexively default to tactics as a first resort. This is the rookie's mistake in issues management and crisis avoidance.

framework for using the tactics effectively can be established, and the implementation of the plan can be accomplished in a flexible, effective, and cost-effective way.

Communication Tactics

Communication tactics are the specific communication techniques that will be employed to convey the messages to the ultimate audiences. The tactics part of the plan is a substantive inventory of the communications activities to be undertaken. It is what will actually be done to send the messages. As a result, it tends to get the most attention.

Because communication tactics involve what people actually do, they may tend to drive the communication planning process. It is easy for people to focus on interesting tactics ("let's hold a press conference," "let's do a Facebook page," "let's launch a Twitter campaign") regardless of the purpose or whether sufficient resources are available for effective execution.

Choice of tactics should be driven by two general considerations, each of which requires a degree of discipline.

- First, communication tactics should be driven by the communication strategies. The tactics should not be determined until after there is a clear articulation of the analysis, the business objectives and strategies, and the communication objectives and strategies. There should be at least one strategy that demonstrably accomplishes each objective. And each tactic should demonstrably support at least one strategy.
- Second, tactics should be do-able. Napoleon once remarked, "Amateurs worry about tactics, professionals worry about logistics." What is sustainable should govern tactics. The plan should not, for example, include labor-intensive tactics unless it also addresses staffing and other resources. And it shouldn't promote "gee-whiz" technologies unless it also addresses how those technologies will be obtained and delivered.

There should be specific communication tactics listed to support each strategy (and, as appropriate, each audience).

Communication tactics are deliverable items. They may include:

- Employee memoranda or e-mails
- Press releases
- Website postings
- Press conferences
- Op-ed articles in newspapers
- Advertisements
- Investment community conference calls

Because each tactic is subordinate to a specific strategy to achieve a known objective, it becomes easy to discard tactics that aren't working and replace them with new tactics that are more likely to work.

One virtue the systematic planning process that this template represents is that it allows for prompt mid-course correction without losing sight of objectives. If the objectives, strategies, audiences, and messages are clear, it is easy to adapt the plan to assure it is accomplishing its purpose.

Documents

The documents section of the plan is optional. It is intended to serve as an inventory of specific pieces of writing necessary to execute the communication tactics.

The document section identifies each individual communication required to implement the tactics. Since each piece of communication needs to be drafted, and since all need to be consistent and mutually reinforcing, this section constitutes a work list of documents to be produced before tactics can be executed.

These documents will include:

- Press releases
- Media Q & A
- Employee e-mails
- Employee Q & A
- Call center scripts
- Call center Q & A

Note three different Q & A documents are called out above. Since each is a Q & A format, a document inventory makes it clear that a separate Q & A is needed for three separate audiences. The three Q & As will provide different emphases and different levels of detail, but all three will be consistent with and mutually supportive of each other.

Communication Logistics

The communication logistics section identifies the resources and tools necessary to implement strategies and execute tactics. Like the documents section, it is optional. Like the documents section, it serves as a kind of reality check against tactics. It may include timeline of preparation and execution of tactics. It may also include the resources necessary to prepare the tactics for execution, or the individuals tasked to draft documents, seek approvals, or perform other tasks.

▶ BEST PRACTICES IN ISSUES MANAGEMENT

▪ Focus on the goal, not just on the processes

▪ Get management buy-in

▪ Name an accountable leader

■ Involve all relevant business functions

■ Set tangible communication objectives and measure success against them.

■ Follow the plan, focusing on the goal; adapt the tactics to changes in the environment, but keep the emphasis on the goal.

▶ RESOURCES FOR FURTHER STUDY

Issue Action Publications

Issue Action Publications, affiliated with the Issues Management Council, publishes a range of resources for those with issues management responsibility. It publishes two monthly newsletters:

• Corporate Public Issues and Their Management
• The Issues Barometer.

It also publishes a range of issues management books. It can be found at: http://www. issueactionpublications.com.

Issues Management Council

Issues Management Council is a professional membership organization for people whose job includes issues management. It offers conferences, publications, and other resources. It can be found at http://www.issuemanagement.org/.

▶ QUESTIONS FOR FURTHER DISCUSSION

1. Why is it so important to get management buy-in for an issues management process?

2. What is the optimal relationship between the issues management process and media relations and employee communications?

3. How can an effective plan make issues management more effective?

4. What is the difference between ultimate audiences and intermediate audiences?

5. Why is message discipline so important in issues management?

▶ NOTES

1   http://thebatterycontrolled.com/the-facts/.
2   http://www.energizer.com/programs/Pages/Coin-Lithium-Safety.aspx.
3   http://fleishmanhillard.com/work/energizer-the-battery-controlled/.

4   James E. Grunig and Todd Hunt, *Managing Public Relations* (New York: Harcourt Brace Jovanovich, 1984).

5   The company is a client of one of the authors, and due to confidentiality requirements the author is not permitted to identify the company by name. It is a Fortune 100 company and a leader in the U.S. financial services sector. Several identifying details were left out in order to protect the identity of the company, but all details of its issues management process are accurate.

6   Sun Tzu, *The Art of War*, translated by Thomas Cleary (Boston: Shambhala, 1998), p. 82.

7   "GE's Jeff Immelt on the 10 Keys to Great Leadership," *Fast Company*, April (2004), p. 96.

11 CRISIS COMMUNICATION

*Our greatest glory is not in
never falling,
but in rising every time we fall.*
– Confucius

■ ■ ■

CRISIS RESPONSE ON IDLE

In early 2014 Mary Barra, a long-time General Motors executive, became the company's CEO. Initially there was celebration that a woman had reached the top of one of the largest companies in the world.

But soon after taking over Barra discovered a problem. For more than thirteen years the company had known about a serious safety defect involving a poorly designed ignition switch built into its Cobalt and other car lines. That switch would fail while the vehicle was in motion, turning off the car, and with it the power steering and airbags. More than a dozen people had been killed by the defect, but the company had yet to recall the cars.

In mid-2014 GM had to pay a $35 million fine,[1] and the company would recall more than 20 million vehicles. The company hired a highly respected independent lawyer to conduct a thorough investigation of what happened and why. That report was published at the end of May 2014. It was devastating. Excerpts include:

> The below-specification switch approved in 2002 made its way into a variety of vehicles, including the Chevrolet Cobalt. Yet GM did not issue a recall for the Cobalt and other cars until 2014, and even then the initial recall was incomplete. GM personnel's inability to address the ignition switch problem for 11 years is a history of failures.[2]

CEO Barra seems to have done all the right things upon becoming CEO and discovering the problem. But because the problem itself had gone unaddressed for more than a decade, and because Barra was an executive at GM that whole time—but apparently unaware of this set of challenges—her actions may not be sufficient to keep the trust and confidence of GM's stakeholders, from customers to regulators to investors.

As this book goes to press, the jury is still out on whether CEO Barra can survive and whether GM will be permanently damaged.

The GM story illustrates many of the patterns in effective and ineffective crisis response. Among these:

- A sterling track record, a respected management team, political connections, and financial clout are not sufficient to protect an organization from major reputational, operational, or financial harm.
- The longer it takes to resolve a crisis, the harder it is and the more painful it will be for the company and its leaders.
- Most harm to reputation, trust, confidence, and financial condition is self-inflicted.
- Timeliness and quality of response matter.

This chapter lays out some of the disciplines of crisis communication, crisis management, and effective crisis response.

■ ■ ■

INTRODUCTION

One of the core roles of the corporate communication function is to help organizations and their leaders make decisions and communicate clearly when something goes wrong.

Effective crisis response—including both in what a company does and what it says—provides companies with a competitive advantage and can even enhance reputation. In particular, companies that handle crises well tend to protect those things they hold most dear, including:

- Stock price
- Operations
- Employee morale and productivity
- Business relationships
- Demand for their products
- Support of public policymakers
- Strategic focus

> One of the core roles of the corporate communication function is to help organizations and their leaders make decisions and communicate clearly when something goes wrong.

> Effective crisis response provides companies with a competitive advantage and can even enhance reputation.

Ineffective crisis response can cause significant harm to a company's operations, reputation, and competitive position, and can even put an enterprise's existence in jeopardy. And because time is one's enemy in a crisis, the sooner a company recognizes that business as usual does not apply the sooner it is likely to mobilize its resources to respond effectively in a crisis.

Here is just one tangible example of competitive advantage and disadvantage based on handling crises well or poorly.

Two Oxford University researchers demonstrated the extent to which effective and ineffective crisis response affects a company's enterprise value. Rory F. Knight and Deborah J. Pretty studied the stock price performance of prominent publicly traded corporations that had suffered significant crises. They calculated each company's stock price performance attributable to the crisis—stripping out market movements and other factors unrelated to the crisis that might have affected the stock price, and calculating what they called the "cumulative abnormal returns" for each company.[3]

Knight and Pretty found that companies that mishandled crises saw their stock price (calculated as cumulative abnormal returns) plummet an average of ten percent in the first weeks after a crisis, and continue to slide for a year, ending the year after the crisis an average of 15 percent below their pre-crisis prices.

Companies with effective crisis response, on the other hand, saw their stock fall an average (cumulative abnormal returns) of just 4 percent in the weeks following a crisis, about half the initial decline of companies that mishandled the crisis. More significant, companies with effective crisis response saw their stock price recover quickly, and remain above their pre-crisis price thereafter, closing an average of 7 percent above their pre-crisis price one year after the crisis (Figure 11.1).

> The tangible difference between effective and ineffective crisis response was, on average, 22 percent of a company's market capitalization.

In other words, the tangible difference between effective and ineffective crisis response was, on average, 22 percent of a company's

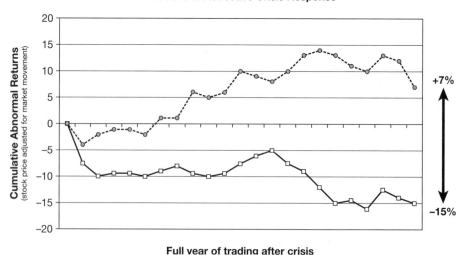

Figure 11.1 Effective v. Ineffective Crisis Response

Source: The Impact of Catastrophes on Shareholder Values: A Research Report Sponsored by Sedgwick Group, by Rory F. Knight and Deborah J. Pretty. The Oxford Executive Research Briefings. Templeton College, Oxford, England, 1997

market capitalization. Knight and Pretty assess the reasons for this disparity, and conclude that the most significant factors are not the scope of financial damage or reduction in cash flows caused by the crisis. Rather, the most important determinant of a company's ability to recover and increase its market capitalization after a crisis is the management team's response. Knight and Pretty conclude that positive stock performance

> springs from what catastrophes reveal about management skills not hith-
> erto reflected in value. A re-evaluation of management by the stock market
> is likely to result in a re-assessment of the firm's future cash flows in terms
> of both magnitude and confidence. This in turn will have potentially large
> implications for shareholder value. Management is placed in the spotlight
> and has an opportunity to demonstrate its skill or otherwise in an extreme
> situation.[4]

Whether a company survives a crisis with its reputation, oper-ations, and financial condition intact is determined less by the severity of the crisis—the underlying event—than by the timeli-ness and quality of its response to the crisis. Institutions that suffer the same very severe crisis can experience dramatically different outcomes based on the timeliness and quality of their respective responses.

> Whether a company survives a crisis with its reputation, operations, and financial condition intact is determined less by the severity of the crisis than by the timeliness and quality of its response to the crisis.

WHAT IS A CRISIS?

A Crisis Is a Crisis Because . . .

A crisis isn't necessarily a catastrophic event, but rather an event that, left to usual busi-ness processes and velocities, causes significant reputational, operational, or financial harm.

But how does a professional communicator know whether his or her company faces a crisis? The question is important because in a crisis timing is critical: Actions that could effectively prevent any harm to a company's reputation on Day 1 may be completely ineffective on Days 2, 5, or 10.

When a company is in a crisis or approaching one, business as usual needs to be suspended, especially the sometimes-ponderous ways decisions get made in complex organizations. Knowing whether such a suspension is necessary is often the first and most difficult deci-sion. The risk for companies and other complex organizations is in failing to recognize that business as usual has ceased to exist, so the usual communication processes—from choice of spokes-person to review and approval protocols—won't work.

It is all too easy for companies to recognize too late that they're in a crisis, because often the organization itself doesn't recognize

> Many crises are not catastrophes, but small-scale interruptions in routine business that, if ignored or handled poorly, can easily escalate to cause significant operational or reputational harm.

it until people outside the organization are already feeling the effects. There is a natural tendency to assume that a crisis is by definition a catastrophe; that a crisis exists only when damage has already been done or only when the event in question is potentially catastrophic. That's much too narrow a view. Many crises are not catastrophes, but small-scale interruptions in routine business that, if ignored or handled poorly, can easily escalate to cause significant operational or reputational harm.

The American sociologist Tamotsu Shibutani defines a crisis as:

> any situation in which the previously established social machinery breaks down, a point at which some kind of readjustment is required . . . A crisis is a crisis precisely because [people] cannot act effectively together. When previously accepted norms prove inadequate guides for conduct, a situation becomes problematic, and some kind of emergency action is required. Since activity is temporarily blocked, a sense of frustration arises; if the crisis persists, tension mounts, and an increasing sense of urgency for doing something develops.[5]

So companies need to be prepared in two ways for crises: they need to understand what constitutes a crisis in the first place; and they need an early warning system that helps them understand when business as usual has ceased to exist—or is likely to cease to exist—and that therefore business-as-usual practices need to be suspended. The corporate communication function is often an important part of that early warning system.

One way to think about crises is suggested by Steven Fink in his book *Crisis Management: Planning for the Inevitable*. Fink describes a crisis as a "turning point," not a necessarily negative event or bad thing. "It is merely characterized by a certain degree of risk and uncertainty."[6] Fink refers to crises as "prodromal," or as precursors or predictors of something yet to come:

> From a practical, business-oriented point of view, a crisis (a turning point) is *any prodromal situation that runs the risk of*:
>
> A. Escalating in intensity.
> B. Falling under close media or government scrutiny.
> C. Interfering with the normal operations of business.
> D. Jeopardizing the positive public image presently enjoyed by a company or its officers.
> E. Damaging a company's bottom line in any way.[7] (Italics in original.)

Fink points out that as a turning point the crisis could go either way:

> If any or all of these developments occur, the turning point most likely will take a turn for the worse . . . Therefore, there is every reason to assume that if a situation runs the risk of escalating in intensity, that same situation—caught and dealt with in time—may not escalate. Instead, it may very conveniently dissipate, be resolved.[8]

Fink's approach to crises anticipates both catastrophic events and also routine dealings that are suddenly the subject of attention. It finds merit in early intervention and affirmative management of business processes as well as the communications about the event.

Our own definition of a crisis integrates much of what Fink and others have suggested:

A crisis is a non-routine event that risks undesired visibility that in turn threatens significant reputational damage.

This "non-routine event" may be the result of a normal business practice that suddenly becomes controversial, or it may be an attack from outside the organization. The crisis consists not in the fact that the event is non-routine, but in the possible consequence of the event: visibility that could threaten damage to the organization's reputation.

> A crisis is a non-routine event that risks undesired visibility that in turn threatens significant reputational damage.

If It Smells and Feels like a Crisis . . .

One quick way to determine whether something that just happened or is about to happen is likely to become a crisis is to convert the descriptions of crises summarized above into questions.

For example, to use Fink's definition, ask:

- Is this situation a precursor that risks escalating in intensity?
- Does it risk coming under close scrutiny?
- Will it interfere with normal business operations?
- Will it jeopardize our public image or bottom line?

If the answer to one or more of these is yes, a crisis exists.

To use our own definition, ask:

- Is this a non-routine event?
- Does it risk undesired visibility?
- Would that undesired visibility in turn threaten reputational damage?

If not, then a company probably does not need to do anything out of the ordinary. But if the answer is yes, the company needs to recognize that the situation is anything but business as usual, and that the company needs to behave and communicate in different ways.

One virtue of these definitions of crisis is that they focus on outcomes: on the effect that the crisis may have on the stakeholders who matter to a company, and how the company can maintain the trust and confidence of those stakeholders as the event plays out.

One problem, of course, is the word "crisis." The very word can cause alarm and even panic. But the original meanings of the word are not nearly as dire. The original Greek word from which

> The original Greek word from which our "crisis" is derived originally meant decision, choice, event to be decided, sudden change for better or worse, turning point, and the power of judgment.

our "crisis" is derived, Κρισισ (*krisis*), originally meant decision, choice, event to be decided, sudden change for better or worse, turning point, and the power of judgment. So a crisis, originally, was a decision that would determine whether a course of events would unfold one way or another, for better or worse—very similar to Fink's view of crisis as turning point.

In Chinese, the character that translates into the English word crisis is *wei ji*, a combination of two ideograms: 危机. *Wei* means danger or fear. *Ji* means opportunity or desire. So the shorthand meaning of *wei ji* is danger plus opportunity. There is some dispute as to whether the two ideograms mean "danger plus opportunity," "dangerous opportunity," or "opportunity for danger." But whatever the syntax or grammar, the thoughts suggest something less clear-cut than a catastrophe.

So one way to think about crises is to think about the need to make a choice. We can define crisis management as the management of decisions one makes at a turning point moment, where our destiny is determined one way or another; toward danger or towards opportunity; where we lose our reputation or gain our reputation.

> We can define crisis management as the management of decisions one makes at a turning point moment, where our destiny is determined one way or another; toward danger or towards opportunity; where we lose our reputation or gain our reputation.

And crisis communication is the engagement of stakeholders in that turning point moment.

A crisis can be acute or chronic. An acute crisis arises suddenly and has potentially significant consequences. In such a crisis, audiences typically expect organizations to act quickly and to communicate in a timely way. The absence of such timely action or communication causes audiences to wonder whether the leader or organization cares, and trust and public support are put at risk. A chronic crisis arises over time, involves a series of events, or presents an ongoing risk. Chronic crises require careful monitoring, consideration, and communication over time. Most of the work in these crises is to prevent negative events by intervening early in processes or with critical audiences. Such crises essentially serve as an early warning of something potentially damaging yet to come.

A crisis can arise from any of three directions:

1. Self-generated—an event or issue that arises from within an organization or that is based on the behavior or misbehavior of the company's employees or executives or from some breakdown in its business processes.
2. Where the organization is a target—an event or issue that arises from outside the organization, but that is directed at it.
3. A crisis unrelated to the organization, but where there is a change in the business environment or the organization's competitive position, and where stakeholders expect a response.

QUICK CHOICES AND THE LEAST BAD OUTCOME

Sometimes organizations and their leaders are presented with situations where all the possible outcomes are bad. The challenge then is to choose the path with the least bad outcome, and to execute actions and communications effectively.

Take US Airways flight 1539, which made an emergency landing in the Hudson River on January 15, 2009. Captain Chesley B. Sullenberger, III, a former US Air Force fighter pilot, a pilot union safety official, and a sometime plane crash investigator with the National Transportation Safety Board (NTSB), exhibited exceptional leadership skills when his Airbus 320 aircraft hit a flock of geese when taking off from New York's LaGuardia airport that afternoon.

The geese took out both of his plane's engines at approximately 3,200 feet as the plane was making a left turn over the borough of the Bronx. With no power in his engines, Captain Sullenberger had a choice to make, and very little time to make it.

- He could try to get back to LaGuardia, flying in a loop back to one of its runways. Downside: If he missed the runway, he'd crash into a highly populated urban setting, in a plane filled with jet fuel. The possibility of massive fatalities onboard and on the ground was high.
- He could cross the Hudson River and try to land at Teterboro, a general aviation airport just across the George Washington Bridge in New Jersey, which he told air traffic controllers he could see. Downside: If he missed the runway, he'd come down in a heavily populated residential area.
- Or he could attempt a controlled water landing in the Hudson River.

He chose the latter, recognizing that a water landing, even in freezing temperatures, was a better (or less bad) option than the risk of fire, explosion, and loss of further life on the ground. While calm, he quickly—almost instinctively—made the tough call.

Using his plane as a glider, he passed the George Washington Bridge at about 900 feet. He brought the plane down in a classic landing position, with the nose just above the tail, allowing the plane, in the words of one witness, to skim across the water like a flat pebble.

Captain Sullenberger not only made the right call on strategy—which choice to make—he also was able to execute the decision effectively, gliding his plane to a landing that didn't result in the aircraft coming apart, or sinking, or flipping over.

The 81-ton plane settled into the river, intact and afloat. The river at the time was filled with ferries, small boats, and the usual Coast Guard, New York Police Department, and New York Fire Department watercraft. Within minutes, the plane was surrounded by rescuers on boats, in helicopters, and in the case of NYPD rescue divers, in the water.

The five-person flight crew kept the passengers calm and led an orderly evacuation. All 150 passengers, including a nine-month old baby, got out. One had two broken legs; others had impact injuries. And some had to be treated for hypothermia. The air temperature was about 30 degrees; the water temperature close to freezing. But all the passengers, and all five crew, survived. New York State Governor David Paterson called the event "A miracle on the Hudson."

According to reports from the passengers and New York City Mayor Michael Bloomberg, Captain Sullenberger then walked through the plane twice to ensure that there was no one left. One witness said that the back of the plane was filled with water to neck-height. Captain Sullenberger was the last to climb into a raft. The last passenger to leave the plane told the news media that in the raft he gave the Captain a hug and called him "our hero."

The next day, US Airways stock rose 15 percent, on a day when the market as a whole rose only a half of one percent.

DECISION CRITERIA: WHAT TO DO AND SAY

Because crisis management is the management of decisions, the starting point in crisis response is to establish decision criteria: how do we decide first what to do, and then what to say. Best practice calls for starting with an understanding of stakeholder expectations. So at a very general level, the decision criterion for what to do and say in a crisis is this: What are the legitimate expectations of our stakeholders? A candid and clear-eyed answer to this question usually establishes a productive universe of choices to make. Another way to ask the question is to divide it into three parts, as follows:

Decision Criterion in Three Parts: What to Do and Say in a Crisis?

What would reasonable members of your stakeholder group . . .
. . . appropriately expect a responsible organization to do . . .
. . . when confronted with this kind of problem?

There are several elements of this decision criterion worth teasing out. The first is that the starting point is to inventory which stakeholders matter in any given crisis. Each stakeholder group can be defined very broadly (e.g., employees) or very narrowly (e.g., those hourly employees who work at a certain facility). But however granular the definition, the key is to start with an understanding of reasonable members of that stakeholder group: not those who are always opposed to what the company may do (but their reaction should be taken into account in planning), nor those who are so disengaged that they will not pay attention. Rather, start with an understanding of those you hope to influence in your crisis response.

The second element is to consider those reasonable stakeholders' appropriate expectations. Not impossible or unrealistic expectations. For example, in the early phases of a physical crisis involving injuries, reasonable stakeholders do not expect the company to know everything that happened: the cause, the number and nature of injuries, etc. But reasonable stakeholders to expect a company to acknowledge that something bad has happened, and to take appropriate steps to contain the damage, remedy the problem, and prevent it from happening again.

The third element is that the expectations are of what a responsible organization would do. Note that the decision criterion is not ". . . expectations of what we should do . . ." Rather, it's of what a responsible organization should do. This is a non-trivial distinction. The authors have found that many companies and other organizations who ask "what should we do" or "what do our stakeholders expect us to do" often deprive themselves of potentially powerful options. There is a human tendency to filter out options that may not seem popular or that resemble actions that did not work in the past. We have often heard management teams exclude choices early in consideration for apparently arbitrary reasons (we won't be able to get budget for it; the boss will be angry if we propose that; we tried something like that in the past and it didn't work . . .). But in our experience, asking the question not about our own organization but about a responsible organization (which could include us) gets us to a more realistic and potentially workable set of choices.

The decision criterion can be answered to a very granular level of detail, for any subset of stakeholders.

But there is one common expectation that is typically held by each stakeholder group to a greater or lesser degree: that the organization cares that something has happened.

> One common expectation is typically held by each stakeholder group to a greater or lesser degree: that the organization cares that something has happened.

So the single largest contributor to reputational and other harm and to loss of trust and confidence in the aftermath of a crisis is perception of indifference, especially when there are victims. Companies, governments, and leaders are forgiven when bad things happen. But they won't be forgiven if they're seen not to care that bad things have happened. This is a lesson that many leaders and PR professionals fail to understand or to act on in the initial early phases of a crisis.

> Effective crisis response consists of a timely and persistent demonstration that the organization cares.

So effective crisis response consists of a timely and persistent demonstration that the organization cares.

Anything that detracts from the perception that the organization or its leader cares diminishes trust and confidence in the aftermath of a crisis.

The crisis guru James E. Lukaszewski, in his 2014 book *Lukaszewski on Crisis Communication: What Your CEO Needs to Know About Reputation Risk and Crisis Management*, says that they key element of a crisis is the creation of victims. Caring about the victims becomes key.

> Crisis-created internal and external victims are the greatest threat to the organization.
>
> A key role for senior management, as well as other managers, is making certain that the needs of victims are tended to immediately, fully and compassionately. The most significant causes of litigation and lousy visibility during crises are the ignored or discredited needs of victims, victims' families, and survivors—and the failure of leadership to aggressively manage the victim dimension.[9]

Lukaszewski notes that managing the victim dimension—attending to the needs of victims, and of those who empathize with victims—is the key to maintaining reputation, trust, and confidence. He notes that while victimhood is a self-designated state and self-sustaining, it is also a self-terminating state. Victims stop feeling like victims when companies offer a simple, sincere, and positive responses to their plight. "Actions, communications, and behaviors that fail to meet these three challenging standards prolong the victimization."[10]

WHAT HAPPENS WHEN YOU DON'T SHOW YOU CARE? BP *DEEPWATER HORIZON*

Consider Tony Hayward, the chief executive officer of BP, in the aftermath of the April 20, 2010 explosion on the oil rig *Deepwater Horizon*. The explosion led to a gush of oil from the base of the well about five miles under the surface in the Gulf of Mexico. That oil continued gushing despite many failed attempts to control the well over a three-month period, ultimately creating the single worst environmental disaster in American history and releasing a total of approximately 4.9 million barrels of oil into the Gulf.[11]

About a week after the rig exploded, Mr. Hayward was quoted in *The New York Times* from an internal meeting where he asked, "What the hell did we do to deserve this?"[12] Stakeholders took the statement as an expression of self-pity for the criticism the company was receiving for its inability to control the well. A few days later Mr. Hayward, speaking of the contractor whose rig BP had hired to explore for oil, said, "This was not our accident. This was not our drilling rig . . . This was not our equipment. It was not our people, our systems or our processes. This was Transocean's rig. Their systems. Their people. Their equipment."[13] While technically a true statement, BP, as the contracting company, was both legally responsible and publicly seen to be the owner of the well site. The statement was seen as an attempt to shift blame and attention from the company to its contractor.

About ten days after that, Mr. Hayward was quoted in the *Guardian* newspaper saying, "The Gulf of Mexico is a very big ocean. The amount of volume of oil and dispersant we are putting into it is tiny in relation to the total water volume."[14] While technically true, the statement came after three weeks of continuous coverage of the spill and its environmental impact, and as waves were carrying the oil onto the beaches of Louisiana, Alabama, and Mississippi. The statement was interpreted as further proof that BP didn't care and that it didn't understand or even acknowledge the public's appropriate concerns about the spill and its aftermath.

The final defining moment in BP's CEO's public commentary came on May 30, forty days after the spill, and after significant criticism that the company and its leaders didn't care. Mr. Hayward held a press conference on a dock on the Louisiana coast. He tried to explain that he did care. He apologized for the impact the spill had on residents of the Gulf, and he tried to show that his interests were aligned with the Gulf residents' interests: "I'm sorry. We're very sorry for the massive disruption that it has caused to their lives. There's no one who wants this over more than I do. You know, I'd like my life back."[15]

The first part of the statement was fine, if forty days late. But the last sentence, wanting his life back, did not work. He clearly meant it as metaphor. But critics pounced and pointed out that 11 rig workers who had died could never have their lives back; that those injured would have their lives changed forever; that residents of the Gulf had their livelihoods affected in meaningful ways. It was the beginning of the end for Mr. Hayward. He lost the trust and confidence of those who mattered most to him, including senior officials in the U.S. government and, eventually, of his own board of directors. He was out of a job several months later.

WHAT HAPPENS WHEN YOU DON'T SHOW YOU CARE? *COSTA CONCORDIA* SHIPWRECK

Consider also the behavior of the captain of the cruise ship *Costa Concordia*. The ship, with more than 4,000 passengers and crew aboard, left the Italian port of Civitavecchia on the evening of January 13, 2012, for a week-long Mediterranean cruise. Several hours later, the ship's captain, Francesco Schettino, deviated from the ship's computer-programmed route and guided the ship close to the shore. The ship hit a large rock that tore a 160-foot gash along the bottom of the ship's hull. The ship began taking on water and lost electrical power. The ship listed to one side, and passengers were ordered to abandon the ship.

Before the evacuation was complete, the Italian Coast Guard recorded a telephone conversation between one of its officers, Gregorio de Falco, and Captain Schettino, who had himself abandoned ship along with his first officer, even while passengers were still struggling to get off the ship. The telephone conversation included heated exchanges between an increasingly frustrated Coast Guard officer and the ship's captain, who had left passengers and crew to fend for themselves while he rescued himself. The recording went viral on YouTube and other social media, and soon became the subject of mainstream news coverage.

According to a translation made by the BBC, parts of the exchange included:[16]

De Falco: Please, now you go aboard.

Schettino: I am on the lifeboat, under the ship, I haven't gone anywhere, I'm here.

De Falco: What are you doing, commander?

Schettino: I'm here to coordinate rescues.

De Falco: What are you coordinating there? Go on board and coordinate rescues from on board. Do you refuse?

Schettino: No, no I'm not refusing.

De Falco: You're refusing to go aboard, commander, tell me why you're not going.

Schettino: I'm not going because there is another lifeboat stopped there.

De Falco: Go aboard: it's an order. You have no evaluation to make, you declared abandon ship, now I give orders: go aboard. Is it clear?

Captain Schettino did not return to the ship. In all, thirty-two people died and dozens were injured. Captain Schettino became a laughing stock and was later arrested by Italian authorities and as of this writing is awaiting trial.

Consider the decision criteria on what to do in a crisis: What would reasonable members of your stakeholder group appropriately expect a responsible organization to do when confronted with this kind of problem? One reasonable expectation is that the captain would coordinate the rescue and be certain that no more passengers were at risk before leaving the ship himself. That is precisely what Captain Sullenberger did in the US Airways Hudson River landing two years earlier. In the *Costa Concordia* shipwreck, the Italian Coast Guard was seen to care about the victims, but the ship's captain, whose foolishness had caused the wreck in the first place, seemed to care only about his own safety.

SHOWING YOU CARE: CHINA'S PREMIER WEN JIABAO AND THE SICHUAN EARTHQUAKE

On May 12, 2008, a massive earthquake struck China's Sichuan province, just months before the world's attention would turn to the Beijing Olympics. Within two hours of the quake China's Premier, Wen Jiabao, was on a plane to the stricken area. He spent eighty-eight hours on the scene, comforting the injured and survivors, and coordinating the government's response.

He spoke loudly to people still buried in debris and reminded the rescue workers to care for their own safety as well. He held the hands of those who lost their families, told them the progress of the rescue efforts, and gave them comfort. In one of the most reported moments of his visit, standing in front of the remains of a destroyed elementary school, the Premier wept as he picked up a child's shirt and a bag that had belonged to one of the victims. In a soccer stadium Premier Wen told excited crowds that the government had deployed all available resources for the rescue effort and more supplies would arrive soon. In the room assigned for the children who lost their family in the quake, the Premier held two children tightly and promised that they would have a safe place to grow up, assured them that many people cared for them, and asked them to cherish life after surviving this disaster. Stepping out of the room, he asked the local officials to assure that the children's psychological needs were met.

Journalists not only from China but also from the United States, Japan, Singapore, and other countries gave significant coverage to the Premier's visit to disaster area. The *New York Times* said:

> Over the past week, as Wen Jiabao toured earthquake-shattered towns and cities across northern Sichuan, he has hollered out words of encouragement to those trapped beneath fallen buildings and shared tearful moments with newly orphaned children . . . His high-profile humanitarian gestures have stood in stark contrast to the response of the rulers of Myanmar, who have been widely denounced for inaction toward the victims of a devastating cyclone.[17]

CNN reported:

> Premier Wen traveled to the disaster areas within hours of the massive earthquake . . . Wearing a hard hat, he was shown standing on rubble and consoling

trapped survivors through a loud speaker. The message is compelling: This disaster is terrible but the government is doing everything it can.[18]

Reuters said:

> Clambering over shattered buildings, tearfully comforting weeping children, hollering into a bullhorn, Chinese Premier Wen Jiabao has become the unusually open and emotional face of his nation's response to calamity.[19]

A reporter from *Lianhe Zaobao*, the largest Singapore-based Chinese newspaper, noted a particular scene. Premier Wen fell down on a slippery stone while he was inspecting the rescue effort and the sharp stone lacerated his arms, but he asked the nurse who came to bind up his wound to take care of others. "If you were there and looking at him, you would shed tears."[20]

As the media provided a constant stream of coverage about the Premier's visit, the public reacted positively. Wang Liangen, a seventy-two year-old retired math teacher from the devastated city of Dujiangyan, watched as the Premier climbed over the wreckage of a school where hundreds of children were buried, and told a *New York Times* reporter that "He really loves the common people, and we can see this is not an act. He has brought the people closer together, and brought the people closer to the government."[21]

On the Internet, people expressed further support for the Premier. Under the pictures that illustrated the Premier's non-stop visit in Sichuan a great many people left messages saying, "Premier Wen, please take a rest." Somebody wrote: "We can't control the earthquake but we are capable of dealing with its aftermath. Facing up to the unpredicted disaster, we must have confidence, calmness, and courage, as well as powerful direction. In this respect, the premier's intensive journey to the front-line waved a flag symbolic of encouragement and inspiration."[22]

SOCIAL MEDIA: UNITED BREAKS GUITARS

Social media has changed both the reach and the speed of criticism of companies and the crises that can define them. In the olden days, a customer who had a negative customer service experience might tell a few friends, or write a letter to the company. Now social media provides a platform that dramatically changes the power equation between institutions and individuals.

Consider what happened when Canadian musician David Carroll had a bad customer service experience while flying from Halifax to Omaha for a performance. He was required to check his guitar, and during a flight layover at Chicago's O'Hare International Airport he noticed baggage handlers mishandling his bags. He tried to bring his concerns to a gate agent's attention, but he couldn't get the agent to respond. He spoke with three separate employees, who in Carroll's words, "showed complete indifference towards me."[23] By the time he arrived in Omaha his guitar was broken, with the neck completely severed.

Carroll spent nearly a year trying to get reimbursed for the damaged guitar. When United Airlines proved unresponsive, Carroll chose to let the world know through his music. On July 6, 2009 he produced a video with friends for less than $200 and posted it on YouTube. The song, "United Breaks Guitars," includes the refrain:

> United, you broke my Taylor guitar.
> United, some big help you are.
> You broke it you should fix it.
> You're liable just admit it.
> I should have flown with someone else or gone by car . . .
> 'Cause United breaks guitars.[24]

Within days 25,000 people had seen the video. Within a week one million had seen it. He was covered by *CNN*. A week later 5 million people had seen the video. By October more than 5 million people had seen it. By April, 2014, more than 14 million individual viewers had seen the video.[25] United Airlines called Carroll to apologize, and said it would use his video as training for customer service.[26]

SOCIAL MEDIA AND THE CHANGE IN POWER DYNAMICS

Social media is changing not only the reach and speed of criticism; it is also changing the power dynamics between institutions—companies, governments, organizations—and ordinary people.

On July 23, 2011, two high-speed trains collided near Wenzhou, China. The Chinese government, through its railways ministry, initially tried to downplay the story: it had not been a crash, but rather a lightning strike. While the government had been able to get away with such mis-direction and unethical communication before, this time social media held the media accountable. As *The New York Times* described, within days of the news of the accident—which killed 40 people and injured 191, Chinese citizens using social media told the more accurate story of what happened, forcing the government to change its tune and its approach to the crisis:

> China's two major Twitter-like microblogs—called weibos here—have posted an astounding 26 million messages on the tragedy, including some that have forced embarrassed officials to reverse themselves. The messages are a potent amalgam of contempt for railway authorities, suspicion of government explanations and shoe-leather journalism by citizens and professionals alike.
>
> The swift and comprehensive blogs on the train accident stood this week in stark contrast to the stonewalling of the Railways Ministry, already stained by a bribery scandal. And they are a humbling example for the Communist Party news outlets

and state television, whose blinkered coverage of rescued babies only belatedly gave way to careful reports on the public's discontent.

While the blogs have exposed wrongdoers and broken news before, this week's performance may signal the arrival of weibos as a social force to be reckoned with, even in the face of government efforts to rein in the Internet's influence.[27]

Later that year, co-author Helio Fred Garcia, invited to China by the government to teach best practices in crisis response, had a conversation with a senior government official, who confessed, "In the past we could command the people's trust. Now we have to earn it, but we don't know how. Social media changes the relationship."[28]

TIMELINESS OF RESPONSE: THE NEED FOR SPEED

Another determinant of success in protecting reputation in a crisis is the speed with which an organization responds. This was true before social media, but becomes even more important in a social media environment.

As in other areas of business, there is a first-mover advantage in crisis response: whoever defines the crisis, the organization's motives, and its actions first, tends to win. Silence on the part of a company is seen as indifference or as guilt, and allows critics, adversaries, the media, and social media to control the communication agenda.

Crisis guru Jim Lukaszewski notes:

> Every hesitation, marginal or confused response will energize victims, survivors, critics, public authorities, folks with their own agendas, and increasingly trigger social media activity.[29]

And after nearly a decade of highly regarded companies proving unworthy of the benefit of the doubt, stakeholders are increasingly withholding the benefit of the doubt when companies are silent in a crisis. Further, stakeholders tend to interpret even routine operational setbacks as integrity lapses. As a result, silence on the part of companies tends to cause an over-reaction among stakeholders, in financial markets, and in the workplace.

When a crisis looms, the usual business processes and decision velocities need to be suspended and decisions need to be made in ways that reassure key stakeholders that a company and its leaders: (1) understand that there's a problem; (2) take it seriously; and (3) are taking steps to address the problem. But many leaders recognize too late that business-as-usual practices have to be suspended.

> First-mover advantage in crisis response: whoever defines the crisis, the organization's motives, and its actions first, tends to win.

> Stakeholders tend to interpret even routine operational setbacks as integrity lapses.

> When a crisis looms, the usual business processes and decision velocities need to be suspended.

> But many leaders recognize too late that business-as-usual practices have to be suspended.

Crises require special handling. Most routine corporate events can be handled by normal communications methods through traditional channels following usual procedures. But when a company determines that it faces a crisis it is important to recognize that routine decision-making processes, routine communications, and routine timeframes can be counterproductive.

In particular, time is an enemy in a crisis. The sooner a company is seen as taking the event seriously, acting responsibly, and communicating clearly, the more likely it is that the company will emerge with its reputation and operations intact. Former *Wall Street Journal* reporter Ronald Alsop, in his book *The 18 Immutable Laws of Corporate Reputation*, states that:

> Crises aren't like fine wines; they don't improve with age. A communications void is highly dangerous during a time of crisis. Silence gives critics time to gain the upper hand and reinforces the public's suspicion that a company must be guilty. Without information from the company, rumors and misinformation can proliferate fast.[30]

The Golden Hour of Crisis Response

Crisis communicators speak of the "Golden Hour" of crisis response: the early phases when the opportunity to influence the outcome is the greatest. The Golden Hour is a metaphor from emergency medicine, first coined by Dr. R. Adam Cowley, a veteran of the U.S. Army Medical Corps, who discovered that wounded soldiers who were brought to a field hospital within an hour of suffering their wounds had a very high likelihood of survival. Soldiers with the same wounds brought in just a half-hour later had a significantly lower probability of survival. The difference was literally a matter of life and death. Dr. Cowley applied this lesson to civilian emergency medicine, and coined the term "Golden Hour" in 1961.[31] It is now an accepted standard in trauma care in dealing with, for instance, heart attacks. The Golden Hour refers not to a precise duration but rather to the observation that incremental delays have a greater than incremental impact on the likelihood of success.

The Rule of 45 Minutes, 6 Hours, 3 Days, and Two Weeks . . .

Ideally, an organization will exercise the first mover advantage, and define the nature of the crisis, its motives, and its actions before a crisis becomes public. But what if it can't? Then it needs to recognize that are specific points in the cycle of mainstream and social media where it is possible overcome existing interpretations and

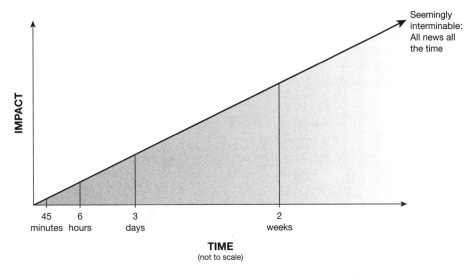

Figure 11.2 (Illustration by Adam Tiouririne)

define the crisis, motives, and actions. Miss one of these points and the organization will suffer increased reputational damage. Worse, the distance between the points, the intensity of the crisis and the potential for reputational harm, grow in almost an exponential fashion as more and more stakeholders begin to form and share impressions of an organization and its response to the crisis (see Figure 11.2).

THE FIRST 45 MINUTES

Give or take, an organization has maximum ability to reshape stakeholder reactions to a crisis in the first moments after a crisis becomes public. During this time, only a small number of people, and possibly only a single reporter or a handful of Twitterers, know about a crisis or are working on or following a story.

If the organization can effectively define the crisis, its motives, and its actions within 45 minutes of the story becoming public, the negative visibility will likely dissipate, even as the event itself continues to unfold. By being seen to care, to do the right thing, the company will maintain trust and confidence and protect its reputation.

But if the crisis remains public without an effective response, more and more stakeholders will be sharing their views, both of the crisis and of the company's insufficient response.

6 HOURS

If a company fails to define the crisis, its motives, and its actions within the first 45 minutes, it is likely to suffer at least 6 hours of reputational distress. As more and more people share information about the crisis, via social networks, social media, e-mail, and mainstream media, the company finds itself needing not only to define itself, but also to overcome the perception that it doesn't care. And even if it is able to engage effectively within a few hours, because so many people will already have posted, shared, or otherwise commented on the crisis, it can take several more hours for the company's commentary to catch up with all that has been written or spoken about it.

3 Days

Once a story hits the daily newspapers, including the newspaper's website and Twitter feed, or makes the evening television news, you can expect it to be alive for several days. During the day the story appears there is likely to be television, radio, and social media commentary about the story, as well as gossip among customers, employees, and competitors, with all the attendant distortion. The day following publication, newspapers that missed the story on Day One are likely to pick it up as their own Day One story. Even newspapers that carried the story on Day One can carry a second-day story of reaction to the first story. And those who come late will themselves carry their own second-day stories on Day Three.

And during this three-day period significantly more people will know about the crisis, form negative opinions about the organization, and share those views. So what it would take to overcome those opinions during the three days will be far greater than what would have worked on the first day.

If you cannot control the story during these three days, expect at least two weeks of negative coverage.

2 Weeks

If it takes more than several days for an organization to define the crisis, its motives, and its actions, then the likelihood is that a significantly higher number of people will know about the crisis, and be guided by critics', adversaries', and the media's interpretations. And it will be even harder to resolve the crisis. And because of the publication schedule of weekly magazines, weekly newspaper sections, weekly blogs, and television programs, and the reactions to all of them, the likelihood is that a controversy will be alive for at least two weeks.

If it takes more than two weeks to define the crisis, motives, and actions, then there's a very good chance of significant damage, sometimes irreparable. We saw that with Tony Hayward and BP: He became untenable as CEO and had to leave the company.

> It is a fundamental mistake for organizations to make decisions about crisis communications on their own routine timelines.

All of this suggests that it is a fundamental mistake for organizations to make decisions about crisis communications on their own routine timelines.

This has translated into a relatively well-established principle in dealing with the news media: fielding an inquiry from a newspaper reporter at 10 a.m. and responding definitively by 11 a.m. can allow one to prevent a story from being published, or to significantly shape what the story will look like. But waiting until 5:30 p.m. to respond to a 10 a.m. inquiry significantly diminishes the likelihood that a story can be shaped: by then the story has already been written and edited, and at best a company can insert a paragraph refuting the central accusation. But the accusation and all the commentary based on it will be in the story.

A similar principle applies beyond the media, where incremental delays can result in greater than incremental setbacks with other critical constituencies, from employees to investors to customers. And in a world of 24-hour news and instantaneous social media, and where seemingly disparate constituencies are linked electronically, a setback with one constituency can quickly cascade to setbacks with others. This is especially the case when the crisis is being fed by an adversary who can embarrass the organization. Whether the adversary is a lawyer bringing suit, a union organizer, a community activist, or an ambitious regulator, the adversary often counts on organizations taking excessive time to respond. This makes the adversary's job much easier, and allowing the adversary to begin a cascade of negative news among many constituencies before the company can develop a sufficient response, at which point it may be too late for the company.

One of the critical roles for corporate communication professionals is to help their organizations understand how core stakeholders are likely to perceive a company's silence or inaction in the wake of a crisis. As the keepers of corporate reputation—and in many cases also keepers of a corporation's conscience—corporate communication professionals need to be on guard to the common institutional barriers to taking crises seriously.

> One of the critical roles for corporate communication professionals is to help their organizations understand how core stakeholders are likely to perceive a company's silence or inaction in the wake of a crisis.

This need for speed is not intended to suggest that a company should communicate reflexively or without careful thought. But it is an argument for establishing a quick response capability with preauthorization to suspend business as usual in order to be able to respond quickly in the aftermath of a non-routine event that risks undesired visibility.

In many ways, the perfect is the enemy of the good-enough: companies often want to be certain of every fact, to dot every "t", and cross every "i" before making any statement. This abundance of caution can be a healthy impulse in normal times. But in the earliest phases of a crisis, something less than perfect, so long as it is accurate, is better than silence. Sometimes just an acknowledgement that the company is aware of a problem, is studying it, and will take appropriate action is sufficient.

CASE STUDY: JC PENNEY

Social media does not increase the dynamics of the Golden Hour of Crisis Response, but it does increase the frequency in which a company needs to use it. Consider JC Penney.

In the back-to-school season in 2011 retailer JC Penney wanted to attract mothers to bring their children to their store to stock-up on back-to-school items—everything from clothing to shoes to school supplies to winter coats. JC Penney, a long-established retailer, was struggling to maintain sales momentum against discounters Walmart and Target as well as office supplies stores such as Staples. Its appeal to moms was convenience: moms could get everything they needed in one place.

But trouble began when a customer noticed an item on Penney's website: a T-shirt for teenage girls. The shirt was adorned with a saying in whimsical typeface: "I'm too pretty to do homework so my brother has to do it for me." Some customers found the shirt offensive. A young woman saw a Facebook posting about the shirt and decided to do something about it. Lauren Todd launched a petition on the social network site Change.org, which allows individuals to initiate petitions online. Change.org, in turn, promoted the petition through Twitter and to parenting blogs, asking people to post directly onto JC Penney's Facebook page. Within six hours than 1,600 people had signed the petition. In ordinary circumstances before the advent of social media, companies had the luxury of taking their time with a response.

But with social media, every minute of delay has the potential to allow exponentially more stakeholders to form a negative impression of a company. JC Penney rose to the occasion. By the end of the day, the company had pulled the shirt from its stores and apologized. It posted on its various sites, "We agree that the 'Too Pretty' T-shirt does not deliver an appropriate message, and we have immediately discontinued its sale."[32] Once stakeholders saw the retailer doing the responsible thing, the controversy abated and the company suffered no meaningful harm to its reputation.

Decision Criterion: When to Engage Stakeholders?

There is a four-question test that leads to a decision to engage stakeholders.

As with the decision criterion of what to do and say, the decision criterion on when to engage stakeholders is grounded on stakeholder expectations. There is a four-question test that leads to a decision to engage stakeholders:

1. Are others speaking about us now, shaping the perception among those who matter to us? Will they be soon?
2. Will those who matter to us expect us to do or say something now?
3. Will silence be seen as indifference to the harm caused, as arrogance, or as guilt?
4. If we wait, will we lose the ability to determine the outcome compared to acting or communicating now?

If the answer to each of these questions is no, then we can wait, watch, and prepare for when the answer becomes yes.

If the answer to each of these questions is no, then we can wait, watch, and prepare for when the answer becomes yes. But if the answer to any one of these is yes, then we need to overcome fear, inattention, and inertia, and engage effectively now.

TEN AVOIDABLE MIS-STEPS

There are ten predictable, avoidable behaviors that organizations typically commit in when a crisis breaks that get in the way of effective and rapid response. The behaviors have two negative effects. First, they make the crisis worse; second, they distract attention from solving the underlying problem, while lulling management into a false sense that the crisis is being dealt with. The ten mis-steps are:

1. *Ignore the problem.* Management seems unaware and is surprised by a crisis that others saw coming, or that they themselves were warned about but chose not to take seriously.
2. *Deny the severity of the problem.* Management takes only minimal steps to address a problem, or downplays its significance, resulting in an inadequate response.
3. *Compartmentalize the problem or solution.* Management mistakenly assumes that others will appreciate its own functional division of labor, and defines the crisis or its solution as specific to a department, division, geographic region, or other compartment, while the constituencies who matter most view the problem as an enterprise-wide crisis and expect an enterprise-wide response.
4. *Tell misleading half-truths.* Management tries to misdirect attention by speaking literally true statements with the intention of misleading, which challenge adversaries or whistleblowers to uncover the full story.
5. *Lie.* Management tells a deliberate untruth with the intention of deceiving.
6. *Tell only part of the story; let the story dribble out.* Management reveals only the smallest amount of bad news it feels compelled to on any given day, but repeats the cycle on subsequent days, leading to multiple bad news cycles. The operative principle of telling bad news is to bundle bad news into as few news cycles as possible, preferably just one.
7. *Assign blame.* Rather than taking meaningful steps to solve the problem, management tries to redirect attention away from itself and to someone else.
8. *Over-confess.* Managements unaccustomed to criticism often implode publicly and turn public statements into private therapeutic sessions in which they unburden themselves of pent-up frustrations.
9. *Panic and undergo paralysis.* Work grinds to a halt as management and employees focus exclusively on the fear or the thrill of the crisis, and companies suffer operational or financial harm from reduced productivity.
10. *Shoot the messenger.* Management creates a culture of punishing those who bring problems to their attention, resulting in problems being buried and compounded.[33]

Corporate communication professionals need to be on guard against these behaviors, and find ways to overcome them quickly.

CONTROL THE COMMUNICATION AGENDA

Speed is one ingredient of effective communication; robust content and effective distribution of the messages are others. One of the goals of crisis communication is to influence the way key stakeholders think and feel, and what those stakeholders know and do. To do so requires controlling the communication agenda, and not allowing the media, adversaries, or the rumor mill define a company's situation.

So crisis communication needs to be grounded in the desired outcome: the end state in the audiences to whom you're communicating.

Content needs to be crafted to sufficiently influence the audience's frames of reference. And the channels through which communication takes place needs to be sufficient to reach audiences effectively.

Once you have determined the goals of communicating and the core messages, the process of communicating is relatively straightforward. Once you've decided what you want to say and to whom, the rule for doing so is the following:

1. Tell it all
2. Tell it fast
3. Tell 'em what you're doing about it
4. Tell 'em when it's over.
5. Get back to work.

1. *Tell it all.* This admonition should not be confused with an instruction to bare the corporate soul and confess every sin and weakness you know of.

    "Tell it all" means bundle everything that will inevitably be known into the smallest number of news cycles possible. Rather than letting bad news drip out over time, take all the pain all at once.

    Further, "Tell it all" should not be confused with saying more than you know, are legally permitted to say, or find it prudent to say. For example, if the crisis is still unfolding, tell only what you know, but all of what you know. If the extent of damage hasn't been determined, don't speculate; say that the extent of damage hasn't been determined. If you have a contractual obligation to keep certain information confidential, don't break the contract. If you know the names of people killed or injured, but the next of kin haven't been notified, don't disclose the names. But in each case you will be advantaged by saying what you do know and the reasons you are not disclosing—for example, "The extent of damage is still being investigated by the fire marshal, and we'll let you know as soon as the investigation is concluded," or "The identities of those killed are known, but we will not release the names until next of kin have been notified."

2. *Tell it fast.* It is common for companies to want to delay disclosure of bad news until the last possible moment. The risk, of course, is that others will be talking about the problems before the company does, and that the negative news can take on a life of its own.

    "Tell it fast" says that to the degree possible, it is better to be the one who brings the news to the public's attention, rather than reacting to someone else's account of the news. Even when the company isn't the first to disclose, "Tell it fast" suggests that speed of communications throughout a crisis is critical: it keeps the company in the driver's seat and prevents the story from getting out of hand. And to the degree that you are susceptible to rumors—which, in a crisis, is often—"Tell it fast" allows you to control or eliminate damaging rumors. (See Decision Criterion: When to Engage Stakeholders, earlier.)

The manner in which one communicates quickly should be based on the specifics of the particular crisis. It could include a press release; it could be an employee meeting or memo; it could be an interview with a reporter. Or it could be all or none of these. But whatever the specific communications vehicle (or combination of several), the tactical goal is to speak completely and quickly so as to take the high ground and control the communications agenda.

3. *Tell 'em what you're doing about it.* It is important, as early in the communication process as possible, to outline the remedial steps that are underway to resolve the underlying issues in the crisis. If such steps haven't yet been determined, it is sufficient to outline the processes being put in place; e.g., "We have launched an investigation, which we expect to be completed soon, to discover the cause of the problem and to identify solutions."

    Many companies (and many lawyers) are reluctant to talk about steps the company is taking because there's so much uncertainty in the early phases of a crisis. They need to overcome this reticence, and to know that the public will expect to be told not only what happened, but what's being done about it.

4. *Tell 'em when it's over.* Similarly, many companies are reluctant to open old wounds when a crisis is resolved. This instinct, while understandable, is counterproductive. There will always be some people whose last interaction with the company was in the context of a crisis. If the crisis is past, and the company has recovered, it needs to update those who matter (and the databases) to let the world know that the crisis has been solved.

5. *Get back to work.* Once the crisis team has been assembled and communication is being handled, don't let the crisis distract attention from the important work of running the company. Too many people want to be crisis managers. The tasks should be clearly assigned; people not directly involved in the crisis communication should be directed to return to prior duties.

    Even those who are needed in some element of crisis communication, such as senior executives, eventually need to stop communicating and get back to work. This includes the CEO, who has many other claims on his or her time than an exclusive focus on the crisis.

CHECKLIST FOR CRISIS RESPONSE PREPAREDNESS:

Have a clear sense of what constitutes a crisis, and know how to mobilize energy and resources quickly.

Designate a senior executive as responsible for crisis preparedness and response.

Test the system with processes that challenge leaders to make tough decisions and act quickly.

Control the agenda. Don't let the media, social media, adversaries, or the rumor mill define your situation.

Keep your focus on the goal: influencing stakeholders. Decisions become clear when you keep stakeholders in mind.

Are you prepared for a crisis facing your organization? Here's a checklist to help you understand your level of preparedness:

1. Have a clear sense of what constitutes a crisis, and know how to mobilize energy and resources quickly.

2. Develop an early warning mechanism/rapid response capability.

3. Designate a senior executive as responsible for crisis preparedness and response.

- Make this executive accountable and provide sufficient resources to conduct a thorough analysis of vulnerabilities, crisis response strategies, and crisis implementation.
- Pre-authorize this executive to take initial response steps without going through usual corporate approval processes.

4. Test the system with wargames, table top exercises, and other processes that challenge leaders to make tough decisions and act quickly.

- Remember that the best plan won't help if executives don't know what to do.

5. Recognize when business as usual needs to be suspended. A quick test:

- Are others speaking about you now, shaping the perception about you among your key stakeholders? Will they be soon?
- Are those who matter expecting you to take prompt action or to communicate with them now?
- Will silence be seen as indifference to the harm the crisis is causing?
- If we wait, will we lose the ability to determine the outcome?

6. Control the agenda. Don't let the media, social media, adversaries, or the rumor mill define your situation.

7. Keep in mind the Golden Hour of crisis response: incremental delays cause greater-than-incremental harm to reputation.

8. Develop messages and tactics with a goal in mind: how do you want your key stakeholders to think and feel, and what do you want them to know and do?

9. In a crisis, assure both self-awareness and situational awareness:

- Coordinate all functions of the crisis response with frequent meetings/conference calls.
- Correct mistakes early.

10. Understand what your stakeholders, adversaries, the media, and others are saying about you.

- Keep your focus on the goal: influencing stakeholders. Decisions become clear when you keep stakeholders in mind.

DEALING WITH RUMORS

A challenge facing nearly every organization in a crisis is the circulation of rumors that, unaddressed, can cause significant reputational harm, sometimes even more damage than the crisis event itself.

Rumors are particularly damaging because they often seem nebulous. It is hard to figure out where a rumor started, how it is building momentum, and where it might end. And people tend to pass rumors along, whether or not they actually believe them.

> Rumors are particularly damaging because they often seem nebulous.

Sometimes rumors are deliberately planted by people who are out to hurt a company or to profit from its distress, such as Wall Street short-sellers, disgruntled former employees, community activists, competitors, and people suing a company.

Once started, rumors can spread among employees, customers, suppliers, lenders, investors, and regulators. Rumors can feed other rumors, and rumors from several different sources can be combined in the retelling from one person to another. And when rumors hit the newspapers, television news programs, radio or the Internet they get formalized and are then seen to be an accurate rendering of reality. Worse, people who may have been skeptical of the original rumor, on seeing or hearing the same thing in the newspapers or on television, often conclude that the news account proves the accuracy of the rumor.

Rumors often ameliorate anxiety, uncertainty, and fear, especially when people feel that a crisis directly affects them. This is commonly the case in employee populations when rumors about layoffs, cutbacks, restructuring, hiring freezes, benefit reductions, or other changes arise. Rumors allow employees to express collective frustration and validate each other's fears. Rumors can also be subversive, providing an alternative communication channel and establishing an unofficial culture.

Because crises are by nature characterized by uncertainty, rumors are a fact of life in crises. The good news is that preventive and remedial actions are possible, allowing professional communicators to minimize the damage from rumors, or even to stop them in their tracks.

One of the important roles corporate communication professionals fill is to be an early-warning and rapid-response mechanism for rumor control. But being effective in preventing or controlling rumors requires an understanding of the psychological

Paradoxically, telling more and telling it faster has the effect of eliminating a rumor.

and sociological factors that drive people to listen to, pass along, and believe rumors. More important, being effective requires companies to act in counter-instinctive ways: to make and communicate decisions faster than they may be accustomed to making them, and to be more forthcoming with information than they otherwise would be.

Paradoxically, telling more and telling it faster has the effect of eliminating a rumor. Most executives are uncomfortable with the notion that they must affirmatively disclose information in order to stop the flow of information. It is a paradoxical situation, but the results will pay off. In other words, if we want others to stop talking about us, sometimes we need to talk about us.

Fighting forest fires is a good analogy. Sometimes it is impossible to fight a forest fire using direct methods such as building a firebreak—a cleared area around the area that is in flames in order to stop a fire from spreading. Firefighters may then engage in a practice called "backburning," where they set a fire to remove fuel (for example, brush) between the spreading edge of a wildfire and the control line established by the fire commanders on the scene.[34]

Just as it is paradoxical to start a fire to put out a fire, so too is communicating to shut down communication. But as with fighting a forest fire, it works, and sometimes it is the only thing that works. The backburn removes the fuel that would feed a fire, just as timely and robust communication removes the fuel—uncertainty and fear—that feeds a rumor. But like a backburn, the communication must be done at the right time and in the right way. Therefore, effective rumor control requires a high degree of both courage and discipline to recognize that counter-instinctive actions in the short term have a predictable, though paradoxical, long-term benefit of preventing rumors from proliferating.

The Morphing of Rumors

As a rumor passes from person to person, it tends to change in predictable ways.

One of the defining elements of rumors is that they are not static. As a rumor passes from person to person, it tends to change in predictable ways, through a process that social psychologists call leveling, sharpening, and assimilation.

In the 1940s two Harvard University psychologists, Gordon W. Allport and Leo Postman, conducted experiments on how the content of rumors changes as the rumor passes from person to person. They concluded that as a rumor travels, it tends to grow shorter, more concise, and more easily grasped and told:

> In subsequent versions, more and more original details are *leveled* out, fewer words are used, and fewer items are mentioned . . .
>
> As leveling of details proceeds, the remaining details are necessarily *sharpened*. Sharpening refers to the selective perception, retention, and reporting of a few details from the originally larger context. Although sharpening, like leveling, occurs in every series of reproductions, the same items are not always emphasized. Much depends on the constitution of the group in which the tale is transmitted. Those items will be selected for sharpening which are of particular interest to the reporter . . .

Assimilation . . . has to do with the powerful attractive force exerted upon the rumor by habits, interests, and sentiments existing in the reader's mind . . . Items become sharpened or leveled to fit the leading motif of the story, and they become consistent with this motif in such a way as to make the resultant story more coherent.[35]

Allport and Postman emphasize that while leveling, sharpening, and assimilation are independent mechanisms, they function simultaneously. The result is that a story becomes more coherent, more interesting, and therefore more believable with each retelling. But like a game of "telephone," later participants in the chain are likely to experience the rumor differently than earlier participants. Indeed, Allport and Postman's conclusions were based, in part, on their own experiments on the "telephone" phenomenon.

But unlike the game of "telephone," rumors do more than simply level, sharpen, and assimilate the stories contained in them. Participants in rumor transmission have an investment both in the content of the rumor and in the status that transmitting the rumor conveys. In particular, some people see retelling a rumor as a status-enhancing activity. Sociologists refer to this as a process of exchange, where information is a commodity with value, and the sender derives status from being seen to be "in the know." The French sociologist Jean-Nöel Kapferer explains:

> Some people see retelling a rumor as a status-enhancing activity.

> By taking others into his confidence and sharing a secret with them, the transmitter's personal importance is magnified. He comes across as the holder of precious knowledge, a sort of front-runner scout—creating a favorable impression in the minds of those he informs.[36]

The sender therefore has an interest not merely in passing the information along, but also in persuading the receiver to believe and act on the rumor. But often in order to achieve desired status the transmitter needs to enhance the details even more than the leveling and sharpening that Allport and Postman found.

And as a rumor changes with each telling, there is a reason for each transmitter to modify, or assimilate, the details of the rumor in ways that increase his or her status. Indeed, rumors cannot continue without exaggeration. This is a process known as snowballing, where the rumor's importance seems to grow with each telling. According to Kapferer,

> Exaggeration is common when it comes to rumors. It is not some kind of pathological or aberrant phenomenon, but rather a logical consequence of communication. Rumors can be viewed as a process of commodity exchange. In the rumor process, once information is shared among too many people, its value seriously diminishes, and the rumor thus stops short. The end of the rumor does not mean disbelief: it means silence.
>
> *Snowballing* is the only way for a rumor to last. It is a necessary condition of rumor persistence. Indeed, identical repetition kills the news value of all information. Were a rumor repeated word for word, without

any modification whatsoever, throughout its diffusion process, its death would be thereby accelerated. If everyone's friends have already heard it, or everyone imagines that they have, nobody would then dare speak of it again: for there would be a high risk of receiving no reward, or worse, of receiving negative reinforcement.

On the contrary, the permanent addition of new details, the systematic inflation of figures (at the outset, one dead man; then five; then one hundred, etc.), amplification and exaggeration are value-boosting devices. They make possible the continuation of communication within a group. Snowballing is not some innate or odd trait that rumors have: a rumor, i.e., a contagious process of information exchange, would not last long without this value-added process.[37]

It is regrettably common for management teams in a crisis simply to dismiss the rumor mill's significance, or to insist that employees get back to work and pay no attention to rumors. This is counterproductive. It is precisely when people are feeling vulnerable that they seek reassurance. And if management does not take their concerns seriously, people will find reassurance from those around them.

The result of inattention to the emotional needs of external stakeholders can be reduced demand for a company's products, decline in stock price, negative media coverage, and increased regulatory scrutiny. Inattention to the emotional needs of employees can include significant distraction, reduced productivity, and—through leveling, sharpening, assimilating, and snowballing—the transmission of ever-more damaging, distracting, and counterproductive rumors. Being a closed environment, employee populations tend to be rumor-incubators, especially when management tends to withhold important information. Such internal rumor processes are sometimes seen by employees to be the only credible sources of information about the company, in contrast to what employees consider to be propaganda from official sources.

Preventing Rumors

Rumors arise and are believed when official information is lacking or is not believed. Rumors can be avoided—along with their attendant negative consequences—if companies recognize the need to provide sufficient clarifying detail and information as early as possible in life of a disruptive event. Kapferer makes this point dramatically: "[Rumors] constitute an informational black market."[38] And the way to prevent a black market is to create a robust legitimate market: in the case of rumors, by diminishing the demand for information, and diminishing its value, by increasing its supply.

So what is a rumor? In *The Psychology of Rumor* Allport and Postman define it as follows:

A rumor, as we shall use the term, *is a specific (or topical) proposition for belief, passed along from person to person, usually by word of mouth, without secure standards of evidence being present.*

The implication in any rumor is always that some truth is being communicated. This implication holds even though the teller prefaces his tidbit with the warning, "it is only a rumor, but I heard . . ."[39]

The most important element of this definition is that a rumor exists in the absence of secure standards of evidence, but is taken by the recipient to be true. But in the presence of secure standards of evidence a rumor will not arise. Allport and Postman elaborate:

> Rumor thrives only in the absence of "secure standards of evidence." This criterion marks off rumor from news, distinguishes "old wives' tales" from science, and separates gullibility from knowledge. True, we cannot always decide easily when it is that secure standards of evidence are present. For this reason we cannot always tell whether we are listening to fact or fantasy.[40]

Allport and Postman give a compelling argument for telling more:

> When people are sure they know the worst, they are unlikely to darken the picture further by inventing unnecessary bogies to explain their anxieties to themselves.[41]

This latter concept—that when people are convinced they know the worst they are unlikely to darken the picture further in order to justify their own anxieties to themselves—can be of critical importance in situations that affect people over time. When people—whether as employees facing corporate downsizing or whose company is for sale, or investors in a corporation under investigation—do not believe they know the worst, they look for the slightest scrap of information to validate their fears. But when employees know what will happen next, what the worst case is likely to be, or that the worst is in fact over, they are less likely to be driven by rumors or look for hidden meanings.

In short, ambiguity provokes anxiety, and anxiety prompts rumors. Conversely, absence of ambiguity reduces anxiety, and in turn diminishes the strength of rumors. Allport and Postman observe: "*Unguided by objective evidence, most people will make their prediction in accordance with their subjective preference.*"[42] And in the presence of objective evidence, it is possible for people to move beyond their subjective preference, even their subjective fears.

For crisis communicators, the challenge is to help clients and employers summon the courage to disclose what is necessary to

> When people are convinced they know the worst they are unlikely to darken the picture further in order to justify their own anxieties to themselves.

> Ambiguity provokes anxiety, and anxiety prompts rumors.

> For crisis communicators, the challenge is to help clients and employers summon the courage to disclose what is necessary to provide objective evidence that helps people move beyond their subjective preferences.

provide objective evidence that helps people move beyond their subjective preferences. The good news is that Allport and Postman provide a way to do so.

Controlling Rumors—Mathematically

Fortunately, rumors tend to follow predictable patterns, and intervention in specific ways can help an organization overcome, or even kill, a rumor.

The breakthrough work on rumors—including how to kill false rumors—was conducted during World War II by Allport and Postman. Much of their work was classified, but after the war it was published, first in *Public Opinion Quarterly* in 1946, and then in their 1947 book, *The Psychology of Rumor*. One of their most significant contributions to the study of rumors was a mathematical formula that described the way a rumor works. The formula further suggests ways to control or eliminate a rumor.

The two factors that influence a rumor are: (1) its importance to the listener (if true); and (2) its ambiguity. In order to control a rumor one must either diminish the level of importance one assigns to the rumor if true, or eliminate the ambiguity around the factual basis of the rumor, or both. Eliminating ambiguity is particularly important if the rumor is in fact completely false. But even where the rumor has some mixture of truth and fiction, eliminating ambiguity about the fiction can help control the rumor and ground it in reality. Once an unambiguous reality is established, it may be possible to reduce the level of importance of the content of the rumor, thereby diminishing its transmission to others.

> Ambiguity can further arise when a company's credibility is weak, when the company sends mixed messages, and when people have become conditioned to mistrust what the company says.

The ambiguity can further arise when a company's credibility is weak, when the company sends mixed messages, and when people have become conditioned to mistrust what the company says. In such cases, even when the company is telling the truth, people are disinclined to believe it. Allport and Postman observe, "Most important of all . . . rumor will race when individuals distrust the news that reaches them."[43]

Allport and Postman elaborate how the two factors of importance and ambiguity work together, and note that there is a mathematical relationship:

THE BASIC LAW OF RUMOR

The two essential conditions of importance and ambiguity seem to be related to rumor transmission in a roughly quantitative manner. A formula for the intensity of rumor might be written as follows:

$$R \sim i \times a$$

In words this formula means that the amount of rumor in circulation will vary with the importance of the subject to the individuals concerned (i) *times* the ambiguity of the evidence pertaining to the topic at issue (a). The relation between importance and ambiguity is not additive but multiplicative, for if either importance or ambiguity is *zero*, there is *no* rumor. Ambiguity alone does not sustain rumor. Nor does importance.[44]

Because the relationship between importance and ambiguity is multiplicative, an incremental decline in either can result in a greater than incremental decline in the scope of the rumor.

Here are some ways to think about the model quantitatively. The elements of the Allport and Postman Model of Rumor Dynamics are:

- $R \sim i \times a$, where:
- R is the rumor: its reach, intensity, duration, and the degree that people will rely upon it;
- i is the importance of the rumor to the hearer or reader, if true;
- and a is the level of ambiguity or uncertainty surrounding the rumor.

In other words, the reach, intensity, duration, and reliance on a rumor is roughly equivalent to the importance one attaches to the rumor if true, multiplied by ambiguity surrounding the rumor, especially surrounding its denial. Note that simply denying a rumor does not eliminate ambiguity; it may even increase it. Rather, eliminating ambiguity requires giving an affirmative factual demonstration that gives people a basis for not relying on the rumor; in Allport and Postman's words, providing objective evidence sufficient to overcome people's subjective preference.

> Eliminating ambiguity requires giving an affirmative factual demonstration that gives people a basis for not relying on the rumor; providing objective evidence sufficient to overcome people's subjective preference.

Here's how the math works. Assume a scale of zero to ten, zero being non-existent and ten being certainty. If both importance and ambiguity are high, say ten, the scope of the rumor will be quite strong:

$$R \sim I \times a$$
$$R \sim 10 \times 10$$
$$R \sim 100$$

In other words, when both the importance and ambiguity are at their highest, ten, the scope of the rumor will be at its highest, 100. But reduce just one of the factors and the scope of the rumor declines considerably. Assume that importance remains high, ten, but that ambiguity can be reduced to three. Apply the model as follows:

$$R \sim i \times a$$
$$R \sim 10 \times 3$$
$$R \sim 30$$

The scope of the rumor has declined from 100 to 30, or by more than two thirds. Reduce both factors and the decline is even more dramatic. Say both are three:

$$R \sim i \times a$$
$$R \sim 3 \times 3$$
$$R \sim 9$$

The scope of the rumor has reduced from 100 when importance and ambiguity were at ten, to just nine when each is reduced to three.

Because anything multiplied by zero equals zero, if either ambiguity or importance is reduced to zero the rumor disappears. Assume that importance is still ten, but ambiguity is completely eliminated, at zero:

$$R \sim i \times a$$
$$R \sim 10 \times 0$$
$$R \sim 0$$

The scope of the rumor is zero, and the rumor disappears.

In practical terms, this formula lets a professional communicator and a management team do several powerful things. Knowing that importance and ambiguity drive a rumor, a company can be far more efficient in identifying what it needs to do and say than if it wasn't so aware. Second, knowing the formula gives clients and bosses confidence that they can influence the interpretation of events. The formula empowers management to focus communications in ways that can have impact on how the company is being perceived. Best of all, the formula can disarm negative information, killing a rumor and preventing further damage.

Dynamics of the News Cycle in Controlling a Rumor

The Allport and Postman model empowers crisis communicators and companies to disclose more sooner, thereby controlling the rumor and decreasing the likelihood of unnecessary reputational harm.

When applying the $R \sim i \times a$ formula, one critical element of success is how early one can influence the two factors that drive rumors, importance and ambiguity. Corporate managements, however, have little appreciation for the need to pre-empt rumors, for the seemingly arbitrary and somewhat confusing deadlines under which journalists work, or for the dynamics of social networks and social media. The Allport and Postman model empowers crisis communicators and companies to disclose more sooner, thereby controlling the rumor and decreasing the likelihood of unnecessary reputational harm.

▶ BEST PRACTICES

Effective crisis communication requires both discipline and flexibility, and a keen focus on the desired outcome of communication. Among the best practices are:

1. Know when to suspend business as usual: have a clear sense of what constitutes a crisis, and how to mobilize energy and resources quickly.

2. Get pre-authorization to use judgment quickly.

3. Find ways to show you care quickly.

4. Use the First-Mover Advantage to control the agenda: Don't let the media, adversaries, or the rumor mill define your situation, your motives, or your actions.

5. Keep in mind the Golden Hour of crisis response: incremental delays cause greater-than-incremental harm to reputation. Note that there are particular points in the cycle of bad news where you can take control of your destiny. The most powerful point is the first:

- 45 minutes
- 6 hours
- 3 days
- two weeks

6. Develop messages and plan tactics with a goal in mind: how do you want your key stakeholders to think and feel, and what do you want them to know and do?

When you've determined this, follow this process;

- Tell it all
- Tell it fast
- Tell 'em what you're doing about it
- Tell 'em when it's over
- Get back to work

7. Be attentive to rumors, and work to eliminate them as quickly as possible. Follow the formula for diminishing or eliminating rumors: $R \sim i \times a$.

▶ RESOURCES FOR FURTHER STUDY

Logos Institute for Crisis Management & Executive Leadership: A research, publishing, and executive education organization run by co-author Helio Fred Garcia, the Logos Institute provides a range of publications, some free of charge, that provide insight, analysis, and tools for managing and communicating about crises. See http://www.logosinstitute.net.

The Lukaszewski Group: run by premier crisis management advisor James E. Lukaszewski, the Lukaszewski Group provides:

- Strategic guidance for senior management during crises and recovery.
- Hands-on management of critical crisis problems.
- Management leadership development during crises.
- Counsel on prevention, readiness, response, and recovery.
  See www.e911.com.

Crisis Manager newsletter is a free electronic newsletter on current crisis topics published by crisis management advisor Richard Bernstein. See http://www.bernsteincrisismanagement.com/newsletter.html.

▶ QUESTIONS FOR FURTHER DISCUSSION

1. How can a company or organization know that it is in a crisis?

2. Why do so many companies fail to recognize until too late that they're in a crisis?

3. Which is more important: the actions one takes in response to a crisis or the communication about the crisis? Why?

4. How can companies or other organizations show they care in a crisis?

5. Why is it so hard to act quickly in a crisis?

6. Has social media changed crisis communication fundamentally? Or has it simply increased the frequency in which crisis communication must be conducted?

7. Why are rumors so hard to prevent and to put to rest?

▶ NOTES

1 Matthew L. Wald and Danielle Ivory , "G.M. Is Fined Over Safety and Called a Lawbreaker," *The New York Times*, May 16, 2014, at http://www.nytimes.com/2014/05/17/business/us-fines-general-motors-35-million-for-lapses-on-ignition-switch-defect.html?module= Search&mabReward=relbias%3As%2C[%22RI%3A7%22%2C%22RI%3A12%22].

2 Anton R. Valukas, *Report to the Board of Directors of General Motors Company Regarding Switch Recalls*, (Chicago, IL: Jenner & Block, May 29, 2014), pp. 1–2.

3 Rory F. Knight and Deborah J. Pretty, *The Impact of Catastrophes on Shareholder Value: A Research Report Sponsored by Sedgwick Group, The Oxford Executive Research Briefings* (Oxford: Templeton College, 1997).

4 Ibid., p. 7.

5 Tamotsu Shibutani, *Improvised News: A Sociological Study of Rumor, by Tamotsu Shibutani* (Indianapolis: Bobbs Merrill, 1966), p. 172. Note: Shibutani uses the gender-specific words "man" or "men" to refer to people in general. Throughout, I will quote him using the gender-neutral "person" or "people."

6 Steven Fink, *Crisis Management: Planning for the Inevitable* (New York: American Management Association, 1986), p. 15.

7 Ibid., pp. 15–16. (Italics in original.)

8 Ibid., p. 16.

9 James E. Lukaszewski, *Lukaszewski on Crisis Communication: What Your CEO Needs to Know About Reputation Risk and Crisis Management* (Brookfield, CT: Rothstein Associates Inc., (March 11, 2013), p. 23.

10 Ibid., p. 25.

11 United States Coast Guard, *On Scene Coordinator Report Deepwater Horizon Oil Spill* (Rep. Washington, DC: United States Coast Guard, 2011), 33.

12 Clifford Krauss, "Oil Spill's Blow to BP's Image May Eclipse Costs," *The New York Times*, April 29, 2010, http://www.nytimes.com/2010/04/30/business/30bp.html.

13 "BP Vows to Clean up Gulf of Mexico Oil Slick," *BBC News*, March 3, 2010, http://news.bbc.co.uk/2/hi/americas/8658081.stm.

14 Tim Webb, "BP Boss Admits Job on the Line over Gulf Oil Spill," *The Guardian*, May 13, 2010, http://www.theguardian.com/business/2010/may/13/bp-boss-admits-mistakes-gulf-oil-spill.

15 "BP CEO On Need To Stop Oil Spill: 'I Would Like My Life Back'," *YouTube*, May 31, 2010, http://www.youtube.com/watch?v=EIA_sL4cSlo.

16 "Concordia Disaster: Coastguard Calls Captain," *BBC News*, January 17, 2012, http://www.bbc.co.uk/news/world-europe-16599655.

17 Andrew Jacobs, "In Quake, Apotheosis of Premier 'Grandpa'," *The New York Times*, May 21, 2008, http://www.nytimes.com/2008/05/21/world/asia/21wen.html?pagewanted=all.

18 Jamie FlorCruz, "China's Government Gives Rare Transparent Look at Disaster," *CNN*, Cable News Network, May 16, 2008, http://www.cnn.com/2008/WORLD/asiapcf/05/15/florcruz.china/.

19 Chris Buckley, "'Grandpa' Wen Comforts China's Earthquake Victims," *Reuters*. Thomson Reuters, May 14, 2008, http://uk.reuters.com/article/2008/05/14/uk-quake-premier-idUKPEK20190120080514.

20 De Xiao, "The Earthquake in the Eye of Foreign Media," *International Herald Leader*, May 16, 2008, http://world.people.com.cn/GB/8212/7248516.html.

21 Jacobs, "In Quake, Apotheosis of Premier 'Grandpa'."

22 Anonymous, Re: "Premier Wen's 88 Hours in Sichuan," May 19, 2008 ; comments posted on http://news.xinhuanet.com/misc/2008-05/15/content_8187939.htm.

23 "United Breaks Guitars," July 6, 2009, music video by David Carroll, http://www.youtube.com/watch?v=5YGc4zOqozo.

24 Ibid.

25 Lessons from "United Breaks Guitars," April 16, 2010, ColumbiaBusiness, Columbia University, on YouTube, https://www.youtube.com/watch?v=_Hd8XI42i2M&noredirect=1

26 "Broken Guitar Song Gets Airline's Attention." CBC News, July 8, 2014.

27 Michael Wines and Sharon LaFraniere, "In Baring Facts of Train Crash, Blogs Erode China Censorship," *The New York Times*, July 28, 2011, http://www.nytimes.com/2011/07/29/world/asia/29china.html?_r=1.

28 Personal interview with co-author by senior official in China Food and Drug Administration, August 28, 2011.

29 Lukaszewski, *Lukaszewski on Crisis Communication*, pp. 13–14.

30 Ronald J. Alsop, *The 18 Immutable Laws of Corporate Reputation: Creating, Protecting, and Repairing Your Most Valuable Asset* (New York: Free Press), 2004, p. 220.

31 For historical roots of the phrase "Golden Hour" in emergency medicine, see "New Techniques Developed for Treatment of the 'Epidemic'" by Robert Locke, the Associated Press, January 18, 1982.

32 "'I'm Too Pretty to Do Homework' T-shirt Yanked," *CBS News,* CBS Interactive Inc., September 1, 2011, www.cbsnews.com/stories/2011/09/01/earlyshow/living/parenting/main20100427.

33 For more on these behaviors, how to recognize them, and how to prevent them, see also *Avoiding Crisis Mis-Steps*, by Helio Fred Garcia, Logos Crisis Monograph Series, 2004, at http://www.logosconsulting.net.

34 http://www.ruralfire.qld.gov.au/level2/M06/introduction.htm.

35 Gordon W. Allport and Leo Postman, "An Analysis of Rumor," *Public Opinion Quarterly*, vol. 10, 1946, p. 505 and 506 (italics in the original).

36 Jean-Noël Kapferer, *Rumors: Uses, Interpretations, and Images*, (New Brunswick: Transaction Publishers, 1990), p. 12.

37 Ibid., p. 108 (italics in original).

38 Ibid., p. 9.

39 Gordon W. Allport and Leo Postman, *The Psychology of Rumor* (New York: Henry Holt & Co., 1947), p. ix, italics in the original.

40 Ibid., p. x.

41 Ibid., p. 1.

42 Ibid., p. 44 (italics in the original).

43 Ibid., p. 3.

44 Ibid., pp. 33 and 34 (italics in the original).

12 CORPORATE RESPONSIBILITY

By Anthony P. Ewing

You cannot escape the responsibility of tomorrow by evading it today.
– Abraham Lincoln

■■■

NIKE'S JOURNEY, PART 1

Nike, by 1996, had built a $5 billion sporting goods business and its "swoosh" logo embodied the celebrity-fuelled American sports culture worldwide. But the global brand that symbolized performance and excellence to millions would soon acquire some truly frightening attributes—greed, exploitation and indifference to human suffering.

Warning signs had appeared as early as 1992, with a *Harper's* magazine story criticizing Nike labor practices in Indonesia. However, the storm of anti-Nike publicity and activism which would inflict lasting damage on the company's reputation did not gather fully until 1995, when concerns over globalization and sweatshops converged, capturing the attention of activists, consumers and policymakers. Between April and August 1995, the CBS television news magazine *Eye to Eye* ran a segment portraying Pakistani children as young as six stitching Adidas and Reebok soccer balls; United States-based labor activists publicized the plight of workers fired for organizing a union in a Salvadoran apparel factory supplying Gap and Eddie Bauer; and state officials freed enslaved immigrants from an El Monte, California, garment sweatshop.

It did not take long for Nike's global business practices to become the focus of intense scrutiny. In less than a year, media coverage of working conditions in Asian factories had turned Nike into the corporate poster child for the inequities of the global economy. The allegations were serious and attention grabbing. Indonesian factory workers making Nike sneakers were paid less than the local minimum wage and required to work excessive overtime. Pakistani children were stitching Nike soccer balls. Factory managers in Vietnam subjected employees to physical, verbal, and sexual abuse and exposed workers to toxic chemicals.

Negative press coverage prompted a broad range of constituencies important to Nike to question the company's motives and business practices. Columnists pointed out the enormous disparities between the price of celebrity-endorsed sneakers sold in the United States and the wages earned by the Indonesian women who made them. Activists accused Nike of ruthlessly exploiting workers and the environment in the company's global pursuit of profit at any cost. Students organized campus protests and boycotts of Nike products, demanding that Nike disclose the location of its subcontracted factories worldwide. Government officials in North America and Europe introduced measures to ban imports of apparel and sporting goods made with child labor. Socially responsible investment funds, using the same strategies they had applied a decade earlier to encourage corporate divestment from Apartheid South Africa, began to screen their investment portfolios for labor and environmental policies, and submit shareholder resolutions urging companies to adopt codes of conduct for their suppliers. Meanwhile, the plaintiffs' bar in the

United States began testing novel legal strategies to hold companies account-able in U.S. courts for the abusive treatment of workers in foreign markets.

Nike's initial response to the rising tide of criticism was instinctively defen-sive. At first, Nike spokespeople denied responsibility for the conduct of the company's supplier and sought to discredit critics. The following is an excerpt from a Nike press release, responding to an allegation the Nike Air Jordan shoes were made in Indonesia for 14 cents an hour:

> One has to question the credibility of an individual whose organiza-tion is largely financed by labor unions opposed to free trade with developing nations. It's also too bad that Kathie Lee Gifford has found it necessary to avoid the media spotlight by pushing Michael Jordan into it.[1]

Nike's high-profile founder and chairman, Philip Knight, responded angrily to criticism of Nike's business practices through letters, press statements, speeches and other public communications, arguing that Nike's presence in developing markets contributes to higher standards of living and that the com-pany does its best to ensure that labor abuses do not occur. In the midst of growing pressure from universities to ensure minimum labor standards in the production of university-licensed apparel, and heated anti-Nike rhetoric on col-lege campuses, Nike cancelled a contract with the University of Michigan in a dispute over applicable codes of conduct. Knight went so far as to withdraw a personal donation to his *alma mater*, the University of Oregon, publicly link-ing his decision to the university's criticism of Nike's labor practices.

But under steady pressure from stakeholders to take meaningful steps to address labor practices in its supply chain, Nike's approach began to change. By necessity and through much trial and error, Nike has become a corporate responsibility leader in the years since the company first attracted a critical spotlight.

■ ■ ■

> [S]ocial accountability is just another management art that corporations are going to have to learn. In the long run, the corporation that does the best job of managing its operations will also do the best job of adapting to social needs.
>
> – Harold Burson, 1973[2]

■ ■ ■

Leading companies know that corporate responsibility mat-ters. Meeting the non-financial expectations of stakeholders helps a company to manage risk, protect its reputation, attract and retain employees, grow its markets and improve its financial performance for shareholders.

> Leading companies know that corporate responsibility matters.

Demonstrating corporate responsibility is a key challenge for business leaders, and effective communication is a central element of every successful corporate responsibility program.

Demonstrating corporate responsibility is a key challenge for business leaders, and effective communication is a central element of every successful corporate responsibility program. Most companies have not had the benefit of spending years at the center of the corporate responsibility debate, like Nike, learning what works and what does not.

This chapter is intended to provide an overview and practical guidance to business leaders, managers and others who seek to better understand corporate responsibility and the challenges of communicating it.

CORPORATE RESPONSIBILITY

Definition

Corporate responsibility: Meeting the expectations of stakeholders; it goes beyond philanthropy and legal compliance.

The first challenge is defining corporate responsibility. Companies often use "corporate responsibility," "corporate social responsibility," "corporate citizenship," "business ethics" and "sustainability" interchangeably to describe corporate initiatives ranging from philanthropy, to legal compliance, to social and environmental programs.

According to economic theory, the sole responsibility of business is to maximize profits. As long as companies obey the law, there are no requirements or duties beyond the financial imperatives of the corporation. Any corporate activity that elevates societal interests above the interests of shareholders is an inappropriate use of corporate resources by company managers. In this orthodox view of the world, there is a strict separation of governmental and corporate responsibilities. An economist might argue that Nike has no responsibility for the activities of its independently owned suppliers and Nike's efforts to improve working conditions in its supply chain constitute mismanagement.

Few companies take such a narrow view. The definition of the role of business in society has evolved from a focus exclusively on shareholder returns, to the acknowledgment by business of a much broader group of corporate stakeholders and range of responsibilities.[3]

For some observers, corporate responsibility means companies simply follow the rules. Corporate responsibility comprises the ethics programs, codes of conduct and compliance efforts necessary to meet legal and regulatory requirements.

Compliance is just the starting point for any discussion of corporate responsibility.

But compliance is just the starting point for any discussion of corporate responsibility. When apparel companies were accused of running sweatshops in the early 1990s, a common corporate response was to deny any legal responsibility over factories the companies did not own. Legal precision did nothing to improve conditions for workers, however, and stakeholders were not satisfied. Corporate stakeholders expect legal compliance;

increasingly they demand voluntary standard setting beyond the legal minimum. Smart companies realized that irrespective of legal liability, their credibility was tied to acknowledging responsibility for working conditions in their supply chain and setting standards that exceeded legal minimums. When U.S. companies manufacture products in developing countries, advocates and customers expect the companies to adhere to U.S. levels of health and safety and environmental protection in their foreign factories, even if local standards are lower or unenforced.

Many corporate responsibility initiatives go beyond compliance to set minimum standards for business conduct, and for social and environmental performance within a company's "sphere of influence," even in the absence of legal requirements or enforcement.

Increasingly, business leaders understand that corporate responsibility also goes beyond philanthropy, such as charitable giving. While corporate philanthropy is expected, charity alone no longer meets stakeholders' expectations for corporate responsibility.[4]

General Electric (GE), for example, has adopted a comprehensive corporate responsibility definition for its own operations by combining the traditional financial notion with compliance and a broader concept of ethical decision-making: "Good corporate citizenship comprises strong economic performance over time, rigorous legal and accounting compliance, and going beyond compliance when there are opportunities to create benefit for society and the long-term health of the enterprise."[5]

For the purposes of this chapter, corporate responsibility encompasses corporate efforts to meet the non-financial expectations of stakeholders.[6] Under this definition, corporate responsibility goes beyond philanthropy and legal compliance. Stakeholders include investors, employees, business partners, suppliers, customers, governments, regulators, international organizations, non-governmental organizations (NGOs), and the communities where businesses operate. Most of the examples in this chapter are of companies seeking to set minimum social and environmental standards for their operations or those of their business partners.

The Business Case

Companies face constant pressure to act responsibly.

Global business practices are a particular focus of scrutiny. The globalization of business and communication means that the activities of companies in foreign markets are no longer invisible to stakeholders at home. Stakeholders routinely call attention to the broader social impact of corporate activities on the communities and societies where they operate.

Human rights are now a business concern. Alongside governments, companies are viewed as a source of human rights abuse, as well as international actors with the capacity to promote human rights. Over the last twenty years, human rights advocates have shined a spotlight on human rights conditions in a wide range of transnational industries including oil and mining; the manufacturing of consumer goods;

> Human rights are now a business concern.

agriculture on farms that produce food for global markets; pharmaceuticals; and the internet and communications sector. The abuses at issue include child and forced labor, discrimination, dangerous and unhealthy conditions for workers and communities, privacy violations, and complicity in human rights abuses committed by governments. The United Nations Human Rights Council has endorsed a set of Guiding Principles on Business and Human Rights detailing the responsibilities of both states and business enterprises.[7]

Environmental performance has been the most prominent focus of corporate responsibility efforts. Following the 1989 *Exxon Valdez* oil spill in Alaska, environmental groups and institutional investors came together to promote principles for corporate environmental conduct.[8] Since then, environmental sustainability has become an element of corporate strategy. In response to sustained pressure from stakeholders, companies are setting policies on climate change, natural resource management and environmental stewardship. Sustainability advocates promote "triple bottom line" reporting that accounts for a company's economic, social and environmental performance.[9]

Corporate governance, financial reporting, and corporate compliance continue to be central concerns of stakeholders, fuelled by corporate scandals and the financial crisis. Companies operating in the United States have adopted corporate ethics and compliance programs in response to regulations such as the U.S. Sentencing Guidelines, the Foreign Corrupt Practices Act, stock exchange regulations and the Sarbanes-Oxley Act.

For many years, companies have used corporate philanthropy to burnish corporate reputation, improve corporate relationships and support good works. Stakeholders increasingly look to the private sector to go beyond traditional corporate giving to align philanthropy with business strategy and use the considerable resources and expertise of business to tackle social problems.[10] Calls for pharmaceutical companies to provide universal access to life-saving drugs are just one example.

Pressure for greater corporate responsibility comes from many sources. It can take the form of socially responsible investment funds and customer preferences for responsible brands (market-based pressure), government regulation of business activity or civil litigation against companies (legal pressure), and advocacy campaigns and media coverage targeting corporations (public pressure).

Companies have responded to increased scrutiny of business practices, calls for greater corporate accountability, and the expanding definition of corporate responsibilities in many different ways, ranging from hostility and inaction to acknowledgement, engagement and the transformation of business strategy. For some companies, corporate responsibility efforts are simply a means to meet minimum requirements or silence critics. Companies that take corporate responsibility seriously, however, define corporate responsibility broadly and make the business case for their efforts.

> Companies that take corporate responsibility seriously, however, define corporate responsibility broadly and make the business case for their efforts.

Opportunities to do business and do good are not mutually exclusive, nor are they less valuable for having a positive business impact. This marriage of business opportunity with global need can create a model that our Company and others will see as an opportunity to deliver more than financial performance and have a far-reaching impact.

> – Jeffrey R. Immelt, chairman and CEO, GE[11]

I don't think our fiduciary duty is to put shareholders first. I say the opposite. What we firmly believe is that if we focus our company on improving the lives of the world's citizens and come up with genuine sustainable solutions, we are more in synch with consumers and society and ultimately this will result in good shareholder returns. . . . Why would you invest in a company which is out of synch with the needs of society, that does not take its social compliance in its supply chain seriously, that does not think about the costs of externalities, or of its negative impacts on society?

> – Paul Polman, chief executive, Unilever[12]

The business case for adopting responsible corporate practices includes:

- Managing and mitigating risk
- Protecting and enhancing reputation, brand equity and trust
- Attracting, motivating and retaining talent
- Improving operational and cost-efficiency
- Ensuring a "license to operate"[13]
- Developing new business opportunities
- Creating a more secure and prosperous operating environment[14]

Effective corporate responsibility improves the bottom line by managing risk. Market-based pressure poses the risk of lower sales and a higher cost of capital. Legal pressure presents the risk of liability and less operating flexibility. Public pressure puts at risk a company's most valuable intangible assets—corporate reputation and brand equity. All of these risks, if left unmanaged, can affect company financials.

In the best cases, corporate responsibility creates competitive advantage. By adopting sustainable water management practices, Central American coffee suppliers make themselves more attractive to coffee buyers like Starbucks, whose stakeholders demand minimum environmental standards. By partnering with human rights groups to set standards for internet companies seeking to protect the freedom of expression and privacy of their users, Google, Microsoft and Yahoo! can respond to government internet censorship and surveillance in a way that balances human rights concerns and business objectives.

High-profile brands like Nike, Starbucks, and Google have been thrust into corporate responsibility leadership and led efforts to set standards for social and environmental performance. Pressure often spreads from leaders to an entire industry sector. Nike's early standard-setting efforts influenced the adoption of supplier codes by other apparel and sporting goods companies. Starbucks was the first major coffee company to offer Fair Trade Certified coffee, but since then the largest coffee retailers have followed suit. The experience of the first industries targeted by human rights, labor and environmental activists—the apparel, sporting goods, extractive, and agricultural industries—is shaping second-generation corporate responsibility strategies in healthcare, financial services, and information technology.

COMMUNICATING CORPORATE RESPONSIBILITY

Corporations may be tempted to communicate instead of improving performance; to report only what is legally required; or to say nothing at all.

Communicating corporate responsibility presents companies with a unique set of challenges. Corporations may be tempted to communicate instead of improving performance; to report only what is legally required; or to say nothing at all. But corporate responsibility communications will fail if the company ignores corporate critics or asserts responsibility without action to back it up.

Effective corporate responsibility communications are accurate, credible, and transparent. Companies that excel understand their diverse audiences and available tools; and seek to adopt best practices for communicating corporate responsibility. The most powerful communications make meeting stakeholder expectations part of corporate strategy and a condition of business success.

Audiences

Corporate responsibility audiences include every traditional stakeholder—customers, employees, and investors—and extend to include the media, investment analysts, regulators, policymakers, international organizations and the vast array of nongovernmental groups active on these issues.[15] Leading companies take into account the expectations of all key audiences and make sure that stakeholders understand their efforts.

Choosing language carefully is particularly important. Corporate responsibility topics may be unfamiliar both for the audience and for the spokespeople. An abstract concept like human rights, for example, can be difficult to explain in corporate settings, but employees and other corporate audiences will easily understand the importance of adequate working conditions, non-discriminatory treatment, and protections against abusive treatment. Translating corporate responsibility for every audience is a necessary skill for effective communicators.

Tools

Communicating corporate responsibility employs all of the traditional corporate communication tactics, as well as unique corporate responsibility tools, such as codes of conduct, monitoring initiatives, training and education programs, and due diligence.

CODES OF CONDUCT

A code of conduct is often a company's first step. The past twenty years have witnessed an explosion of voluntary codes.

A code of conduct communicates minimum standards for employees, suppliers, or business partners. Codes also convey messages to corporate stakeholders generally. Royal Dutch Shell's 1997 revision of its Statement of General Business Principles was a first step toward restoring Shell's reputation among stakeholders after the public criticism surrounding Shell's conduct in Nigeria. The changes made by Shell, particularly acknowledging the company's responsibility to "express support for fundamental human rights in line with the legitimate role of business," signaled an important corporate policy change and implicitly acknowledged that Shell had been wrong to insist that the company had no role to play advocating human rights with the governments where Shell operates. The about-face was so abrupt that *The New York Times* editorial page, which two years earlier had excoriated Shell for its failure to intervene, applauded Shell's new statement of principles in an editorial titled, "Citizen Shell."[16]

The content of a code communicates a company's priorities and can help define the limits of a company's responsibility. A code also provides an opportunity to reference widely accepted standards. More and more companies, for example, reference the Universal Declaration of Human Rights and core International Labour Organization Conventions as the common standard for corporate human rights programs.[17]

While codes are a useful tool, they create an expectation of compliance that can lead to criticism if companies fail to live up to the standards they set.

Monitoring

Setting standards creates an expectation of further communications that demonstrate compliance. Companies participating in the UN Global Compact, for example, must communicate annually with stakeholders about progress implementing the Global Compact principles. Companies seek to ensure code compliance by monitoring performance through audits, surveys, inspections, and other means.

A challenge for companies is how to handle monitoring results. Companies are justifiably reluctant to make public the results of internal monitoring of social and environmental performance. It often goes against corporate culture and practice to publicize any internal processes, let alone internal processes that reveal poor corporate performance. While many companies keep code monitoring results confidential, a number of companies have begun to share this information with external parties, report instances of noncompliance, or summarize findings in public reports. The Fair Labor Association (FLA), a multi-stakeholder initiative to improve working conditions in apparel production, summarizes the findings of independent monitoring visits to factories producing apparel for participating apparel brands. The FLA publishes tracking charts of individual factories that detail noncompliance findings and remediation efforts by participating companies. In the internet sector, the Global Network Initiative (GNI) reports publicly on independent assessments of member companies' compliance with the GNI Principles on freedom of expression and privacy.[18]

Compliance programs with the highest levels of transparency make all monitoring results public. The Accord on Fire and Building Safety in Bangladesh, established by certain apparel retailers and trade unions following the 2013 Rana Plaza factory collapse, for example, makes public detailed factory inspection reports by an independent safety inspector.[19]

TRAINING AND EDUCATION

Corporate responsibility initiatives increasingly focus less on standards enforcement and more on education and training to improve performance. Many of the first companies to adopt codes and monitoring are shifting from a policing to a partnership approach to code compliance, seeking to identify key performance indicators that address the root causes of code violations, and then partnering with suppliers to build their capacity to achieve sustainable social and environmental compliance. In factories where excessive working hour violations are common, for example, the Fair Labor Association has sought to educate factory management that less frequent overtime results in higher quality, fewer accidents, and less employee turnover.[20]

THE CORPORATE RESPONSIBILITY TO RESPECT HUMAN RIGHTS

In 2011, the UN Human Rights Council unanimously endorsed the Guiding Principles on Business and Human Rights, detailing steps businesses can take to meet their responsibility to respect human rights.[21] The Guiding Principles are an influential source of guidance for companies seeking to manage human rights impacts as part of their corporate responsibility efforts. The Principles also elaborate important concepts for effectively communicating corporate responsibility. These include the following.

Due Diligence

The scope of a company's human rights due diligence must be sufficiently broad to identify, prevent and mitigate any human rights risks. Companies must assess both actual and potential human rights impacts; prioritize the risk of severe human rights impacts; and look for human rights impacts with which the company may be involved either through its own operations; or linked to its operations, products or services by its business relationships. Human rights due diligence is a dynamic, ongoing activity. New activities or relationships; major decisions or operational changes; and external developments can trigger the need for reassessment.

Transparency

Transparency is an essential feature of the Guiding Principles, which call for companies to track and communicate their human rights performance. Business enterprises whose operations pose risks of severe human rights impacts are expected to report formally on their performance. All companies should be prepared to communicate externally when concerns are raised by or on behalf of affected stakeholders. Human rights reporting should track what due diligence reveals, and include sufficient information for third parties to evaluate whether or not a company's response to a particular human rights impact is adequate.

DUE DILIGENCE

The most effective corporate responsibility efforts anticipate and prevent issues before they become stakeholder concerns. Due diligence—information gathering, research, stakeholder outreach and impact assessments designed to identify, prevent and mitigate risk—has become a key feature of effective corporate responsibility programs. Robust due diligence earns credibility among stakeholders.

As part of its human rights due diligence program, the multinational food company Nestle partnered with the Danish Institute for Human Rights to conduct a series of human rights impact assessments that seek to better understand the scope and magnitude of the human rights impacts resulting from the company's business activities. By reporting publicly on its due diligence process, including the findings in specific country operations and the steps the company has taken to address its actual and potential impacts, Nestle has embraced a level of transparency that allows stakeholders to evaluate the company's efforts.[22]

NON-FINANCIAL REPORTING

> *By all indications, non-financial reporting is on a trajectory to becoming standard business practice in the early 21st century.*
>
> Allen L. White, 2005[23]

To communicate corporate responsibility results to diverse stakeholders, and in some cases to meet regulatory requirements, companies are reporting publicly on non-financial performance. So-called "triple bottom line" reporting adds social and environmental performance to traditional financial reports. Almost all of the world's 250 largest companies are publishing non-financial reports.[24]

The strongest corporate responsibility reports communicate accurate information that is complete, relevant and measurable. Complete information provides a full picture of a company's actions and performance. When addressing efforts to enforce minimum labor standards, for example, it is insufficient for a brand that subcontracts most of its manufacturing to communicate only efforts to enforce standards in its own facilities. Relevance in corporate responsibility communications is analogous to materiality in financial reporting. If a reasonable stakeholder would consider certain information to be relevant, companies should seek to disclose it. The fact that a pharmaceutical company prices life-saving drugs below cost in developing countries is relevant for investors concerned about the role of the private sector providing access to medicines. Finally, companies should provide information that is measurable. The objective is to go beyond mere compliance to demonstrate corporate action. Investors and other stakeholders want to be able to compare corporate responsibility efforts over time and establish a basis for measuring future performance. While metrics for corporate environmental performance are well developed, quantifying social performance, such as human rights conditions, is still an emerging discipline.

Effective corporate responsibility reports:

• Prioritize issues
• Place a company's efforts in the context of business objectives and strategy

- Reference best practices and widely-accepted standards;
- Provide sufficient detail for stakeholders to make their own assessment of performance
- Serve as a basis to measure future performance
- Acknowledge obstacles and challenges, such as issues for which a single company's efforts are insufficient

Corporate responsibility reports demonstrate actions taken, serve as the basis for third party assurance, and are a means to share results and best practices. Some reports feature a management discussion of corporate responsibility issues, along the lines of the management discussion and analysis required in corporate financial reports. Companies have strengthened their reporting by asking independent experts to publicly critique their reports. Chiquita, Gap, Nike, and Ford, for example, have included statements from independent experts in their non-financial reporting. Feedback from stakeholder groups can be a valuable resource for companies seeking to better understand the issues, information and metrics of greatest interest for external stakeholders.

Efforts are underway to standardize non-financial reporting. The Global Reporting Initiative (GRI) is a multi-stakeholder process that provides a voluntary reporting framework for companies to report their economic, environmental, social and governance performance and impacts.[25] The GRI Guidelines help companies to present a balanced picture of their corporate responsibility performance, promote comparability of corporate responsibility reports, serve as an instrument to facilitate stakeholder engagement, encourage incremental reporting, and seek to establish performance indicators for key issues. Hundreds of companies, including BP, Ford, GE, Nike, Shell, and Starbucks, use the GRI Guidelines as the basis for their corporate responsibility reporting.

While companies often begin corporate responsibility reporting as a way to communicate with external stakeholders, many companies find that the process itself—gathering information from across the organization, identifying the issues that matter to stakeholders, and developing targets and ways to measure results—proves to be most valuable as a means to drive corporate responsibility strategy internally throughout the company.

CASE STUDY: NIKE'S JOURNEY, PART 2

Nike's efforts to restore its reputation and demonstrate responsible practices parallel the emergence of corporate responsibility as a corporate discipline. Nike has implemented almost every innovation in the field. In 1992, the company adopted a code of conduct and set minimum labor standards for its suppliers. Since then, Nike has acknowledged responsibility for social and environmental conditions in its supply chain and changed the way it sources certain products to improve environmental performance and reduce the risk of labor violations. Executives have engaged in the public debate over globalization and in conversations with the company's critics. Nike joined governmental and industry-wide efforts to eliminate sweatshops and participates actively in multi-stakeholder partnerships to develop factory standard-setting and monitoring mechanisms, and to support programs for workers and communities. Nike created the position of vice president for corporate responsibility to lead the company's efforts and signal the issue's importance. The company launched internal monitoring of its supply chain, expanded its compliance to include external third-party monitoring, and made its audit results public. Nike signed on to international corporate responsibility initiatives like the United Nations Global Compact[26] and references international human rights, labor and environmental standards in its own standards. Nike established a Corporate Responsibility Committee of its Board of Directors and began issuing a Corporate Responsibility Report on its social and environmental performance in 2001. The company's corporate responsibility reporting has become increasingly detailed, robust and transparent, setting quantifiable environmental and social performance targets that seek to connect corporate responsibility efforts with the company's return on investment:

> Corporate responsibility must evolve from being seen as an unwanted cost to being recognized as an intrinsic part of a healthy business model, an investment that creates competitive advantage and helps a company achieve profitable, sustainable growth.[27]

Communication has played a key role in every step of Nike's journey through the complicated terrain of corporate responsibility. At first, Nike did a poor job communicating corporate responsibility. In 1997, a *Wall Street Journal* article questioned whether Nike's public relations efforts on employment practices had done any good at all. A year later, in a speech to the National Press Club, Nike CEO and Chairman Philip Knight was acknowledging the company's responsibility for the business practices of Asian manufacturers and announcing unilateral initiatives to adopt United States air quality standards for foreign factories, raise the minimum working age to eighteen for all footwear manufacturing workers, and permit the external monitoring of Nike suppliers. Nike's response to stakeholder pressure shifted from merely asserting, to actively demonstrating corporate responsibility.

The cultural change at Nike since then has been dramatic, a point the company readily acknowledges:

> From our early years up to the 1990s, the stakeholders we thought most about were athletes and consumers. In the

1990s, we ignored an emerging group of stakeholders. We learned a hard lesson . . . Non-governmental organizations, trade unions and others have opened our eyes to new issues and viewpoints, and have enabled us to draw on their experience and expertise. This does not mean that we will always agree with our stakeholders, but we know from experience that constructive engagement is usually the approach that brings about the best insight to the challenges we all have an interest in addressing.[28]

Today, the company embraces both transparency and stakeholder engagement, each a best practice for communicating corporate responsibility. Its 2012 Corporate Responsibility Report notes:

We believe that transparency is a central component of a responsible business strategy and that reporting is critical in delivering transparency. Reporting is the main tool we use to provide critical information to our stakeholders about how we manage corporate responsibility issues and impacts. . . . Our stakeholders help us to prioritize key issues and develop our corporate responsibility policies. We engage with stakeholders because we learned early on in our corporate responsibility journey the importance of engaging and listening. We see engagement with multiple stakeholders as a key enabler of both risk mitigation and innovation.[29]

▶ BEST PRACTICES

Companies that communicate corporate responsibility effectively tend to follow six rules.

1. Demonstrate responsibility; do not assert it.

2. Get the facts.

3. Engage critics.

4. Earn credibility.

5. Connect corporate responsibility to business strategy.

6. Be transparent.

1 Demonstrate Responsibility; Do Not Assert It

As in all corporate disciplines, actions speak louder than words when communicating corporate responsibility. Managers must resist the temptation to demonstrate corporate responsibility via press release. Corporate communications face a high threshold to meet stakeholder expectations, especially when audiences are highly skeptical. So-called "greenwashing"—presenting an environmentally responsible public image that is unfounded or intentionally misleading[30]—has become sufficiently widespread that stakeholders have formed groups devoted to exposing the worst corporate offenders. Many audiences assume that corporate statements, if they are not misleading or outright false, will be self-serving and provide only a limited perspective. Few companies can reasonably expect external audiences to take their statements at face value.

Corporate communications and marketing should support, not drive, corporate responsibility programs. The most effective communications are actions that address the expectations of stakeholders. Enforcing minimum labor standards in your supply chain is more effective than issuing a statement to explain why the company was unaware that its main supplier fired employees for attempting to organize or that a subcontractor routinely administered pregnancy tests to prospective employees.

Attempting to "spin" issues of corporate responsibility is even worse. In the 1990s, the U.S. energy company Unocal faced intense criticism over its pipeline project in Burma from activists who alleged that the company was complicit in human rights abuses committed by the military to clear the pipeline route. In a 1996 internal e-mail to a Unocal spokesperson, a company executive advised a colleague how to evade difficult questions: "By saying we influenced the army not to move a village, you introduce the concept that they would do such a thing; whereas, by saying that no villages have been moved, you skirt the issue of whether it could happen or not."[31] Communication that misleads never meets stakeholders' expectations. In fact, Unocal knew of Burma's poor human rights record before the company invested. Companies that view corporate responsibility as simply a public relations issue, or that fail to take any meaningful action to improve performance or address deficiencies, unnecessarily increase their legal, regulatory and reputational exposure. In 2005, facing various lawsuits and engaged in merger discussions with Chevron/Texaco, Unocal ultimately settled the lawsuits and agreed to compensate the Burmese villagers who had sued the company for complicity in forced labor and other human rights abuses.

Assertions of corporate responsibility without the appropriate due diligence, policies, and procedures in place to back them up do more harm than good. Critical stakeholders will quickly point out any inconsistencies between word and deed. Whenever a company talks about corporate responsibility, the communication should be based on corporate action. The first act is usually some form of due diligence.

2 Get the Facts

Responsibility begins with accurate information. Companies often find themselves in crisis mode when they first address corporate responsibility. Facing accusations of irresponsible practices—sweatshop working conditions, complicity with human rights violations, poor environmental practices—companies must first provide accurate information.

Without a clear understanding of conditions on the ground, companies cannot respond to critics or improve corporate responsibility performance. Sporting goods manufacturers were caught flat-footed in 1995 when media accounts portrayed thousands of children stitching soccer balls in Pakistan. Nike, Reebok, and other companies had codes of conduct that prohibited child labor, but had failed to conduct due diligence or implement the standards beyond their principal Pakistani suppliers. When challenged, the industry could not say confidently that its supply chain was free of child labor. In fact, children were stitching soccer balls at home in an extensive subcontracting network.

The critical first step for the sporting goods industry to demonstrate corporate responsibility was commissioning local experts to survey the role of child workers in soccer ball production. Contrary to the most sensational media accounts, the survey found that the worst forms of child labor were not prevalent and the number of young children affected was smaller than originally reported. Sporting goods brands, once they understood the reality on the ground, convinced their suppliers to eliminate home stitching and monitor the age of workers.

Accurate information not only informs smart business decisions, it minimizes the legal and regulatory risks associated with public communications. Allegations of corporate irresponsibility often prompt calls for government regulation of corporate conduct. Companies that provide policymakers with reliable information and demonstrate that they are taking an issue seriously can reduce pressure for regulation. When U.S. chocolate manufacturer Hershey Foods was confronted with news accounts of child trafficking and slave labor on West African cocoa farms, the company's initial response was one of bewilderment: "[N]o one . . . had ever heard of this. Your instinct is that Hershey should have known. But the fact is we didn't know."[32] Shortly thereafter, under threat of U.S. legislation that would ban cocoa imports from West Africa, chocolate companies and the global cocoa industry mobilized around the issue, and commissioned independent research to assess working conditions. Companies averted legislative or regulatory action by committing to a voluntary, industry-wide program to eliminate the worst forms of child labor from cocoa production.

Accurate information is just as important for advocates who seek to improve corporate performance. A common set of facts provides a basis for engagement and collaboration among stakeholders. In 2001, after Mexican police intervened in an apparel factory labor dispute, factory customers Nike and Reebok worked with independent factory monitoring and labor rights organizations to establish common findings on factory conditions, worker sentiments, and applicable law. Agreement on the origins of the dispute allowed the apparel companies and their various stakeholders to work with factory management to reinstate illegally fired workers and protect the right to organize. The collaborative effort based on common facts resulted in the first independent union in the Mexican maquiladora sector and met the expectations of key corporate stakeholders.

3 Engage Critics

The catalyst for a company to address corporate responsibility, more often than not, is public criticism. The first instinct of corporate managers accused of corporate irresponsibility is to defend the organization by ignoring or attacking its critics. Both tactics are likely to backfire.

In December 1995, *The New York Times* ran an editorial arguing that the world's largest oil company, Royal Dutch Shell, had failed to shoulder its responsibility to intervene with the military government of Nigeria on behalf of the activist Ken Saro-Wiwa.[33] In 1994, Shell had called in Nigerian government security forces to protect its facilities from violent attacks and quell unrest in the area of its oilfields. Saro-Wiwa, a prominent political opponent of the Nigerian dictatorship and of Shell's operations in Nigeria, was arrested by government security forces for allegedly inciting a riot and sentenced to hang in a trial widely criticized as corrupt and politically-motivated. Initially, after Saro-Wiwa was found guilty, Shell argued that it was "not for a commercial organization to interfere with the legal processes of a sovereign state." After a storm of public criticism following Saro-Wiwa's execution, however, Shell changed its policy on human rights engagement, asserting its right and responsibility to make its position known on any matter which affects the company, its employees, customers, shareholders or community.[34] Learning from its experience as the focus of intense criticism, Shell now regularly engages critics, participates in multi-stakeholder initiatives like the Voluntary Standards on Security and Human Rights and the UN Global Compact, and actively monitors human rights risks wherever the company operates.

Shell's competitor BP faced a similar issue in Colombia. Human Rights Watch accused BP of complicity with Colombian security forces that had a record of human rights abuse.[35] Rather than adopt an exclusively defensive posture, BP entered into dialogue with critics and, along with Shell, other energy companies and human rights advocates, joined a process convened by the U.S. and British governments to develop the Voluntary Standards on Security and Human Rights.[36] BP made engaging critics a key element of its business strategy as the lead partner in a consortium building a natural gas pipeline from Georgia to Turkey. The pipeline project generated initial opposition from human rights and environmental groups. When Amnesty International released a report critical of BP and the human rights impact of the pipeline,[37] BP engaged Amnesty in dialogue, and sought to address some of the human rights concerns by incorporating international human standards in the legal agreements governing the project. According to one BP executive, the dialogue was valuable: "Our work with Amnesty International was an eye-opener; they viewed things in a way we never would have."[38] Engaging its main critic and taking stakeholder concerns seriously earned the company credibility.

Most companies, however, are exceedingly cautious and reluctant to engage critics. In 2003, The Coca-Cola Company received a letter from Human Rights Watch expressing concern over hazardous child labor in the production of sugar cane in El Salvador, sugar that is purchased to make Coke.[39] In a series of communications with Human Rights Watch, Coca-Cola sought to distance itself from the issue of working conditions in the sugarcane fields by asserting its responsibility only for conditions at its direct supplier, the large processing mill covered by Coca-Cola's Guiding Principles for Suppliers. While Coca-Cola deserves credit for a certain level of engagement, the company's response is reminiscent of Nike's initial response to allegations of child labor and Shell's original position on raising issues with host governments. By adopting a legalistic approach and distancing itself from controversy rather than engaging critics and exploring possible remedies, Coca-Cola may have missed an opportunity to manage a supply chain risk to its reputation, gather accurate information, and promote human rights in the communities where it both sources and sells its product.

A company may not agree with or ultimately adopt the recommendations of a human rights organization or labor union, but engaging that external stakeholder in honest dialogue can earn credibility and demonstrate a corporate commitment to addressing the issues at stake. Engaging reasonable critics can also provide valuable information and expertise, and set the stage for collaboration or partnership.

4 Earn Credibility

Communicating corporate responsibility places a high premium on credibility. Demonstrating responsibility through actions, conducting due diligence to establish the facts, and engaging critics earns credibility. Companies also earn credibility by submitting to third-party assessments, adopting widely accepted standards, acknowledging obstacles and partnering with stakeholders.

The most powerful corporate responsibility communication comes from third parties. The opinions of credible experts and independent stakeholders almost always carry greater weight than corporate assertions, especially in an atmosphere of deep mistrust of corporate motives. Independent third-party monitoring was one of the first expectations of stakeholders when companies began to adopt voluntary codes of conduct. A single statement of support from a respected former critic can do more for a company's reputation than years of corporate communication.

Adopting widely accepted external standards earns credibility. Voluntary corporate standard-setting is often criticized as a self-serving tactic designed to head off stricter government regulation. Companies can counter this argument by adopting standards for corporate conduct that are widely accepted by stakeholders. Corporate human rights policies, for example, increasingly reference international standards, such as the Universal Declaration of Human Rights, ILO Conventions, and the UN Guiding Principles on Business and Human Rights.

Acknowledging problems earns credibility. Reasonable stakeholders put corporate responsibility efforts in perspective. There is a limit to corporate influence; a single company cannot solve systemic problems affecting social and environmental conditions wherever they operate. When a company cannot meet the nonfinancial expectations of stakeholders, it should explain why. Failing to acknowledge problems and limitations is more likely to damage credibility than addressing stakeholder concerns directly.

Many corporate responsibility reports are notable for the candor with which they acknowledge failures and address obstacles to improved performance. In 2003, Gap Inc. issued its first Social Responsibility Report. In addition to describing the company's internal and third-party factory monitoring process, the report detailed the regional distribution and frequency of specific violations of Gap's Code of Vendor Conduct. While Gap's reporting prompted media coverage of the poor factory conditions it revealed,[40] Gap's candor earned the company credibility among stakeholders:

> We think this goes far beyond the public relations fluff that other companies put out a lot of the time. By making some very candid admissions, they are taking an important first step toward cleaning up the problems.
> – Bob Jeffcott, Maquila Solidarity Network

Partnering with stakeholders earns credibility. Nike has worked to restore its credibility among stakeholders by partnering with competitors, labor, government, and experts to improve working conditions in foreign factories. Stakeholder engagement allows a company to identify issues of concern, tap needed expertise, build relationships, and communicate corporate responsibility performance in a highly targeted fashion. Stakeholder dialogue is gaining prominence as an effective means to rebuild corporate reputation.[41]

Voluntary "multi-stakeholder" programs bring together diverse actors to tackle common problems on the corporate responsibility agenda. These partnerships allow companies to share information, resources and responsibilities. Sector-specific initiatives like the Global Network Initiative and the Fair Labor Association draw strength and credibility from the participation of diverse stakeholders.

5 Connect Corporate Responsibility to Business Strategy

Stakeholders expect corporate responsibility to be an integral part of business strategy. Investors who value information on social and environmental performance want companies to explain what the company is doing to incorporate sustainable practices in the company's long-term strategy. Customers, employees, and partners look for signals that initiatives reflect an ongoing organizational commitment rather than an *ad hoc* response to an isolated issue. The most effective communications demonstrate how a company's corporate responsibility efforts advance key business objectives.

Corporate responsibility efforts are most effective when they are integrated, well-understood and rewarded at all levels of an organization, from the boardroom to the factory floor. Every business function in an organization should be able to state the business case for corporate responsibility. As with all corporate strategy, corporate responsibility initiatives carry the greatest weight when sponsored by the company's CEO and most senior executives. But unlike traditional business disciplines such as marketing and investor relations, there is no well-defined way to conduct corporate responsibility throughout a company. Functional responsibility for corporate responsibility initiatives can be found in legal departments, operations, sourcing, government relations, investor relations, and corporate communications.

> Every business function in an organization should be able to state the business case for corporate responsibility.

Leading companies adopt initiatives that align business and corporate responsibility objectives. According to Michael Porter, "Companies need to move away from defensive actions into a proactive integration of social initiatives into business competitive strategy."[42] When companies redefine products, markets and operations taking into account societal needs, benefits and harms, business can create "shared value" for both the enterprise and society.[43] The global food company, Unilever, for example, by taking steps across its operations to reduce the company's environmental impact, also strengthens its brand, creates opportunities to innovate and reduce costs, and reduces risk in its raw material supply chains.[44]

6 Be Transparent

Transparency is the most important of all the best practices for communicating corporate responsibility. Since the very first corporate responsibility efforts, stakeholders have sought more transparency from companies, and expectations of greater transparency continue to grow.

Transparency—communicating accurate information that is complete, relevant and measurable (see "Non-financial Reporting," earlier)—allows stakeholders to make their own assessments of corporate performance. As a rule of thumb, more information is better than less. High levels of transparency earn greater credibility with stakeholders and critics, create incentives for continuous improvement, and encourage the adoption of best practices.

Of course, there are drawbacks to communication. Companies that embrace full disclosure risk becoming the target of critics. No compliance program can eliminate all violations, and it only takes one media exposé to damage corporate reputation. The risk is substantial for a company that has never disclosed before or a company that has been the focus of intense attention. Many companies make public only what is required by law. That is often a short-sighted strategy.

In the apparel industry, for example, mounting pressure to eliminate sweatshops created a need for transparency that eventually outweighed corporate concerns over proprietary information and public criticism. At first, apparel brands relied on their own codes of conduct and monitoring. Stakeholders, however, expected greater assurance about apparel supply chains. For years, companies resisted calls by advocates for full disclosure of factory locations. A number of well-known brands joined multi-stakeholder programs with varying levels of independent monitoring and public disclosure of monitoring results. Despite its experience as a target of criticism, in April 2005, Nike announced that it would disclose every contract factory worldwide where its products are made, reversing the company's longstanding position against factory disclosure. Nike determined that the benefits of full disclosure outweighed the risks of publicizing individual violations. By unilaterally disclosing all of its contract factory locations and supporting industry-wide approaches to improve working conditions in apparel factories, Nike also used its corporate responsibility strategy to level the playing field among well-known apparel brands and competitors. Six months after Nike, Levi Strauss followed Nike's lead by disclosing the locations of its own suppliers. Nike's principal rival, Adidas, ultimately disclosed factory locations in 2008.

The trend is toward greater transparency. Most companies active on corporate responsibility issues have concluded that the benefits of communicating outweigh the risks of not communicating at all. Industries more recently under the corporate responsibility spotlight, such as internet and communications companies, have built robust public reporting requirements into their corporate responsibility programs. Companies must overcome any cultural bias against public disclosure and seek levels of transparency sufficient to establish facts, demonstrate corporate responsibility performance and earn credibility among stakeholders.

> The benefits of communicating outweigh the risks of not communicating at all.

► RESOURCES FOR FURTHER STUDY

Elkington, John, *Cannibals with Forks: The Triple Bottom Line of 21st Century Business*, Oxford: Capstone, 1997.

Ewing, Anthony P., "What Executives Need to Know (and Do) About Human Rights," Business & Human Rights Resource Centre (February 2013), available at http://www.business-humanrights.org/Links/Repository/1017323/.

Harvard Business Review on Corporate Responsibility (2003).

MacKinnon, Rebecca, *Consent of the Networked*, New York: Basic Books, 2012.

Ruggie, John Gerard, *Just Business: Multinational Corporations and Human Rights*, New York: W.W. Norton & Company, 2013.

Vogel, David, *The Market for Virtue: The Potential and Limits of Corporate Social Responsibility*, Washington: Brookings Institution Press, 2005.

Websites

BSR (Business for Social Responsibility), http://www.bsr.org

Business & Human Rights Resource Centre, http://www.business-humanrights.org

Ceres, http://www.ceres.org

Ethical Corporation, http://www.ethicalcorp.com

Fair Labor Association, http://www.fairlabor.org

Global Network Initiative, http://www.globalnetworkinitiative.org

Global Reporting Initiative, http://www.globalreporting.org

Institute for Human Rights and Business, http://www.ihrb.org

United Nations Global Compact, http://www.unglobalcompact.org

Noteworthy Corporate Responsibility Reports

The Coca-Cola Company, http://www.coca-colacompany.com/sustainability/

Ford Motor Company, http://corporate.ford.com/our-company/sustainability

General Electric Company, http://www.gecitizenship.com

Microsoft, http://www.microsoft.com/about/corporatecitizenship/en-us/reporting/

Nestle, http://www.nestle.com/csv

Nike, http://nikeinc.com/pages/responsibility

PVH, https://www.pvh.com/corporate_responsibility.aspx

Shell, http://www.shell.com/global/environment-society.html

Starbucks, http://www.starbucks.com/responsibility

Unilever, http://www.unilever.com/sustainable-living-2014/

▶ QUESTIONS FOR FURTHER DISCUSSION

1. How has the meaning of corporate responsibility evolved over time?

2. What is the relationship between corporate responsibility and corporate communication?

3. Why is transparency important to stakeholders?

4. How can corporate responsibility be integrated throughout a company's operations?

5. How can corporate responsibility create competitive advantage?

▶ NOTES

1 Nike press release, June 6, 1996.

2 *Social Responsibility or "Telescopic Philanthropy": The Choice is Yours*, remarks by Harold Burson, Founding Chairman, Burson-Marsteller, Columbia University, Graduate School of Business, March 20, 1973.

3 Cf. Milton Friedman, "The Social Responsibility of Business is to Increase its Profits," *The New York Times Magazine*, September 11, 1970; Peter Drucker, "The New Meaning of Corporate Social Responsibility," *California Management Review*, vol. 26, no. 2, Winter 1984.

4 In a survey of U.S. consumers, most defined corporate responsibility as a commitment to employees or communities. Fleishmann-Hillard/National Consumers League, Rethinking Corporate Social Responsibility, 2006, available at www.csrresults.com/FINAL_Full_Report.pdf.

5 General Electric Company, Our Actions: GE 2005 Citizenship Report, 2005, p. 4.

6 Communicating financial performance is covered in Chapter 8, Investor Relations.

7 John Ruggie, "Guiding Principles on Business and Human Rights: Implementing the United Nations 'Protect, Respect and Remedy' Framework," Report of the Special Representative of the Secretary-General on the issue of human rights and transnational corporations and other business enterprises," UN doc. A/HRC/17/31, March 21, 2011.

8 The Ceres Principles address protection of the biosphere, sustainable use of natural resources, reduction and disposal of wastes, energy conservation and product safety. CERES Principles, 1989, available at http:// www.ceres.org/coalitionandcompanies/principles.php.

9 See, for example, John Elkington, *Cannibals with Forks: The Triple Bottom Line of 21st Century Business*, 1997.

10 See, for example, Michael E. Porter and Mark R. Kramer, "The Competitive Advantage of Corporate Philanthropy," *Harvard Business Review*, December 2002.

11 General Electric Company, *Our Actions: GE 2005 Citizenship Report*, 2005, p. 3.

12 Quoted in Jo Confino, "Unilever's Paul Polman: Challenging the Corporate Status Quo," *Guardian Sustainable Business*, April 24, 2012.

13 By earning the trust of stakeholders and acting in ways that meet societal expectations,

companies maintain a so-called "license to operate," a non-legal dimension of corporate responsibility.

14 See, for example, World Economic Forum, Values and Value, 2004.

15 NGOs engaged in the corporate responsibility debate include human rights organizations, environmental groups, labor unions, and development organizations.

16 *The New York Times*, "Citizen Shell", March 31, 1997, p. A14.

17 For a list of codes that reference human rights standards, see Business & Human Rights Resource Centre, www.business-humanrights.org/Documents/Policies.

18 Global Network Initiative, *Public Report on the Independent Assessment Process for Google, Microsoft, and Yahoo* (January 2014).

19 Accord on Fire and Building Safety In Bangladesh, Inspection Reports, available at http://www.bangladeshaccord.org/inspection-reports/.

20 Fair Labor Association, Widespread Overtime and Why It Doesn't Work, 2009, available at www.fairlabor.org/images/WhatWeDo/SpecialProjects/scope_how_may09.pdf.

21 John Ruggie, "Guiding Principles on Business and Human Rights: Implementing the United Nations 'Protect, Respect and Remedy' Framework," Report of the Special Representative of the Secretary-General on the issue of human rights and transnational corporations and other business enterprises," UN doc. A/HRC/17/31, March 21, 2011.

22 The Danish Institute for Human Rights and Nestle, *Talking the Human Rights Walk: Nestle's Experience Assessing Human Rights Impacts in its Business Activities* (2013).

23 Allen L. White, *New Wine, New Bottles: The Rise of Non-Financial Reporting* (Business for Social Responsibility, June 20, 2005).

24 KPMG, *The KPMG Survey of Corporate Responsibility Reporting 2013* (2013).

25 Global Reporting Initiative, G4 Sustainability Reporting Guidelines, 2013.

26 The UN Global Compact is a voluntary corporate citizenship initiative that calls on companies to integrate into their core business operations ten principles on human rights, labor rights, environmental protection and transparency.

27 Nike, Inc., FY05–06 Corporate Responsibility Report, 2007, p. 7.

28 Nike, Inc., FY04 Corporate Responsibility Report, 2005, p. 11.

29 Nike, Inc., FY10–11 Corporate Responsibility Report, 2012, pp. 79, 82.

30 *Oxford English Dictionary* (1999). See BSR and Futerra, *Understanding and Preventing Greenwash: A Business Guide* (July 2009).

31 E-mail from Unocal Director of Information Carol Scott to Unocal Media Contact and Spokesperson David Garcia, cited in Doe I v. Unocal Corp., 9th Cir., filed September 18, 2002.

32 Robert M. Reese, Senior Vice President of Hershey Foods, quoted in Bob Fernandez, "Hershey 'Shocked' by Report," *The Times Union* (Albany, NY), June 24, 2001, p. A7.

33 *The New York Times*, "Shell Game in Nigeria", December 3, 1995, p. E14.

34 Royal Dutch/Shell, Statement of General Business Principles, March 17, 1997.

35 Human Rights Watch, Colombia: Concerns Raised by the Security Arrangements of Transnational Oil Companies, April 1998.

36 See generally, Bennett Freeman, "Drilling for Common Ground," *Foreign Policy Magazine*, July/August 2001.

37 Amnesty International UK, *Human Rights On the Line*, May 2003.

38 Jay Pearson, Regional Coordinator, BP p.l.c., UN Global Compact Learning Forum, Nova Lima, Brazil, December 2003.

39 Human Rights Watch, *Turning a Blind Eye: Hazardous Child Labor in El Salvador's Sugarcane Cultivation* (June 2004).

40 See, for example, Michael Liedtke, "Gap Inc. Says Some of its Factories are Sweatshops," *Associated Press*, May 13, 2004.

41 See, for example, Sheila Bonini, David Court, and Alberto Marchi, "Rebuilding Corporate Reputations," *The McKinsey Quarterly*, June 2009.

42 "CSR—A Religion with Too Many Priests?," *European Business Forum*, issue 15, autumn 2003.

43 Michael E. Porter and Mark R. Kramer, "Creating Shared Value," *Harvard Business Review*, January–February 2011.

44 Unilever, Unilever Sustainable Living Plan 2013, 2013.

13 PUBLIC RELATIONS CONSULTING: CONSULTING AND CORPORATE COMMUNICATION— THE NEXUS

By Louis Capozzi, Chairman, retired, MSL Group

Talk low, talk slow, and don't talk too much.

– John Wayne

- ▶ Management Lesson from Consultants
- ▶ Overview: The Public Relations Consulting Business
- ▶ The History of Public Relations Consulting Firms
- ▶ Agency Structure and Areas of Practice
- ▶ Financial Management

■ ■ ■

MANAGEMENT LESSONS FROM CONSULTANTS

I've spent about half my career in corporate life, and half in consulting firms. When I took the job as CCO (chief communication officer) of Aetna, someone stopped me in the hall and asked, "How could you give up the excitement of Madison Avenue for life in a stodgy insurance company?"

I answered that I "gave up anxiety for frustration." When you work for a firm, you worry all the time. Will clients like my advice? Will they pay their bills? Will I make my numbers? Most of those concerns go away when you join a large organization, but they're replaced by other challenges.

Life inside the company offers a number of unique management problems. In many organizations, mastering the process is critical. You go to many more meetings where the outcomes are vague at best. And politics often trumps logic.

To overcome the challenges of corporate life pay attention to the practices of consultants. By adopting a "consulting" mentality, corporate communicators can maximize their impact and minimize their frustration.

Lead, don't manage. Develop an action bias. Treat the people you staff like "clients." Organize for efficiency. Drive hard for results, and quantify them. Develop a deep understanding of the business. Know the numbers cold.

Here's hoping you will find the principles in this chapter a recipe for successful management of communication, whichever side you sit on.

■ ■ ■

Public Relations Consulting =

The business of providing advice and counsel, as well as communication services, to clients for a fee. Reputation is key.

OVERVIEW: THE PUBLIC RELATIONS CONSULTING BUSINESS

This chapter covers the business of public relations consulting. That's as opposed to the "profession" of public relations, which covers everyone who works in public relations—from corporate communicators to those in associations and non-profits, to government communication staff.

> Public relations consultants work in firms that offer communication advice and services to clients—for a fee.

Public relations consultants work in firms that offer communication advice and services to clients—for a fee. Consultants must balance the interests of clients, employees and the firm's owners. This "triple squeeze" creates unique challenges for managers and adds an extra dimension of reward—and stress—to what is already a challenging profession.

Clients want great work and service, at a reasonable price. Employees want new challenges and opportunities, as well as a chance to advance in status and pay. Owners want growth and a fair return on their investment. It sounds simple, yet these three dynamic factors are in constant tension. To provide great work

> That means longer work hours and lower wages for the staff. That's where the tension exists.

and service, you need to hire more and better people—and pay them more. That drives down profits for the owners. To boost the profits, you need to get higher productivity out of your existing staff. That means longer work hours and lower wages for the staff. That's where the tension exists.

Managing the "triple squeeze" poses substantial challenges. But with the right perspective and the right skills, great results can be achieved.

This chapter attempts to bring the experience of working in a public relations consulting firm—often called "the agency business"—to life.

THE HISTORY OF PUBLIC RELATIONS CONSULTING FIRMS

Public relations consulting began as an industry in the early 1900s. And at the beginning it was an industry dominated by individual counselors—larger than life figures who helped shape the reputations of entire industries and became legends in the field.

The Pioneers

An ex-newspaperman named Ivy Lee created one of the first consulting firms in 1904. His clients included the Pennsylvania Railroad, Standard Oil, and Guggenheim. He's credited with inventing the press release at a time when he had to convince clients that they had an obligation to inform reporters about events before they learned about them elsewhere.

Lee is often called the "father" of modern public relations consulting, an honorific he often shares with Edward Bernays. Nephew to Sigmund Freud, Bernays was the first to offer clients influence on public opinion. He coined the term "public relations counsel" and taught the first course on the subject at The University of New York (now New York University) in 1923. In that same year, Bernays wrote *Crystallizing Public Opinion*, a book counselors would find instructive and prescient today.

An associate of Bernays', Carl Byoir, founded the first large-scale public relations consulting business in 1930. It became one of the most recognized firms in the business, and was eventually taken over in 1980 by Hill & Knowlton, then the largest firm in the industry. Byoir created the March of Dimes for President Roosevelt, but the roots of his firm were deeply embedded in work for large industrial clients.

Another pioneer, John W. Hill, who started Hill & Knowlton in 1927 after an eighteen-year career as a journalist, shared that focus on industry. It would become the world's largest public relations firm by the mid-1960s, and it remains a leader in the field today. Founded in Cleveland, Ohio, the firm built its business on work for the American Iron and Steel Institute. Hill moved the firm's headquarters to Manhattan in 1934, and began the growth of New York City as a major center for the public relations consulting business.

Yet another pioneer with beginnings in business-to-business communication, Harold Burson, began his firm as a one-man-band in 1947. In 1952 he met an advertising man named Bill Marsteller whose client, Rockwell Manufacturing Company, was looking for a PR firm. They won the account together, and then merged their businesses. Burson-Marsteller became one of the world's largest and most respected public relations consulting firms, a reputation it still enjoys today. Harold, age ninety-three at this writing, still goes to the office every day and is considered the "dean" of public relations consulting.

The Modern Landscape

Today's public relations industry would be unrecognizable to its pioneers. In 1968, the first year records were kept by the O'Dwyers Newsletter, the largest firm in the world was Hill & Knowlton with $6.5 million in fee income.[1] The largest firms today are global giants, each exceeding $500 million in fee income with employees numbering in the thousands. They are big businesses and, mostly, part of even bigger communication conglomerates.

Beginning in the 1960s, most large PR firms were being bought by advertising agencies. While the ad agencies reported to brand managers or marketing directors, the PR firms were counseling the CEO. The ad agencies saw public relations as a way to move up the ladder, and to broaden their offering to clients.

By the 1980s, consolidation in the advertising industry began. As a result, a new force emerged in the communication industry—the publicly traded communication holding company. And within those holding companies most of the largest global public relations networks now reside.

The first of the holding companies was Interpublic. Founded in 1960 with advertising giant McCann Erickson as its base, the company bought literally hundreds of advertising, public relations and marketing communication firms. Today, two of the largest and most successful PR firms live within Interpublic—Weber Shandwick, among the very largest, and Golin Harris, which also ranks in the top tier of the industry.

The largest of the holding companies today, Omnicom, was founded in 1986. DDB Needham merged with BBDO in a deal the industry dubbed "the Big Bang." Omnicom went on to acquire another large ad agency, TBWA Worldwide. It owns three large, powerful public relations firms: Ketchum, Fleishman Hillard, and Porter Novelli.

Another holding company giant emerged in 1985 when Martin Sorrell bought a shell company called Wire and Plastic Products on the London Stock Exchange, and began acquiring communication firms. He bought J. Walter Thompson advertising, which owned Hill & Knowlton public relations. Later, acquisitions of Ogilvy (with Ogilvy PR), Y & R (with Burson Marsteller and Cone & Wolfe) and Grey Advertising (with GCI) gave WPP an enormous public relations portfolio.

The newest of the holding company giants, Publicis, began as a French advertising agency and grew through a series of dramatic acquisitions, including Saatchi & Saatchi advertising, and another holding company called Bcom3. The Bcom3 acquisition brought American advertising giant Leo Burnett into the Publicis Groupe, and also top ten PR firm Manning Selvage & Lee, now MSLGroup.

In this holding company environment, public relations firms have thrived. The industry has enjoyed fantastic growth, and the PR operations now represent significant portions of the groups' revenues and profits.

Today, the world's largest public relations firms manage networks of dozens of offices across the globe. Budgets for a single client often exceed the size of even the largest firms a few decades ago. The size, scope and influence of public relations consultants has grown to put the industry on the same level as any other communication discipline.

> Budgets for a single client often exceed the size of even the largest firms a few decades ago.

Specialty Firms

While the huge global networks dominate the industry today, a large number of high-quality specialty firms have also developed, in both industry segments and audience sensitivities.

Financial communication consultants, such as Saard Verbinnen, Citigate, Brunswick, Kekst and Financial Dynamics, specialize in advising clients on mergers, acquisitions and other financial matters. Such transactions require intense, focused efforts at high levels. When faced with such a situation, many clients turn to these specialists to work with the lawyers and investment bankers on the communication aspects of the transaction. Their depth of expertise, and their ability to dedicate staff to an intense, but short-lived assignment, make them effective partners on financial deals.

In recent years large-scale healthcare consultancies that specialize in the marketing of prescription drugs have emerged. Firms like Chandler Chico, Noonan/Russo, and

Spectrum Science help clients navigate the difficult waters of drug communication in this highly regulated sector.

Technology specialty firms grew up in the dot.com era that began in the 1980s, and several survived the bursting of that bubble in the late '90s. Waggener Edstrom, Text 100, Broedeur, and others offer specific technical expertise, insights and relationships that help technology clients communicate effectively. A large trade press, an acutely interested business press, and an increasingly wired public need to be factored into technology communication programs, both on line and in traditional media.

The public affairs arena has spawned specialty firms offering clients specialized skills, unique experience and personal contacts to can help them deal effectively with the government. Firms like APCO, Quinn Gillespie, and Penn Shoen often employ former government officials to assist their clients. Often Republicans and Democrats will team up to offer the broadest possible representation in Washington. Jack Quinn, for example, was President Clinton's White House Counsel, while his partner, Ed Gillespie, was the Republican National Chairman.

> You can find a firm for nearly every niche, from strawberries to skateboarding.

There are a wide range of other specialty firms as well, including food and nutrition, fashion, travel and entertainment. There are also firms that specialize in audience segments, like children or moms or elders. You can find a firm for nearly every niche, from strawberries to skateboarding.

Small to Mid-Sized Firms

Finally, there exists a vast network of small to mid-sized public relations consultancies—literally thousands of independent consultants and firms ranging in size from a few people in a small local market, to dozens operating on a national or even sometimes a global basis.

Trade Associations

As the public relations industry grew, the need emerged for trade associations that represent firms' mutual interests. Today, such organizations exist in most countries, and regional or global coordinating bodies have also been formed.

In the U.S., the Council of Public Relations Firms (CPRF) was formed in 1998, and now represents more than 100 PR consulting firms across the country, including most of the industry giants. It represents the premier global, mid-size, regional, and specialty agencies across every discipline and practice area. The Council's mission is "to advance the business of public relations firms by building the market and firms' value as strategic business partners." Activities include advocacy, setting industry standards, management programs and events that convene the leadership of the industry.

The CPRF publishes a wide range of useful information, from a code of professional conduct to information helping clients select and manage their agencies. (Their website is http://www.prfirms.org.)

Associations similar to the Council exist in most countries of the world. Some of the largest are the PRCA in the U.K., Assorel in Italy and GPRA in Germany. These individual country associations come together under the umbrella of a global organization called ICCO, the International Communications Consultancy Organisation.

ICCO acts as an "association of associations." It convenes the leaders of nearly thirty national associations in Europe, the Americas and Asia to share information, perspectives and ideas. The ICCO board includes a representative from each member country, and builds relationships among firm leaders around the world. It publishes an annual World Report on the state of the industry, has developed a global standard of practice called the Stockholm Charter, and shares information on member organizations at http://www.iccopr.com.

AGENCY STRUCTURE AND AREAS OF PRACTICE

How Clients Use Consulting Firms

Firms can offer an external view, and often have experience in areas not covered by the in-house communication staff. Additionally, the input of external advisors often carries weight internally, especially when other staff functions—such as the lawyers—bring in their own "experts" to advise management.

> Firms can offer an external view, and often have experience in areas not covered by the in-house communication staff.

Firms often provide creative idea development as well. Even in the largest internal departments, the same few people are usually charged with developing new creative ideas and angles for promoting the interests of the organization. Because consulting firms are larger collections of people, and because people can be brought in who do not regularly work on one particular client, new perspectives can be brought to bear and fresh ideas emerge.

Many clients use consulting firms to manage specific programs that are well contained and can be delegated to the firm with a minimum of staff oversight. Examples might be a sponsored event, or a product marketing program. Large multinational organizations in particular rely on firms with global networks to manage broad global campaigns.

Finally, clients employ consulting firms to accomplish work efficiently. In any internal department, there will be small teams assigned to specific jobs. Even the largest departments, like the one I ran at Aetna in the 1980s (with nearly 200 staff) might only have two or three people on any one specific area of practice. As a result, the internal department has a limited ability to delegate work to the lowest possible level. As a result, senior people might often find themselves dealing with matters that could be much more efficiently performed by lower level employees. Public relations consulting firms are designed to offer this kind of efficiency to clients.

How Consulting Firms Organize

Most firms use a "pyramid" structure to offer clients all of the advice and services they require. The largest number of employees are at the bottom of the "pyramid"— assistant account executives (AAEs). These are the firm's lowest level professional employees. Many are right out of school, perhaps having done an internship as part of their education.

AAEs do the most routine jobs for clients, putting together contact lists, monitoring the media, writing reports and, yes, stuffing envelopes! Since they have the lowest salaries, their services can be offered to clients at the lowest rates.

> As the seniority of the employees increases, from AAE to Account Executive, up to Supervisor, VP or Senior VP, the number of employees in that group decreases, and the salaries, and concomitant billing rates go up.

As the seniority of the employees increases, from AAE to Account Executive, up to Supervisor, VP or Senior VP, the number of employees in that group decreases, and the salaries, and concomitant billing rates go up.

In addition to this "pyramid" structure, larger, full-service agencies generally organize by practice area. Typical structures would include corporate and financial, healthcare, consumer marketing, and technology practices. These practices would be organized in the firm's key offices, and also globally.

Finally, many larger firms organize around clients. Global account teams, organized in support of a multinational client, might often be as large as a practice area, and in many cases be larger than any one of the firm's offices. Global Account Directors manage these teams, as well as the global and headquarters client relationships.

FINANCIAL MANAGEMENT

> Two financial skills are critical for the agency manager—budgeting and firm profitability.

Public relations consultancies are both professional service providers and businesses. A successful consultancy must manage both the quality of its work and the financial performance of its business in order to be successful.

Two financial skills are critical for the agency manager—budgeting and firm profitability.

Budgeting

Budgeting client assignments correctly ensures the firm will be properly compensated for its work. Most firms use estimates of hours or man-days required to provide clients with budgets for their assignments. Tightly constructed, explicit budgets protect the interests of both the firm and its clients. Poorly prepared budgets cause financial and relationship issues.

Budgeting two ways improves accuracy and helps check for omissions. One way to budget involves making a list of all the tasks involved in a project, and deciding the level of staffing required (how many people and at what level for how many hours) to accomplish each task. As a cross check, a second budgeting method can be employed—simply estimating how many people will work on the assignment, and for how long. Both budgets must include detailed estimates for the "out of pocket" expenses—all the things that must be purchased to accomplish the task.

Agency Financial Metrics

Most consulting firms estimate annual revenues at the beginning of the year, then adjust their expectations quarterly based on actual experience.

Revenue budgets include confirmed contracts with clients, estimated income from existing clients who have not yet signed contracts (discounted by their likelihood for success) and an estimate of new business income for the year (based on past experience).

Expenses are generally managed as a percentage of income. Most firms target their total compensation ratio (salaries and benefits) at between 50 percent and 53 percent of income. General and administrative expenses should be between 20 percent and 22 percent, and occupancy costs (rent) should be held under 7.5 percent. With the ratios at this level, the firm should be able to make a 15–20 percent pre-tax profit.

Good Financial Management

No one likes to be surprised by a budget that's out of line. An adage in the consulting business is that you win clients with ideas, and you lose them over money. Good financial management means "no surprises."

> An adage in the consulting business is that you win clients with ideas, and you lose them over money.

Use monitoring systems to avoid budget surprises. Communicate often with clients. Money may not be easy to discuss, but it's very important to preserving a positive relationship. Know your client's preferences with regard to billing. Do they have monthly cutoff dates for processing bills? Do they require detailed activity reports with invoices?

The firm's owners don't like surprises either. Monitor your financial performance closely. Report changes as they are emerging, and communicate the steps you are taking to adjust for those changes.

In the end, financial success equals firm success. It's a business, and the metric for business is revenue growth and profitability. By monitoring and managing your financial performance, you can concentrate on what's really important—the quality of your work and the satisfaction of your employees and clients.

MANAGING CONSULTANTS AND CONSULTANCIES

> The old adage, "the inventory goes down in the elevator every night" applies.

Public relations firms are only as good as the people they can attract and retain in their businesses. The old adage, "the inventory goes down in the elevator every night" applies.

Managing a consultancy presents unique challenges. Firms attract and reward entrepreneurs. "Star power" attracts business. But at the same time teamwork is the key to success. No individual can be as strong as the firm overall—best teams win.

On top of that, work in a consultancy can be extremely stressful. Pressure-packed workloads, looming client deadlines and financial pressures combine to create a difficult work environment.

> The key to success is a truly collaborative culture-a culture that puts the firm first, that promotes a spirit of teamwork, saying we're stronger together than we are as individuals.

The key to success is a truly collaborative culture—a culture that puts the firm first, that promotes a spirit of teamwork, saying we're stronger together than we are as individuals. Add to that an honest, open dialog and a climate of trust and mutual respect and you've got the ingredients for a successful consulting firm.

Dr. W. Edwards Deming's theory of management works perfectly in a consulting firm environment. His philosophy of "joy of work" and intrinsic rewards sets the stage for creating a successful corporate culture in a consulting firm. (See the Expert Perspectives box below.)

EXPERT PERSPECTIVES: THE DEMING SYSTEM OF PROFOUND KNOWLEDGE

Professor Howard Gitlow is Executive Director of the University of Miami Institute for the Study of Quality in Manufacturing and Service. He is one of the world's leading authorities on Dr. W. Edwards Deming, whose management theory has become the foundation for many successful companies today.

According to Dr. Gitlow, Deming's theory of management, called *The System of Profound Knowledge*, promotes "joy in work" and will "unleash the power of human resource contained in intrinsic motivation. Intrinsic motivation is the motivation an individual experiences from the sheer joy of an endeavor."

Dr. Gitlow describes Deming's theory of management as based on four paradigms:[2]

1. People are most effectively motivated and inspired by a mix of intrinsic and extrinsic rewards. Intrinsic motivation comes from the sheer joy of performing an act, and releases human energy that can be focused into improvement and innovation of a system.
2. Management's job is to improve and innovate the processes that create results, not just to demand results.
3. Management's function is to optimize the entire system so that everyone wins.

Managers must understand that individuals, organizations, and systems of organizations are interdependent.

4. Cooperation works better than competition. In a cooperative environment, everybody wins. Customers win products and services they can brag about. The firm wins returns for investors and secure jobs for employees. Suppliers win long-term customers for their products. The community wins an excellent corporate citizen.

According to the model, says Dr. Gitlow, leaders who practice these four Deming paradigms can increase quality and simultaneously decrease costs. Waste and rework is reduced. Staff attrition and litigation decrease, and customer loyalty increases. The key is to practice *continuous improvement* and think of a business as a system, not as bits and pieces. (See the sidebar on General Systems Theory, page 38.)

CLIENT SERVICE: A CREATIVE COLLABORATION

Building and maintaining positive partnerships with clients may be the most important skill a consultant possesses. Fortunately, some data exist on the drivers of client satisfaction.

> Building and maintaining positive partnerships with clients may be the most important skill a consultant possesses.

Tom Harris, founding partner of Golin Harris (now Golin), a leading consulting firm, conducted a study of the key drivers of client satisfaction. Table 13.1 shows the top elements on the list. (The higher the percentage, the more important the factor is to the clients.)

Table 13.1 Harris survey of the key client satisfaction drivers

Technical Elements

Overall quality of work	70%
Meets deadlines, keeps promises	66%
Creativity	50%
Quality of writing	49%
Thorough attention to detail	58%

Relationship Elements

Chemistry	74%
Client Service	73%
Quality of my account team	73%
Quality of management	69%
Stability of Staff	54%

In fact, "chemistry" was the highest-ranked element.

As you can see, relationship elements score as high or higher than technical skills in driving client satisfaction. In fact, "chemistry" was the highest-ranked element.[3]

The following precepts can serve as a guide for success in managing client relationships.

1. *Listen before talking and acting.* Good listening skills are a key to good consulting skills. Says one often-quoted anonymous pundit: "Before you shoot off your mouth, make sure your brain is fully loaded."

2. *Know your client's company and industry.* Read everything you can about the client's industry, and master their jargon. Study the mysteries of the client's organization, and discern how and where public relations fits into the puzzle.

3. *Be passionately supportive of the client's product or service.* Clients want their consultants to love them. Never underestimate the client's enthusiasm for their product. Passion sets apart the great consultants. And don't *ever* serve Coke at a Pepsi meeting.

4. *Manage expectations; deliver on promises.* Clients want their consultants to slay dragons, drink the blood of the bad guys, and bring them stars beyond their reach. Be careful about what you promise. And be compulsive about delivering once you do.

5. *Be available, respond quickly, and meet deadlines.* When clients ring the doorbell, answer quickly. Information, public opinion, and the media move at a light-speed pace. Consultants must be speedy, on time and on target.

6. *Lead the relationship.* Anticipate events that will affect your client. Develop new ideas. Remember why the client hired you in the first place, and live up to that standard every day.

7. *Be true to your client.* Stay true to the strategy you and your client have agreed on, and use the methods and processes you have defined together in advance.

8. *Make quality your cornerstone.* Produce impeccable work in every way. Sloppy writing or typing means sloppy thinking. And evaluate results together, using methods you've agreed on in advance as well.

9. *Communicate often.* Communicate with both your team and your client. Use phone calls, personal visits, and e-mails to keep a constant dialog intact with your client. Monitor activity of the company, competitors, and the industry and send news along to the client when you find it. Also, be sure to keep your team in the loop on all of your interactions with the client.

10. *Bill accurately, clearly, and promptly.* Remember, money is the root of all evil. It's the consultant's job to make it easy for clients to pay the bill. Be sure there's no disconnect between their view of the budget and yours. And remember, clients don't share your sense of urgency about payment.

11. *Watch your language.* Our words define us. Avoid statements that demean your advice—phrases like "we came up with this idea." Consultants don't "come up" with ideas, they think and plan strategically and make thoughtful recommendations. They "build" or "engineer" ideas and solutions.

Even with the greatest care and commitment to success, sometimes client relationships go awry. You know your client is unhappy when:

- They don't return your calls
- There is tension in the air
- Conversations feel strained
- Sarcasm creeps into their dialog

Bad client relationships are no fun. And they're not good for business either. Watch for the warning signs. Be over-sensitive to displeasure. Draw them out—and show genuine interest in solving the problem. Look for an acceptable solution, and ask for their feedback.

> Done well, client service is a joy. Done badly, it's a nightmare.

Done well, client service is a joy. Done badly, it's a nightmare.

CASE STUDY: STAY TRUE TO WHO YOU ARE

I'm in a bar in Berlin with my client, Jules Prast, the VP of Corporate Communications at Philips. We'd been working together for several years. My firm, MSL Group, handled most of the Dutch electronics giant's product PR, while two other firms took on their technology and corporate work.

We'd been asked by the client to create a collaborative spirit between our firms—to avoid making passes at each others' assignments, to look for opportunities to cooperate, and to participate together in the overall planning and strategic direction of the Philips communication effort.

MSL, the biggest of the three firms and the one with the largest book of Philips business, had worked hard to create the collaborative relationship with the other firms. It wasn't hard for us—collaboration and collegiality were already hallmarks of our firm's corporate culture.

That night, though, after the second beer, Jules leans across the table and offers me the opportunity to pitch for the entire global account.

I nearly spilled my beer, so flabbergasted that I went on instincts and politely refused: "How can you ask me to collaborate with the other firms on the one hand, and then quietly sneak behind their backs to steal their business?"

We talked about it for a while, and in the end I told Jules that when he had decided to fire the other firms—and told them about it—then I would be happy to pitch for their assignments.

Months went by. Another meeting, in another bar—this one in New York City—and Jules gave me the news that the other two firms had been dismissed. We agreed on a plan for the pitch, and several weeks later we met in London and were awarded the global account.

Reflecting back on that experience, Jules told me: "I offered you the business on a silver plate and you turned it down. The way you handled that showed style and character, and deserved my respect."

> As chairman of MSL I had built the firm around a culture of collaboration, collegiality and mutual respect. By staying true to that culture, I ended up winning what would become the agency's largest global account for many years.

PITCHING AND WINNING NEW BUSINESS

Differentiating your firm in new business, and standing out from the pack as a result, is one of the greatest challenges facing public relations consultants.

Great client service helps you retain and grow your current clients. But every consultancy needs a robust new business initiative to attract *new* clients to the firm as well.

Differentiating your firm in new business, and standing out from the pack as a result, is one of the greatest challenges facing public relations consultants. The solution lies in a well-organized, well-planned, well-rehearsed, and well- presented approach.

Organizing the Pitch

Right from the beginning, you need a plan. How will you get off to a winning start? How can you engage the client in a dialog? How will we bring our ideas to life?

First, pick the team. Think about the levels of people needed and the specific expertise the client requires. Bring the team together to develop the pitch plan, and get them working right away on gathering background materials. Solicit their questions and ideas on how to shape the proposal.

Next, analyze the client. Use your networking and research skills to find out what you can about both the organization and the individuals involved. Learn about the issues, the corporate culture, their past and other agency relationships, and the personalities of the people you'll meet with. Dig to discover who you're competing with; this can provide you with clues on how to differentiate yourself.

Rank the make-or-break factors. What's going to win this pitch, or lose it? Is it experience, chemistry or the enthusiasm of the team? Do your firm's size and resources make a difference? Is the organization looking for a consultant who really knows the business and industry? Will a blockbuster creative idea tip the decision in your favor, or will the decision be made on price?

Best Practices: Presenting to Win

Consultants put an enormous amount of effort into a new business presentation, often investing the full estimated profits of the account for the first year. They pour over secondary data, conduct original research, and analyze the competition. The best strategic minds in the firm work to gain insights that will help the potential client succeed. Creative teams develop ideas that sizzle.

But all of that effort can go to naught without a well-planned and well-executed presentation. Here are some of the ways consultants create successful presentations.

1. *Never sacrifice the long-term reputation of the firm for short-term gains.*
2. *Plan carefully.* Analyze the audience you'll be talking with. Who is the decision maker? Who will be your team leader? How will you present—standing, sitting, from the front of the room? What visuals will support your recommendations? And what are your audio/visual needs?

    Where will you present? At the client's offices or your own? Be sure to check out the room in advance.

    How many people will sit at the table? Are there the right number of chairs?
3. *Listen first, then talk.* Find a way to engage the audience in a dialog. Begin by asking them to introduce themselves, and to tell you a little about their jobs. Ask them what they hope to see or learn from the presentation. Confirm the schedule—how long do they have to meet with you?
4. *Home in on their key needs.* Don't sell the client a drill, when what he really needs is a hole. Be sure you spend the bulk of your time on the client's key issues.
5. *Don't let the presentation do all the work.* Avoid the trap of endless PowerPoint slides with lists of bullets. Yes, they keep you on track and remind you what to say next, but they're boring and visually dead. At the same time, watch out for too many Power Point gimmicks. Remember, you are a consultant imparting important advice. An entertaining presentation is helpful; a silly one detracts from your gravitas.
6. *Be careful with criticism.* Consultants often make a classic mistake, effectively telling the prospective client "You have big problems, but we can save you." It's important to tell clients what they need to hear, not necessarily what they want to hear. But remember, they are not your client yet, and you should be very careful with the way you talk with them about problems or negative issues. It might be a good idea to ask the client to explain a negative situation, allowing them to give their view before you characterize the situation yourself.
7. *Rehearse, rehearse, rehearse.* When your team is ready and the presentation's complete, do a dry run, working out everyone's role and walking through the pieces of the presentation. Next, do a formal rehearsal. It's often helpful to invite a senior consultant who has not been involved in the program to act as a "pitch doctor," listening to the rehearsal and offering feedback. Finally, do a "walkthrough" rehearsal, where you work out where everyone will sit, how they will move about the room, where they will stand to present and how the visual aids will be positioned.
8. *Pay attention to emotions and politics.* Once you've done your homework on the client, you should know the interpersonal dynamics of the people in the room. Be sure you understand their hot buttons, the issues they feel defensive about, statements that might potentially offend them.
9. *Go the extra mile.* Competition in pitches among consultants is fierce. Doing just enough to satisfy the requirements set by the prospective client will almost never

win the day. Think about how to stretch the brief, go beyond what's expected and bring something extra to your presentation. If you don't, you can be sure your competition will.

10. *Present to the individual.* Make sure you connect with each and every person in the room. Make good eye contact.

11. *Rehearse the Q & A.* You should anticipate every question the client will ask and develop a plan for answering. Make sure everyone on the team gets a chance to speak during the Q & A. Rehearse their answers. Be careful about building on each other's points. One amplification is fine. Two begins to get risky. Three, and you may as well have said, "What that dummy meant to say was . . ."

> A relentless approach to preparation will pay great dividends in your new business effort.

A relentless approach to preparation will pay great dividends in your new business effort.

Be a "slave to structure." Listen, and ask the right questions. Always allow time for rehearsal. Learn to stop editing the presentation in an effort to make it "perfect," and spend the time instead on the critical factors for success.

ETHICS IN PUBLIC RELATIONS CONSULTING

Companies like Johnson & Johnson have "credos" or statements of "values."[4] The public relations profession, too, has codes of conduct. But consulting offers unique challenges for consultants and their firms.

The trade associations, including the Council of PR Firms in the US and The International Communications Consultants Organisation, ICCO, offer guidelines specifically tailored to consulting. They establish behavioral guidelines and uniform standards to guide professional behavior.

THE ICCO STOCKHOLM CHARTER

Public Relations consultancies are professional service firms who help clients influence opinions, attitudes and behavior. Along with this influence comes responsibility to our clients, our people, our profession and society at large.

Objective Counsel and Advocacy

Public relations consultancies may not have interests that might compromise their role as an independent consultant. They should approach their clients with objectivity, in order to help the client adopt the optimum communication strategy and behavior.

Society

An open society, freedom of speech and a free press create the context for the profession of public relations. Consultants operate within the scope of this open society, comply with its rules, and work with clients that share the same approach.

Confidentiality

Trust (the future equity of a good reputation) is at the heart of the relationship between a client and a public relations consultancy. Information that has been provided in confidence by a client and that is not publicly known should not be shared with other parties without the consent of the client.

Trust (the future equity of a good reputation) is at the heart of the relationship between a client and a public relations consultancy.

Integrity of Information

Public relations consultancies should not knowingly mislead an audience about factual information, or about the interests a client represents. Consultancies must make their best efforts to strive for accuracy.

Delivering Promises

Consultancies must work with clients to establish clear expectations in advance about the output of their efforts. They must define specific goals for communication actions and then work to deliver on their promises. Consultancies must not offer guarantees which are not supportable, or which compromise the integrity of the channels of communication.

Conflicts

Consultancies may represent clients with conflicting interests. Work may not commence for a new and conflicting interest without the current client first being offered the opportunity to exercise the rights under any contract between the client and consultancy.

Representation

Consultancies may refuse to accept an assignment based on the personal opinions of the firm's management or the organization's focus.

Consultancies may refuse to accept an assignment based on the personal opinions of the firm's management or the organization's focus.

Governance and Business Practices

Public relations consultancies are committed to ethical behavior and implementation of best business practices in dealing with all audiences.[5]

While the association codes are a helpful beginning, they have their weaknesses. They apply only to members, and are usually too general for any kind of enforcement. Also, association members are unwilling to criticize their peers and avoid getting involved in the process.

So, consultants are often on their own in defining what's ethical and what's not. They must consider ethics in terms of their relationships with clients, with the media and in the firm itself.

Knowing the difference between right and wrong is generally pretty easy. It's the gray areas that cause problems. Consultants are well advised to pursue their clients' interests in an ethical manner both in counseling the client and representing them in public.

Be sure you clearly understand what the client is asking of you. Advise your client to do the right thing. Show the client how your advice can resolve the problem and help reach a solution.

> While you're putting the client's best foot forward with the media, always tell the truth and always be on your best professional behavior.

With the media, act ethically as the client's representative. Remember that reporters don't share your client's interests. Understand the client's vulnerabilities as you advocate on their behalf. While you're putting the client's best foot forward with the media, always tell the truth and always be on your best professional behavior. Assume nothing is "off the record."

Avoid innuendoes and claims that are misleading. Never misrepresent your identity or motives. And remember not to burn bridges with a reporter—you'll have other clients to advocate for in the future.

Choosing Clients to Represent

A consultant's clients define who they are. Ask yourself if this is really a client for whom you want to work. Is the client doing the right thing? Will you have an impact? Will you be proud to present the client's point of view?

Often, a consultant's personal values can conflict with the client's agenda. That's especially true on broad public policy issues like abortion, contraception, guns, tobacco, liquor or equal rights. Employees of a consultancy must be able to decline to work on client accounts that conflict with their personal values. If a subject makes them uncomfortable, for whatever personal reason, they have to know that they can "opt out" without fear of penalty or retribution.

Ethical decisions can be tricky, and often the right answer is elusive. But consultants can be guided by one simple piece of advice from Spike Lee, "Do the Right Thing."

RESOURCES FOR FURTHER STUDY

Ongoing developments in the public relations industry are available by visiting the following websites:

Council of Public Relations Firms, http://www.prfirms.org
Institute for Public Relations, http://www.instituteforpr.com
Jack O'Dwyer's Newsletter, http://www.odwyerpr.com
PRWeek magazine, http://www.prweek.com
Paul Holmes' newsletter, http://www.holmesreport.com
Public Relations Society of America, http://www.prsa.org

Suggested additional reading materials available online include:

"Careers in Public Relations Firms: Opportunities in a Dynamic Industry," prepared by the Council of Public Relations Firms, http://www.prfirms.org.
"Hiring a Public Relations Firm: A Guide for Clients," prepared by the Council of Public Relations Firms, http://www.prfirms.org.
"Standards for Conducting a PR Firm Search, Principles and Practices," prepared by the Council of Public Relations Firms, http://www.prfirms.org.
"Working with Your Public Relations Firm," prepared by the Council of Public Relations Firms, http://www.prfirms.org.

Perspectives on firm management can be gained from:

Gitlow, Howard, *Quality Management Systems, a Practical Guide* (Boca Raton: St. Lucie Press, 2001).
Maister, David, *Managing the Professional Services Firm* (New York: Free Press, 1997).

QUESTIONS FOR FURTHER DISCUSSION

Negotiation Exercises

Exercise #1: As a consultant at a public relations firm, you receive a request from your client for support. He tells you he has a great piece of news about a groundbreaking new business-to-business technology his company has developed and is about to introduce to the marketplace. You and your team have analyzed the story, and have concluded that it will only appeal to a business audience. Your client, though, insists that you pursue broad consumer media. "I want you to get the CEO on Oprah," he insists. You know you'll be lucky to get coverage in general business magazines.

Work in teams, with one team playing the role of the client, the other the consultant. Then switch roles.

Exercise #2: Your consulting firm has written copy for a client's print ad and e-brochure, and the client has rejected it. She said the work was so bad that she had someone on her staff rewrite it, and she refuses to pay your bill. As the senior manager on the client account, you review the situation and conclude that the original instructions from the client were wrong.

Again, have one team play the role of the client, the other the consultant, and then switch.

Exercise on Ethics

A reporter contacts your firm, asserting that you could save lives by giving out details about a client's research on a life-saving medicine. The client has shared the information with you on a strictly confidential basis, since the public launch of the drug is six months in the future. You know the information is not for public release, but lives hang in the balance.

What should you do?

▶ NOTES

1   O'Dwyer's, 271 Madison Avenue, New York, NY 10016.
2   Gitlow, Howard, *Quality Management Systems: A Practical Guide*, Los Angeles: CRC Press, 2000.
3   Thomas Harris, Study of Client Preferences, 1997.
4   Johnson & Johnson, 2012 Annual Report.
5   The text of the Stockholm Charter, reproduced in this sidebar, is available at http://www. iccopr.com/Member-Benefits/Stockholm-charter.aspx

14 CHALLENGES AND OPPORTUNITIES IN CORPORATE AND ORGANIZATIONAL COMMUNICATION

The greatest challenge of communication is the illusion that it has taken place.
— George Bernard Shaw

Firms gain sustainable competitive advantage by cultivating intangible and inimitable assets, based on their ability to maintain the confidence of key stakeholder groups.

An organization's reputation is the sum of how its various stakeholders view it. But all too often companies leave such stakeholder perceptions to chance.

Enlightened companies know that an effective corporate or organizational communication process can both enhance and protect its reputation. And they also know that the reputation, while an intangible asset, provides a number of tangible benefits to the company.

Fordham University Business School professor Kevin T. Jackson describes the benefits of a strong reputation in his book *Building Reputational Capital*:

> A critical mass of credible evidence is showing a link between superior corporate reputations and financial performance . . . Companies with above-average overall corporate reputation scores demonstrate greater ability to sustain or attain an above-average return on assets.[1]

Professor Jackson also elaborates some of the benefits such a reputation provides, noting that firms gain sustainable competitive advantage by cultivating intangible and inimitable assets, based on their ability to maintain the confidence of key stakeholder groups:

> Companies compete for clients, customers, investors, partners, employees, suppliers, and the support of local communities. A good reputation erects an intangible barrier that rivals stumble to get over. You can cut marketing expenses, command top dollar for your services, erect barriers to competition, and enjoy expanded latitude in decision-making. By itself, this competitive advantage ensures stronger long-run returns to better-reputed firms.[2]

Effective engagement with stakeholders and a strong reputation create a barrier to competition.

A significant challenge for those who run corporate or organizational communication functions is to manage the ways the organization engages its key stakeholders. Because an organization competes for the positive attention of the groups who matter to it, how it engages those stakeholders has meaningful bottom-line impact. As Professor Jackson notes, effective engagement with stakeholders and a strong reputation create a barrier to competition. But ineffective engagement, and weak reputation, make it easier for competitors to penetrate those barriers.

Chapters 2 through 13 focused on tangible ways to organize and manage the various forms of corporate and organizational communication, including communication intended to engage particular stakeholder audiences.

The communication function is entitled to be at the table. It must earn the right to contribute.

A further challenge is to exercise leadership to align all the functions with each other and with the operational, legal, financial, and administrative functions that collectively define the work of any organization.

A related challenge is for the communication function to be a respected participant in corporate deliberations, not an afterthought. Leaders of enlightened companies include reputational considerations—and the input of those whose primary job is to protect and enhance reputation—at the table when they make decisions. But that doesn't mean that the communication function is entitled to be at the table. It must earn the right to contribute.

EARNING A SEAT AT THE TABLE: DEFINING THE PROFESSIONAL COMMUNICATOR'S ROLE

Former U.S. Secretary of State Henry Kissinger—who knew a thing or two about bureaucratic infighting—observed that leaders listen to advisors whose views they think they need, not those who insist on a hearing because of the organizational chart.

> Leaders listen to advisors whose views they think they need, not those who insist on a hearing because of the organizational chart.

As public relations becomes increasingly important to senior executives, many professional communicators find themselves marginalized, as CEOs take advice from lawyers, friends, and others rather than from their chief communication officers. Professional communicators who aspire to work at the top levels of their organizations need the grounding necessary to become trusted advisors to their senior-most executives.

There are several reasons the communication function gets marginalized. Sometimes the marginalization is self-inflicted; often it is imposed by other functions such as corporate law, finance, or even by the CEO. But whether self-inflicted or imposed by others, the marginalization typically is grounded in how the communication function – and hence the leaders of that function – are defined. These include:

- *Being cast as an implementer.* The head of communication is seen as a doer rather than as a leader.
- *Being cast as a tactician.* Whether the head of communication is implementing or managing the function, communication is seen as solely as a tool or tactic, and not as part of the strategic focus of the enterprise.
- *Being cast as part of a functional area.* The head of communication is seen as a writer, or as a media person, or as a technology person, and not as having enterprise-wide standing to offer advice beyond the narrow functional area.

There are a number of ways to overcome this marginalization. At the very least, professional communicators need to learn the objective and subjective factors that leaders use to choose whom to listen to, and develop the skills and temperaments necessary to become trusted advisors to management. Three skills, or areas of expertise, are especially necessary.

First, in order to speak for the organization, and to have standing to advise on how the organization should communicate, a communicator must have a thorough knowledge of the organization's operations and of finance, product development, marketing, and human resources.

> A communicator must have a thorough knowledge of the organization's operations and of finance, product development, marketing, and human resources.

The communicator must have a worldview that includes knowledge of issues that affect the company.

The communicator must possess the art of giving advice and of building trust.

Executives who wouldn't dream of micromanaging the work product of the engineering department or the corporate law department have no problem micromanaging the work product of professional communicators.

The top communicator in the company needs to be demonstrably the most gifted communicator in any meeting of senior executives.

The primary value of a senior communication executive is less about transmitting information than about predicting how the stakeholders who matter to senior management are likely to behave.

Second, the communicator must have a worldview that includes knowledge of issues that affect the company, its industry, the marketplace in general, and emerging social trends.

And third, the communicator must possess the art of giving advice and of building trust, everything from thinking problems through from the perspective of senior executives to offering insights that would not otherwise occur to a senior management team.

But these three approaches, while necessary, are not sufficient. Part of the challenge to be overcome is the very word, communication. Unlike the skill-set needed for nearly every other business function, communication is a skill that every executive thinks he or she possesses. Because non-communication executives often assume that communicators' key competence is speaking and writing, they assume that the function is something anyone could do well if only they had the time. After all, they've been speaking since they were young children, and reading and writing since at least first grade. The same cannot be said of manufacturing, engineering, finance, or law.

As a result, executives who wouldn't dream of micromanaging the work product of the engineering department or the corporate law department have no problem micromanaging the work product of professional communicators. Or of bypassing the professional communicators until it's time to distribute what has been drafted (often poorly) by others.

There are several ways to overcome this perception. The first is for the professional communicator to model communication excellence in everything he or she does. The top communicator in the company needs to be demonstrably the most gifted communicator in any meeting of senior executives.

But the bigger challenge is to frame the communication role as something more than words on paper or in electronic format; as more than the simple transmission of information from the company to its audiences. The key is to define the communication role in terms of the stakeholder groups who matter to executives. The primary value of a senior communication executive is less about transmitting information—the typical definition of communication—than about predicting how the stakeholders who matter to senior management are likely to behave.

One of the most important roles of the professional communicator is to provide a perspective on stakeholder behavior that an organization would not otherwise have access to. In this sense, the professional communicator's role is like a lens: to provide a corrective perspective to bring into focus what may be unclear to the executive team.

The corrective perspective works in both directions: the professional communicator helps a management team understand how any given stakeholder group is likely to think, feel, and behave in any given circumstance; the communicator also helps bring a company's desired perception into focus for the stakeholder group.

A corrective perspective

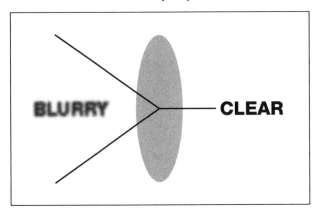

Figure 14.1
(Illustration by Lisa Wagner)

We have long believed that professional communicators are valued not because of our communication skills, but rather because of our ability to predict how groups who matter to management are likely to behave, and further to predict how to get those groups to behave in more beneficial ways. In this sense professional communicators, when we do our best work, function as applied anthropologists.

> Professional communicators, when we do our best work, function as applied anthropologists.

Like any anthropologist, the best communicators undertake rigorous observation of the behavior of individual groups. Such groups could include any or all of the following:

- Customers
- Employees
- Investors
- Regulators
- Legislators and federal and state executive branch officials
- Business partners
- Lenders
- Suppliers and vendors
- Communities in which a company does business
- Competitors
- Academics and other thought leaders such as think tanks and industry experts
- Industry associations
- Contract sales force, such as agents, brokers, and dealers
- The news media
- Society at large
- Any subset of any of the above.

The best communicators further diagnose the values systems, social relationships, and power relationships within any given group, and among various groups. They understand what drives behavior within those groups, and understand how particular decisions are triggered and how the group's behavior plays out.

They can advise on how any given action or communication is likely to be interpreted by the group in question and how the behavior of any one group is likely to influence the behavior of the others.

Finally, professional communicators help mobilize the resources of their organizations to affect the behavior of those groups in ways that are more beneficial; that enhance the groups' relationship with the organization and that affirmatively contribute to a better reputation.

So the knowledge base of professional communicators is not just the mechanics of communication, or the industry or sector of the organization. Rather, like any anthropologist, the knowledge base involves understanding how to influence the groups that matter to the organization. Most of the chapters of this book address ways to assure the most effective engagement of these groups.

In most organizations there are structures to deal with each specific stakeholder group. So the sales force deals with customers; human resources deals with employees; finance deals with bankers and investors; corporate law with regulators and legislators, and so on.

> The only standing structure whose mandate includes understanding all stakeholder groups, and the links among them, is the corporate or organizational communication function.

But the only standing structure whose mandate includes understanding all of these stakeholder groups, and the links among them, is the corporate or organizational communication function. Those who preside over corporate or organizational communication need to understand these links, and to be able to harvest the best knowledge about any given stakeholder group. So the professional communicator needs to be able to diagnose behavior and prescribe a response beyond the individual silos that create artificial barriers between functional areas in a company. This cross-silo insight is a core competence, and one of the keys to reversing the marginalization of the function.

> The ability to see patterns early, and to help a company influence the way a pattern plays out, can be greatly valued by a company's management team.

The ability to see patterns early, and to help a company influence the way a pattern plays out, can be greatly valued by a company's management team. The ability to engage management with a discussion of patterns and predictions of group behavior allows a professional communicator to argue persuasively in favor of taking difficult business decisions, even decisions that are contrary to the advice of other members of management who have their own expertise, such as lawyers, finance officers, or scientists.

> The professional communicator should generally avoid discussion of communication tactics and implementation with senior management.

Finally, to overcome the marginalization of the function, and to demonstrate value beyond what is otherwise seen as the tactical practice of communication, the professional communicator should generally avoid discussion of communication tactics and implementation with senior management. Rather, the focus should be more strategic, on the outcomes that are desired among the stakeholders who matter: what do we want our customers, employees, investors, communities, and other core stakeholders to think, feel, know, and do? What do we need to do or not do, to say or not say, to cause them to think, feel, know, and do these things? Only after reaching agreement on desired end states should discussion focus on the mechanics of making that happen: on the tactics of communication. (More on being strategic follows later in the chapter.)

HISTORICAL PERSPECTIVE: EDWARD L. BERNAYS AND THE ROOTS OF APPLIED ANTHROPOLOGY

The seminal thinking about public relations as applied anthropology dates to the 1920s. The father of modern public relations is Edward L. Bernays, who worked on the U.S. government committee that shaped U.S. public opinion during World War I, and who was the first person to call himself a public relations counselor. In 1923 Bernays taught the first university course in public relations—at New York University, where Fred and John and many of this book's contributors teach. And that year he also published the first book on modern public relations, *Crystallizing Public Opinion*, of which the book you are reading is a successor. Bernays described public relations as "the vocation of the social scientist who advises clients on social attitudes and on the actions to take to win support of the public upon whom the viability of the client depends."[3]

Bernays writes, "The public relations counsel is first of all a student . . . [whose] field of study is the public mind. His textbooks for this study are the facts of life . . . He brings the talent of his intuitive understanding to the aid of his practical and psychological tests and surveys."[4]

Bernays adds:

> The public relations counsel must discover why it is that a public opinion exists independently of church, school, press, lecture platform, and motion picture screen—how far this public opinion affects these institutions and how far these institutions affect public opinion. He must discover what the stimuli are to which public opinion responds most readily. To his understanding of what he actually can measure he must add a thorough knowledge of the principles which govern individual and group action. A fundamental study of group and individual psychology is required before the public relations counsel can determine how readily individuals or groups will accept modifications of viewpoints or policies.[5]

Bernays' description of public relations has direct bearing on professional communication for many reasons, not least of which is that it doesn't mention the mechanics of communication at all. Rather, it focuses on how those who matter to a company think and feel, and how to get them to think and feel differently. It focuses on social attitudes and on the actions a company must take to win support. It describes the public relations counselor as a social scientist—essentially 1923 vocabulary for an applied anthropologist. Even the title of his book, *Crystallizing Public Opinion*, focuses not on the mechanics of communication but on the outcome.

Bernays' description also recognizes that the most effective way to change groups' perception is to act in certain ways; that communication needs to be grounded first in the action a company takes. He says that a public relations practitioner is:

> Bernays' description recognizes that the most effective way to change groups' perception is to act in certain ways; that communication needs to be grounded first in the action a company takes.

as much an advisor on actions as he is the communicator of these actions to the public . . . He acts in this capacity as a consultant both in interpreting the public to his client and in helping to interpret his client to the public. He helps to mould the action of his client as well as to mould public opinion.[6]

Bernays also recognized that groups—in modern vocabulary *stakeholders* such as those listed above—behave in predictable, if shifting, ways:

The public relations counsel works with public opinion. Public opinion is the product of individual minds. Individual minds make up the group mind. And the established order of things is maintained by the inertia of the group. Three factors make it possible for the public relations counsel to overcome even this inertia. These are, first, the [overlapping] group formation of society; second, the continuous shifting of groups; third, the changed physical conditions to which groups respond. All of these are brought about by the natural inherent flexibility of individual human nature.[7]

And finally, Bernays notes that the interaction between a company and its critical stakeholders isn't a one-time event, but rather continues over time, and each interaction is shaped by prior interactions and reactions:

Action and interaction are continually going on between the forces projected out to the public and the public itself. The public relations counsel must understand this fact in its broadest and most detailed implications. He must understand not only what these various forces are, but he must be able to evaluate their relative powers with fair accuracy.[8]

Bernays recognizes that the value of the public relations counselor—and today the value of the any professional communicator—is the ability to advise on the ongoing engagement between a company and its critical stakeholders, and in particular how a company's engagement is likely to influence how that stakeholder group is likely to think, feel, and behave across a number of scenarios.

Bernays' description of public relations—as a vocation applied by a social scientist who advises a client on actions to take in order to win support of the public on whom the client's viability depends—is a good way for a professional communicator to see his or her role.

THE FUTURE OF CORPORATE AND ORGANIZATIONAL COMMUNICATION AND PUBLIC RELATIONS

Public relations has see extraordinary growth in the U.S. over the last ten years. That growth is likely to continue.

This growth is due mainly to three trends, according to John Paluszek, senior counsel to Ketchum Public Relations and past president of the Public Relations Society of America:

- PR is important today to every major institution: for-profits, not-for-profits, governments, and religions.
- Increasingly, institutions recognize that they practice many kinds of communication with many stakeholders, and that they must all be coordinated, which is the proper role of public relations or its subset corporate communications.
- Public relations is being practiced around the globe.

Paluszek, at a Professional Development Seminar sponsored by the M.S. Degree Program in Corporate Communications and Public Relations at New York University, said that the profession is at its pinnacle, in terms of challenges and opportunities, and that his only regret is "that I am not starting out now."

EXPERT PERSPECTIVES: SIX CHALLENGES FACING THE PUBLIC RELATIONS PRACTITIONER TODAY

By Judy Voss, APR, Director of Professional Development for the Public Relations Society of America, the world's largest organization for public relations professionals (http://www.prsa.org)

Successfully conquering today's challenges will give you the experience and perspective you need to secure your company's reputation, and keep you employed for a long time to come. From my point of view, these six challenges are the most critical to address first.

1. "Tell the truth. Prove it with action."

Ethics is at the top of my list of challenges. I'm quoting two Arthur Page Society principles in the subhead above. (The Arthur W. Page Society can be found at http://www. awpagesociety.com.) Page, a pioneer in the practice of public relations, served as the first vice president of public relations for AT&T beginning in 1927. He set the standards for the position as it related to strategic public relations in corporate management. He counseled corporations and several U.S. presidents, always managing their reputations supported with ethical conduct. The Page persona is missing today.

I asked a colleague, Tom Vitelli, APR, Fellow PRSA, assistant vice president, Communications for Intermountain Health Care, Salt Lake City, UT, about challenges he sees in the field. Ethics is also at the top of his list. He comments: "Ethics are a foundation for credibility, and credibility is a foundation of business development. Ethical lapses undermine the achievement of business goals, so, as a practical matter, PR firms and professionals really have no choice but to behave ethically."

Public relations professionals who aspire to sit at the management table, to develop policy and participate in strategic planning to meet business goals must choose to demonstrate ethical behavior. You must think ethics, feel ethics, communicate ethics. That is your challenge.

> Leaders who dare to think or act without considering ethics should be prepared for a downfall with no sympathy from their publics. Or their public relations counselor after the fact. Period.

Your CEOs and CFOs must be counseled to do the right thing in all cases at all times. Period. Corporate leaders read newspapers and watch CNN. They see dishonest corporate leaders getting caught and going to jail. So those leaders who dare to think or act without considering ethics should be prepared for a downfall with no sympathy from their publics. Or their public relations counselor after the fact. Period.

2. Social Media

Second on my list of challenges facing the PR practitioner today is how to keep up with ongoing changes in social media. As a professional, you must pay attention to technology *plus* experience it yourself in order to learn just how powerful the new tools are. You obviously have to know the media habits of your publics. In today's segmented markets you may choose to reach them using twitter, Facebook, blogs, and whatever else is coming next to get your company's message to them and engage with them. After all, in this day of participative journalism, social media is how your publics are reaching you, talking about your company, offering their opinions about your company's reputation. Integrating social media venues with the "old fashioned" television and radio broadcasting, print advertising and direct mail continue to be a challenge.

3. Globalization

> Our friends are closer – so are our enemies.

Third on my list is the globalization of companies. The fact that corporations buy or partner with their counterparts in other countries means having to understand language and culture barriers. Certainly technology has shrunk the world. Our friends are closer – so are our enemies.

As much as the practice of public relations emphasizes working things out—solidifying relationships and building a better community—not everyone is listening. Americans are finding out just how much some of the world hates us. The process of globalization is where we have the most to learn and gain. Globalization, in the long run, will impact individuals, jobs, our economy, security, and power base.

4. The Media

Another colleague I turned to for the challenges she faces is Melissa May, APR, a public relations and communications consultant. She cites such media challenges as journalists' failure to fully explore topics and their focus on titillating news. She says: "I've been troubled by the habit of some journalists to print ideological language and concepts as if they are reality, using the language of extremists and incorporating it into journalistic lexicon . . . lending the terms credibility by repeating them."

She points out: "Some terms used by reporters today may have started out as quotes by people on one side of an argument, but they soon were incorporated into coverage as standard language, skewing the perception of these issues by readers, listeners, and viewers. It seems more and more that reporters come into interviews with their minds made up and are simply looking for quotes to reinforce the story they have already written."

And on the other side of the media, she continues: "People are only following—reading, watching, listening to—media that supports and reinforces their beliefs and perspectives. It's facilitating peoples digging into their preconceived notions . . . they're not being challenged to open their minds to new approaches, new ways of thinking about an issue."

5. Building Trust

Closely tied to all other challenges, building trust just may be the most difficult. Post-election recounts demonstrate continuing distrust with voting systems and the people behind them. Ongoing religious wars and hard economic times also cultivate mainstream distrust. So where do you start? As Tim McMahon states in this book's Chapter 9, "Relations are built on trust. To be trusted, be trustworthy." Start with yourself. Expanding trust and trustworthiness to your friends can be a strong framework for building trust with colleagues and communities, both online and in-person.

6. Survival

The guidance you're receiving while reading this book will help prepare you to meet the challenges listed above. In addition, I see the list of character traits below as "must-haves" for the new millennium public relations professional. To not have them is an additional, very personal challenge.

- *Ambition*—searching for opportunities to showcase your strengths and move up in the world.
- *Knowledge*—keeping up with changes, and wanting to participate with the social media tools and whatever the future holds.
- *Energy*—eating, sleeping and staying fit. Doing what you have to do to be proactive and responsive at work.

- *Joy*—liking what you do; enjoying your job while helping others carry out their own job.
- *Curiosity*—being inquisitive not only about work but also your entire environment; developing your perspective.
- *Caring*—having integrity and sincerity as a base for coming into the public relations profession in the first place; staying in touch with these feelings as you grow in your career.

Back to the Arthur W. Page Society for one more principle: "Conduct public relations as if the whole company depends on it." We continue to see from today's headlines and the pr practitioner's capabilities to manage their company's reputation, that indeed, the whole company does depend on it.

Becoming Truly Strategic

The most enlightened companies see communication as a strategic asset; as what in the military is known as a "force multiplier." Effective communication can help a company meet its business goals faster and better; ineffective communication can be a drag on performance.

> Many communication people default to the tactical. But enlightened communicators at all levels default to the strategic—to the goals that communication is intended to accomplish, and the most effective ways to accomplish those goals.

One key to success is for those who run the communication function to organize communication strategically: focused on accomplishing defined business and communication goals.

Many communication people default to the tactical – to discussion of press releases, or e-mails, tweets, clicks, or of other tools of the trade, leading to self-marginalization. But enlightened communicators at all levels default to the strategic – to the goals that communication is intended to accomplish, and the most effective ways to accomplish those goals. Over time this strategic emphasis can become habitual, and can lead to even greater contribution to an organization's success.

> Being habitually strategic means making judgments based on the goals to be accomplished, as one's first resort and not as an afterthought.

Being habitually strategic means making judgments based on the goals to be accomplished, as one's first resort and not as an afterthought. It means conditioning one's behavior to resist the temptation to leap to tactics but rather to consider consequences of various forms of action and communication. And because, as Aristotle taught us (see Chapter 2), we are what we habitually do, we become strategic by deliberately and persistently behaving in goal-oriented ways, and remaining focused on a specific outcome.

Individuals become habitually strategic when they persistently weigh alternative courses of action against desired outcomes, and act on the choices that most clearly lead to those outcomes. Organizations become habitually strategic when their leaders insist that all parts of the organization act strategically as a first resort. This means encouraging strategic thinking by, among other things, rewarding strategic decisions even if they sometimes fail, and discouraging immediate defaults to the tactical even when they sometimes succeed.

Habitually strategic organizations set clear goals and hold managers accountable for reaching those goals; they persistently reinforce those goals. The classic contemporary example of a corporation behaving strategically is General Electric, which, under the tenure of chief executive officer Jack Welch, had very clear goals and strategies and held managers accountable for meeting those goals and fulfilling those strategies. Tactical execution that advanced those strategies was encouraged; tactics that distracted from the fulfillment of the strategies were discouraged, even when they were otherwise incrementally attractive. The best-known General Electric strategy during that period was to be number one or two in each of its areas of business, or to exit that sector.

Jack Welch's successor as General Electric CEO, Jeffrey Immelt, told *Fast Company* magazine the most important lesson he learned from Welch. Immelt said, "Every leader needs to clearly explain the top three things the organization is doing. If you can't, you're not leading well."[9]

Habitually strategic organizations also establish a culture of accountability, insisting that their values be lived and not merely posted on websites. And, not surprisingly, these companies find it easier to survive significant setbacks with minimal reputational, operational, and financial harm. Because all players in a company know what is expected, they manage to avoid many of the crises and much of the self-inflicted damage that plague companies who have not developed these habits. And when the inevitable negative event happens, the company is able to respond quickly and effectively, to take responsible action, and to communicate in ways that restore or maintain the confidence and trust of its core stakeholders.

> Habitually strategic organizations establish a culture of accountability, insisting that their values be lived and not merely posted on websites.

Those who head corporate and organizational communication can contribute to an organization's strategic success in two ways: first, they can use communication as a strategic tool that allows all stakeholders to understand what the organization's mission, vision, and values are. Second, they can establish a strategic focus for each of the elements of corporate and organizational communication: employee communications, community relations, media relations, investor relations, and so forth. They assure alignment of the various functions in support of a corporation's larger corporate goals.

WHAT IS STRATEGY?

The word "strategy" is much-used and misunderstood in business and in communication. Its origins lie in warfare: the skills necessary to command an army. The English word "strategy" comes from the ancient Greek verb στρατηγεω (strategeo), to be a general or to command a military force. That verb, in turn, derives from the noun for army, στρατοσ (stratos), and the verb to lead, αγειν (agein). So the classical meaning of a strategist is a leader of a military force, what we would call a general. The word carried that meaning for much of Western history, from the Greeks to the Romans to the nineteenth century in Europe.

Not surprisingly, then, the first prominent modern use of the word was by a military officer writing about warfare. It appeared in the classic volume on military affairs, *On War*, by the Prussian general and head of the Prussian War College, Carl von Clausewitz. His 1832 book, ostensibly about the qualities necessary to conduct a military campaign, has become a classic of military strategy, governing much U.S. war planning (except for the Vietnam war and the war in Iraq). But *On War* is useful not merely as a book about warfare. It is in many ways the seminal book on strategy itself, both military and civilian, and can provide valuable insights into business management and leadership in general and into the leadership of communication in particular.

Indeed, the Strategy Institute of the Boston Consulting Group argues that the principles elaborated upon in *On War* are essential to understanding contemporary business strategy:

> Clausewitz' *magnum opus* . . . deserves, now more than ever, the full attention of the modern business strategist for accomplishing the unlikely feat of offering new ways to order thinking in disorderly times and provides steadiness in charting strategy in an unstable environment.[10]

In Clausewitz, the Boston Consulting Group finds a kind of thinking that is not restricted to military matters, but rather is an integral part of leadership—leadership that applies to business management, and also leadership as it applies to those who run communication. The key is "ordered thinking"—that is, thinking that proceeds in a certain sequence and is directed toward certain outcomes. In a time of rapid social and technological change, the more unstable the environment, the greater the need for such ordered thinking.

Too often communication is seen as soft—as sentimental, and as intended to make people feel good. But using ordered thinking to help an organization accomplish tangible goals can help change the perception of the communication function internally. A strong leader can cut through the misperception, emotion, and clutter, and can use Clausewitz' principles to guide his or her communication organization to more closely resemble the hard science of management.

The Boston Consulting Group notes:

> It is the true strategist . . . who can benefit most from the work of Carl von Clausewitz because *On War* is quintessentially a philosophy of strategy that contains the conceptual seeds for its constant rejuvenation. It is a philosophy that fuses logical analysis, historical understanding, psychological insight, and sociological comprehension into an encompassing exposition of strategic thought and behavior. It is a philosophy that effectively prevents strategy from ever degenerating into dogma.[11]

The Boston Consulting Group describes why Clausewitz' way of organizing thinking and courageous behavior is so important:

> In its ultimate consequence, the philosophy of Clausewitz demands that commanders and executives not merely think when formulating strategy but that they arrive at a stage where they literally think strategy.[12]

In other words, by following Clausewitz one can learn to become *habitually strategic*. Over the years co-author Fred Garcia has found that following Clausewitz holds one of the keys to effective stewardship of the organizational communication function. Clausewitz' principles can help professional communicators think clearly and organize their activities in ways that predictably help enhance an organization's reputation, operation, financial performance, and enterprise value. The ordered thinking, and the rigor that it represents, also appeals to executives and begins to neutralize the objection that communication is soft or sentimental.

Among the strategic principles Clausewitz lays out that have particular relevance to the communication function are the following

ENDS AND MEANS: EYES ON THE PRIZE

Clausewitz' most famous utterance is the observation that *war is the continuation of policy by other means*. It is part of a continuum, a tool in the service of a much broader process. But it is only a tool. Clausewitz writes:

> The political object is the goal, war is the means of reaching it, and means can never be considered in isolation from their purpose.[13]

Means can never be considered in isolation from their purpose. This is the essence of habitual strategic thinking. This is Clausewitz' breakthrough concept that informs contemporary business leadership, and that can inform leadership of organizational communication.

> Effective communication is merely the continuation of business by other means.

The corollary to Clausewitz' observation *that war is the continuation of policy by other means* is that *effective communication is merely the continuation of business by other means*. The specific ways to communicate with stakeholders are tools in a continuum of tools, all in the service of some clearly-articulated business goal. And just as war is not the goal but the means, communication is not the goal, but simply the means to some other end. And since means can never be considered in isolation from their purpose, this view sees communication as the continuation of business, not as something separate from business—and in particular not as an afterthought.

> Communication is not the goal, but simply the means to some other end.

The principle of the objective, as Clausewitz' principle is called, helps the habitual strategic thinker to avoid impulsive—and self-indulgent—rushes to the tactical. Rather than doing what feels good, or what has always been done, the enlightened communication leader considers the situation as it presents itself and as it is likely to evolve, identifies a clear goal or end state toward which the resources of the enterprise will be directed, and prescribes the means that are most likely to accomplish the goal or end state.

The leader further evaluates tactical options based on the likelihood they will contribute to the achievement of the goal, not because they make the leader feel good, or defer short-term pain or embarrassment. The test of whether any given tactical response should be taken is its alignment to the goal. Means can never be considered in isolation from their purpose.

So one begins to manage communication by understanding a business goal: either a desired business outcome, or a change in the business environment. This may include enhancing employee productivity, selling more products, changing a regulatory requirement that impairs organizational performance, and so forth.

Communicating effectively, in turn, begins with *a clear communication goal*: a change in the emotional, intellectual, or behavioral predispositions of target stakeholders. This may include improving employee morale, increasing demand for a company's products, changing regulators' minds, and so forth.

Focusing on how those who matter to management—employees, customers, investors, regulators, adversaries—think and feel, and how they are likely to think and feel in the future, is a critical part of habitual strategic thinking in communication.

It is all too common for communication professionals to measure output: the number of employee meetings held, the number of press releases issued, the number of stories published. But these are measures of process, not of the goals. They are at best a weak proxy for effectiveness. Rather than focus on process, a more meaningful measure of communication impact is the degree that the communication goals—changes in stakeholders' attitudes and opinions—have been accomplished.

ACTION AND REACTION

Communication is an act of will directed toward a living entity that reacts.

A second Clausewitz concept that informs contemporary business leadership and communication is his observation that war is less like art and more like commerce; he calls it an "act of will directed toward a living entity that *reacts*."[14]

Communication is also an act of will directed toward a living entity that reacts. That living entity is the group of stakeholders who matter to management; the reaction is how that group is likely to think and feel and what it is likely to do in any given post-communication scenario.

The effective communicator grounds all planning and implementation on the desired reaction among critical stakeholders.

The effective communicator grounds all planning and implementation on the desired reaction among critical stakeholders.

Communication is not merely the transmission of information, but the predictable reaction to that information by the audience to which it is directed.

BUILDING IN FLEXIBILITY

The third principle of Clausewitz that informs communication is his notion of *friction: the innumerable small barriers to effective implementation of a strategy.* As Winston Churchill observed, "You'll never get to your destination if you stop to throw a rock at every dog that barks along the way." Clausewitz takes account of the inevitable distractions that interfere with the implementation of a plan:

> Everything in strategy is very simple, but that does not mean that eve-
> rything is very easy. Once it has been determined, from the political
> conditions, what a war is meant to achieve and what it can achieve, it is
> easy to chart the course. But great strength of character, as well as great
> lucidity and firmness of mind, is required in order to follow through
> steadily, to carry out the plan, and not to be thrown off course by
> thousands of diversions.[15]

Similarly, in communication, the important principles are very simple. (Many are described in Chapters 2 through 13.)

But implementing the simple principles can be complicated, especially in an environment of instantaneous linked communication, where all stakeholders have near-simultaneous access to information about a company, both positive and nega-tive. It can be very difficult to keep the various communication disciplines aligned with each other and with the communication and business goals, especially as each discipline works to respond to issues that arise with the stakeholder group over which it has responsibility.

The "thousands of diversions" Clausewitz speaks about can be a defining part of many communication tasks. For example, in many large corporate media relations departments, a common complaint is that the media relations staff spends so much of their time fielding incoming press inquiries that they rarely get the opportunity to think strategically and to affirmatively shape stories. One of the challenges for communication leadership in such circumstances is to create structures that are immune from the day-to-day crush of incoming inquiries and to focus intently on self-generated media visibility.

Being strategic in communication involves recognizing that there will always be real internal and external obstacles to implementing any communication plan effec-tively. But that shouldn't deter one from developing the plan and being diligent in its implementation. Rather, recognizing the likelihood of obstacles allows the leader to plan for the inevitability of distraction, and to build processes to overcome, ignore, prioritize, or otherwise manage through those distractions. To use the Churchill anal-ogy, the leader needs to recognize the likelihood that dogs will bark along the way, and build a plan that permits the organization to not allow the barking dogs to deter it from the most productive course.

Clausewitz' successor in the development of Western military strategy was Helmuth von Moltke, who served as Chief of Staff of the Prussian (and after unifica-tion, the German) General Staff for thirty years in the mid- to late nineteenth century. He famously observed that *no plan survives its initial implementation*. Rather, each plan needs to be continuously adapted to take account of individual tactical encounters that modify what is possible and what is likely to be accomplished in the short term. But this observation does not minimize the importance of planning. Rather, it places a premium on having a clear and powerful set of goals and strategies, and recognizes that individual tactics will change as the plan is implemented. The goals and strategies, however, are unlikely to change; only the tactics, which will need to be adapted to reflect the situational reality. But the tactics are merely means, and means can never be considered in isolation from their purpose. So if the planned tactics should become ineffective in accomplishing their goals, they should be discarded in favor of other, more promising tactics.

Moltke writes:

> No plan of operations extends with certainty beyond the first encounter with the enemy's main strength. Certainly the commander in chief will keep his great objective continuously in mind, undisturbed by the vicissitudes of events. But the path on which he hopes to reach it can never be firmly established in advance. Throughout the campaign he must make a series of decisions on the basis of situations that cannot be foreseen. The successive acts of war are thus not premeditated designs, but on the contrary are spontaneous acts guided by military measures. Everything depends on penetrating the uncertainty of veiled situations to evaluate the facts, to clarify the unknown, to make decisions rapidly, and then to carry them out with strength and constancy.[16]

The communication leader needs to develop a robust plan that clearly manifests the goals and strategies, but remains sufficiently flexible to deal with mid-course corrections based on results of the initial tactical implementation of the plan.

So the communication leader needs to develop a robust plan that clearly manifests the goals and strategies, but remains sufficiently flexible to deal with mid-course corrections based on results of the initial tactical implementation of the plan. He or she needs to develop structures to penetrate the uncertainty of veiled situations, to evaluate facts, and procedures to make tactical decisions quickly.

■ ■ ■

The key to successful corporate and organizational communication is to have clarity about the destination—the reputation that will help a company better accomplish its goals—and of the best path by which to get there.

It has been said that if you don't know where you're going, any road will get you there.

The key to successful corporate and organizational communication is to have clarity about the destination—the reputation that will help a company better accomplish its goals—and of the best path by which to get there. That path typically includes assuring that all of the communication functions of an organization are strategically grounded, well-managed, and aligned with each other and with the broader activities of the enterprise. When they are, the destination is reached faster and more effectively; and the journey is considerably more enjoyable.

▶ NOTES

1   Kevin T. Jackson, *Building Reputational Capital: Strategies for Integrity and Fair Play That Improve the Bottom Line*, (Oxford: Oxford University Press, 2004), p. 12.

2   Ibid.

3   Glenn Rifkin, "At 100, Public Relations' Pioneer Criticizes Some of His Peers," *The New York Times*, December 30, 1991, p. D6.

4   Edward L. Bernays, *Crystallizing Public Opinion* (New York: Boni and Liveright, 1923), p. 52.

5 Ibid., pp. 96–7.

6 Ibid., p. 57.

7 Ibid., p. 139.

8 Ibid., p. 77.

9 "GE's Jeff Immelt on the 10 Keys to Great Leadership," *Fast Company*, April, 2004, page 96.

10 *Clausewitz on Strategy: Inspiration and Insight from a Master on Strategy*, ed. and with comm. Tiha von Ghyczy, Bolko von Oetinger, and Christopher Bassord, a publication of The Strategy Institute of the Boston Consulting Group (Boston: John Wiley & Sons, 2001), p. 2.

11 Ibid., p. 4.

12 Ibid., p. 37.

13 Carl von Clausewitz, *On War*, ed. and trans. Michael Howard and Peter Paret (Princeton: Princeton University Press, 1976), p. 87.

14 Ibid., p. 81 (italics in the original)

15 Ibid., p. 178.

16 *Clausewitz on Strategy*, p. 55.

INDEX